MISSOURI READER

MISSOURI

READER

FRANK LUTHER MOTT
Editor

UNIVERSITY OF MISSOURI PRESS
Columbia, Missouri

PREFACE

This is a collection of writings about Missouri by Missourians. The field from which I have selected materials is rich and varied; and I have wandered through it with singular editorial pleasure, plucking something charming here, something profound there, something funny somewhere else. Missouri is a state of extraordinary variety—in its topography, its population, its culture, its activities, its history. This versatility I have tried to indicate in the selections chosen.

Most of the contents of this volume belong to belles-lettres on some level or other, though a few expository articles, short but significant, have seemed to demand a place in order to round out the book. In chronology, selections range from the early explorers and settlers to the present; in literature, from the immortal Mark Twain to the well-forgotten Commodore Rollingpin; in topics, from Jessie Benton Frémont's *Souvenirs of My Times* to Senator George G. Vest's "Eulogy on the Dog." Arrangement into topical sections is occasionally arbitrary, a selection sometimes seeming to belong to two (or perhaps three) categories as appropriately as to the one in which I have chosen to place it.

Any well-read person who leafs through this book of selections will miss some of his favorites; others will say that this or that was not worth including. Such are the perils the anthologist must accept. It is a consoling thought, however, that probably few readers will fail to find some things herein that are new and interesting to them—and perhaps not a few pieces that may broaden their understanding of Missouri and its culture.

Two or three highly regarded writers, though Missourians by the accident of birth, are omitted because they have written nothing distinctively Missourian. (One refuses to admit, for example, that Missouri was the original "Waste Land"!) Two or three other authors I might otherwise have included were omitted because of difficulties in arranging copyright permissions.

The editor owes much to William Peden for his assistance in this work. He started the project when he was Director of the University of Missouri Press. We then planned to collaborate as co-editors, but other commitments prevented Professor Peden from carrying out a design so pleasantly conceived. Nevertheless, he suggested some selections that might otherwise have escaped me, and he has been good enough to help in other ways. I am grateful also to Ralph H. Parker, University Librarian, for advice and encouragement in this work, as well as to Robert Morris, Director of the University Press, for unfailing aid and cooperation.

I wish I could name here all the persons who have been helpful and kind in connection with this anthology. Many have made suggestions, others (especially the librarians) have helped in digging out materials for articles and headnotes, most of our writers have been generous in the matter of copyright permission fees, everyone with whom I have talked or corresponded concerning this project (over a term of three or four years) has been interested in it, and many good friends have been no less than enthusiastic in their encouragement.

Finally, the statement that this is a book "about Missouri by Missourians" requires a little definition. Some old-timers incline to the conservative view that a man is not a true Missourian unless he, or his father, or perhaps his grandfather, was born within the state. However, for the purposes of this anthology, I have taken a more liberal stand. A few of the writers represented herein were little more than transients among us, but I think I know Missouri well enough to assume that if anyone lives here for only a few years he never quite gets over it.

FRANK LUTHER MOTT

Columbia, Missouri
July 1, 1963

CONTENTS

GENERAL

THE STATE OF MISSOURI

WALTER WILLIAMS

Walter Williams was born in Boonville in 1860 and died in Columbia in 1935. He was editor successively of the Boonville Advertiser *and the* Columbia Herald *in the years 1884–1908. He was president of the National Editorial Association in 1895, and the first president of the American Association of Schools and Departments of Journalism. For a decade he was a member of the Board of Curators of the University of Missouri; but he resigned that position to become dean of the world's first school of journalism, which he had been active in founding at the University. He was president of the University of Missouri from 1930 until his death.*

Dean Williams was a world traveler, and his influence as an educator was felt especially in the Orient. He was the author of several books, some dealing with the history of his native state. While a member of the commission in charge of the Louisiana Purchase Exposition at St. Louis in 1904, he wrote The State of Missouri, *from the introduction to which we excerpt the following paragraphs.*

Walter Williams was a great Missourian, and it seems fitting that these passages, written in that golden style for which he was famous in his editorial page and on the platform, and expressing his regard and affection for his state, should lead off the selections in this volume.

A State is the product of its people. In field and mine and forest are found the tools. The character of the population who use these tools decides. In this is Missouri finely fortunate. Three gates opened wide to the Missouri territory in the early days. The Spanish came by the lower water gate in search of gold; the French by the upper water gate in quest of adventure or led by Marquette's noble missionary zeal; through the mountain gate from the eastward came the Virginians, their children of Kentucky and in later times the Scotch-Irish descendants, the men and women from north and east and from beyond the sea, all seeking homes, where there was blue sky and elbow-room and freedom. The Spanish are remembered by an occasional name of town or river and the French in the same wise or by some ancient family tree. The colonists from east of the Appalachians seeking homes were the real founders of the early State. They builded homes. They constituted a brave, intelligent, patriotic citizenship. They founded a state in the wilderness and equipped it with all the machinery of government a year before the congress of the United States could make up its mind to admit the sturdy youngster to sit full-privileged at the republic's council table. They were of genuine pioneer stock. Some peoples will not bear transplanting; even in the wilderness others are architects of States.

Of the latter were the settlers in Missouri, hardy, dominant and daring. Missouri, a very Titan for strength, is the product of their handiwork, while every State from the Father of Waters to the Golden Gate shows their skill in commonwealth-construction. In struggles with savage beast and untamed man the pioneer Missourian showed persistent heroism and hardihood. They were his children who in the strife between the States enlisted to the number of beyond 100,000 in the Union army and more than 50,000 in the Confederate service, keeping the State's quota full, without draft or enforced enlistment, not merely in one but in both armies, a record unexampled among the States north or south. They were church-going and school-encouraging. They had respect for law. . . .

If Missouri, which is capable of supporting as large a population in proportion to area as Egypt, equalled that land in population there would be 64,000,000 people in this State instead of less than 3,500,000 [4,320,000 in 1960]. God forbid that that time should ever come. Let us always live far enough apart to be neighborly. But there is room enough without crowding for several million more inhabitants of Missouri—and unfeigned welcome! The State is 328 miles in extreme length from north to south and contains 69,415 square miles. Its entire population could be placed, allowing to each a space of six square feet, upon less than a third of a square mile. In area Missouri is slightly larger than England and Wales, which have 32,500,000 [45,400,000 in 1960] population. It is more than four times as large as the mountain republic of Switzerland, which has about the same population. . . .

The soil of Missouri is capable of yielding varied products more largely than the soil of any country in the world. Here is space and to spare for millions upon millions of intelligent, thrifty, industrious citizens.

Missouri has had an interesting and important history. At least three times within the three-quarters of a century of its life as a sovereign State has it been the central figure of national political affairs swaying the policies of the republic. The great Grecian mathematician asked for a spot upon which to rest the lever with which he would move the world. In Missouri may be found a broad area, filled with every help to material prosperity, blessed with noble citizenship, whose sons and daughters are to aid in moving the world nearer to the ideal of human life. The State has given great men to the nation, the chief product of any State. Four hundred Missourians were asked to name the leaders of the State's thought, the men who had done the most for Missouri and through Missourians for the world. The majority named Thomas Hart Benton, Frank P. Blair, John S. Phelps, B. Gratz Brown, R. P. Bland, Hamilton R. Gamble, James S. Green, and Edward Bates, statesmen; James S. Rollins, the father of the State University; Sterling Price and A. W. Doniphan, soldiers; James B. Eads, engineer; E. M. Marvin, preacher; Eugene Field, poet; and George C. Bingham, artist.

The spirit of Missouri is the spirit of progress, tempered by conservatism. It rejects not the old because of its age, nor refuses the new because it is not old. It is the spirit of a community, conscious of its own secure position, somewhat too careless at times of the world's opinion, hospitable, generous, brave. The dream of the greatest statesman is a nation of useful citizens dwelling in happy homes. In Missouri the dream finds realization.

The noble Latin motto of the State has ever expressed—and does— the spirit of the united citizenship: "Let the welfare of the people be the supreme law." Nobler motto there could not be for commonwealth or citizen. . . .

THE GEOLOGY OF MISSOURI

E. B. Branson and W. D. Keller

Edwin Bayer Branson was born in Kansas and received his bachelor's and master's degrees from that state's university. He earned his doctorate at the University of Chicago. In 1910 he began a distinguished career of forty years in the Geology Department of the University of Missouri. He died while Missouri: Its Resources, People, and Institutions *(1950) was in press.*

Walter David Keller was born in North Kansas City, Missouri. He has received degrees from the University of Missouri, the Missouri School of Mines, and Harvard University; and he has been a member of the Geology faculty at the University of Missouri since 1926.

The paragraphs which follow constitute the introduction and the conclusion of an essay in the above-named volume, issued by the Curators of the University of Missouri and now out of print.

The oldest visible things in Missouri (approximately 1,300,-000,000 years old) are the igneous rocks (granites and porphyries) that

Reprinted by permission of Walter D. Keller.

appear at the surface in the southeastern part of the State. Igneous rocks are those which originated by solidification from a hot liquid.

We may imagine ages ago an earth without life, and with lava at the surface and molten rock below. In what is now southeastern Missouri the lava solidified to very fine-grained gray, pink, or reddish rocks with fewer larger crystals of quartz and feldspar scattered throughout. These lava rocks are called porphyries, a name derived from the texture wherein large crystals occur in a groundmass of finer crystals. The walls of the "Royal Gorge" south of Ironton are porphyry.

Beneath the insulating cover of porphyry other molten material solidified slowly to form a coarse-grained granite, like that occurring in the quarries near Graniteville. Missouri granite is composed of pink feldspar and clear, glassy quartz mineral grains.

Granites, other igneous rocks, and older metamorphic rocks (rocks that have been changed mineralogically or structurally in the solid state by very high temperature and pressure) have been found by drilling to underlie all parts of the State. South of Kansas City, these rocks are about 2,500 feet below the surface, and in the northwest corner of Missouri they are probably more than 4,000 feet below the surface, although no drillings have penetrated that far. These old basement rocks, along with other ancient exposures in other states, upon weathering, furnished all of the materials which accumulated to form the younger overlying rocks in the State. One of the functions of geology is to explain how the older rocks give rise to the younger.

The primitive land surfaces were bare igneous rocks with no vegetation, and no animals on them. Even the streams and the seas contained no animals or plants which left fossil remains. But primitive soils developed on the rock through weathering as it operates today. Wind and rain, freezing and thawing, atmospheric gases, and moisture broke down and softened the fresh rock surfaces. The crisp feldspar minerals (combinations of potassium, sodium, and calcium with aluminum, silicon, and oxygen) were decomposed to become earthy clay minerals (hydrogen, aluminum, silicon and oxygen) which contributed toward a soil mantle, or to dust and mud if carried away. The sodium and calcium were dissolved in ground water, and were carried to the ocean by streams.

The resistant, inert quartz particles became silt, sand, and gravel in the soil and stream beds. Boulders and pebbles were loosened by weathering.

Eventually an ocean invaded the valleys and rose high on the rounded igneous and metamorphic rock hills in Missouri. The gravel and boulders accumulated on the old eroded surface, and were cemented to form conglomerates which we find today. Sand was washed down the streams, onto the beaches, and over the old sea floors to give rise to the sand-stones which overlie the old igneous rocks. Clay mud was washed far out or into quiet arms of the ancient sea and upon compaction became shale as we see it today.

The calcium and magnesium which went in solution to the ocean became limestone or dolomite (calcium-magnesium limestone) on the clear water portion of the ocean floor, like the lime deposit on the bottom of a tea kettle. Hence sedimentary rocks—conglomerates, sand-stones, shales, and limestones—were developed as sediments which ac-cumulated from weathered rock products carried into ancient seas that covered Missouri millions of years ago. Sedimentary rocks are charac-teristically layered, bedded, or stratified.

The porphyries of southeast Missouri, besides being the oldest ex-posed rocks, and contributing to the formation of sedimentary rocks, are the country rock for important iron ores. At Iron Mountain, in St. Francois County, a rich deposit of hematite iron ore (Fe_2O_3, iron 70 per cent, oxygen 30 per cent) has been partially depleted, but mining is being continued and additional ore reserves are being blocked out. The large open cut in the top of Pilot Knob Mountain and underground work testify to the tremendous quantity of iron ore which has been re-moved from the old porphyry rocks.

Beautiful red granite is quarried for building and monumental stone at Graniteville.

The Elephant Rocks Park at Graniteville features large boulders of granite which are rounded, weathered granite blocks that were sepa-rated by joints (cracks) which opened after solidification.

The "shut-ins" of southeast Missouri are usually developed where streams flow from a low wide-cut flood-plain area on relatively easily erodable sedimentary rocks into narrow (hence, "shut-in"), steep-walled canyons incised into relatively resistant hard igneous rocks. The streams seem to have assumed their courses on sedimentary rocks when they covered all of the igneous rocks of the region. As the streams deepened their valleys they cut into resistant igneous rock bosses and are super-imposed in their present valleys. . . .

Missouri lies within that part of our continent which is generally free from serious earthquakes, but on December 16, 1811, a quake of very high intensity occurred in the New Madrid region of southeast Missouri. Other severe quakes and minor after shocks occurred for several months. No deaths were known to have resulted because the area was almost uninhabited, but if a similar quake were to occur under present populated conditions, the loss of life and property would be great. Fissures were opened in the ground, and craterlets and mounds of sand were formed during the movement. The largest surface manifestation of the New Madrid earthquake was the dropping of the basin which filled with water to form Reelfoot Lake in eastern Tennessee, a short distance from the Missouri boundary. The lake is 60 to 70 miles long, 3 to 20 miles wide, and in some places 50 to 100 feet deep. The forest trees in the area were more or less completely submerged. Further adjustment in the earth's crust has continued to take place northward toward St. Louis, as is indicated by the infrequent slight shocks which have occurred.

Earthquakes are the tremors or vibrations which arise from fracturing of rocks within the earth. Other causes of quakes are of so little consequence that they need not be mentioned. Stresses may develop near the earth's surface, or at some depth, until they exceed the strength of the rocks, which then fail or break. Movement along the break may be in a vertical or horizontal direction, or both, which is technically termed a "fault."

Faulting in an area may consist of short intermittent movements spaced at various intervals through a long time. Where faulting takes place near the earth's surface, fault scarps (surface expressions) may persist. Usually erosion keeps pace with the faulting and obliterates quickly any surface effects. Subsequent erosion has removed almost all surface expression of many faults in Missouri which are known to geologists. In such cases the presence of a fault is recognized by the pronounced and abrupt change in the rocks which are in contact across a fault zone.

A complex area of faulting in Ste. Genevieve County, and other pronounced faults occur westward across St. Francois, Washington, and Crawford counties. Faults are also known in southwest Missouri. In Lincoln County, a fault has cut across the Mississippi River from Illinois and continues northwestward between the towns of Winfield and Foley. It grades into a fold or bend in the rocks which flattens out farther to the west. Other areas of gently folded rocks are common in Missouri.

Rocks under stress may be bent (folded) or broken (faulted). The magnitude of forces involved in such deformation is almost incomprehensible. The geologic processes which involve those large scale movements within solid rock are called "diastrophism."

From a wide regional viewpoint, the earth (rock) structure of a wide band across Missouri from Cape Girardeau toward Kansas City is an asymmetrical elongate dome. The top of the structural dome lies between Fredericktown and Ironton from which the rocks dip downward gently toward the northwest and south, but more steeply toward the northeast and east. A broad, gentle structural trough extends from St. Louis northwestward in the direction of Maryville. The structural "grain" of Missouri, which is northwest-southeast, is clearly seen on a geologic map of the State.

The surface of Missouri may be conveniently divided into the Ozark Region, Old Plains, Old Plains modified by glaciation, and River Plains. The Ozark Region is the hilly part of southeast Missouri. West of the Ozark Region are the Old Plains of rather level topography. The Old Plains modified by glaciation are, in the main, north of the Missouri River. The River Plains are mainly in the valleys of the Mississippi River, the Missouri River, and the Grand River, but they extend along many other stream valleys.

MISSOURI IS *ALL* AMERICA

IRVING DILLIARD

Irving Dilliard is claimed by two states—Illinois and Missouri. He was born in Illinois, and for most of his life has kept a home for himself and his family just across the river from St. Louis, at Collinsville. But for twenty-five years he was on the staff of the St. Louis Post-Dispatch, *for several years as editor of its editorial page, and he still contributes to that paper. Thus he has been identified through most of his adult life with Missouri affairs and Missouri life.*

Dilliard is well known as lecturer, author, and freelance writer. His chief field of scholarly interest has been that of legal biography.

The following pages are taken from the introduction to a book of Missouri photographs by Allyson Painter, for which Dilliard wrote a delightful textual commentary. The book has the title, "I'm from Missouri!" Where Man and Mule Shaped the Heart of a Nation.

Let's start by looking at a map.
Let's see just where Missouri is.
The best guide of all is the Mississippi. Within the United States there is no orientation to compare with the mighty river which rises far up toward the North Star and joins the sea where gazers at the heavens can almost glimpse the Southern Cross.

From "I'm from Missouri!" by Irving Dilliard, copyright by Hastings House, Publishers.

So find the Father of Waters. Then follow half way down the great channel of the continent's life blood. There is Missouri. Some five hundred miles of twists and turns of the highway of the Indians are Missouri's eastern boundary. Now look half way down the bends and loops which wash Missouri's morning side. That Y which slants to the west is the confluence of the Mississippi and Missouri Rivers.

The Missouri is the Mississippi's longest arm, if itself it is not the Mississippi above their confluence. Is the Missouri really the upper Mississippi? Many geographers believe so and the way the lighter waters of the Mississippi disappear in the brown Missouri tends to bear them out. But we shall not investigate that question. For us it is enough that the Missouri, as the map calls it, reaches across the state. Some two-fifths of Missouri's 69,674 square miles lie above its east-west course, about three-fifths below.

And so Missouri is practically centered on the nation's two great rivers.

Let's do some rough measuring. Our eye tells us that Missouri is approximately half way between the Rocky Mountains and the Appalachians. From the Lake of the Ozarks it is just about as far east to Lake Ontario as it is west to Great Salt Lake. At first glance Missouri appears closer to the Atlantic than to the Pacific. Yet is it?

Count the states between Missouri and the Atlantic, Illinois, Indiana, Ohio, Pennsylvania, New Jersey. Five. Count the states westward to the Pacific. Kansas, Colorado, Utah, Nevada, California. Five again. Now count up and down. Between Missouri and Canada are Iowa and Minnesota. Two states. South from Missouri to the Gulf of Mexico are Arkansas and Louisiana. Two again. Starting with Missouri there are equal numbers of states east to the Hudson and west to the Golden Gate. Also equal numbers north to Rainy River and south to the Rio Grande.

Now let's see what we can learn with a piece of string. Put one end down at Lamar, in Southwestern Missouri, where the thirty-third President was born. Stretch the string to Calais, Maine, most distant point to the northeast still in the country. Using the distance as a radius, swing the arc south, west and northward to the Pacific Coast. The distance from Harry S. Truman's birthplace to the pine forests of Maine is just about equal to the distance from his rural hometown to the palms of Santa Barbara, California.

Move the string to Bethany, in northern Missouri. That is the *Country Town* where Edgar Watson Howe set type as a boy and lived among his *Plain People*. Extend the string southeast to Key West. Then stretch it in the opposite direction from Bethany. The point on the string which touched our Caribbean extremity is just about on the impounded Canadian snow waters behind Grand Coulee Dam.

Intersect lines from Southern California to Maine and from Florida to the Pacific Northwest and where these lines cross there is Missouri. Other tests and measurements would only confirm what we now see: Missouri is the heart of the United States. Missouri is the middle of the nation. The rest of the country lies around Missouri.

But Missouri is more than the heartland. The heart is also the whole. Missouri is *all* America in one place. It is the 48 states of the Union joined together, superimposed on one another, fused into a composite of many outlooks and moods and experiences and ways of thinking and speaking and doing things.

Missouri is abolitionist North with its belief in equal rights for all men and women. It's plantation South which clings to old ideas of a leisure society. It is the industrial East, busy, noisy, mechanical, commercial. It is the grazing West, miles on miles of pasture and prize livestock in every direction.

In May, Missouri is Virginia and billowing apple orchards pink-white for blossomtime. In late June, it is the beginning of the Great Plains and waving, golden-ripe wheat of Kansas, Nebraska, and the Dakotas. In August, Missouri is Illinois' blazing cornland prairie. It is rocky New England farmyards, bright with larkspur and hollyhocks along rail fences. It is sun-baked mine fields of Oklahoma, New Mexico and Arizona. It is broad patches of cotton and bent pickers with their bulging bags from Alabama, Mississippi and Louisiana.

In Missouri's cities and towns are Pennsylvania foundries and Massachusetts mills, Connecticut factories and New Jersey laboratories. Missouri has country clubs with golf courses from fashionable Long Island and crossroads stores from Hoosier Indiana; two-room country schools from Yankee Maine and white-painted wayside churches from Buckeye Ohio. And Missouri has cathedrals and universities with antecedents in the Old World.

Missouri is itself as well. Missouri is ancient, rounded-down Taum Sauk Mountain, old enough to be the great-grandfather of that young upstart, Pike's Peak. It is a galaxy of surging, dancing springs, the most beautiful collection of natural fountains anywhere. Missouri is unspoiled streams like the Current River, where fish and fishermen play together by day, where campfires light the water's edge at night.

Missouri's central position on the continent, its joining of North, East, South, and West, its place at the meeting of the great rivers have given the state a role in the national pageant which bears on every other part.

Here black-robed explorers arrived by canoe. Here came early adventurers and seekers after fortune from France and Spain. From remote settlements fur traders and miners pressed into the wildness among the

Indians. Here opened the Gateway to the West. Here passed mule pack trains to Santa Fe and covered wagons bound for Oregon. Here stopped the Mormons for a while and from their Missouri cabins they went to the Far West. The Gold Rush hurried by on its way to California.

Along the Missouri-Kansas border tempers flared and burned in the years leading to the Civil War; by night men of color and bondage were slipped across the Mississippi to Illinois, the underground railroad and freedom. After Fort Sumter, Missouri was the largest state battleground. Here families divided, brother fought brother and hardly a community but had its clash of muskets and swords. Across Missouri the first trans-Mississippi railroad pushed its proud little trains. The Pony Express galloped away with a Missouri rider in its cloud of dust. Germans and Irish, Italians and Bohemians brought their songs, habits and beliefs from overseas. Industry followed agriculture and on farm and in village, town and city, man and the mule he drove shaped the heart of a nation.

As Missouri is all parts of America so is Missouri all kinds of people. It is important people whose names are in history books and headlines and it is nearly four million ordinary people who help elect Presidents and Congresses and so make America what it is. All these are Missourians: strawberry pickers at Cassville, corncob pipe makers at Washington and Boonville, peony growers at Sarcoxie, saddle craftsmen at St. Joseph, mushroom raisers at Hermann, chair and basket weavers at Branson, singing and dancing choruses of St. Louis' Municipal Opera, timber cutters on the hills around Van Buren, streamliner engineers at Kansas City, surgery miracle workers at Washington University, rivermen at Cape Girardeau.

Missouri is a host of celebrated native sons and daughters, many of them distinguished and some notorious. Little Florida, in Monroe County, gave the world a boy named Sam Clemens who grew up to be Mississippi pilot Mark Twain and the literary father of Tom Sawyer and Huckleberry Finn and Becky Thatcher. In a three-story brick house near the riverfront in St. Louis, Eugene Field took his first steps, ran barefoot and stored memories for his poems of childhood.

Missouri's Linn County village, Laclede, sent "Black Jack" Pershing to World War I, the Argonne, Belleau Wood, Chateau-Thierry and St. Mihiel. Randolph County's hamlet, Clark, produced "Soldier's Soldier" Omar Bradley for World War II, Twelfth Army Group and the pounding drive of Missouri clerks and farmboys across the Rhine and towards Hitler's Reichschancellery.

From Diamond Grove, in Newton County, a boy born in slavery rose to renown as George Washington Carver, botanist, agriculturist and educator. From Nashville, in Barton County, Harvard's astronomer,

Harlow Shapley, climbed up to search among the constellations. Jesse James, who put daylight through too many men, first saw light of day on a farm near Kearney, Clay County. The first murals observed by painter Thomas Hart Benton were those which Nature unrolled on the hills around Neosho each autumn. Thomas Stearns Eliot, Nobel prize poet, spelled out his first lines in St. Louis, and Langston Hughes, poet of protest against racial injustice, sounded his first words in Joplin.

Most notable of all of course is a very human, ordinary, likeable and determined man named Harry S. Truman who, through the workings of American party politics, happened to be Vice-President of the United States when Franklin D. Roosevelt died in 1945. This typical Missourian served almost four years in the White House and then, by all precedents should have been defeated when he asked to be elected in 1948 to succeed himself. But this average American, this field artillery Captain in World War I, this haberdasher—local politician—Senator went to the whistle stops. He talked man to man from the back platform of his campaign train to anybody who would listen. Poll takers quit sampling opinion weeks before election day, so sure were they that he was beaten. Columnists chose his opponent's cabinet. But the man from Independence who spoke everyone's language scored the biggest surprise in American politics. He won over the confident and polished Governor of New York by more than two million popular votes and 114 electoral votes. All the way back to Washington's day, there had been no upset to compare with Harry Truman's.

Ginger Rogers, Betty Grable, Jack Oakie, Jean Harlow, Martha Scott and other stars of the movie screen came from Missouri soil. So did Bernarr MacFadden, physical culturist, of Mill Springs; Dale Carnegie, success lecturer, of Maryville; James Cash Penney, merchant, of Hamilton; Mary Margaret McBride, radio entertainer, of Paris; Tex Rickard, prize fight promoter, of Kansas City; Frederick Gilmer Bonfils, ripsnorting Denver publisher, of Troy; Homer Croy, novelist and humorist, of Nodaway County; and Sally Rand, fan dancer, of Cross Timbers.

But Missouri is not just the men and women who have gone out from its boundaries to fame and fortune. Missouri is also those who have come from a thousand other places. Cross into Missouri and we are where native Kentuckian George Graham Vest appealed to a jury to spare Old Drum, the hound dog, as "the one absolutely unselfish friend that man can have in this world, the one that never deserts him, the one that never proves ungrateful or treacherous." Enter Missouri and we are where Virginia-born George Caleb Bingham painted pictures of the *Jolly Flatboatmen* and the *Fur Traders,* where the frontier artist recorded the pioneer democracy at work—the stump speaking, the county election and the verdict of the people.

Missouri is where native North Carolinian Thomas Hart Benton became famous as "Old Bullion." Where an Ozark constituency kept sending Richard P. Bland back to the House of Representatives until all the country called him "Silver Dick." Where Champ Clark's followers sang a tune about "quit kickin' my dog around," threw their hats when he was elected Speaker and wept when he failed to win the presidential nomination that went to Woodrow Wilson. Where James A. Reed sharpened the tongue that made him the scourge of the Senate.

Missouri drew a Hungarian emigrant named Joseph Pulitzer who found the German culture of St. Louis in the '70's immediately receptive to the crusading journalism which he launched in his fearless *Post-Dispatch*. Missouri attracted William Rockhill Nelson who, through *The Kansas City Star,* changed a frontier town into a modern city. Missouri held a firm attachment for Civil War correspondent "Little Mack" McCullagh, who wrote a chapter in the history of American newspaper reporting for his *St. Louis Globe-Democrat.* For nearly 40 years Missouri has been the studio of world-famous editorial cartoonist, Daniel Robert Fitzpatrick, who helps shape his times and foretell the future with bold, incisive strokes of black crayon which lampoon buffoonery, expose corruption and castigate the faithless in high place.

Enter St. Louis by way of Eads Bridge and we are where Louis Dembitz Brandeis of Kentucky and Harvard hung out his shingle as a freshman lawyer. From that little office at Broadway and Chestnut, a stone's throw from the Old Courthouse, spread the influence of a social and economic philosopher and a wise and just judge of the Supreme Court. Stop at Columbia and we are where the University of Missouri, first state university west of the Mississippi, gave a teaching refuge to Thorstein Veblen, exile from Wisconsin, Cornell, Chicago and Stanford. For seven years mid-Missouri was sanctuary for that original thinker and his criticisms of American social, business and educational systems.

Missouri is where Rabbi Leon Harrison, from Liverpool, won distinction as a brilliant pulpit orator. It is where witty, dramatic Bishop William A. Quale, descendant of Manxmen, became eminent as a Methodist preacher, church administrator and lecturer. It is where kindly, bearded, raw-boned missionary Daniel Sylvester Tuttle rose to Presiding Bishop of the Episcopal Church. It is where tall, genial Irish John J. Glennon conducted his long Roman Catholic ministry which led to a Cardinal's red hat from the hands of Pope Pius XII.

So it is that Missouri is all kinds of people in many kinds of places. People like Tom Horn, who ran away from home to Santa Fe to be a government scout and interpreter and to start his short, strange career in the robust West which ended at Cheyenne on the gallows. People like adventurous fur trader Pierre Laclede Liguest and play writer Augustus Thomas. Like three-crown prize fighter Henry Armstrong and uninhibited editor William Marion Reedy of *The Mirror*. Like southpaw first baseman George Sisler, poet Sara Teasdale and log hauler Sam Grant, veteran of the Mexican War. Like political boss Tom Pendergast, romantic novelist Winston Churchill and that daring, buckskin-clad bundle of frontier femininity "Calamity Jane" Canary. Like horse trainer Missouri Ben Jones, who sent Whirlaway streaking into racetrack history.

Places like Cardiff Hill with its kerosene lighthouse for river pilots, *Lover's Lane, St. Joe,* the Shepherd of the Hills country, and Wilson's Creek where the Secessionists took a bloody first-round battle from the Federals in August, 1861, and Gen. Nathaniel Lyon fell dead on the field. Places large and places small, known and unknown. Places named Jonesburg, Grubville, Pumpkin Center and Owls Bend. Places down on the map as Mammoth and Minimum, Liberal and Radical, Huzzah and Braggadocio, Ponder and Peculiar, Cureall and Success, Enough and Enon.

Missourians live under an assortment of roofs. Their architecture is as diverse as will be seen almost anywhere. Flats, bungalows, mansions and ranchhouses trace back to primitive styles of basket weave, mud and straw walls and log cabins. Many Ozark families are at home in houses built of logs placed in mountainside clearings. Along the Mississippi are old French houses whose design came from the Creole South. Walls of upright logs set in the earth or on stones at Ste. Genevieve are a curiosity much studied by architects and historians. Steep roofs and broad, sheltering porches mark these French architectural survivors. In Missouri River towns and wherever else the Germans settled are compact, solid brick houses, built close to the sidewalk with garden and fruit tree space to the rear. Throughout the farming country north of Jefferson City are hundreds of two-story classic revival homesteads. In Missouri, home may be a pre-Civil War mansion, built in the style of an Italian country house, with a stone tower to command a view of the Mississippi. It may be a unit in a housing development in what was once St. Louis' Kerry Patch. It may be a trailer camp at the edge of Highway 66 or a houseboat on the Gasconade.

Our inventory of Missourians and the places in which they live could go on for a long time. Now that we have met Missourians in substantial numbers, let's listen to them talk a while. . . . Some Missourians talk with a magnolia drawl. Some have the twang of New England, some the burr of the Rockies. At Drury College and St. Louis University, at

Westminster and Principia, speech ranges from Harvard to Mills and from Carleton to Millsaps. But most Missourians talk the Main Street languages of the Middle West.

This typical speech, so students of dialects have determined, is the only form of American speech which is not undergoing radical change. Instead it is spreading and modifying the dialects of the rest of the United States. It is the speech which, however much Oxonians may deprecate it, promises to become standard American speech. Already, so such careful observers of speech trends as the Hermans report, the Middle Western dialect is spoken by more than ninety millions among the one hundred and fifty-five millions in the United States.

Reading personality from the talk of Rolla, Wright City, Warrensburg and Kirksville, these students of dialect find that it falls between the hurried excitability of New Yorkers and the unworried calmness of Southerners. Missouri talk bespeaks welcome good fellowship and pleasure at being host.

Missouri's weather runs the full round of the seasons and then some. There are days when the climate is straight from Albany and Bangor. Sometimes the weather is St. Paul's, Denver's or Washington's. Many summer days are like Palm Springs, Wichita, Miami or San Antonio. The year begins with drifting snow and winds that drop the mercury to zero. With March come scudding clouds and the first warm days when country folks and small town dwellers plant potatoes and sow onions, radishes and lettuce. April lives up to its reputation for showers and May brings on blossoms and flowers. Then comes summer's green and if rains are spaced out gardens and lawns and pastures stay lush until frost.

October is Missouri's month of months. Skies are blue and warm sunshine lights the sumac and sassafras whose leaves grow in brilliance as the days shorten. Under the chill harvest moon shocks of corn turn into Indian wigwams. Yellow pumpkins gleam between the rows and flocks of fattening fowls are pleasant harbingers of the seasonal feasting at family reunions which round out the year. There may be snow for Thanksgiving yet on Christmas it can be warm enough for baseball. Cold as kraut or hot as blazes, Missouri's weather is never indifferent. It always can be talked about.

Missouri's table is set from many kitchens. A meal may begin with French onion soup or Russian borscht. It may include Irish corned beef and cabbage or German hot potato salad or Italian spaghetti and ravioli or Hungarian goulash. Sooner or later everyone eats cornbread, country sausage, barbecued ribs, chicken and dumplings, wheat cakes and honey, gooseberry pie, watermelon preserves, green tomato pickles, biscuits and sorghum, and strawberry shortcake.

Missouri serves dishes from Boston and Richmond, New Orleans and El Paso, Bemidji and Kalamazoo. But Missouri is an exporter, too. There can hardly be a kitchen in the country which does not prepare some of its food the way housewives fix it in Missouri. Missouri's hickory smoked ham, its apple dumpling with nutmeg sauce, its spring greens and its roast Ozark turkey hold their own with the top dishes of any state or region.

Missouri is a lop-eared he-hawer, slow but sure, which has pulled his share and more in mud and mountains around the world. It is the channel catfish and the small mouth black bass, the mallard, the squirrel and the rabbit. It is the red flash of the cardinal and the hoarse call of the crow. It is Jack in his pulpit and lace along the road for Queen Ann. It is the corn-cob pipe, square dance and quilting bee; the country fair, potluck supper, school picnic and moonlight boatride. It is old Arrow Rock Tavern, Louis Sullivan's pioneer skyscraper, and the fiery race between the *Natchez* and the *Robert E. Lee.* It is machine politics in the cities and tent revivals in the hills. It is *Frankie and Johnny, The Missouri Waltz,* and *St. Louis Blues.*

THE PRONUNCIATION OF "MISSOURI"

ALLEN WALKER READ

Allen Walker Read pursued his doctorate under Robert L. Ramsay, long a respected member of the University of Missouri faculty and an authority in the field of place-name studies. Later, Read became a member of the staff preparing the great American Dictionary at the University of Chicago, and is now a professor in the Department of English Language and Literature at Columbia University.

The following paragraphs are pickings from Read's definitive study, "Pronunciation of the Word 'Missouri,'" published in American Speech *in its December, 1933, number (Vol. VIII, pp. 22–36).*

Before allowing others to have their say on the matter, the editor of this volume wishes to record his observation that the almost invariable pronunciation of old-timers in this state, and of most Missouri leaders (as the present governor and both of our U. S. senators) is Muhzooruh, *the first and last vowels sounding like* a *in* sofa *(the inverted* e *in the system of symbols used by the International Phonetic Association).*

Reprinted from *American Speech,* December, 1933. By permission of the author.

Many, however, at this time, thirty years after the publication of the Read study, say Muhzoory; *and it seems likely that this pronunciation may eventually prevail because of its almost universal use by radio and television announcers.*

. . . In 1889 Eugene Field wrote:

> He lives in Mizzoura, where the people are so set
> In ante-bellum notions that they vote for Jackson yet.

This spelling was exploited most successfully by Augustus Thomas, in his play "In Mizzoura," produced in Chicago in 1893. . . .

A hornet's nest of controversy was aroused in 1897 by the action of the school board of Columbia, the seat of the state university. On October 4 of that year, on the motion of Walter Williams, then editor of a local newspaper, the *Herald* . . . the board passed this resolution: "Resolved, That this board hereby instructs the teachers employed in the Columbia school district to teach the pronunciation of the name of the state, Miz-zou-ry." Editorially Mr. Williams supported the motion:

It is only in late years that there has been any difference of opinion upon this subject. The old-fashioned said either Mizzourah or Mizzouri, the best educated the latter. Recently, however, there has sprung up in this state a preference for a pronunciation that gives the hissing sound of "s" to the letters and we hear, among our newly imported friends, that the name should be M-i-s-s-o-u-r-i. This is not euphonious; it is contrary to established usage; it is incorrect. It is a fad that should not be transplanted into our state.

A man has a moral and legal right to pronounce his name as he pleases, and no one ought to say him nay. So the people of the state have the same right. In neither case have dictionaries, or foreign universities, or "culchaw," authority to make any change.

. . . [But another] group of commentators frankly believed in setting aside popular usage and following the authority of dictionaries and literary people. The *St. Joseph News* admitted:

The majority of Missourians certainly pronounce it Mizzourah. Mr. Gray [state inspector of the building and loan associations] says that was the pronunciation he heard when he was a boy, and he says truly that is the pronunciation of the plain people of the state today. These same plain people are very careless in pronunciation, and the majority of them may say "I have went" and "I seen your friend," but that does not make either of these sentences good grammar, even in Missouri.

Therefore, the *News* concluded, the educators and literati outside the state have the right to determine correctness. The *St. Louis Globe-Democrat* took the same side, using other arguments:

One pronunciation often heard makes the last syllable "rah." This is clearly a corruption or mannerism, and can be dismissed as unwarranted. The final syllable has the sound of "ree," though not too much prolonged. Perhaps to say it has the short sound of "i" would be more exact. That point is easily disposed of, but not so with the two "s's." Have they the sharp sibilant sound of "s" or the flat sibilant sound of "z"? The professors of the Columbia State University recently pronounced in favor of "z," and their usage hereafter will be "Miz-zoo-ree." Numerous protests have been made against this ruling. If "Miz-zoo-ree," it is asked, why not "Miz-iz-zippi"? Both are Indian words, one meaning muddy waters and the other great waters. The aboriginal root must be the same, and to vary the sound needlessly is mere caprice. Many other Indian names contain the "Miss," and in no other case is the syllable changed to "Miz."

The letter "z" brings up the tail of the alphabet, and was not admitted to the Roman schools until the time of Cicero. Missouri demands the best that is going, and will not accept an alphabetic straggler or tramp without whose aid the Romans rose to greatness. . . . Therefore "Mis-soo-ree" seems to be supported by analogy as well as alphabetical dignity.

. . . Further comments seem to show that the influx of the form "Missoory" was largely the work of the reforming school teacher. Frederick M. Crunden, librarian of the St. Louis Public Library, reported:

I had always said "Mizzoura" until Thomas Metcalf, of the high school of Normal, Illinois, corrected us to "Missouri." As far as I have observed, all the people throughout the state call it "Mizzoura," but in St. Louis the custom seems to be to call it "Missoury."

And said the *Franklin News:*

We do not know of a person in Howard County who says Missoori. In fact, the only person we ever knew who invariably said Missoori was an elocution teacher in Kirksville. This teacher introduced Missoori to the State Normal School there as the very latest—just from the East. It was evident from the comment among the students that the pronunciation was an innovation—that they had not been accustomed to it.

And so it is today. Note how the people you meet pronounce the name and you will observe that nine out of every ten say Mizzoury, or something very near that.

. . . Colonel William F. Switzler, one of the most erudite of Missouri's historians, rallied, he said " 'round the flag of grand old M-i-z-z-o-o-r-a-h, with a soft accent on the r-a-h." Many papers took him as their authority. Said the *Plattsburg Democrat-Lever:*

We certainly hope the pronunciation of the name of this state advocated by the *Columbia Herald* will not become general usage. It is neither euphonious nor suggestive of anything imperial. It sounds too much like something insignificant or diminutive, like Johnny or Sammy. Let it be Missoura, with the short sound of "a."

And the *Macon Times:*

Now either the question must be decided on popular usage or on the exclusive usage of the learned few. The learned few have for forty years pronounced it Missouri, giving the "s" the sound it has in Mississippi, and we take it that Mizzouri is simply a hybrid between the two and not approved by either. Therefore the *Times* is with the unwashed masses of the state as says Mizzoura.

. . . Dozens of editors called for legislative action, similar to that in Arkansas, many of them not so much anxious to enforce a particular pronunciation as desirous of having some authoritative way established. One writer favored the pronunciation Missouro, in order that the abbreviation of the state name, "Mo.," would be justified. . . .

As an aftermath [of the controversy of 1897] a committee was formed, with Dr. John R. Kirk as chairman, to secure the opinions of two hundred important Missourians—senators, editors, state officials, business men, and others. It was found that eighty percent favored the form "Mizzoory."

. . . The present [1933] governor of Missouri, Hon. Guy B. Park, gave his opinion in the *Milan Standard:*

I've lived in Missouri all my life and have never heard any true Missourian pronounce the name of the state in any other way than "Mizzourah." When you give the final letter the sound of "i" it is all wrong to me.

. . . The dictionaries, gazetteers, and geographies have been at great variance with local usage. [Here follows a list of such pronunciations, but Doctor Read refers in a footnote to his own statement of basic principle, as set forth in another article in *American Speech,* Vol. VIII (February, 1933), pp. 44, 46]:

In his *Spelling Book* of 1803 Noah Webster enunciated the principle that has been accepted in modern lexicography: "The true pronunciation of the name of a place is that which prevails in and near the place. . . ."
. . . The student of language may well take upon himself the mantle of critic, but he must realize that he is not talking then about what is correct. That can be determined simply by impartial observation of selected speakers in the locality of the place named.

. . . [The pronunciation of the final vowel in the word *Missouri* like the *a* in *sofa*] has, in defiance of spelling, shown remarkable vitality. An actual counting of heads in Missouri would show, I believe, that it has the decided majority, perhaps that of two-thirds. It is so widespread even elsewhere and so well supported by phonetic tendencies that in the present day it is passed on like any other non-spelling pronunciation, as "wimmen" for women and "hickup" for hiccough. It is on the defensive, however, and many of those who normally use it admit they do so incorrectly, except a certain group (among them Senator James Reed) who hold that it is the most validly Missourian usage and maintain it against all criticism. . . .

THE PIONEERS

THE EARLIEST WHITE SETTLERS IN MISSOURI

ALEXANDER MAJORS

Alexander Majors, who has been called Kansas City's first millionaire, made his fortune in the freighting business on the Santa Fe Trail. He was much interested in the beginnings of the Pony Express; note the reference to him in Dick Swearingen's graphic description of the first run of that famous mail service a little further along in this book. Majors' Seventy Years on the Frontier *was edited by Colonel Prentiss Ingraham, best known as writer of dime novels about "Buffalo Bill" Cody; and Cody himself wrote an introduction to the Majors book of recollections. It is from the second chapter of that work that we take the descriptions of Missouri in the eighteen-twenties and thirties which follow.*

There was about one-fourth of the entire territory of Missouri that was covered with timber, and three-fourths in prairie land, with an annual growth of sage-grass, as it was called, about one and one-half feet high, and as thick as it could well grow; in fact the prairie lands in the commencement of its settlement were one vast meadow, where the farmer could cut good hay suitable for the wintering of his stock almost without regard to the selection of the spot; in other words, it was meadow everywhere outside of the timber lands. This condition of things would apply also to the States of Illinois, Iowa, and some of the other Western States, with the exception of Missouri, which had a greater proportion of timber than either of the others mentioned. The timber in all these States grew in belts along the rivers and their tributaries, the prairie covering the high rolling lands between the streams that made up the water channels of those States.

Many of the streams in the first settling of these States were bold, clear running water, and many of them in Missouri were sufficiently strong almost the year round to afford good water power for running machinery, and it was the prediction in the commencement of the settlement of these States by the best-informed people, that the water would increase, for the reason that the swampy portions in the bottom lands, and where there were small lakes, would, by the settlement of the country, become diverted, its force to run directly into and strengthen the larger streams for all time to come. And to show how practical results overthrow theories, the fact proved to be exactly the reverse of their predictions. There has been a continuous slow decline in the natural flow of water-supply from the first settlement of the country. Many places that I can now remember that were ponds or small lakes, or in other words little reservoirs, which held the water for months while it would be slowly passing out and feeding the streams, have now become fields and plowed ground. Roads and ditches have been made that let the water off at once after a rainfall. The result has been that streams that used to turn machinery have become not much more than outlets for the heavy rainfalls that occur in the rainy season, and if twenty of those streams, each one of which had water enough to run machinery seventy years ago, were all put together now into one stream, there would not be sufficient power to run a good plant of machinery. The numerous springs that could be found on every forty or eighty acres of land in the beginning, have very many of them entirely failed. . . .

All the first settlers in the State located along the timber belts, without an exception, and cultivated the timber lands to produce their grain and vegetables. It was many years after the forest lands were settled before prairie lands were cultivated to any extent, and it was found later that the prairie lands were more fertile than they gave them credit for being before real tests in the way of farming were made with them. The sage grass had the tenacity to stand a great deal of grazing and tramping over, and still grow to considerable perfection. It required years of grazing upon the prairie before the wild grass, which was universal in the beginning, gave way, but in the timber portions the vegetation that was found in the first settling of the land gave way almost at once. In two years from the time a farmer moved upon a new spot and turned his stock loose upon it, the original wild herbs that were found there disappeared and other vegetation took its place. The land, being exceedingly fertile, never failed to produce a crop of vegetation, and when one variety did appear and cover the entire surface as thick as it could grow for a few years, it seemed to exhaust the quality of the soil that produced that kind, and that variety would give way and something new come up. . . .

The first settlers in the Mississippi Valley were as a rule poor people, who were industrious, economizing, and self-sustaining. From ninety-five to ninety-seven per cent of the entire population manufactured at home almost everything necessary for good living. A great many of them when they were crossing the Ohio and Mississippi to their new homes would barely have money enough to pay their ferriage across the rivers, and one of the points in selling out whatever they had to spare when they made up their minds to emigrate was to be sure to have cash enough with them to pay their ferriage. They generally carried with them a pair of chickens, ducks, geese, and if possible a pair of pigs, their cattle and horses. The wife took her spinning wheel, a bunch of cotton or flax, and was ready to go to spinning as soon as she landed on the premises, often having her cards and wheel at work before her husband could build a log cabin. Going into a land, as it was then, that flowed with milk and honey, they were enabled by the use of their own hands and brains to make an independent and good living. There was any quantity of game, bear, elk, deer, wild turkeys, and wild honey to be found in the woods, so that no man with a family, who had pluck and energy enough about him to stir around, ever need to be without a supply of food. At that time nature afforded the finest of pasture, both summer and winter, for his stock.

While the people as a rule were not educated, many of them very illiterate as far as education was concerned, they were thoroughly self-sustaining when it came to the knowledge required to do things that brought about a plentiful supply of the necessities of life. In those times all were on an equality, for each man and his family had to produce what was required to live upon, and when one man was a little better dressed than another there could be no complaint from his neighbor, for each one had the same means in his hands to bring about like results, and he could not say his neighbor was better dressed than he was because he had cheated some other neighbor out of something, and bought the dress; for at that time the goods all had to come to them in the same way—by their own industry. There was but little stealing or cheating among them. There was no money to steal, and if a man stole a piece of jeans or cloth of any kind he would be apprehended at once. Society at that time was homogeneous and simple, and opportunities for vice were very rare. There were very few old bachelors and old maids, for about the only thing a young man could do when he became twenty-one, and his mother quit making his clothes and doing his washing, was to marry one of his neighbor's daughters. The two would then work together, as was the universal custom, and soon produce with their own hands abundance of supplies to live upon.

The country was new, and when a young man got married his father and brothers, and his wife's father and brothers, often would turn out and help him put up a log cabin, which work required only a few days, and he and his spouse would move into it at once. They would go to work in the same way as their fathers had done, and in a few years would be just as independent as the old people. The young ladies most invariably spun and wove, and made their bridal dresses. At that time there were millions of acres of land that a man could go and squat on, build his cabin, and sometimes live for years upon before the land would come into market; and with the prosperity attending such undertakings, as a general thing he would manage in some way, when the land did come into market, to pay $2.25 per acre for as much as he required for the maintenance of his family.

Men in those days who came to Missouri and looked at the land often declined to select a home in the State on account of their having no market for their products, everybody producing all that was needed for home consumption and often a surplus, and they were too far away from any of the large cities of the country, without transportation of either steamboats or railroads (for it was before the time of steamboats, much less railroads) to make them markets for business and trade. Men in the early settlement often wondered if the rich land of the State would ever be worth $5 per acre.

Missouri at that time was considered the western confines of civilization, and it was believed then that there never would be in the future any white settlements of civilized people existing between the western borders of Missouri and the Pacific Coast, unless it might be the strip between the Sierra Nevada Mountains and the Pacific Ocean, which the people at that time knew but little or nothing about.

In 1820 and 1830 there were a great many peaceable tribes of Indians, located by the Government all along the western boundary of Missouri, in what was then called the Indian Territory, and has since then become the States of Kansas, Nebraska, and Oklahoma Territory. I remember the names of many of the tribes who were our nearest neighbors across the line, and among them were the Shawnees, Delawares, Wyandottes, Kickapoos, Miamis, Sacs, Foxes, Osages, Peorias, and Iowas, all of whom were perfectly friendly and docile, and lived for a great many years in close proximity to the white settlers, even coming among them to trade without any outbreaks or trespassing upon the rights of the white people in any way or manner worth mentioning.

There was a long period existing from 1825 to 1860 of perfect harmony between these tribes and the white people, and in fact even to this day there is no disturbance between these tribes and their neighbors, the whites. The Indian troubles have been among the Sioux, Arapahoes, Cheyennes, Apaches, Utes, and some other minor tribes, all of which, at the present time, seem to have submitted to their fate in whatever direction it may lie. There is one remark that I will venture here, and it is this, that while the white people were in the power of the Indians and understood it, we got along with the Indian a great deal better than when the change to the white people took place. In the early days white men respected the Indian's rights thoroughly, and would not be the aggressors, and often they were at the mercy of the Indians, but as soon as they began to feel that they could do as they pleased, they became more aggressive and had less regard for what the Indian considered his rights. Then in the early days Indians were paid their annuities in an honest way, and there was no feeling among them that they were mistreated by the agent whose duty it was to pay them this annuity.

I was acquainted with one Indian agent by the name of Major Cummings, who for a long time was a citizen of Jackson County, and for a great many years agent for a number of the tribes living along the borders of Missouri. There never was a complaint or even a suspicion, to the best of my knowledge, that he or his clerks ever took one cent of the annuities that belonged to the Indians. The money was paid to them in silver, either in whole or half dollars, and the head of every family received every cent of his quota. Therefore we had a long period of quiet and peace with our red brethren. It is only since the late war that there has been so much complaint from the Indians with reference to the scanty allowances and poor food and blankets.

DANIEL BOONE FINDS "ELBOW-ROOM" IN MISSOURI

TIMOTHY FLINT

Timothy Flint was a man of vigorous mind, an itching heel, and a ready pen. A graduate of Harvard, he entered the Congregational clergy and soon found himself a church missionary and circuit rider in the West. He spent several years up and down the eastern edge of what is now the State of Missouri, settling for three years (1816–1819) at St. Charles, where he founded a church and a school. He liked St. Charles and a few years later bought a farm near there, but did not live upon it long.

Flint later devoted most of his time to literary labors as magazine editor, novelist, biographer, and recorder of his own experiences. Perhaps his best remembered book is his first one—Recollections of the Last Ten Years (1826).

Doubtless Flint was moved to write his life of Boone because of the old hunter's choice of the St. Charles region for a home when he removed from Kentucky. There old Boone was held in high respect, though he had his land-title troubles after Missouri passed out of Spanish control; but by the time Flint was a neighbor of his, Congress had granted him 850 acres in the Femme Osage district.

The following pages are taken from Flint's biography, the full title of which runs: The First White Man of the West, or the Life and Exploits of COL. DAN'L. BOONE, the First Settler of Kentucky; Interspersed with Incidents in the Early Annals of the Country. *Of course, Dan'l was not "the first white man of the West."*

After Boone was established in Missouri, he made many journeys

farther to the West, exploring, hunting, trapping. He often visited his
sons and their families, who had settled in the Boon's Lick region of
central Missouri. There is even a somewhat hazy tradition that he once
traveled as far west as the Yellowstone. He died in 1820 and was buried
beside his wife near his adopted home. But in 1845 Kentuckians dis-
interred the two bodies from their resting place in the region in which
he had found refuge and transported them to Frankfort, where Ken-
tucky, which had deprived him of extensive lands half a century before,
now gave him a good six feet of earth for burial, and erected a monu-
ment over his remains.

Among others who made these loose and unfortunate entries
[of land titles in Kentucky] was Daniel Boone. Unaccustomed to the
forms of law and technical precision, he was guided by his own views
of what was proper and requisite, and made such brief and general
entries, as were afterwards held not sufficient to identify the land. He
had discovered and explored the country when it was all one vast wilderness—unoccupied, and unclaimed. He and a few other hardy pioneers,
by almost incredible hardships, dangers, and sacrifices, had won it from
the savage foe; and judging from his own single and generous mind, he
did not suppose that question would ever be made of his right to occupy
such favorite portions as he might select and pay for. He did not think
it possible that any one, knowing these circumstances, could be found
so greedy or so heartless, as to grudge him the quiet and unmolested
enjoyment of what he had so dearly earned. But in this he was sadly
mistaken. A set of speculators and interlopers, who, following in the
train of civilization and wealth, came to enrich themselves by monopo-
lizing the rich lands which had thus been won for them, and by the aid
of legal advisers, following all the nice requisitions of the law, pounced,
among others, upon the lands of our old pioneer. He was not at first
disturbed by these speculating harpies; and game being plenty, he gave
himself little uneasiness about the claims and titles to particular spots,
so long as he had such vast hunting grounds to roam in—which, however, he had the sorrow to see daily encroached upon by the new settlements of the immigrants.

But the inroads made by the frequent settlements in his accustomed
hunting range, were not the only annoyances which disturbed the simple habits and patriarchal views of Boone. Civilization brought along
with it all the forms of law, and the complicated organization of society and civil government, the progress of which had kept pace with
the increasing population. . . .

Influenced by these feelings, he removed from Kentucky to the great
Kanahwa; where he settled near Point Pleasant. He had been informed

that buffaloes and deer were still to be found in abundance on the unsettled bottoms of this river, and that it was a fine country for trapping.
Here he continued to reside several years. But he was disappointed in
his expectations of finding game. The vicinity of the settlements above
and below this unsettled region, had driven the buffaloes from the country; and though there were plenty of deer, yet he derived but little success from his trapping. He finally commenced raising stock, and began
to turn his attention to agriculture.

While thus engaged, he met with some persons who had returned
from a tour up the Missouri, who described to him the fine country
bordering upon that river. The vast prairies—the herds of buffaloes—
the grizzly bears—the beavers and otters; and above all, the ancient and
unexplored forests of that unknown region, fired his imagination, and
produced at once a resolve to remove there.

Accordingly, gathering up such useful articles of baggage as were of
light carriage, among which his trusty rifle was not forgotten, he started
with his family, driving his whole stock of cattle along with him, on a
pilgrimage to this new land of promise. He passed through Cincinnati
on his way thither in 1798. Being enquired of as to what had induced
him to leave all the comforts of home, and so rich and flourishing a
country as his dear Kentucky, which he had discovered, and might almost call his own, for the wilds of Missouri? "Too much crowded,"
replied he—"too crowded—I want more elbow room." He proceeded
about forty-five miles above St. Louis, and settled in what is now St.
Charles county. This country being still in the possession of the Spanish,
the ancient laws by which these territories were governed were still in
force there. Nothing could be more simple than their whole system of
administration. They had no constitution, no king, no legislative assem-
blies, no judges, juries, lawyers, or sheriffs. An officer, called the Commandant, and the priests, exercised all the functions of civil magistrates,
and decided the few controversies which arose among these primitive
inhabitants, who held and occupied many things in common. They suffered their ponies, their cattle, their swine, and their flocks, to ramble
and graze on the same common prairies and pastures—having but few
fences or inclosures, and possessing but little of that spirit of speculation, enterprise, and money-making, which has always characterized the
Americans.

These simple laws and neighborly customs suited the peculiar habits
and temper of Boone. And as his character for honesty, courage, and
fidelity followed him there, he was appointed Commandant for the district of St. Charles by the Spanish Commandant. He retained this command, and continued to exercise the duties of his office with credit to
himself, and to the satisfaction of all concerned, until the government
of the United States went into effect.

ASHLEY'S HUNDRED

JOHN G. NEIHARDT

John Gneisenau Neihardt was born in Illinois in 1881. He lived for many years in association with Indian tribes in Nebraska and the Dakotas, sometimes representing the federal Office of Indian Affairs; and he came to know Indian character, customs, and religion probably more intimately than any other writer. But much of his later life has been spent in Missouri. He was literary editor of the St. Louis Post-Dispatch *1926–1938 and later lived for a time at Branson, in the Ozark lakes region. In 1947 the University of Missouri conferred the honorary degree of Doctor of Letters upon him and the next year invited him to become poet in residence and lecturer at the University.*

Although famous chiefly for his epic cycle of narrative poems dealing with the explorers, fur traders, and Indian wars of the early West, Neihardt wrote some strong short stories early in his literary career, many fine lyric poems, and a distinguished novel based on Indian customs and theology entitled Black Elk Speaks.

The following lines are taken from the first poem of his epic cycle (though the second to be published), The Song of Three Friends *(1919) and includes the first section and a part of the second.*

Who now reads clear the roster of that band?
Alas, Time scribbles with a careless hand
And often pinchbeck doings from that pen
Bite deep, where deeds and dooms of mighty men
Are blotted out beneath a sordid scrawl!

One hundred strong they flocked to Ashley's call
That spring of eighteen hundred twenty-two;
For tales of wealth, out-legending Peru,
Came wind-blown from Missouri's distant springs,
And that old sireny of unknown things
Bewitched them, and they could not linger more.
They heard the song the sea winds sang the shore
When earth was flat, and black ships dared the steep
Where bloomed the purple perils of the deep
In dragon haunted gardens. They were young.
Albeit some might feel the winter flung

Upon their heads, 'twas less like autumn's drift
Than backward April's unregarded sift
On stout oaks thrilling with the sap again.
And some had scarce attained the height of men,
Their lips unroughed, and gleaming in their eyes
The light of immemorial surprise
That life still kept the spaciousness of old
And, like the hoarded tales their grandsires told,
Might still run bravely.

                                For a little span
Their life-fires flare like torches in the van
Of westward progress, ere the great wind 'woke
To snuff them. Many vanished like a smoke
The blue air drinks; and e'en of those who burned
Down to the socket, scarce a tithe returned
To share at last the ways of quiet men,
Or see the hearth-reek drifting once again
Across the roofs of old St. Louis town.

And now no more the mackinaws come down,
Their gunwales low with costly packs and bales,
A wind of wonder in their shabby sails,
Their homing oars flung rhythmic to the tide;
And nevermore the masted keelboats ride
Missouri's stubborn waters on the lone
Long zigzag journey to the Yellowstone.
Their hulks have found the harbor ways that know
The ships of all the Sagas, long ago—
A moony haven where no loud gale stirs.
The trappers and the singing *voyageurs*
Are comrades now of Jason and his crew,
Foregathered in that timeless rendezvous
Where come at last all seekers of the Fleece.

Not now of those who, dying, dropped in peace
A brimming cup of years the song shall be:
From Mississippi to the Western Sea,
From Britain's country to the Rio Grande
Their names are written deep across the land
In pass and trail and river, like a rune.

Pore long upon that roster by the moon
Of things remembered dimly. Tangled, blear
The writing runs; yet presently appear

Three names of men that, spoken, somehow seem
Incantatory trumpets of a dream
Obscurely blowing from the hinter-gloom.
Of these and that inexorable doom
That followed like a hound upon the scent,
Here runs the tale.

                When Major Henry went
Up river at the head of Ashley's band,
Already there were robins in the land.
Home-keeping men were following the plows
And through the smoke-thin greenery of boughs
The scattering wild-fire of the fruit bloom ran.

Behold them starting northward, if you can.
Dawn flares across the Mississippi's tide;
A tumult runs along the waterside
Where, scenting an event, St. Louis throngs.
Above the buzzling voices soar the songs
Of waiting boatmen—lilting *chansonettes*
Whereof the meaning laughs, the music frets,
Nigh weeping that such gladness can not stay.
In turn, the herded horses snort and neigh
Like panic bugles. Up the gangplanks poured,
Go streams of trappers, rushing goods aboard
The snub-built keelboats, squat with seeming sloth—
Baled three-point blankets, blue and scarlet cloth,
Rum, powder, flour, guns, gauderies and lead.
And all about, goodbyes are being said.
Gauche girls with rainy April in their gaze
Cling to their beardless heroes, count the days
Between this parting and the wedding morn,
Unwitting how unhuman Fate may scorn
The youngling dream. For O how many a lad
Would see the face of Danger, and go mad
With her weird vixen beauty; aye, forget
This girl's face, yearning upward now and wet,
Half woman's with the first vague guess at woe!

And now commands are bellowed, boat horns blow
Haughtily in the dawn; the tumult swells.
The tow-crews, shouldering the long cordelles
Slack from the mastheads, lean upon the sag.
The keelboats answer lazily and drag

Their blunt prows slowly in the gilded tide.
A steersman sings, and up the riverside
The gay contagious ditty spreads and runs
Above the shouts, the uproar of the guns,
The nickering of horses.

                              So, they say,
Went forth a hundred singing men that day;
And girlish April went ahead of them.
The music of her trailing garment's hem
Seemed scarce a league ahead. A little speed
Might yet almost surprise her in the deed
Of sorcery; for, ever as they strove,
A gray-green smudge in every poplar grove
Proclaimed the recent kindling. Aye, it seemed
That bird and bush and tree had only dreamed
Of song and leaf and blossom, till they heard
The young men's feet; when tree and bush and bird
Unleashed the whole conspiracy of awe!
Pale green was every slough about the Kaw;
About the Platte, pale green was every slough;
And still the pale green lingered at the Sioux,
So close they trailed the marching of the South.
But when they reached the Niobrara's mouth
The witchery of Spring had taken flight
And, like a girl grown woman over night,
Young Summer glowed.

HENRY DODGE AND DUFF GREEN

Floyd C. Shoemaker

Floyd Calvin Shoemaker, though born in Florida, was brought to Missouri at an early age. He received his higher education at the State College at Kirksville and the University of Missouri; from the latter he received two earned degrees and later an honorary doctorate. Since 1910 he has been officially connected with the State Historical Society of Missouri (executive secretary and librarian 1915–1960), retiring to the po-

Reprinted from *Missouri's Struggle for Statehood, 1804–1821* by Floyd C. Shoemaker. By permission of the author.

sition of consultant after half a century of more active service. He is the
author of several books and many articles in historical journals—par-
ticularly in the Missouri Historical Review, *of which he was long editor.*
In 1955 he was officially dubbed "Mr. Missouri" by resolution of the
State Senate.

The sketches of two leading Missouri pioneer figures here presented
are taken from Shoemaker's most important book, Missouri's Struggle
for Statehood, 1804–1821.

General Henry Dodge, or "Honest Harry Dodge" as he was
affectionately called by the West, was born at Port Vincennes, October
12, 1782, of English and Scotch-Irish parents. His minority was spent
under his mother's guidance in Kentucky and later under his father's
direction in upper Louisiana. His military career began early in 1806
and continued for nearly three decades; his civil career covered a period
of over half a century. The former won him a place in popular favor
next to that occupied by General Jackson; the latter raised him to the
high honor of being appointed the first Governor of the original Territory of Wisconsin and also of holding that office two terms after the
separation of Iowa Territory; of being elected the Territorial Delegate
to Congress from Wisconsin, when a change in national politics had
lost him his former position; and finally of being elected the first United
States Senator from the State of Wisconsin. Although not a great man
either in war or in politics, Dodge was an eminently successful one in
both. His talents were essentially those of a leader, having been so
endowed by nature in both mind and body and so trained by an active
life among frontiersmen and Indians. Since the achievements of Dodge
in the field are familiar to students of western history, we will turn to
his less known though perhaps equally interesting and valuable career
in politics.

In politics Dodge was a staunch Democrat, and a warm, personal
friend of Jackson and Benton. As the chief executive of Wisconsin Territory he exerted the greatest influence in the enacting of good laws,
both by forceful and decisively worded messages and by his direct influence over the members of the legislature. He had that rare faculty of
being able to maintain his prerogatives as an official without making
enemies. His success in dealing with scores of Indian tribes both in
peace and war was marked and to them he was one of the most feared
and respected men in the west. The red sons of the forest and plain,
whether enemies or friends, relied on the word of Henry Dodge when
the threats and promises of other leaders had failed to move them. His
strong common sense and fundamental honesty is shown in his refusal

either to meddle in the fight over the location of the capital of Wisconsin Territory or to accept as a gift any lots in Madison.

After entering the halls of Congress, he always felt bound by the instructions of his legislature even though at times these were contrary to his personal convictions. He consistently advocated internal improvements, an adequate military force on the frontier, a duty on lead, and cheap land. His convictions on the land question were so statesmanlike that we marvel at the comparative silence of his biographers on this subject. As Governor of Wisconsin Territory in his second annual message of November 7, 1837, he said: "Land was the immediate gift of God to man, and from the earliest history of the world was designed for cultivation and improvement, and should cease to be an object of speculation." "Speculators in the public lands have purchased large tracts east of the Mississippi in this Territory, which remain waste until they will sell for the highest prices; thereby retarding the growth and settlement of the Territory to the great injury of the actual settler." On February 24, 1853, in supporting the Homestead Bill, Senator Dodge delivered what must be regarded as one of the most truthful, prophetic, and powerful speeches that found its way into the record. That speech is now almost forgotten, but before its centennial can be observed, not only scholars but men of affairs and all progressive citizens will be familiar with the fundamental truths it contains. We can recall but few instances in American history where our statesmen and writers have as thoroughly appreciated so great an evil, so succinctly described it, and so accurately perceived its remedy as Senator Dodge did in this exposition of the land question. The following extract has been selected from that speech:

The soil of a country is the gift of the Creator to His creatures, and, in a government of the people, that gift should not become the object of speculation and monopoly. Springing from the earth and destined to return to it, every man desires to possess some of it, wants a spot he can call his own. It is a deep and absorbing feeling which no people have manifested more strongly than the Americans. If you desire to render this Republic indestructible, to extinguish every germ of agrarianism, and secure for ages the quiet enjoyment of vested rights, you should give an interest in the soil to every man who asks it. If every quarter section of the public land was the *bona fide* property of an actual settler, it would do more to perpetuate our liberties than all the constitutions, State or National, which have ever been devised. Incorporate every man with the soil, throw around him the blessed endearments of home, and you bind him in an allegiance stronger than a thousand oaths.

When we recall that these words were spoken not by a rabid demagogue or a pauper social disturber, but by an old man in his seventy-first year, who was a United States Senator, who held large landed interests, and who based his statements on a personal experience in public life that had covered nearly half a century, then the weight of their truth is increased tenfold.

If it were not too much of a digression we would be glad to enter even briefly into the private life of this celebrated "Captain of Aggressive Civilization," to describe his views on such questions as religion and slavery, to eulogize his remarkable mother, Nancy Ann Hunter, who alone in the annals of this nation gave birth to two United States Senators, Henry Dodge and Lewis F. Linn, and to expand upon this, the only example in our history, of a father and son—Henry Dodge and Augustus Caesar Dodge—sitting together first in the lower house of our national legislature and finally in the Senate chamber.

Interesting as is the life of Henry Dodge, we do not regard it more fascinating than was the checkered career of General Duff Green. In several respects Duff Green was one of the most remarkable of those men who framed Missouri's first constitution. He was beyond dispute the most versatile man in the convention; and became its greatest politician. In this latter capacity he attained a national reputation. Later he achieved honor as a diplomat, and finally in his old age received posterity's blessing by constructing a railroad and founding a city.

A native of Kentucky, Duff Green was related to some of the best and oldest families in Virginia. At an early age he taught school, studied law and was admitted to the bar, and sold goods as a country merchant. Having immigrated to Missouri Territory about 1817 he engaged in politics, mail contracts, speculation, and also had a large law practice. He established the first mail stage line west of the Mississippi river; and founded the town of Chariton, being its first postmaster. After the framing of Missouri's first constitution, Duff Green was elected a representative from Howard county in 1820 to the State legislature and in 1822 was elected a State Senator. In 1821 he was chosen Brigadier-General of the first brigade of the first division of the Missouri militia, and owing to his holding this office together with his services in Kentucky in the War of 1812, he was always known as General Duff Green. In 1823 Green became owner and editor of Benton's organ, the *St. Louis Enquirer,* and two years later purchased and edited the *United States Telegraph* at Washington. From that time to his death in 1875, he was always more or less before the public. As editor of the *Telegraph* he became one of the most powerful factors in national politics, and is credited with having been one of the chief instruments in the election of Jackson in 1828. His paper was then given the government patronage, and this placed Green in good financial circumstances. His subsequent break with Jackson in 1830, his support of Clay in 1832 and of Calhoun in 1836, did not ruin him, as it did many other politicians. His paper continued to wield the greatest influence, and was known for its aggressiveness and independence, and for its large and philosophical views on national finance.

General Green visited Europe frequently on important public missions, conferring with leading statesmen and crowned heads. In 1843 he was sent to Mexico to aid in conducting negotiations for the acquisition of Texas; and under President Taylor's administration was again dispatched there on public business.

In later life he took the contract for constructing the Tennessee Railroad from Dalton, Georgia, to Knoxville, Tennessee, and was one of the founders of the former city. In the lives of few men are there crowded so many different and dramatic events as are revealed in Green's career. In many ways it is an epitome of the biography of the entire convention of 1820.

THE MAD WOLF

JOSEPH E. BADGER, JR.

Joseph Edward Badger, Jr., later well known to readers of dime novels as "Harry Hazard," was born in Illinois in 1848; but when he was sixteen his father, then chief clerk in the Quartermaster's Department at Jefferson City, moved his family to the capital city. Joe attended Bryant's Business College in St. Joseph for a time, but he soon found his true vocation in writing western pieces for Bonner's New York Weekly *and then for Beadle's dime novel series. For a long time he turned out stories for Beadle at the rate of one every five or six weeks.*

The latter part of Badger's life was tragic. When competition in cheap books virtually wrecked the business of Beadle & Adams in the latter 1870's, he turned to the trade of cigar making and later ran a billiard hall in Blue Rapids, Kansas. After an accident, followed by a term of poor health, he committed suicide in 1909.

The narrative which follows is taken from No. 25 of Beadle's Boys' Library, entitled Round the Camp Fire; or Snow-Bound at "Freeze-Out" Camp.

"I hev knowed men that would ruther lie than to eat when they was hungry, but I never tuck no stock in sech onnat'ral critters. It's a p'izen bad practice, an' I'm sorry to see that some o' you boys is kinder got a leanin' that-a-way—'specially when you come back from a hunt whar you hain't had overly good luck.

"Ef you'd only take a fri'ndly warnin' an' pattern by *me,* you'd be better off, an' I'd be spared many a sleepless night which I lay awake all the time a-grievin' over the awful bounders which you told, to 'splain *why* you didn't kill what you'd orter done."

"We were talking about wolves," hastily interposed one of the party . . . evidently fancying that the veteran's discourse was taking a turn too personal to be interesting to all parties. "Did you ever know of a human being whom a mad wolf bit?"

"They's mighty few things I hain't see'd or heared tell of in my time. But of them all, I don't know of a more curiouser sarcumstance than what happened after old Hark Triplett was bit by a mad wolf which he had ondertook to p'izen.

"That was a long time ago, when I was a right smart chunk of a boy, livin' 'long o' my uncle down in old Mizzouri, at a little town called Bitter Crick. 'Twas a little place, as I said afore, but jest the liveliest town in seventeen States, 'cordin' to its size. The stage run through it every week, an' we hed a malishy comp'ny, an' a brass band, an' a spellin' school, an' a tavern, an' *more* dogs! Why it wasn't nothin' out o' the common to see as many as seventeen dog-fights all a-goin' to oncet!

"A mighty lively little town, but old Hark Triplett bu'stit it wide open when he ondertook to p'izen a old he wolf that'd stolen a couple o' his sheep—clean bu'sted it up, an' now I don't reckon thar's a single stick or stone o' the hull city left!

"When Hark found out that it was a wolf that was makin' so free with his sheep, he 'lowed he'd putt a stop to the fun, an' takin' a chunk o' the mutton that the wolf had left, he scorched it over a fire, then tied it onto the eend of a trail-rope, mounted his mule an' sot off draggin' the bait ahind him, crossin' back an' forth atween his place an' the hills, so's to make sure the wolf, in comin' out after its supper that night, would cross the trail an' foller it up ontel he found the bait.

"When tired o' this work, Hark got down an' wettin' the bait, sprinkled some strychnine over it, then went back home fer to git sleep enough so he could wake up airly enough to find the dead wolf afore anybody else, or they might try to cheat him out o' the pelt an' the bounty which the State offered fer wolf-scalps.

"He was up an' out afore day, but it chainced that the wolf hed over-slept hisself, not findin' the bait ontel just afore Hark come along.

"The p'izen was just beginnin' to work, an' no sooner did Hark stick his nose through the bushes than the wolf up an' jumped onto the old man, takin' a piece o' meat clean out o' his shoulder.

"The old man was so s'prised an' skeered that he tumbled over an' over, yellin' like mad, an' afore he could think to use his gun, the wolf was gone, runnin' like the devil was at its tail, right down through the town.

"In course the dogs turned out, an' tackled the wolf an' made sech a fuss an' 'fernal rumpus that everybody in town turned out, most of 'em b'lievin' that the world was comin' to a eend. An' ef it wasn't, that skrimmage was fated to be the eend o' Bitter Crick, anyway!

"The wolf was mad, in course, fer p'izen al'ays makes 'em that-a-way, an' though a thousan' dogs, more or less, was piled onto him, he fit like a four-legged devil, an' bit or clawed 'most every pup in the hull kit an' boodle!

"Old Triplett come up, jest a-snortin', but he was too late to save even the skelp o' his wolf, which didn't sweeten his temper any, as you kin guess.

"It all come out how he'd p'izened the wolf, but that didn't skeer nobody then, fer they none of 'em knowed how the p'izen worked on critters; but they found out afore the week was over, fer old Triplett went stark ravin' mad from that wolf-bite!

"The fust anybody knowed was when his oldest gal come runnin' in one mornin' airly, sayin' her dad hed ett his old woman an' all the rest o' the young-'uns up, then made a break fer tall timber, runnin' on all fours an' a-growlin' an' a-snappin' an' a-kerryin' on fer all the world like a wolf, in nothin' but his shirt-flaps!

"Course we all turned out to hunt him up, but even then nobody didn't think what was the matter, raaly, layin' it all onto the jim-jams, fer the old man soaked up whisky like a sponge, an' his credit was good fer a bar'l at any time.

"Even when we trailed him to a hole 'mongst the rocks, an' pulled him out by the heels, an' he pitched into us all, tooth an' toe-nails, frothin' at his mouth an' growlin' like a wolf, we didn't raaly think what was the matter, an' handled him as easy as we could, though every time he socked his teeth in, they held on ontel the mouthful o' cloth or flesh, or whatever it was, tore clean out. An' I reckon thar was nigh a dozen of the crowd that he drawed blood from afore we could master him.

"Even then, when he was tied hand an' foot, he fit so desprit that we couldn't tote him home, an' so sent fer a ox-sled that was the nighest thing in the haulin' line.

"But we hadn't much more'n got started fer town, when the old man bu'sted out in a new place, a-yowlin', snarlin', snappin', and yellin' so that the oxen was frightened so bad that they set up a cavortin' that eended only when they bu'sted thar yoke, an' then went off through the bresh, tail-on-eend, as though a million hornets was after 'em!

"Somebody went fer a waggin then, but afore it come the old man hed chawed a great holler in the nigh runner o' that sled, actin' so turribly ferocious that nobody dar' try to putt a gag into his mouth.

"He kept up sech a screechin' that the hosses wouldn't stan when they did come, so we tuck them out, an' pitchin' the old man inside, hauled the waggin home ourselves.

"When we got thar, his mouth was full o' splinters which he chawed out o' the waggin-bed, but we throwed a thick blanket over his head, an' so manidged to git him into the house, tyin' him tight down to the bed afore we tuck the blanket off.

"But it all wan't no use. He died thet same day sufferin' the most awfulest torments, an' from the way things went with him, some in town begun to think that thar was somethin' wuss the matter with him than only the jim-jams, though the idee was so turrible that nobody didn't dast speak right out.

"The truth come out soon enough—too soon fer them as hed bin bitten or scratched by old Triplett—fer the dogs that the wolf hed chawed begun all goin' mad together.

"The word spread like the small-pox, an' everybody as hed guns turned out an' tuck to killin every dog, big an little, old an young, he or she, that they could find.

"It was like the Fo'th of July or a pitched battle the way them old guns 'sploded!

" 'Lection day wasn't nowhar 'longside them times in old Bitter Crick.

"Everybody that hedn't been hurt in ketchin' old Triplett got together, an' threatenin' to shoot down anybody that dared to raise a finger ag'inst it, tuck pris'ners all that hed bin marked by the old man durin' that skrimmage, an' tied 'em hand an' foot down to thar beds, to wait an' see ef thar was any signs o' thar goin' mad like the old man hed done.

"When this was done, an' all the dogs killed, an' all the cows an' hosses an' hogs an' sech-like dumb animules, was fast tied or penned up, then the rest of us began to breathe more free like, thinkin' every danger was guarded ag'inst.

"An' so it would 'a' bin ef old Hark hed bin bit by a mad-dog, 'stead of a wolf what hed bin p'izened, but as it was, the fun was only commencin', nur it didn't stop ontel the hull town of Bitter Crick was swept away, an' the hull kentry 'round about fer miles an' miles was made a desert waste, whar green things never growed ag'in.

" 'Twas the very next day that a mighty cur'ous sight was see'd.

"An old ox-sled come a-r'arin' an' a-t'arin' down the middle o' town, wavin' its tongue from side to side, like it was the live tail to a power-ful big sarpint, fastened onto the wrong eend! Nur they wasn't no oxen nur nothin' hitched onto it fer to make eet go! 'Peared like the durned fool thing hed gone plum crazy an' sot out on a 'pendent rampage!

"It'd wheel and turn around an' chase people wherever it could see anybody, an' bang up ag'inst the doors when they run in an' shet 'em, just as though it was a livin' thing.

"Everybody was scar't most to death, thinkin' thar must be witches to work in it, an' nobody knowed what it all meant ontel we hearn the rattle o' waggin-wheels, an' saw the same waggin that old Triplett hed bin hauled home in, come jest a-boomin' 'round the corner, swingin' its tongue like the sled did; an' then we knowed what was up.

"Both the ox-sled an' the waggin hed gone mad 'cause old Triplett hed bit 'em!

"We looked on out o' the upper winders, or from the house-tops, or in the trees, wherever we'd run to git out o' the way o' that p'izen sled, an' from thar we see'd a monstrous queer sight—ef we didn't, then I wouldn't say so!

" 'Peared like them two old go-carts hed eyes fer to see with, sense they run straight at each other, r'arin' up on eend an' slashin' thar tongues together like mad, makin' more noise than a harrycane an' thunder-storm b'iled down into one!

"In natur, the sled was the clumsiest, but its tongue was the heaviest an' strongest, an' bimeby it broke the waggin tongue short off. But the old go-cart was gritty, an' didn't give up so easy, but would putt on a bulge an' run clean over the sled, givin' it a nasty kick as it passed, with each wheel, while the sled would h'ist its hind-end an' make the waggin bed rattle at every thump, then whirl around an' slosh its tongue ag'in the wheels as p'izennasty as you please.

"But it was these under-kicks that won the battle fer the sled. I reckon they turned the waggin sick to its stummick; anyhow, the waggin purty soon turned tail an' run fer it, the old sled follerin' after, hot-foot, nur they didn't neither on 'em stop ontel they was clean out o' sight, an' riz the hill south o' town, an' pitched over it onto the rocks at the foot into the crick."

"And that ended the matter, I suppose?" asked Pretty Poll, sober as a deacon in meeting.

"So we all thought, but thar was whar we was badly fooled.

"We all run to the hill, an' saw that both sled an' waggin hed bin smashed into kindlin' wood, but true as I'm tellin' of ye, gentlemen, each one o' them bits o' wood was up an' a-fightin' each other like all possessed! An' not only that, but they was a-lammin' away at the trees an' stones, an' so chuck-full o' p'izen was they that whatever they tetched went crazy-mad right off, the trees takin' to thrashin' each other like a harrycane was playin' through thar limbs, an' the rocks a-bumpin' each other ontel they cracked, an' even then the pieces went on a-fightin'! I tell you gentlemen, it was jest turrible fer to see an' hear!

"We knowed it was no use a-fightin' ag'inst sech luck, an' so we jest ketched up what critters we could, packin' onto them the most vallible things as lay handy, then lit out o' thar fer dear life never haltin' ontel we put the Mizzouri ahind us, fer we knowed them mad things'd never try to cross runnin' water."

"How did it turn out? What became of the people you left behind, tied to their beds?" asked Woodcock Andy.

"I never went back thar ag'in, but them as did, said they reckoned some o' them mad sticks must 'a' 'tacted the houses, or mebbe them as the ox-sled bumped ag'inst jest afore it tackled the waggin, went mad too an' shook around so lively that they scattered the fire what we left in the stoves an' fire-places, an' that spread an' spread ontel everythin' in an' around the town was burnt up. In course the trees that went mad, died, an' so was easy to burn.

"Anyhow, the hull place was made like a salt desert, an' never nothin' growed thar any more, all 'long of old dad Triplett ondertakin' to p'izen that wolf.

JOE BOWERS

This ballad based on the gold rush to California is very widely disseminated throughout the country, and has many versions. The one here given is that printed in H. M. Belden's Ballads and Songs Collected by the Missouri Folk-Lore Society.

My name is Joe Bowers;
I've got a brother Ike;
I came from old Missouri,
All the way from Pike.
I'll tell you why I left thar
And why I came to roam

And leave my poor old mammy
So far away from home.

I used to court a gal thar,
Her name was Sally Black.
I axed her if she'd marry me;
She said it was a whack.
Says she to me, "Joe Bowers,
Before we hitch for life,
You ought to get a little home
To keep your little wife."

"Oh, Sally, dearest Sally,
Oh, Sally, for your sake
I'll go to California
And try to raise a stake."
Says she to me, "Joe Bowers,
You are the man to win;
Here's a kiss to bind the bargain,"
And she hove a dozen in.

When I got in that country
I hadn't nary red,
I had such wolfish feelings
I wished myself 'most dead;
But the thought of my dear Sally
Soon made them feelings git,
And I whispered hopes to Bowers—
I wish I had 'em yit.

At length I went to mining,
Put in my biggest licks,
Came down upon the boulders
Just like a thousand bricks!
I worked both late and early,
In rain, in sun, in snow—
I was working for my Sally;
It was all the same to Joe.

At length I got a letter
From my dear brother Ike,
It came from old Missouri,
All the way from Pike;
It brought to me the darndest news
That ever you did hear.

My heart is almost burstin',
So pray excuse this tear.

It said that Sal was false to me,
Her love for me had fled,
She'd got married to a butcher—
The butcher's hair was red.
And more than that, the letter said—
It's enough to make me swear—
That Sally had a baby;
The baby had red hair.

Now I've told you all
About this said affair,
'Bout Sally marrying a butcher,
That butcher with red hair.
But whether 'twas a boy or gal child
The letter never said;
It only said the baby's hair
Was inclined to be red.

FIRST RUN OF THE PONY EXPRESS

DICK SWEARINGEN

Dick Swearingen was born in 1896 on Pershing Farm, outside Laclede, Missouri, attended school in Brookfield and Trenton, and for sixteen years worked as a cowboy and ranch hand in the state of Nevada. At one time he was a cattle buyer for the Great Western Meat Company. From 1924 until his retirement in 1956 he was a switchman for the Kansas City Terminal Railroad.

His wife Martha, represented in another part of this book, collaborated with Dick in the writing of this narrative, which first appeared in Junior Scholastic, *March 22, 1960.*

Johnson William Richardson pushed back his sombrero and stared at his boss with a look of dismay on his wind-whipped face.

"The mail train'll be more than two hours late, you say, Mr. Majors?"

Alexander Majors, tall and black-bearded, nodded gravely. As part-

From *Junior Scholastic,* March 22, 1960. © 1960 by Scholastic Magazines, Inc. Reprinted by permission.

owner of the newly organized Pony Express mail service to the West, he had been hoping his first run would go out on schedule.

Billy Richardson tugged at his drooping black mustaches. "Come on, girl," he said, and led his trembling bay mare back through the crowd that hemmed them in.

Once inside the Pony Express stables, Billy patted the XP brand on the quivering flank. "Souvenir hunters!" he snorted. "Two hours more out there and you wouldn't have a hair left in your mane or tail! And these fancy togs! . . . ."

Billy looked at his red flannel shirt and the blue trousers tucked inside embroidered, silver-trimmed boots. He was a lean five feet six, with black curly hair reaching his shoulders.

In the late afternoon of April 3, 1860, hundreds of town and country folk milled about the Overland Express Office in the town of St. Joseph, Missouri, western terminus of the railroad and telegraph. From a flag-draped stand a brass band kept repeating the familiar "Camptown Races," "Hail Columbia," and "Dixie Land."

Two hours passed. Billy fidgeted with his hardware—a rifle, two revolvers, and a horn. His lunch was tucked in the pocket of his fine buckskin jacket—a handful of biscuits, some bacon, and a canteen of cold tea.

Seven o'clock came, and with it a whistle from the mail train. The mare pricked up her ears. Billy straightened the "mochila," a light leather blanket that fitted over his saddle and carried on each of its four corners a hard leather box known as a "cantina."

Quickly the postmaster padlocked the mail into the cantinas. Short speeches by Mr. Majors and the mayor, the boom of a cannon, cheers, pistol shots—and the Pony Express was on its way! Waving to the crowd, Billy Richardson cantered down to the Missouri River and onto the ferryboat *Denver,* where he changed from the "fancy togs" to work clothes.

Once across the river, he galloped away down a muddy road into the gathering darkness. In little more than an hour he covered the twenty miles to Troy, his first "swing" station. Here, in less than the two minutes allowed, he "swung" the mochila to the back of a waiting pony and sped away.

Two more "swings" and Billy galloped into his rest station at Granada, Kansas, seventy miles from "St. Joe." He found his relief man, Don Rising, hopping from one foot to the other.

"Where you been?" snapped Don through bristling brown mustaches that belied his sixteen years.

"Train late," explained Billy. "I've made up a half hour. See you do as well!"

And Don Rising had done just that by the time he reached his rest station, Marysville, seventy miles away. Here he threw the mochila to Jack Keetley, who sped away up the Oregon Trail into Nebraska.

So the mochila passed from pony to pony. In ten days, less than half the time required by stagecoach or mule-back, the mail was relayed two thousand miles to Sacramento, California.

From Sacramento the river boat *Antelope* carried William Hamilton and his mustang down the river to San Francisco. At 11:30 on the night of April 13th, Hamilton rode down the gangplank into a city ablaze with bonfires. Bells, whistles, and brass bands greeted the arrival of the Pony Express.

Somewhere on the trail during those ten days, two Pony Express riders had met and passed each other. At four o'clock on the afternoon of the day that Billy Richardson had left "St. Joe," San Francisco had cheered the eastbound mail on its way. Amid pistol-shots and the blaring of bands, a nankeen pony, his mochila decked out with miniature American flags, had trotted up the gangplank of the *Antelope*.

At Sacramento, Warren Upson had saddled the strongest, toughest mustang in the corral, for it was snowing in the Sierras.

As he climbed into the mountains, swirling snow blotted out familiar landmarks. "I had to trust to my compass and my pony's instinct," he related. "Once, as we were picking our way around a cliff, the mustang stopped short and refused to budge. I waited. Pretty soon, not fifty yards ahead, thousands of tons of snow came thundering down the mountain side and filled the pass!"

Leading his pony, Upson toiled over the hump where the air was so thin he could scarcely breathe. When he finally stumbled into his rest station at Carson City, Nevada, he had conquered the worst 85 miles of the entire route. The success of the Pony Express was assured.

For braving dangers such as these, the boys received $50 a month and up, depending on the hazards of the trail. In addition, they had lodging and food.

At his rest station, a rider was supposed to take it easy and wait for the mail coming in from the opposite direction. But suppose his relief man were sick or missing? Then he must carry on.

Jack Keetley, known as the "Joyous Jockey of the Pony Express," held the record for continuous riding. In 31 hours he covered 340 miles! "Part of the time I was sound asleep," said Keetley, "but I lived up to the oath I took when I joined The Pony."

By this oath, the boys had promised not to swear, to drink, or to fight, but to be honest and faithful in their duties. To each Mr. Majors gave a Bible and to all this guiding rule: "Think first of the mail, second of your pony, last of yourself."

For the most part, the eighty riders of the Pony Express obeyed this rule as they carried the mail through scorching deserts and blinding blizzards.

Once Thomas King's pony stumbled on a mountain trail, throwing its rider and sending the mochila over a cliff. Tommy, at the risk of his life, crawled down the mountain side and brought back the mochila.

George Little was only sixteen at the time he joined up. When his pony collapsed in a snowdrift, he cut open the cantinas, stuffed the mail inside his shirt, and plodded on.

Only one mail was lost to the Indians, but the pony of Jose Zowglatz came in with arrows sticking from its shoulders and the body of Jose slumped over the saddle. Another pony galloped in with only the mochila, its rider left somewhere on the trail.

The trail had 190 stations. The stops ranged from hotels to holes dug into the hillside and lined with willow saplings.

"But we could sleep anywhere," said a pony rider. "Even though sometimes we had to do our own cooking, we relished our grub—mostly beans, bacon, buffalo meat, and hominy biscuits."

But the boys hungered for sweets. Johnny Frey solved that problem. On his route lived the widow Hargis and her four daughters, all good cooks. At the sound of a special blast from Johnny's horn, out came the girls to fill his hands with cookies. One day they called, "Stick out your fingers, Johnny!" And they slipped over his fingers small round cakes with a hole in the center. "That," say the old timers, "is how the doughnut came to be."

Up and down the trail, too, went the story of how Johnny Frey lost his shirt tail. A Miss Betsey, who was making a log cabin quilt, begged Johnny for his red tie to brighten it up. Johnny refused. So one day Betsey saddled her horse and rode down the trail to meet him. Suspecting her intentions, Johnny put spurs to his pony. Betsey whirled and galloped alongside. Snatching at his tie, she missed and grabbed his shirt tail instead. It came off in her hands and into the log cabin quilt.

By October, 1861, telegraph wires spanned the continent, and the Pony Express was no longer needed. During the last run, just outside Sacramento, the pony Bill Cates was riding fell on him. Bill's leg was broken. A passing stagecoach offered to carry him and the mail to Sacramento. "No," said Bill. "Put me into the saddle. This last mail has to go through by pony." A passenger in the coach spoke up. "I was a pony man once," he said. "I'll take your place." And he carried the mochila to the end of the trail.

THE CIVIL WAR
IN MISSOURI

THE CENTRALIA MASSACRE

RICHARD S. BROWNLEE

Richard S. Brownlee was born in Brookfield, Missouri, where his great-grandfather had founded the Brownlee-Moore Bank shortly after service in the Confederate Army.

Brownlee has received four degrees from the University of Missouri —an A.B. in history, a Bachelor of Journalism, and master's and doctor's degrees for graduate work performed mainly in the field of Missouri history.

Dr. Brownlee became director and secretary of the State Historical Society of Missouri in 1960. He has contributed many articles and reviews dealing with Missouri history and archeology to various journals. His Gray Ghosts of the Confederacy: Guerrilla Warfare in the West *was a selection of the Civil War Book Club in 1959; it is Chapter XII of that fascinating and valuable history that is reprinted below.*

September 27, 1864, dawned clear and cool. Bill Anderson arose from his blanket at Singleton's, and restless and impatient for news, mounted thirty of his men and rode into Centralia to get St. Louis newspapers. At his right hand trotted little Archie Clement, his flat eyes blinking, his perpetual smile a grimace. Bloody Bill found Centralia sleeping, and he waked the hamlet of one hundred people with pistol shots and yells. For three hours his boys sauntered around the village, terrorizing the inhabitants, demanding and getting breakfast, and looting the depot, stores, and houses of pro-Union men. Several guerrillas got drunk, and in their excitement set the depot on fire. At midmorning the Columbia stage rolled in, and its passengers were hauled off and gleefully robbed. One of them was United States Representative James S. Rollins, on his way to a political meeting. Rollins, a pistol under his nose, did some magnificent impromptu acting, passing himself off as a local farmer and an ardent supporter of the Confederate States of America. He finally managed to slip away to hiding in the attic of Sneed's Hotel. One of the guerrillas rifled his valise and put on a shirt which bore the elegant initials of the congressman. About noon the westbound North Missouri train from St. Charles whistled in the distance, and Anderson's men piled ties on the track and hid to await its arrival. The engineer, James Clark, saw the smoking depot but

Reprinted from *Gray Ghosts of the Confederacy: Guerrilla Warfare in the West* by Richard S. Brownlee. By permission of the author and of Louisiana State University Press. Copyright 1958 by Louisiana State University Press.

did not reverse his engine because there was a gravel train behind him. As the cars pulled up to the depot the guerrillas surrounded them, fired their pistols into the windows, and as the passengers dismounted, they robbed them. Twenty-five unarmed Union soldiers were on board, and these were lined up and marched down the platform by Archie Clement with a guard of fifteen men.

In a few minutes Bloody Bill rode his horse in front of the Union captives and began to question them. Finding out that most of them were on furlough, the guerrilla told them that his men needed their uniforms and ordered them to strip. The miserable prisoners did as they were directed, and soon stood naked or in long underdrawers under the guerrilla guns. Anderson then asked if any were officers or noncommissioned officers. There was a long moment of hesitation, and then one man, Thomas Goodman, stepped forth, and although believing that he would be instantly shot, admitted that he was a sergeant of Missouri Engineers. Anderson carelessly ordered Goodman out of the line, and turning to Clement, told him to "muster out" the soldiers. Little Archie, a Colt revolver in each hand, grinned at his master, turned and fired point blank at the soldiers. The rest of the guard also began shooting. The Union soldiers died with amazement marked on their faces. One of them bounded out of the line, wounded, knocked down a guerrilla, and having no other refuge, crawled under the wooden station dock. It was set on fire, and when the man was forced by the flames to crawl out, he was pistoled. The North Missouri train was then set ablaze, and without engineer or passenger was started west toward Sturgeon, five miles away. The engine whistle was tied down, causing the boiler to empty a short distance from town. The burning cars sent a column of oily black smoke into the clear noon air, which was observed for miles. Anderson mounted his men at once, and they rode back down to Single-ton's, shouting and singing. During the morning they had discovered a case of boots, and each rider had several pair hung over his horse's neck, filled with whiskey from a large keg they were unable to carry off. Sergeant Tom Goodman was taken along, his feet tied under a horse. When they reached camp Anderson, roaring with laughter, congratulated him on his courage and let him go.

Major Johnson and his mounted Union infantry from Paris marched into Centralia at four o'clock that afternoon. He found the town in a state of shock, the women and children screaming and crying, the men standing around white-faced with disbelief. Learning that only thirty men had been with Anderson, Johnson divided his command, leaving half of it under Captain Adam Theis to restore order in town. Then, in spite of warning that there were many guerrillas in the neighborhood, he took the rest of his force out of Centralia south on Anderson's trail. A mile from Centralia he saw ten horsemen to his front who retreated rapidly before him, as they had been ordered to do by Todd and Anderson. Johnson pressed rapidly after them and into an ambush. Nearing the Singleton farm, the Union force topped a gentle rise in the prairie and saw, to what must have been their complete horror, a line of two hundred dismounted guerrillas standing silently to their horses at the foot of a sloping hill. Major Johnson was a brave officer. He knew many of his men were recruits, all had been trained to fight on foot as infantry, and he saw that he could not retreat. He calmly dismounted his company, sent his horses back where they were held, and formed a twenty-yard line of battle.

The guerrillas were astounded. One of Todd's men, John Koger, suddenly said in a voice that could be heard up and down their line, "The fools are going to fight us on foot," and then added, "God help 'em." George Todd roared for the guerrillas to mount, and led by screaming Bill Anderson, they charged up the hill at the Union infantry. Johnson's men fired one volley with their single-shot Enfield muskets. That volley, downhill, was high, and only three of the partisans were hit. "Hank" Williams, one of Anderson's men, pitched from his horse, dead, and Frank Shepherd, shot through the head, dashed his brains and blood over the leg of Frank James, who rode next to him. Richard Kenney was fatally wounded. In the next minute the guerrillas, their terrible revolvers popping, had ridden into the terrified Union infantry, through it, and had scattered its horses. Frank James stated that some of the soldiers were desperately biting cartridges, attempting to reload; some were trying to fix bayonets; others simply threw down their rifles and looked up dazed. In a few minutes most were dead, shot through the head. Major Johnson, courageously firing his pistol, went down before the guns of seventeen-year-old Jesse James. The guerrillas roared back into Centralia and rode over Theis's men. Captain Theis got to his horse, and with a few troopers raced west to the blockhouse at Sturgeon. He and only eighteen others reached there safely. Frank James, mounted his horse "Little George," and Archie Clement followed Theis under the rifles of the Union post in their excitement. In little more than an hour the Thirty-ninth Missouri Infantry had lost 114 men and two officers killed, two men wounded, and six men missing. The guerrillas rode back to Singleton's, killing all the wounded they could locate. Joking little David Pool counted the dead at Singleton's by jumping from one body to another, crowing, "If they are dead I can't hurt them, I cannot count 'em good without stepping on 'em. When I get my foot on one this way I know I've got him."

Major Johnson and many of his men were stripped, and it was reported at the time that their bodies were mutilated. This atrocity story was not so.

The almost complete destruction of Johnson's command panicked the entire area. It was several days after the massacre and fight at Centralia before federal cavalry in the area began to feel out cautiously after the guerrillas. By that time Anderson, Todd, and Thrailkill had separated and faded into hiding in Howard County.

SHELBY AND HIS MEN

JOHN N. EDWARDS

John Newman Edwards was born in Virginia in 1838, but came to Missouri at an early age. He left the editorship of his Lexington, Missouri, paper to join Shelby's men early in the War Between the States; he was appointed a brigade adjutant and later commanded a division with the rank of Colonel. After the peace at Appomattox, he retreated with Shelby and the remnants of his army into Mexico. There he became a friend of the Emperor Maximilian and Empress Charlotte. When he returned to Missouri, he wrote Shelby and His Men; or, The War in the West *(1867), from which the following passages describing the encampment at Fulton, Missouri, are taken. In 1868 Edwards, in partnership with John C. Moore, established the* Kansas City Times.

Later Edwards worked with Stilson Hutchins on the St. Louis Dispatch, *and when Hutchins left that paper to found the* Times, *of the same city, Edwards accompanied him and continued a prominent figure in Missouri journalism until his death in 1889.*

The camp at Fulton was delightful, amusing, instructive, and retired. Shelby never relaxed for a moment the vigor of his drill nor the manly exercises of his troopers. The short cavalry Enfields were here distributed to the troops, and the two brigades were splendidly armed, with the exception of Slayback's regiment, which had lances, tipped with steel and decorated with gay flags made by fair hands. This was one of General Magruder's ideas, and Shelby, to retain Slayback mounted, readily espoused it, and distributed the pikes among the men, fully determined, however, to arm them as well as the others upon the occasion of another battle. It seemed very much like going back in the service of warfare two hundred years to see these fine, athletic Missouri marksmen handling the clumsy and unwieldy lances, more dangerous to horses and the rear ranks of a column than they could ever be to the enemy, even in the opinions of their most sanguine advocates.

The reckless dare-devils of the division began, by and by, to grow restless and yearn for the dangers of the war-path and the excitement of actual conflict—so much so that it required all of Shelby's iron firmness and resolution to restrain now and then some madcap frolic. Once, while he was away, half a dozen or more came to Fulton on passes and concluded to have a general egg-nog. It was necessary to be very circumspect, for Lieutenant Miller Wilds was doing provost-marshal duty in the town, and Captain Maurice Langhorne, commanding the escort, was cantoned just below headquarters, both vigilant officers and very Jeffries in the execution of their duty. However, Frank Gordon, D. A. Williams, Charley Jones, Henry Belles, Dick Berry, John Brinker, John Thrailkill, and several others, not forgetting the inimitable, sociable, agreeable, witty, and gallant Joe Moreland, had an elegant supper prepared at Madam Mourner's, the keeper of a very fashionable and first-class restaurant, which supper was to be washed down with great bumpers of egg-nog in lieu of champagne. Bob Lawrence was the moneyed man, and invested just one thousand Confederate dollars in five gallons of as fine new corn whisky as ever ran through a smuggled still escaping the fierce edict of Lieutenant-General Holmes. The party concentrated at nine o'clock, and, after a neat little speech by Moreland, the attack on the viands commenced, which lasted two hours, and then the drinking began. C——, a protégé of Moreland's, was close behind him, and as some spirits went down others arose in proportion.

The night sped, and the low, unearthly glimmer of a waning moon shuddered in through the open windows and upon the wrecked argosy of the supper-table. Either history or romance tells us that the great love of Cardinal Richelieu for Anne of Austria, Queen of Louis XIII, was turned into greater hate by her promising him that if he would dance the *Saraband,* an Oriental dance, in appropriate costume with turban and bells before herself and maids in waiting, she would smile upon his guilty and consuming passion. He did so, to their intense amusement, but the giddy Queen violated her obligations, and laughed at the ridiculous Cardinal. No one could ever tell what inspired Moreland with the mad freak, but sure it was that he insisted upon C——'s dancing the *Saraband* too, and commenced to wind the folds of a huge table-cloth around his head and to smear his flushed face with yellow ochre to give it the true Oriental tinge, the rest of the company dancing and singing around in great glee. C—— looked about him with imploring eyes, seeking sympathy, yet found none. Fortunately the door was open, and as a last resort he made a dash for it, the improvised turban trailing behind and the ochre gleaming yellow in the moonlight. "Halt!" again cried Moreland, but C—— merely swerved a little as the bullet whistled past, and three other shots followed in quick succession. Dark, dank, broad-rimmed, and treacherous, a huge tan vat lay directly across the track of the flying racer, and barred it with an unknown depth. Short time for reflection. Before was hope, help, succor, safety—behind a deadly revolver echoing through the midnight and a pitiless voice shouting: *"Saraband, Saraband!"* One moment and no more. Straight and upright as a war-horse he leaped out into the darkness and disappeared for a moment beneath lime, ooze, half tanned hides, and the smell of a charnel house. There came a wild shout from the reckless crowd, and all was still again. The alarm had been given. Wilds and his guards swarmed out to see what the matter was; the rollicking rioters dispersed in every direction—for Shelby was known to be unusually severe on his officers of late for drinking, and only Moreland was nabbed on the scene of his exploit—caught red-handed in the very act.

Moreland was marched off in triumph to the guard-house, where all the ridicule of his position flashed upon him, and he sent for Colonel Buster, commanding the post, to ask him for release before Shelby arrived. Buster soon came, and for two hours Moreland amused and delighted him with his varied and brilliant conversation.

"Sit down, Colonel," he said, with the old habitual politeness of manner, and a humorous light in his fine black eyes, "and I will explain to you the science of electricity and the important part it performs in animal and vegetable life." From electricity he went on to describe what purported to be the maelstrom off the coast of Norway. "But, sir," he said, "no maelstrom exists there; Bayard Taylor traveled over the entire sea and didn't find a whirlpool big enough to engulf a man who refused to dance the *Saraband*." From whirlpools he went to wines, and told about Metternich and his Johannisberg; Madame Cliquot and her Champagne; the Mumm and the pale Anjou; from wine to women was an easy transition, and he described "Edith of the Swan's neck; the wife of Harold; how the Lady of Beauty, so faithfully and so tenderly, in loneliness and in ruin, loved her apathetic, senseless, discrowned King Charles VII"; the Medici with their pills and philters; the female Pope and the male nun of Italy; Guenever and her guilty loves; and then compared the relative merits of Tennyson's "charge of the light brigade" with that by Judge A. A. Meek, of Alabama, winding up his eloquent discourse by asking: "If it is entirely consistent with your duty, Colonel, and I presume you have discretionary powers in the matter, it would be a personal favor if you will release me before 'Old Joe' gets back." Buster laughed heartily in spite of his official dignity, and asked why he had shot at C——. "Why, really, Colonel, he refused to execute that most remarkable dance, the *Saraband*," and drawing nearer and

speaking in a low, confidential tone: "I only shot at him some four or
five times." It is needless to say that Moreland was released, and the
affair kept hid as long as possible; but Shelby, hearing of it as he heard
of everything going on wrong, administered a rebuke to the entire party
few of them will ever forget.

A chronicle like this of a graceless frolic should never be tolerated
in literature, only as it may serve to show the innerworking of a division which carried its chivalry and *abandon* to the very summit of perfection. Shelby knew he commanded Southern volunteers, and to foster
their pride and independence, he overlooked many acts that would have
gained disgrace for the offenders in the "Old Army." The code was
recognized, dueling tolerated, insults were to be avenged, and an in-
sulted officer must either fight or resign. It is easy to understand then
why the men glorified in their organization and held its honor as a
priceless gem. By just such a system of administration was he enabled
to school them for great things. It was pride which held them at Mine
Creek, pride at Newtonia, and pride which carried them from every
desperate position into which they were rushed on more than a dozen
occasions.

Had the Confederacy been rich enough, Shelby would have had for
his soldiers splendid arms, magnificent accouterments, silver spurs,
scarfs, plumes, and all the pomp of war. It would have been a household division—an *élite* corps like Napoleon's cuirassiers of the Old
Guard, and he would have so impressed this upon them that the charges
and assaults would have been irresistible.

A volunteer who has no romance in his disposition, and who has no
pleasure in the reckless frolic or the daring escapade, soon sickens and
dies with lumbago or pleurisy. He must be always ready to dance, drink,
flirt, race, and be shot at. He must look upon war as an accomplishment, in which every gentleman should excel, and be prepared at all
times to draw his sword for love and for duty. The French were attacking some castle upon an island in the Rhine during the wars of
the Fronde, says the author of "Guy Livingstone," and it was hot work.
The black mousquetaires of Louis XIII, clad in all the coquetry of lace
and fringed scented gloves, stood saucily by, laughing loud and boister-
ously at each successive repulse of the lines-men. Finally the infantry
shouted to the gentlemen to advance—they wanted to see the crack
corps beaten also. Right up to the breach went the mousquetaires and
carried it, leaving two-thirds of their number upon it, too. The general
made the entire army defile past their guidon and salute it. This was
the kind of spirit Shelby infused into his own ranks, and this is why the
officers were ever ready for fun and frolic.

JOE STINER

This Civil War ballad was printed in the Springfield Leader, *October 16, 1933, based on the recollection of M. I. Mathis, of that city. The lines refer to the Battle of Wilson Creek, and attempt to get what fun is possible out of the bloody business that was transacted not far from Springfield on August 10, 1861. A variant text in H. M. Belden's* Ballads and Songs *(pp. 362–363) is entitled "Joe Slinsworth." Belden observes that "Dutch" was a common name for "German" in early times, and continues: "The German element was strong in St. Louis, especially after the Revolution of 1848; and these revolutionaries would naturally be opposed to slavery and range themselves on the Union side. Presumably [this was] a camp song of the Confederates in Missouri."*

My name is Joe Stiner
I came from Amsterdam;
I am a full-blooded Dutchman
From that there is no sham.
I came off to this country—
They say the land is free,
Oh, there I makes much money
Oh, that's the land for me.

One day as I was drinking
Mine glass of lager beer,
And thinking of no danger
In this great country here,
They all cries out "This Union,"
"This Union!" very loud.
And they makes us walk together
In one very big Dutch crowd.

Now they say we got to fight
This Union for to save,
Mine God and Himmel did I think
Such a country we should have.
The first thing that we done
Was to take old General Frost
And shoot the women on our way
Through Camp Jackson as we crossed.

Then next we came to Rolla
Oh, how the secessionists flew
We made them get in every style

It was such glorious fun.
Then next we came to Springfield,
And there we stopped and stayed
Until our General Lyon
Had got his plans well laid.

They say that Price has got
Most all his secessionists
Camped way down on Crane creek
'Twas in a pretty fix.
And so we goes down there
Within about four miles,
When our batteries they did crack
And our rifles they did play.

What I seen there
I never shall forget,
Seemed like the ground was all alive
With secessionists.
Their blamed old rifles shot so true,
I can not tell you why.
They strike us in our stomachs
And they hit us in our eyes.

They kills our General Lyon
And they makes our Siegel run
Solomon hid in the college,
I'll tell you it was no fun.
They kills our men, they took our guns,
They knocked us into fits.
And many a prisoner, too, they took
But I gets up and gets.

Now I am in Springfield,
My legs were almost broke,
And for the want of lager beer
I was so nearly choked.
This blamed old secessionist country,
Will never do for me,
I vamish runs, I gets away,
For the city of St. Louis.

When I gets there
May I be roasted done,
If ever I shoot secessionist again

For money, love or fun.
I sits myself down by my frau,
I hears my children cry,
And this shall be my Dutch prayer—
I bid you all goodby!

ST. LOUIS

RECOLLECTIONS OF EARLY ST. LOUIS

JESSIE BENTON FRÉMONT

Jessie Benton, daughter of Senator Thomas Hart Benton, married the dashing young Army officer, John C. Frémont, in 1841, the year before he set out on the first of the three exploratory expeditions that he led to the Oregon country—adventures that earned him the common appellation of "The Pathfinder." Since Frémont served as one of the first two United States senators elected from California in 1850–1851, just as Benton was finishing his long term in that body, Jessie Benton Frémont for two years found herself with both husband and father serving as senators in Washington.

Mrs. Frémont was a lady of great charm and strength of character, and was the author of several books of sketches and memoirs. The following passage describing her girlhood recollections of St. Louis is taken from her book Souvenirs of My Time *(1887).*

Although St. Louis was not more than a *petite ville* in numbers, yet it had great interests and had a stirring life, much of which revolved about my father, who was the connecting link and powerful friendly intermediary between these interests and the Government.

General Clarke, of Lewis-and-Clarke exploring fame, was ending his days quietly in St. Louis where he had charge of all Indian affairs for that whole region; a distinguished-looking white-haired man who understood his trust and governed kindly and wisely.

When Washington Irving was out there a war-dance was held in the large council yard that he might see real Indians at their real life. I was very young, and the whole horrible thing, as they grew excited, threw me into a panic. . . .

St. Louis was on the border of an immense and almost unexplored Indian country. The caravans of merchandise going through it to Santa Fé ran all the risks you ever read of among Bedouins on the desert; the hunters and trappers, as well as the merchants, started off into the unknown with only the one certainty—that danger was there; and when they came back—if they did—it was as from underworld. Jefferson Barracks below St. Louis was a large and important military post which was kept busy enough. It ended much hard Indian warfare when they at last captured Black Hawk. I saw him when he was a prisoner at the Garrison —a real Indian and real old warrior, captive but not subdued.

The governing religion was of course Catholic as this had been so lately a French possession and its chief people were the French settlers who were also the chief traders in furs. Priests and Sisters of Charity in their special black dress were everywhere in the streets, so were the army officers in service-worn uniforms, and the French peasant women wore, as in France, their thick white caps, sabots and full red petticoats with big blue or yellow handkerchiefs crossed over the white bodices; and with the Indians painted and blanketed gliding along in files towards the enclosure around General Clarke's quarters one would have been puzzled to say whose country it was now. On the levee negro boat-hands sang wild chants as they "loaded-up"; but already keen-featured, sallow men were going quietly but alertly in and out of warehouses, and council yard and fur trading houses—"white clover" which ate its way into possession of the pear-orchards and made them town lots, and built square ugly meeting-houses near the cathedral, and married the French girls, and generally changed the face of St. Louis' "French" nature.

The houses were built in the Creole way; a courtyard surrounded by a four-sided house with broad galleries all round, which sat peacefully in the midst of trees and gardens and orchards on the gentle slope looking to the wide muddy torrent of the Mississippi and the flat green plain beyond of "the Illinois." There was only one "main" street—very village-like and not over a mile long. The dwelling-houses were placed just where they preferred without regard to any future plan. The Bishop's garden and the Cathedral (where was the appalling picture of St. Bartholomew) were on a handsome scale, but bordered by little alleys of roughly-paved short streets. From these, by a garden gate in a high wall, you could go in to a great garden which was part lawn and part orchard, and well off from the street would be the large quiet house with polished inlaid floors and handsome, old mahogany furniture. They lived a most comfortable and unceremonious life among themselves and were friendly and hospitable to those they felt to be friends, but, apart from the chosen few, had open antipathy to *"dose American."*

As in France, the young people in marrying did not go from home but had a part of the large house assigned them, and three generations under one roof seemed to blend smoothly in the family whole. . . .

Coming back to Saint Louis always in springtime, even after the mild winters of Washington the contrast was charming. The Potomac was a wide and beautifully blue river, but it did nothing, and was nothing more than a feature in the landscape, while here the tawny swift Mississippi was stirring with busy life, and the little city itself, was animated from its thronged river-bank out through to the Indian camps on the rolling prairie back of the town.

And it was such an embowered fragrant place in that season; the thickets of wild plum and the wild crab-apples which covered the prairie embalmed the air, and everywhere was the honey-scent of the locust. What the elm is to some New England towns the locust was to Saint Louis; the narrow streets were bordered by them and they were repeated everywhere. My father had an affection for this tree and had planted a great many about his house when he first settled there—long before he was married. In my young day these were fine large trees. A line of them made a delicate green screen to the wide galleries which ran the length of the house, on both stories, and their long clusters of vanilla-scented blooms made part of our home-memories. . . .

Not only did the blossoming town seem *en fête,* but everybody seemed light and gay, and my father, freed from the official and exacting life of Washington, reverted to his cheerful out-door life. The long gallery of the parlor-floor was his place when at home, even if light rains were falling. He never breathed in-door air when he could be, head uncovered, in a bath of sunshine. His "settee" and a table, and "a colony of chairs" for others, made his favorite settlement, where the early light breakfast of coffee and bread and fruit was taken—by any number who might chance to come. I *never* heard the word *"trouble"* applied to household arrangements. For all we knew, everything grew ready to be served.

The day begins early in warm climates, and from early morning on, there was a coming and going of varied but all welcome friends. There came governing citizens to talk of political affairs. Much had to be only personal information in those days before railways and telegraphs, and when the plans of an administration were only talked over confidentially with its friends. The father of Mrs. Grant was one of my father's old friends and political allies of that time. . . .

There, too, came officers of the army. My father was their comprehending friend. Himself an old officer, and for twenty years Chairman of the Senate Military Committee, he was their sure and intelligent friend. . . .

The French neighbors enjoyed coming for their chat, and invariably brought some fine fruit or flower for Madame, who fully appreciated both the kindly feeling and the fine skilful cultivation.

There too came many priests who were soldiers in their missionary work, and had as stirring adventures to relate as the trappers and hunters who knew they were always welcome to my father. . . .

My Grandfather Benton's library in Greek, Latin, French, Spanish and English, had been his joy while he lived and made the atmosphere in which my father grew up—guided by his mother and his father's close friend, a clergyman, like himself an Oxford man, who put my father at his Greek Testament when he was but eight; at which age my grandfather's death left him the eldest son in a family of seven children. . . .

In Washington all our lessons were had at home but my father did the important part of appointing studies and preparing us for our teachers, making broad and lucid what they might have left as "parrot-ing," as he expressed it. Here in Saint Louis we were let to go to school; chiefly for the practice in French among other children.

It makes me smile to look back at that word "school" which had not the first idea of studies, of punctuality, or discipline attached to it as I knew it. The going there each morning was as good as playing truant. *Never* could it happen that children of any position left the house alone, or even together. We were big girls of eight and ten and every one knew us, and the distance was only a short mile between houses and grounds of friends; but to go without a maid was never dreamed of. We should have greatly preferred our French nurse, Madeleine, but she was not sufficiently important for such duty. Our mother's maid, "aunt" Sara, was. She had been trained from her youth up for her post—as was the Southern custom—and understood "manners." Erect, silent, holding a hand of each, she drilled us in manners as we went along. When we passed the small house of M'âme Desirée where she in *very* negligée loose gown patted her muslins on the sunny gallery, we had to stop if she spoke to us.

M'âme Desirée was the clear-starcher and fine-muslin genius of Saint Louis; too fat now, but still a most handsome quadroon who had a gay word for every passer-by. M'âme Saraah was a crony of hers, and when she would give us the good day and praise our neatness and good condition (as all due to M'âme Saraah!) we had to wait and listen politely: "You can't hurry her, because she is a poor working woman and it would hurt her feelings"—aunt Sara had never heard the words, but her conviction was that "Time was made for slaves," and not for little young ladies.

Then the garden doors of many pleasant enclosures would be open and, the various Madame Augustes or Madame Caddys* would be out in the fresh of the morning and the ladies themselves—also in most easy negligée—going about their grounds. If they saw us we would be called in and *cette bonne Sara* asked after Madame and praised for her *petites*. And with deliberation (time no object), some pretty fruit would be chosen for us and we would recommence our walk to stop again and again; for, "Madame Auguste is a lady and you can't hurry her"—in fact, there was no hurry anywhere.

* The younger sons were usually called *Cadet* as the descriptive addition to the Pierre or Auguste or what not: the Americans got this into "Caddy," and "Mr. Caddy" and "Madame Caddy" hardened into use from repetition.

When we did reach the school we were consigned to Madame Savary who did not teach, but who looked after us; a small vivacious Swiss-Frenchwoman with a mania for making preserves and doing fine sewing. Monsieur Savary was capable of far more than was required of him. I think he had put away his pride and resigned himself to what he could, not what he would, do. He was a spare tall man with flat black hair and gold spectacles and always wore a short-waisted very long and full-skirted frock coat of gray, with collar and cuffs of black velvet, a sort of uniform for teachers which you often see in old-fashioned French illustrations. He was quiet, gentle and forbearing, and had need to be so as there were about thirty girls, from six to sixteen—of course not a fraction of a boy in a French school—and not one with any intentions of study or habit of discipline; good-natured enough, but trying. They may have learned something. *We* were there only for easy handling of familiar French; and except some spelling, and reading aloud in *Telemachus,* I do not recall anything of lessons. . . . By one o'clock aunt Sara had come for us to go home and as this was our dinner hour we made no delays.

In French schools Thursday is the holiday. Saturday and Sunday, they think, make too much holiday together. But to us Americans the Sunday was not a holiday in their sense, where after mass all their children were taken around among their elder relations and it was a family fête-day.

We did not go on Saturdays to school. That day our mother had us get our Sunday-school lessons with her—telling us many interesting things and making them, as all our home lessons were, a real pleasure and improvement. Our Sunday dresses were decided on and each thing reviewed and put in order that no delay might come. All our dolls and toys and weekday story-books were put away until Monday; and then we had as wild a play as big grounds and good health and early youth could give. In this our French nurse Madeleine was a great factor; she was so gay and knew such beautiful songs and danced such queer dances in her pretty carved sabots that we doted on her.

Her family had come away from France, from near Bordeaux, because of the cholera. . . .

Sometimes, in a summer's day you feel, before you see why, a chill in the air. Something has changed; and though the day looks the same its sweetness is gone. So, in the summer I was about eight, this bright careless Saint Louis life seemed to chill over. At first we were only told we were not to go to school. Then, we were to play only with each other in our own grounds and no more little friends visited us or we them. The friends who came to my father on the long gallery were as many as ever, but they and he himself no longer had any pleasant leisure, but were quick and busy in coming and going, and all looked grave. The tears were all the time on Madeleine's face and constantly she was on her knees telling her beads and praying and sobbing. We saw many, many funerals passing. Our house was on a sloping hill, and we saw to all sides of the square. Then, soon, drays with several coffins piled on jolted fast along the rough street, or a wagon-load of empty coffins would cross another street. Madeleine would run in from the gallery hiding her eyes; "Ah, *Mon Dieu,* it is all funerals on every side —*C'est le cholera."* . . . Our house was a "diet-kitchen"; good soups, preparations of rice, and well-filtered and purified water, it became the occupation of the house to keep ready.

All the water was brought in large barrels from the river and poured bucket by bucket, into great jars of red earthenware, some of them five feet high. These jars had their own large cool room paved with glazed red brick and level with the street. The jars of drinking water and for cooking were clarified of the mud of the river by alum and blanched almonds, and then filtered. So much was needed now that even we children were useful in this sort of work. In that cool dark room the melons used to be kept, but there were no melons or fruit now—we ate only rice and mutton and such simple things.

The sad summer ended as all things must end, bad or good. *Tout passe.* When all seemed safe, suddenly my mother was taken down with cholera, and the nurse who had become blinded by one shock recovered her sight from this other. It was a bad illness, but with that one brush of the dark angel's wing our home stood as before.

It so chanced that my marriage connected me still more closely with Saint Louis and all the interests of its neighboring countries because of their connection with the explorations of Mr. Frémont.

I would go with him to the Delaware Indian country on the frontier and stay until the expedition was ready to start; sometimes returning to Washington, and sometimes remaining in Saint Louis. The frontier of then is now Kansas, and its Indians and wolves and unbroken green stretches of prairie are only a memory; and the present conditions of quick travel and quicker information must almost prevent your having a clear idea of the uncertainties of those journeys. . . .

With all my happy memories of Saint Louis, think how hard it was to go back there to the feeling that met us in '61—in the beginning of the war.

Everything was changed. There was no life on the river; the many steamboats were laid up at their wharves, their fires out, the singing, cheery crews gone—they, empty, swaying idly with the current. As we drove through the deserted streets we saw only closed shutters to warehouses and business places; the wheels and the horses' hoofs echoed loud and harsh as when one drives through the silent streets late in the night.

It was a hostile city and showed itself as such.

One gentle touch from the past softened this. My cousin herself was absent, and her family was in France, but she had written to her man-of-business to meet us and take us to her beautiful house where we had always felt at home. More than ever it seemed home now; the old butler, "uncle" Vincent, slow and gray, met and welcomed us, and from the wall smiled down in lasting youth and sweetness the young cousin who had known but seventeen happy and beloved years. Into that upper parlor where the closer family life had left its impress many troubled men came and found moments of rest. My cousin insisted we should use the house as we needed and it became the Headquarters of the Western Department. . . . And there came General Sherman while waiting orders—out of favor because he had said not 60,000 nor 90,000 men, nor 200,000 could end the war. And there General Grant was given his first command—and many and many a link of historical interest connects with that stately house which was now all that was left me of past days. . . .

Of all wars none can approach a civil war for distressing complications. I went there in July with brown hair, and came away in November gray.

A later memory is of a beautiful day of honors and good-will and a revival of old friendly feelings which came comfortingly, and remains the governing impression.

In the summer of '68 I was invited to come to Saint Louis and unveil a statue of my father. It was a bronze, cast in Munich, and on the pedestal were his words which time had made into a prophecy, though for many years they had the usual fate of ideas in advance of the public. I had seen persons smile significantly to each other, some even touch their foreheads with a gesture to intimate that much thinking on this subject had warped his mind—it is so much easier to imagine one's self superior than to be really so. "Men said he was mad, now they asked had he a God?"

For on this pedestal, where the bronze hand of the statue points *west,* are the words:

"THERE IS THE EAST."
"THERE LIES THE ROAD TO INDIA."

The large Park was filled with a holiday crowd—over forty thousand, I was told. The children of the public schools, dressed in white, and, boys as well as girls, carrying large bunches of roses—my father's favorite flower, were grouped, many thousands of them, around the base of the slight rise on which the statue had been placed; toward the valley below, the trees and shrubbery had been cleared, leaving an open view of the line of the Pacific Railway. . . .

As the veil fell away from the statue, its bronze gilded with the warm sunshine, the children threw their roses at its base; at the same moment the out going train to San Francisco halted and saluted with whistles and flags; and when the speaker of the day dwelt on the public schools, and homestead laws, which had been cherished measures of my father's, who felt for all children, women and helpless people, all knew he deserved the words of praise given him.

ELIPHALET COMES TO ST. LOUIS

WINSTON CHURCHILL

Winston Churchill was born in St. Louis in 1871. He was twenty-eight when he published his most successful novel, Richard Carvel, *a romance of the Revolutionary War, which was an outstanding best seller of its time. The Crisis, from which the following pages are taken, deals with the Civil War, and was almost as successful as* Richard Carvel. *Churchill was rather Victorian in his attitudes toward life, but his historical novels were well researched, well written, and certainly profitable.*

Churchill spent most of his life in New Hampshire, and he once ran for governor of that state on the Progressive ticket.

Faithfully to relate how Eliphalet Hopper came to St. Louis is to betray no secret. Mr. Hopper is wont to tell the story now, when his daughter-in-law is not by; and sometimes he tells it in her presence, for he is a shameless and determined old party who denies the divine right of Boston, and has taken again to chewing tobacco.

When Eliphalet came to town, his son's wife, Mrs. Samuel D. (or S. Dwyer, as she is beginning to call herself), was not born. Gentlemen of Cavalier and Puritan descent had not yet begun to arrive at the Planters' House, to buy hunting shirts and broad rims, belts and bowies, and depart quietly for Kansas, there to indulge in that most pleasurable of Anglo-Saxon pastimes, a free fight. Mr. Douglas had not thrown his bone of Local Sovereignty to the sleeping dogs of war.

To return to Eliphalet's arrival—a picture which has much that is interesting in it. Behold the friendless boy as he stands in the prow of the great steamboat *Louisiana* of a scorching summer morning, and looks with something of a nameless disquiet on the chocolate waters of the Mississippi. There have been other sights, since passing Louisville, which might have disgusted a Massachusetts lad more. A certain deck on the *Paducah,* which took him as far as Cairo, was devoted to cattle —black cattle. Eliphalet possessed a fortunate temperament. The deck was dark, and the smell of the wretches confined there was worse than it should have been. And the incessant weeping of some of the women was annoying, inasmuch as it drowned many of the profane communications of the overseer who was showing Eliphalet the sights. Then a fine-linened planter from down river had come in during the conversation, and paying no attention to the overseer's salute cursed them all into silence, and left.

Eliphalet had ambition, which is not a wholly undesirable quality. He began to wonder how it would feel to own a few of these valuable fellow-creatures. He reached out and touched lightly a young mulatto woman who sat beside him with an infant in her arms. The peculiar dumb expression on her face was lost to Eliphalet. The overseer had laughed coarsely.

"What, skeered on 'em?" said he. And seizing the girl by the cheek, gave it a cruel twinge that brought a cry out of her.

Eliphalet had reflected upon this incident after he had bid the overseer good-by at Cairo, and had seen that pitiful coffle piled aboard a steamer for New Orleans. And the result of his reflections was, that some day he would like to own slaves.

A dome of smoke like a mushroom hung over the city, visible from far down the river, motionless in the summer air. A long line of steamboats—white, patient animals—was tethered along the levee, and the *Louisiana* presently swung her bow toward a gap in this line, where a mass of people was awaiting her arrival. Some invisible force lifted Eliphalet's eyes to the upper deck, where they rested, as if by appointment, on the trim figure of the young man in command of the *Louisiana.* He was very young for the captain of a large New Orleans packet. When his lips moved, something happened. Once he raised his voice, and a negro stevedore rushed frantically aft, as if he had received the end of a lightning-bolt. Admiration burst from the passengers, and one man cried out Captain Brent's age—it was thirty-two.

Eliphalet snapped his teeth together. He was twenty-seven, and his ambition actually hurt him at such times. After the boat was fast to the landing stage he remained watching the captain, who was speaking a few parting words to some passengers of fashion. The body-servants were taking their luggage to the carriages. Mr. Hopper envied the captain his free and vigorous speech, his ready jokes, and his hearty laugh. All the rest he knew for his own—in times to come. The carriages, the

trained servants, the obsequiousness of the humbler passengers. For of
such is the Republic.

Then Eliphalet picked his way across the hot stones of the levee,
pushing hither and thither in the rough crowd of river men; dodging
the mules on the heavy drays, or making way for the carriages of the
few people of importance who arrived on the boat. If any recollections
of a cool, white farmhouse amongst barren New England hills disturbed his thoughts, this is not recorded. He gained the mouth of a
street between the low houses which crowded on the broad river front.
The black mud was thick under his feet from an overnight shower, and
already steaming in the sun. The brick pavement was lumpy from much
travel and near as dirty as the street. Here, too, were drays blocking
the way, and sweaty negro teamsters swinging cowhides over the mules.
The smell of many wares poured through the open doors, mingling
with the perspiration of the porters. On every side of him were busy
clerks, with their suspenders much in evidence, and Eliphalet paused
once or twice to listen to their talk. It was tinged with that dialect he
had heard since leaving Cincinnati.

Turning a corner, Eliphalet came abruptly upon a prophecy. A great
drove of mules was charging down the gorge of the street, and straight
at him. He dived into an entrance, and stood looking at the animals in
startled wonder as they thundered by, flinging the mud over the pave-
ments. A cursing lot of drovers on ragged horses made the rear guard.

Eliphalet mopped his brow. The mules seemed to have aroused in
him some sense of his atomity, where the sight of the pillar of smoke
and of the black cattle had failed. The feeling of a stranger in a strange
land was upon him at last. A strange land, indeed! Could it be one with
his native New England? Did Congress assemble from the antipodes?
Wasn't the great, ugly river and dirty city at the end of the earth, to be
written about in Boston journals?

Turning to the doorway, he saw to his astonishment a great store,
with high ceilings supported by columns. The floor was stacked high
with bales of dry goods. Beside him was a sign in gold lettering, "Carvel
and Company, Wholesale Dry Goods." And lastly, looking down upon
him with a quizzical expression, was a gentleman. There was no mistak-
ing the gentleman. He was cool, which Eliphalet was not. And the fact
is the more remarkable because the gentleman was attired according to
the fashion of the day for men of his age, in a black coat with a deal of
ruffled shirt showing, and a heavy black stock wound around his collar.
He had a white mustache, and a goatee, and white hair under his black
felt hat. His face was long, his nose straight, and the sweetness of his
smile had a strange effect upon Eliphalet, who stood on one foot.

"Well, sonny, scared of mules, are you?" The speech is a stately drawl very different from the nasal twang of Eliphalet's bringing up. "Reckon you don't come from anywhere round here?"

"No, sir," said Eliphalet. "From Willesden, Massachusetts."

"Come in on the *Louisiana?*"

"Yes, sir." But why this politeness?

The elderly gentleman lighted a cigar. The noise of the rushing mules had now become a distant roar, like a whirlwind which has swept by. But Eliphalet did not stir.

"Friends in town?" inquired the gentleman at length.

"No, sir," sighed Mr. Hopper.

At this point of the conversation a crisp step sounded from behind, and the wonderful smile came again on the surface.

"Mornin', Colonel," said a voice which made Eliphalet jump. And he swung around to perceive the young captain of the *Louisiana.*

"Why, Captain Lige," cried the Colonel, without ceremony, "and how do you find yourself to-day, suh? A good trip from Orleans? We did not look for you so soon."

"Tolluble, Colonel, tolluble," said the young man, grasping the Colonel's hand. "Well, Colonel, I just called to say that I got the seventy bales of goods you wanted."

"Ephum!" cried the Colonel, diving toward a counter where glasses were set out,—a custom new to Eliphalet,—"Ephum, some of that very particular Colonel Crittenden sent me over from Kentucky last week."

An old darkey, with hair as white as the Colonel's, appeared from behind the partition.

"I 'lowed you'd want it, Marse Comyn, when I seed de Cap'n comin'," said he, with the privilege of an old servant. Indeed, the bottle was beneath his arm.

The Colonel smiled.

"Hope you'se well, Cap'n," said Ephum, as he drew the cork.

"Tolluble, Ephum," replied the Captain. "But, Ephum! Say, Ephum!"

"Yes, *sah.*"

"How's my little sweetheart, Ephum?"

"Bress your soul, sah," said Ephum, his face falling perceptibly, "bress your soul, sah, Miss Jinny's done gone to Halcyondale, in Kaintuck, to see her grandma. Ole Ephum ain't de same nigger when she's away."

The young Captain's face showed as much disappointment as the darkey's.

"Cuss it!" said he, strongly, "if that ain't too bad! I brought her a Creole doll from New Orleans, which Madame Claire said was dressed finer than any one she'd ever seen. All lace and French geegaws, Colonel. But you'll send it to her."

"That I will, Lige," said the Colonel, heartily. "And she shall write you the prettiest note of thanks you ever got."

"Bless her pretty face," cried the Captain. "Her health, Colonel! Here's long life to Miss Virginia Carvel, and may she rule forever! How old did you say this was?" he asked, looking into the glass.

"Over half a century," said Colonel Carvel.

"If it came from the ruins of Pompeii," cried Captain Brent, "it might be worthy of her!"

"What an idiot you are about that child, Lige," said the Colonel, who was not hiding his pleasure. The Colonel could hide nothing. "You ruin her!"

The bluff young Captain put down his glass to laugh.

"Ruin her!" he exclaimed. "Her pa don't ruin her! eh, Ephum? Her pa don't ruin her!"

"Lawsy, Marse Lige, I reckon he's wuss'n any."

"Ephum," said the Colonel, pulling his goatee thoughtfully, "you're a damned impertinent nigger. I vow I'll sell you South one of these days. Have you taken that letter to Mr. Rénault?" He winked at his friend as the old darkey faded into the darkness of the store, and continued: "Did I ever tell you about Wilson Peale's portrait of my grandmother, Dorothy Carvel, that I saw this summer at my brother Daniel's, in Pennsylvania? Jinny's going to look something like her, sir. Um! She was a fine woman. Black hair, though. Jinny's is brown, like her Ma's." The Colonel handed a cigar to Captain Brent and lit one himself. "Daniel has a book my grandfather wrote, mostly about her. Lord, I remember her! She was the queen-bee of the family while she lived. I wish some of us had her spirit."

"Colonel," remarked Captain Lige, "what's this I heard on the levee just now about your shootin' at a man named Babcock on the steps here?"

The Colonel became very grave. His face seemed to grow longer as he pulled his goatee.

"He was standing right where you are, sir," he replied (Captain Lige moved), "and proposed that I should buy his influence."

"What did you do?"

Colonel Carvel laughed quietly at the recollection.

"Shucks," said he, "I just pushed him into the street, gave him a little start, and put a bullet past his ear, just to let the trash know the sound of it. Then Russell went down and bailed me out."

The Captain shook with laughter. But Mr. Eliphalet Hopper's eyes were glued to the mild-mannered man who told the story, and his hair rose under his hat.

"By the way, Lige, how's that boy, Tato? Somehow after I let you have him on the *Louisiana,* I thought I'd made a mistake to let him run the river. Easter's afraid he'll lose the little religion she taught him."

It was the Captain's turn to be grave.

"I tell you what, Colonel," said he; "we have to have hands, of course. But somehow I wish this business of slavery had never been started!"

"Sir," said the Colonel, with some force, "God made the sons of Ham the servants of Japheth's son forever and forever."

"Well, well, we won't quarrel about that, sir," said Brent, quickly. "If they all treated slaves as you do, there wouldn't be any cry from Boston-way. And as for me, I need hands. I shall see you again, Colonel."

"Take supper with me to-night, Lige," said Mr. Carvel. "I reckon you'll find it rather lonesome without Jinny."

"Awful lonesome," said the Captain. "But you'll show me her letters, won't you?"

He started out, and ran against Eliphalet.

"Hello!" he cried. "Who's this?"

"A long Yankee you landed here this morning, Lige," said the Colonel. "What do you think of him?"

"Humph!" exclaimed the Captain.

"He has no friends in town, and he is looking for employment. Isn't that so, sonny?" asked the Colonel, kindly.

"Yes."

"Come, Lige, would you take him?" said Mr. Carvel.

The young Captain looked into Eliphalet's face. The dart that shot from his eyes was of an aggressive honesty; and Mr. Hopper's, after an attempt at defiance, were dropped.

"No," said the Captain.

"Why not, Lige?"

"Well, for one thing, he's been listening," said Captain Lige, as he departed.

Colonel Carvel began to hum softly to himself:—

> " 'One said it was an owl, and the other he said nay,
> One said it was a church with the steeple torn away.
>   Look a'there now!'

"I reckon you're a rank abolitionist," said he to Eliphalet abruptly.

"I don't see any particular harm in keepin' slaves," Mr. Hopper replied, shifting to the other foot.

Whereupon the Colonel stretched his legs apart, seized his goatee, pulled his head down, and gazed at him for some time from under his eyebrows, so searchingly that the blood flew to Mr. Hopper's fleshy face. He mopped it with a dark-red handkerchief, stared at everything in the place save the gentleman in front of him, and wondered whether he had ever in his life been so uncomfortable. Then he smiled sheepishly, hated himself, and began to hate the Colonel.

"Ever hear of the *Liberator?*"

"No, sir," said Mr. Hopper.

"Where do you come from?" this was downright directness, from which there was no escape.

"Willesden, Massachusetts."

"Umph! And never heard of Mr. Garrison?"

"I've had to work all my life."

"What can you do, sonny?"

"I callate to sweep out a store. I have kept books," Mr. Hopper vouchsafed.

"Would you like work here?" asked the Colonel, kindly.

The green eyes looked up swiftly, and down again.

"What'll you give me?"

The good man was surprised. "Well," said he, "seven dollars a week."

Many a time in after life had the Colonel reasons to think over this scene. He was a man the singleness of whose motives could not be questioned. The one and sufficient reason for giving work to a homeless boy, from the hated state of the *Liberator,* was charity. The Colonel had his moods, like many another worthy man.

The small specks on the horizon sometimes grow into the hugest of thunder clouds. And an act of charity, out of the wisdom of God, may produce on this earth either good or evil.

Eliphalet closed with the bargain. Ephum was called and told to lead the recruit to the presence of Mr. Hood, the manager. And he spent the remainder of a hot day checking invoices in the shipping entrance on Second Street.

SHIRT-WAIST GIRLS IN SAILOR HATS

WILLIAM MARION REEDY

Reedy's Mirror, *a St. Louis weekly of politics, literature, social comment, and news, furnished important encouragement for the new movement in American poetry in the first and second decades of the twentieth century, and probably exerted a considerable political influence, espe-*

cially in St. Louis. It is remembered chiefly for its publication of the
work of Edgar Lee Masters, Vachel Lindsay, Carl Sandburg, Edwin
Arlington Robinson, and Robert Frost; but it was also a center for the
literary activity of its home city and gave first publication to such writ-
ers as Sara Teasdale, Zoë Akins, and Orrick Johns.

Reedy was born in St. Louis in 1862 and died there in 1920. He
became editor of the Mirror *two years after it was founded in 1891, and*
placed his own name in the title in 1913. He was an essayist of no
little charm and force. The following piece has been selected from his
column "Reflections"; it appeared on May 10, 1900.

Life has its compensations. We are likely to forget that there
are many things to mitigate the horrors of the approaching political
campaign. It is our duty not to forget. There is no use giving up all our
minds and hearts and souls to politics. There are things that we can
turn to, from the din and clamor, with much gratefulness. And chief of
them is the shirt-waist girl in the sailor hat, who now begins to make
her appearance. The shirt-waist girl in the sailor hat is the institution
that makes us bless the dog days. She makes us bless even the dog days
that are complicated by tom-cat and poll-parrot politics. She is serene,
bland, cool. There is nothing in the wide world quite so refreshing to
the spirit. There is no combination of feminine fashion so bewitching
as the fashion of which the shirt-waist and sailor hat are the salient
features. The sailor hat gives you a chance to look into her eyes,—frank,
clear eyes. The sailor hat lets out a wisp of hair across the forehead or
just down over the ear and the breezes play with the wisp of hair and
give to the face's expression a bewitching elusiveness. The sailor hat is
jaunty. If the girl walks before you, or to one side of you, the sailor hat
vouchsafes you a glimpse of the shape of her head. The shirt-waist gives
one the idea of buoyancy about a girl. There's an unpretentious honesty
of shape about it that proclaims its charm is more than half inflation.
The shirt-waist is at once trim and abandoned. It is at the same time
careful and negligent. In some vague way it is delightfully indicative
of girlish independence and self-reliance. The garment makes the girl
appear gratifyingly less of the creature of the tailor, more a human
being, less of a bit of upholstery. The shirt-waist is an enormous relief
from the stuffiness of so many women's garbs. It makes her look comfortable, untrammeled and well ventilated, and the impression from
her makes the observer feel something of the same escape from the con-
finement of ordinary clothing. The girl in the shirt-waist and under a
sailor hat, appears as if all the winds have liberty to play about her and
blow her cares away. The shirt-waist has the merit of helping to display

the feminine form without any taint of indecency. A loose shirt-waist, nicely belted in, enhances the artistic value of the hips in the general anatomical outline. The tight sleeves of this season's patterns have just the suspicion or a tendency to make the arms curve and bring the hands in toward the waist, thus suggesting what the artists tell us of the secret of the charm of the old Greek vases—that is, that their lines are modeled upon those of women standing with arms akimbo or with fingers clasped atop of their heads. The curves of the bust and of the hips are both shown in play when walking, and the girls come towards us as beautiful as those bearing good tidings, or they depart from us with an ease and grace that proclaim they have no care. The shirt-waist girl in the sailor hat is clean-cut, individual. No matter how universal the style, every girl makes it her own. The fashion is one that does not make women the same. The raiment has an air as if the wearer means business, and her business just now is to look enticing. Much more will the girl in question suggest to him who has his eyes open. The value of those suggestions is that they will take one's mind off political candidates, platforms, problems, off dull business and his own personal discomfort, as the weather warms up. There's nothing that makes the warm spell uncomfortable for man so much as its effect in concentrating his consciousness upon himself as a most important personage with relation to everything else. There's nothing can take a man out of himself like a glimpse of youth and innocence and freshness and grace. And all these are the especially insistent qualities and characteristics of the shirt-waist girl in the sailor hat. She is the entity beside which the most self-important man is made sure to feel his unimportance, and she is the one eternal thing of life, of which politics and business and art and science and war and religion are but the broken and somewhat distorted glimpses of imperfect mind. The girl—and above all girls, the shirt-waist girl in the sailor hat—is the World's Desire. She is not only what she is of herself, she is clothed on with all we deem her to be, with the best of ourselves, with the finest of our youth, the most radiant of our dreams, the tenderest of our thoughts. The shirt-waist girl in the sailor hat is a picture, a poem, a preachment, a prayer. If she appeal not to us, then truly are we dead to all fine things else—to hope, to faith, to duty, to aspiration, to charity—and our being poisons the universe. It were better for us and for others had we never been born.

THE RETURN OF A POET

ORRICK JOHNS

Orrick Johns was born in St. Louis in 1887, the son of George S. Johns, an able crusading journalist for many years on the staff of the Post-Dispatch *and eventually its editor. The son was by turns journalist, critic, essayist, poet. It was as a poet that he became most widely known. He turned from free verse to a crisper rhymed form. Like his father, he had a strong social consciousness, notable, for example in his "Second Avenue," which won the $1,000* Lyric Year *prize in 1912. He belonged to the Reedy literary group while in St. Louis, and was for a time a member of the* Mirror *staff. He took his own life in 1946.*

The following passage is from Time of Our Lives: The Story of My Father and Myself, *a book that combines a biography of his father with his own autobiography. It is chosen because of its pleasant description of the Meramec country, and also its story of the integration of poetical composition with physical labor. The later parting of the ways between father and son because of ideological differences was a tragedy to both.*

Coming back from New York to St. Louis I have always experienced a flattening of the emotions because of the topography of the journey. Daleville, Indiana, is not a dale, but a table, and Terre Haute is not "High Land." Hillsboro, Illinois, would not vary by a ten meter hill from one end to the other. St. Louis is the center of a flat plain, a disk the surface of which is uniform. But southwest, about fifteen or twenty miles, running parallel with the curve of the Mississippi, lies lovely rolling country. All of our lives we had been familiar with the Meramec River. I remember bathing there as a terrified kid of four with the Byars and the Johns families. Father and Byars wore suits with long drawers and the women had dress costumes with stockings and shoes. Byars never went into the water without a cork life-preserver.

The Meramec Hills are really distant foothills of the Ozark Mountains, and one can drive due southwest, reaching higher and higher levels all the way to the Arkansas border. The neighboring land had been bought in huge tracts by August A. Busch, son of Adolphus Busch and heir to the brewing house of Anheuser-Busch. Busch had built a rustic inn on one of the hills and a golf course, which later became the Sunset Hill Golf Club. Father bought his original forty acres from Busch and later, when he inherited his share of the estate in St. Charles, expanded them to double that extent. Part of Busch's holding was General Grant's old farm a few miles away, where Grant had grubbed a living before the Civil War and cut wood which he hauled into the city to sell.

Father's house, of variegated rubble rock and plaster, sat on a hill facing the old woods and underbrush. In a letter to me he described the early spring shrubs: "I have a shadbush, sometimes called the Juneberry, about forty feet high in my woods, the earliest flowering tree in these parts. It looks like a big ball of snow in the bare woods where not a leaf or flower is yet to be seen. I have kept twenty acres of the original forest untouched by the axe, clearing a little, only about the house. The procession of the season is visible first in the Shadbush, the Wild Plum, and the Redbud; then the Pink Dogwood, and the Wild Crab-apple, of which there are two groves." He said: "I call the three poplars at my door the Brothers Karamazov. One is straight as a die, the other leans, but the third, Ivan, is crooked as a dog's hind leg."

Nearly all of the place was under cultivation. A German farmer, originally owner of much of the land, with a house at the entrance to the drive, did most of the work with his wife and young family. He had planted all the kinds of vegetables that would grow in the climate, some marvelous Belleville asparagus, everbearing strawberries, a few acres of grain and alfalfa. He also tended the young orchard of peaches, pears and apples, which father had put into what we farmers call "the west pasture."

My stay of three weeks at "Cragh Darragh" turned into three years in St. Louis, and Peggy soon joined me there. I had determined to equip myself with a profession at last, and during that summer produced about fifty pages of advertising layouts with text, which I sent to the various advertising agencies in St. Louis. Eventually I was hired by the Gardner Advertising Agency at $35 a week.

In the meantime, with little to do, I became the bookkeeper of the Johns farming enterprise, which very quickly revealed a discouraging balance on the red ink side. Henry Richards, the farmer, would take truck loads of stuff—he insisted on using a horse and wagon—to the commission merchants at Sappington and Fenton, towns in the neighborhood, where he sold it for disastrously low prices; while he bought manure, pig-chow, straw and bran at high prices. Added to these losses was the salary of $75 a month which poor Richards received for his losing operations.

My brother, John Jay, was more successful. That harassed youth, on his way to a smart school every morning, took a Ford truck full of strawberries to the hotels in St. Louis and these sales turned in a profit. I tried to impress the sorrows of a gentleman farmer on the chief victim, George S. Johns. Usually I met with optimistic predictions:

"When the orchard begins to bear" (it never did); or, "That new alfalfa will cut down the feed bill."

Mother was the center of the ménage. It doubled her work, but she was a fountain of energy. There were two cows, a population of hens and cocks, pigeons that produced squab for the table, and, for a time, beehives and rabbits. Mother became an adept handling bees, with a hat, veil and gloves. She did not milk—there was a man for that—but she skimmed the cream, made the butter, cottage cheese and clabber; and spiced and smoked her own hams, bacon and shoulders. When prohibition came she made wine and beer, and was known for miles around as "Moonshine Min." For hours in brown jumpers she worked up-ended over the flower beds; and I have seen her—impatient with the hired man—pushing the lawn mower and squirting the hose on the lawn and flower beds. She kept flocks of baby chicks in the bathroom that she shared with father and he would come down to breakfast grumbling because he had not found room to move around in when he bathed and shaved.

I was especially interested in what seemed to me the fate of the old farmers. Henry Richards was a good example. These people had tilled St. Louis County for decades and furnished St. Louis with food. They drove all night over the bad roads with slow horses, to the early markets in the city. Tempted by prices that seemed to them a small fortune offered for the land by city dwellers who wanted estates in the country, they sold out and thereafter became a distracted, uprooted and very unhappy people, usually keeping the money they had been paid in a corner of the mattress and watching it disappear day by day. They had to accept jobs as hired men on their own ancestral lands. Of course they looked down on the newcomers from their superior old fashioned morality and agricultural knowledge; but the newcomers dominated.

One night I went into Richards' kitchen. There was a big coal range in it, an old horsehair sofa, a table covered with a blue cloth, a shelf filled with baskets of vegetables, crates of berries piled in the corner. The china and pans were neatly arranged in cabinets. There was a chromo-lithograph calendar, and a colored print of "Custer's Last Stand at Little Big Horn," on the wall (for years the annual gift of the Anheuser-Busch brewery to bars and patrons). The one family bedroom was off to the front of the house. The talk was all about a horse named Molly, at least twenty years old, and now fatally ill in the barn. The children were in tears, Richards and his wife in abject despair. They felt the death of Molly almost as keenly as if she had been one of the family. Father came in with the veterinary—and a revolver in his pocket. They both begged Richards to let them shoot the horse and he finally consented. The shot was heard outside and the family burst into a wail.

Richards was a sandy, ruddyfaced man with a pale long mustache and a beaten look. Two of his daughters had been seduced by city men and one of them had disappeared. His wife was bent almost to a right angle by farm work. In the neighborhood were many such families, who met two or three times a week in the little stone Lutheran church and cursed the invaders.

A year or two later I wrote a play about these landless farmers called "The Price of Vegetables" which two managers in New York said they wanted to produce. The last minute upsets, which are commonplace on Broadway, interfered.

The changes in the seasons in Missouri were abrupt and dramatic. The climate in that part of the state is by no means kindly at its extremes. There are long, unrelieved hot weeks in summer, and the winters can be bitterly cold. I remember times when we were actually iced in for days at a time. No car could get through the roads. Tree branches fell with the weight of glistening ice. The lower branches of the spruce were frozen to the ground, and wires to the city were all down. In such weather mother fed the winter birds on a big tray outside her window; chickadees, juncos, downy woodpeckers and longspurs. Only the hardy all-season cardinals found their food somehow in spite of the snow. When the snow disappeared the place looked senile and battered, with the stumps of brown weeds, stiff, naked golden rods, fallen limbs, dried yellow cornstalks, dried gumbo pods in the garden, the peach stones and shrivelled apples still hanging on the trees. Then the spring would come in, beginning with the shrubs, and the woods from April first would take on color. Peggy and I collected and dated some fifty kinds of wild flower; wild anemone, bloodroot, bellwort, Indian tobacco, a kind of phlox that Richards called goldenlocks, woodbettony, and so on.

It is difficult to convey to the reader nowadays what it meant then to a city-bred poet to have the run of a big outdoor place. I was out all day, and I made of it the most productive period of my life. In the morning I would write stanzas under the apple trees, spend a few hours spading earth or chopping wood, then take my rough draft somewhere and work over it for the rest of the day and half of the night. I do not think there are many occupations that more effectively give one the sense of life than the writing of verse. The first intimation may be a phrase or a line—which ultimately may become the last line—but which carries the explosive burden of the whole poem. The labor of perfecting the lines may take a day, or a week; or possibly the final word and cadence will not come until years later. The excitement of breaking into a fresh thought, with the absolutely appropriate combination of sound and meaning that the thought requires, has no equal that I know.

SUNSET (ST. LOUIS)

SARA TEASDALE

Sara Teasdale was born in St. Louis in 1884 and died in New York from an overdose of sleeping tablets in 1933. She was a person of great sensitivity, and is said by one critic to have been "torn between a longing for life and a terror of it." She had many friendships among the American poets of her time; but after she removed to New York in 1929 she lived very much in seclusion. Her Love Songs *received a Pulitzer Prize in 1918; it had gone through five printings within a year.*

Hushed in the smoky haze of summer sunset,
When I came home again from far-off places,
How many times I saw my western city
    Dream by her river.

Then for an hour the water wore a mantle
Of tawny gold and mauve and misted turquoise
Under the tall and darkened arches bearing
    Gray, high-flung bridges.

Against the sunset, water-towers and steeples
Flickered with fire up the slope to westward,
And old warehouses poured their purple shadows
    Across the levee.

High over them the black train swept with thunder,
Cleaving the city, leaving far beneath it
Wharf-boats moored beside the old side-wheelers
    Resting in twilight.

KANSAS CITY

THE MAN WHO MADE THE *STAR*

WILLIAM ALLEN WHITE

William Allen White worked on Kansas City newspapers for about four years, 1891–1895. Though he was born in Emporia, Kansas, and made that town famous by spending most of his life there, and though most of his work on Kansas City newspapers dealt with Kansas affairs, we shall here claim him for Missouri on the basis of his short residence in our state. And we make this presumptuous claim partly because we wish to include in this volume his famous biographical sketch of William Rockhill Nelson, which appeared in Collier's *June 16, 1915, shortly after Nelson's death. Here, then, with all of White's warmth and color, is the tribute of one great editor to another—and incidentally an important chapter in the history of a great city.*

In the beginning, thirty-five years ago when this generation was young, Kansas City sprawled on a half dozen ugly yellow clay hills rising from the west bank of the Missouri River, a "mean city," if ever there was one. Mud streets, wooden sidewalks covered with wooden awnings over the business thoroughfares that slouched or staggered toward the river; cribbed vice reeking and stinking through all the north part of the town, and the catfish aristocracy of the unreconstructed South sulking on the hills about the town; a dozen railroads pouring thousands of Western immigrants into the Union Station every day—vigorous, hustling young men and their wives and children pressing into the great plains to take homesteads and grow up with the country; a few pioneering packing houses near the Kawsmouth beginning to turn the great herds of the prairies into food; Northern hustlers and Southern families dividing the town into factions; the larcenous bark of the real estate vendor forever dinning into the consciousness of visitors, and over all and through all the slambang a vast opium eater's dream of power and glory and wealth and splendor that was to come—such was the Kansas City of the late seventies.

Into this gorgeous nightmare of promise came William Rockhill Nelson in 1880 to found the *Kansas City Star.* When he died, thirty-five years later, April 13, 1915, to be exact—he left a newspaper which is reckoned by men who know as one of the first dozen newspapers in the world; an organ of public opinion that is the expression of the universal world spirit of his age, translated through his personality into an intensely individual thing.

Reprinted by permission of William L. White.

At first Kansas City had some trouble cataloguing Mr. Nelson. He was thirty-nine years old, with better than a fair education, and with more of the air of a man of the world than most men about him. He was nearly six feet tall and stout. He had a massive dignity that large men sometimes have. In the nature of the times, if he had been of another sort, people might have called him "Bill." For years thousands of people in Kansas City did refer to him as "Bill" Nelson, but no one called him "Bill." Sooner would one address a heroic statue of Buddha as "Bud." Time came when they referred to him as "Baron Bill" of Brush Creek, or as "The Baron of Brush Creek," for he was of the baronial type, but distinctly not of the "Bill" type. No man survived that day as Mister. The town had to do something with his name; so, early in his career in Kansas City, he became "Colonel." Not that he was ever a colonel of anything: he was just coloneliferous. When he came to Kansas City, in that early day a young man of thirty-nine, the strong, raw, noisy, lawless, conscienceless community, drunk and dressed up with optimism, spoke to something gay and adventurous in his nature, and on his part it was a case of love at first sight.

He was a typical upper-class American then when the upper crust of our society was about where our middle class is to-day. Back of him was blood—good governing blood; his forbears' names are in city charters and regimental rosters of the Revolution; one was a judge, one a Congressman, one a Quaker pioneer, and one a two-fisted Irishman; his father was a prominent citizen of Indiana in the middle of the last century. There was no tradition of wealth behind him, but much tradition of responsibility. And the middle-aged person with a boy's head on his shoulders who came bolting into Kansas City in 1880 had in his head an assortment of varied memories. There were memories of days when he had been a rebellious young blade in Fort Wayne—too irrepressible for the public school and too energetic for Notre Dame, a Catholic school, where his father, an Episcopal vestryman, had sent the youth in the hope of curbing his insurgency; memories of a try at the law; an attempt at holding a petty office in the court; an adventure in the real estate business; an excursion into cotton planting and storekeeping in Georgia; a rather successful journey into practical politics, when he helped manage the Tilden campaign in Indiana, and a real fortune made and lost in railroad contracting and bridge building.

He was considerable of a man of the world for those hilarious days of the new Kansas City, and carried a certain consciousness of his distinction in his heart; and so, while he doubtless never resented the

"Bill" business which would have been his natural portion, probably he also never exactly encouraged the familiarity of the fresh, crisp gentry of the place who but a few short years before had to be tied while they were collared and shod! So, because he would not get drunk with them, would not be bribed by them or bribe with them, would not share with them when they cut a melon in city graft, and would not brawl with them, but wore his clothes well, knew and observed the proprieties un-consciously, though not punctiliously, and preferred the society of his kind, he was knighted colonel, and from the first held in a sort of shivery respect.

When the *Star* was founded there were four other Kansas City daily papers. The *Times* and the *Journal* were the party thunderers, and there was a ragpicker or so and a plunderer in the field. The *Times,* being Democratic, represented the unconquered confederacy, made heroes of the James boys, regarded all Republicans as horse thieves, and fre-quently was called upon to punctuate its editorial utterances with a horse pistol. It was a fire-eating, blood-and-thunder, partisan sheet, of the type long since vanished from American journalism. The *Journal,* which was Republican in politics, sang softly as the organ of commerce and business progress, and spoke even in that remote day for the rail-roads and the banks. Its editor was in politics. He had a vision for the betterment of humanity—chiefly through prosperity—but something of the idealism of the fifties and sixties, something of what the war really meant, clung to him, and made the *Journal* rather more than respectable —a force for such righteousness as the times would permit.

Into this field came the *Star*. Mr. Nelson had tried his wings as an editor in Fort Wayne. He desired a wider field. He brought with him a few years' experience—and something better: a genuine passion for the newspaper business. In politics he was a mugwump, who had come into his independence by renouncing the Democratic party after it had refused to renominate Tilden in 1880. And a mugwump in that time and place was in a sore plight. Naturally he was taken for a blackmailer. Otherwise, why should he not line up with one of the parties?

And another suspicious thing—the *Star* printed the news: all of it. In those days and in that part of the West money was used as naturally to suppress the news of unpleasant episodes—not of a political nature —as ligatures to suppress bleeding. It took the community some time to discover that the *Star* would not take money. It had but a meager tele-graphic news service, and was filled with articles reprinted from other papers and from magazines and books. Once in those gala days when

the old *Kansas City Times* was having the low resorts raided in order
to catch certain prominent Kansas City Republican statesmen, the *Star*
was running Emerson's Essays in short chunks scattered through the
paper, and columns of book reviews, with editorials on Mr. Howells as
a new force in American letters. It was awful. To be a gentleman; to
be a mugwump; to refuse honest money for a peccadillo about professional ethics; to devote more space to Henry James than to Jesse in
Jesse's home town, and still to be a big, laughing, fat, good-natured,
rollicking, haw-hawing person who loved a drink, a steak, a story, and
a fight—strong men shuddered and turned away from the spectacle.
They couldn't be sure whether he was crazy or they were!

One of the earliest ructions the *Star* had was over the town "opera
house." It was on the second floor over a store, and the *Star* called attention first to the fact that it was poorly built, and second to the fact that
the narrow stairway from the single public exit made it a fire trap. The
simple answer of Colonel Coates, the owner of the opera house and the
leading citizen of the town, was that Colonel Nelson was a blackmailer.
That answer sufficed for the public; it was used to blackmailers. But
that answer did not satisfy Colonel Coates. And a few weeks later, after
the article denouncing the editor of the *Star* as a blackmailer had appeared in another paper, Colonel Coates came to the *Star* office and said:
"You were right, and I was wrong. The opera house is unsafe, and it is
a fire trap." And the plans and specifications for the New Coates Opera
House, which was the pride of Kansas City for a quarter of a century,
were soon ready for the contractor.

This was probably the first notable demand the *Star* made for better
living conditions in the new town. The later life of Mr. Nelson was a
continuous battle for civic and State improvement. His life's aim resolved itself into a fight—there were so many fights, some of the battles
waging simultaneously, that perhaps campaign is a better word than fight;
so let us say that his latter activities resolved themselves into a campaign for the "more abundant life" of men and women in his city, in
his State, in his sphere of influence throughout the Missouri Valley. It
is therefore of interest to examine this campaign for a moment. Looking back over the *Star*'s files of that early day one is impressed with the
fact that the motive in the contest was somewhat newspaper enterprise.
It was one of the *Star*'s things. There was a certain pride of achieve-
ment in the accomplishment of the new opera house, which had youth
and fire and pleasure in it. As the years go on, and we see in the *Star*'s
files other struggles appearing day after day, we find that the motives

behind these militant activities have been slowly growing into a policy. It is too much to presume that this policy was conceived in advance in Mr. Nelson's mind.

The human heart and head do not initiate omniscience—except in retrospect. It was gay old General Sherman who said it was unwise to give a reason for an action before doing it, because so many better reasons might turn up afterward.

The career of the *Star* for thirty-five years seems to be going in a straight line to a definite end, from that first tiff over the rattletrap opera house down to the present fight for the city improvement bonds. And yet it is not the best praise of Mr. Nelson to declare that he looked ahead and saw all that was coming. But given a heart fundamentally honest, and a mind keen to express newspaper enterprise in the terms of public welfare, such a policy as the *Star*'s unwavering, consistent, indomitable policy is the natural result.

When the paper was but a year old it attacked the horse-car monopoly in a mayoralty campaign. The attack won; the *Star*'s candidate was elected over the opposition of the older papers—not because the *Star* was supporting him, but because the *Star* was able to state the situation clearly—to make the fight intelligently. The franchise that was granted in competition with the old horse-car monopoly developed into the cable system. And the cable system climbed over the yellow clay hills of Kansas City, dipped into the great ravines and dived across the valleys; and because Kansas City had a street-car system that permitted it to widen out and to become a city in its rough environment, it went ahead of Leavenworth, St. Joseph, and Omaha, and took first place as a Missouri River town beyond the Mississippi. Of course Mr. Nelson did not see this when he supported the anti-monopoly ticket. Business judgment, the bread-and-butter side of the problem, the business men and advertisers of that day were naturally with the order that was. They stood with the horse-car monopoly. But newspaper enterprise, plus fundamental honesty, gave Mr. Nelson vision to see that the *Star*'s interests were with the people's interests, and the people's interests were with the anti-monopoly crowd, so he went in. And he never had to apologize for that fight.

So it was with every battle in the thirty-five years' campaign. Time and time again he was whipped; the people couldn't see it the *Star*'s way. But never could they quote the *Star* of one campaign against the *Star* in another. Always Mr. Nelson took the honest side. The big, laughing, good-natured, kindly spoken man who came bursting into

Kansas City with a newspaper that printed all the news, and yet never seemed to let its emotion express itself in black type or broken columns, but let its facts arouse their own emotions in the readers, had no gift of prophecy. His clairvoyance consisted in seeing from day to day and from year to year the essentially honest and workable plan for that day and for that year, and advocating it with all the enthusiasm of a nature built on almost grotesquely large lines, physically, mentally, morally; a nature vastly kind and intensely curious about a most interesting world; a nature literally bubbling with love of life and men and founded on a large and humorous charity that never remotely approached cynicism of any kind. It was this hulking, jovial, irrepressible soul, moving like a cumulus cloud through its earthly habitat, steadfastly, slowly, never turning, never breaking, never cyclonic, that reacted upon passing events about it, and made the policy of the *Star*. And the policy of the *Star* gave color to the opinion and economic status of the people of the region known as the Missouri Valley.

Of course the town was many years getting into its consciousness the real meaning of the *Star* in its life. Yet to the few men who met Mr. Nelson even in those first years of his editorship his purpose seems to have been fairly clear. For when the circulation of the paper was growing beyond its press—a miserable little flat-bed press with a capacity of 3,000 an hour—the man to whom he turned for credit when he needed a modern press was Colonel Kersey Coates, whose "opera house" the *Star* had emptied. And Colonel Coates guaranteed the notes and the press came. It was first used on the *Star*'s fourth birthday. "And do you know," said Colonel Nelson many years after to a younger friend who had graduated from the *Star* and in his own office was putting in some new bit of machinery, "do you know I was so happy about that press that I couldn't sleep the first night it was in. I'd get up and look at the paper—gaze at it—it was a kind of holy picture to me, and then I'd go to bed and get up and look at it all over again—every page, every advertisement, and go back to bed." He laughed the great roaring, guttural laugh that came surging up from his pyramidal body into his massive face and threw back his fine gray head as he said: "And 'y gad I'm a good deal that way now; I never have got weaned from the *Star*. I'm likely to get up to-night and look at it and say: 'Well, now, ain't she a daisy!' "

To the hour of his death he kept his enthusiasm, his boyish joy in the passions of his youth. Age never changed his view of life. He was static in the eternal dynamics of his joyous growth.

One of the first jobs of the new press was to print a call for a mass meeting—that was something like a riot—to protest against the exten-

sion of a thirty-year street-car franchise without transfers. The city council had passed the franchise. The mass meeting gave the mayor reasons
for vetoing it. The press was not paid for. The expenses of the *Star* with
the old press had not been met by its income. Mr. Nelson's notes were
baled in a considerable stack in the Armour bank, and the Armour bank
was the political bank of the town in those days. And the politics of the
town was for the franchise. But that did not affect the *Star*'s policy. And
the franchise was lost.

"No," he said again to his young friend, new to proprietorship, in
discussing the mass-meeting incident. "It wasn't so much courage; I
have no more courage than the rest of them. But I saw those scoundrels
[he said damned scoundrels, but we'll forget that] putting all kinds of
pressure on the mayor—from all the so-called respectable and business
element—to tie the people up in a knot, and I had faith that the people
would not stand it, and then," he laughed, "you know all the other
papers were in the scheme, and there was too much competition in that
line—so I took the chance." And he won, and the people began to have
faith in the *Star* and to expect its leadership.

And here is a curious element of his strength. It was faith in the
Star, not faith in Mr. Nelson, that inspired the people. The town was
growing. Excepting a few thousand people who remembered him when
he first came to town, no one knew the editor of the *Star.* He did not
attend the riotous mass meeting that upheld the mayor in his veto. He
had served on no committees. He had never appeared on a speaking
program at a dinner or a meeting, and all his life Mr. Nelson shunned
crowds. He went from his house to his office and back again in the first
years of his editorship alone; later he rode in a carriage, still later in a
coupé, and finally in a limousine. Being born to a social purple, he had
no social ambitions. While the editor of a paper in St. Louis was so
eaten up with social vanity that he printed the names of the occupants
of the reserved seats at a circus to get his name in the society columns
of his own paper, Mr. Nelson's name rarely appeared in the *Star*—
except at the top of its editorial columns. Through his entire career Mr.
Nelson cultivated a sort of elaborate anonymity. So, in the contest for
good government, he desired to establish faith, not in himself, but faith
in the *Star.* Therefore he would run for no office, nor would he permit
his name to be considered for an office. "An editor," he declared,
"should be a kind of political monk; he must take a monastic vow
against holding office. For if he doesn't—as sure as God made little
apples—they'll get him. If he has a blind side—society or business or
politics—they'll get him. These rascals [omitting the damn for brevity]
down there at the courthouse and the city hall and down at Jefferson

City, if they knew I'd take any office [again we cut out the qualifying adjective] from dog catcher to President, would be around with their peacock feathers fanning me to sleep."

He felt keenly that the *Star* should receive every ounce of credit it could have without bragging. But W. R. Nelson in his eyes was a person whose inconsequential attitude would have delighted the heart of Mr. Toots. He was accessible enough. Always his office door was open. The humblest citizen of Kansas City could and did come to him. But because he preserved his obscurity; because he never served on a committee, or caroused around at uplift meetings in person, few of his own social and financial cult or class knew him. In all the half a million people within twenty miles of the *Star* office, not over a thousand would have known Mr. Nelson if he had appeared on the street. He could have walked into any of a dozen political gatherings he denounced without being identified by the men whose activities he was deploring. So in his later life as in his earlier life, the avenues of sinister approach to him were few.

As the years went by, and the *Star,* which was always independent but never neutral, came to have the character of a real personality in its sphere of influence, the personality of its editor was forgotten for the most part by its readers. And that is a curious thing: for the personality of the editor of the *Star* was infinitely more vivid than was the personality of the *Star.* Some men—even some men with elements of greatness in them—repress the outward expression of themselves. They are gray and leaden and puzzling. Mr. Nelson was one of those men who exude character. To begin with, he looked different from the ordinary run of men. He was big—monumental, with a general Himalayan effect as he loomed behind a desk. He had a great voice; in his emotional moments —which were not infrequent—this great voice rattled like artillery. He loved figures of speech; had a thousand homely similes and often spoke in parables. Moreover he was always doing things that were interesting —outside of his professional career. Stories of his sayings and doings sprang up in his pathway and became legends. Always there were stories of his vast charities; his patience with rascals or fools—or both. He despised a fool and hated a rascal and was forever lending them a humorous tolerance—but never in the *Star.* There the fool and the rascal had scant welcome. But in his private relations with men he was given to a sort of Browningesque forgiveness of the unforgivable, and tolerance of the intolerable.

Perhaps one reason for this seeming duality of characters arose in the fact that he never wrote for the *Star.* Certainly no other editor ever pressed his own dominant personality into a paper more completely than Mr. Nelson put his vigorous personality into the *Star*. But the equation of his personality never got into the *Star* through any peculiarity of his literary style. One comes to know Henry Watterson, now the Last of the Mohicans, and one used to know Charles Dana and Horace Greeley, and one recognized Joseph Medill and the editorial giants of the elder days by what they wrote; by the way they turned phrases; by the quirks of their rhetorical self-illumination.

Mr. Nelson thought he was not a writer. He never put his pencil to paper. He called one of his editors or reporters—he referred to all of his writers as reporters—talked the matter in hand over, and the article, whether it was a news story or an editorial, appeared to run through the mental machinery of the writer. Often some phrase or some group of phrases in the strong, homely, figurative language of Mr. Nelson persisted. If it did persist, it was the meat of the article. But often no phrase of his was preserved in articles that pioneered out into new and daring policies.

Yet the article was more truly his than if he had polished every phrase. It was his vision, his courage, his conception of justice. And the irony of it all is that readers often will read personality only from phrases, from literary style; they do not seem to get personality—not, at least, those intimate traits and those delicious human foibles that make a human being well-beloved—through an exhibition of the major virtues. So even to the millions who came to know and follow the *Star*, the man who made it great by sheer force of his own masterful greatness lived and died a stranger to them. If they met the ruddy-faced, square-shouldered, great-bodied, short-legged, bronze-featured man in the street, if they heard his rumbling, good-natured voice, if they met the radiant sunset of a smile that often glowed in his kindly face, doubtless they would turn their heads and say: "There goes some one!" But only a few of his million readers would have identified him with the upstanding, enterprising, wholesome, good-natured newspaper that brought them daily much of their mental and moral and spiritual pabulum.

Before the *Star* was ten years old it had the lead over all papers in its field. It captured Kansas City in five years, and had taken Kansas in two years more. Because it had gone into city politics, and had taken the honest side intelligently and with incidental courage, Kansas City people trusted the *Star;* and because it was interesting, because it had a distinctly literary flavor and avoided sensationalism, Kansas took the *Star* for her bosom pin. In the first two decades of the *Star's* existence it did not take any considerable part in Kansas politics. Indeed, from 1880 until 1900 there was no black and white of wrong and right in Kansas politics. The Republicans were sordid and narrow, and the Democrats and their heirs and assigns, the Populists, were broad and incompetent. So the *Star* printed the news and scorned the devil, who was rather well intrenched on both sides of every question in Kansas in those days. Nationally, Mr. Nelson supported President Cleveland in office and out, through thick and thin. And the things he stood for the *Star* upheld. Low tariffs, a gold standard, civil service, the overthrow of the plutocracy—these were the fundamentals of the *Star's* politics and policies so far as they affected matters national. But in the first twenty years of its life the *Star* paid relatively little attention to any political matters outside of those in Kansas City.

In city matters Mr. Nelson's vision of righteousness was unfolding rapidly. It was no longer newspaper enterprise that moved him. He was consumed by a fire to serve. In 1892 he went after election thieves mercilessly—even election thieves who had helped to elect the men whom the *Star* had supported. The thieves went to the penitentiary. The next year a fight for cheaper gas consumed Mr. Nelson's interest, and he hired experts, paying them the fancy price that experts demand; he coached his reporters and writers in the cost and price of gas, and made the whole city see what a just price was. Kansas City people knew as much about gas as they knew about arithmetic. And he won his fight. In the winter following the *Star* began to promote organized charity. The editor talked with his young men, sent them out to investigate cases, assigned his editorial writers to reportorial beats so that they would put some well-directed emotion into their editorials; the *Star* gave, and it demanded that others give. It attacked poorly built tenements; it went after loan sharks. Like a great watchdog, it shook shyster lawyers who were bleeding the poor. For years this continued demand for equitable treatment for poverty was a moving passion in Mr. Nelson's heart. As a result appeared the free legal-aid bureau, the municipal farm, the welfare board, the divorce proctor, and, interlocked with these things, came the demand for a park and boulevard system.

Curiously enough, the park and boulevard system of Kansas City is the obvious monument to Mr. Nelson's thirty-five years of activity. And this is because it is a material thing. He literally gave color to the life and thought and aspiration of ten millions of people living between the Missouri River and the Rio Grande in the formative years of their growth as commonwealths—part of the national commonwealth. He and they together were dreaming States and building them, each reacting upon the other. The aspirations of the people were caught by his sensitive brain, and he gave these aspirations back in the *Star* policies. Kansas, western Missouri, Oklahoma, northern Texas, New Mexico, and Colorado form a fairly homogeneous section of our population. That section has grown up on the *Star*. Its religion, its conceptions of art, its politics, its business, its economic scale of living, reflect the influence of the indomitable mind of the man behind the *Star,* just as he gathered and voiced the latent visions of these people and gave them conscious form. These things are of the spirit. But half a hundred miles of paving amid trees and grass and flowers and pergolas, and several thousand acres of flowers and grass and trees in parks—these are material. And so the park and boulevard system of Kansas City stands as Mr. Nelson's monument because it is of the earth—earthy.

Yet, after all, these things of earth and wood and stone are accurate symbols of what Mr. Nelson stood for. These boulevards and these parks, from one end of Kansas City to the other, furnish the setting for tens of thousands of homes of a character almost unique for urban populations. They are, first of all, homes in detached houses. In front of each home is a plot of grass, some shrubs, and a few trees. The house is generally a two-story-and-a-half house, built most frequently of brick or stone. Its cost runs somewhere from five to twelve thousand dollars. A considerable majority of the houses in Kansas City built in the last twenty years are of this character. The apartment and the flat are the exception in Kansas City. Generally speaking, the flat and the apartment are found in the business district, or near it, and they were built in the old days before the park and boulevard system came, and offered cheap real estate, plenty of breathing space, and the opportunity to build the ideal middle-class home. Kansas City, like Los Angeles, is a distinctive middle-class American town. The upper class and the lower class are in the minority. The section of the country in which the *Star* finds its circulation—a section almost as large as Europe without Russia—is a middle-class section. No one is very rich there and few are afflicted with biting poverty. Democracy in government comes nearer finding a realization, and economic equality is more nearly approximated than in any other similar area in the world. And the park and boulevard system of Kansas City, for which Mr. Nelson in his studied anonymity through the *Star,* fought so valiantly and so well—the park and boulevard system of the commercial capital of this kingdom of the Southwest—is as suitable a monument as any material characterization might be of all that the man stood for.

The fight through the Missouri Legislatures and the Missouri courts for the park and boulevard system ended in 1895. Then the parks and boulevards began to grow in Kansas City. And the *Star* found itself in a bitter, almost daily, war with speculating real estate owners. It was no new controversy. From the first year of the *Star's* existence until the day its founder died he had fought just one kind of a battle: the fight between property and men. He took the side of men. With the owner of the fire-trap theatre, with the franchise grabbers, with the election crooks who sought to perpetuate graft, with the waterworks company seeking to prevent municipal ownership, with the gas company for dollar gas—all the differences had been upon the fundamental issue between the rights of men to service that would broaden the lives of the many and the rights of property to profits that would enhance the lives of a few. It was the middle-class fight. And Kansas City emerged a middle-class town.

But all this battling, which may have begun with newspaper enterprise for its impulse, was telling upon the editor of the *Star*. He was thriving on it as a publisher, growing with it as an editor, and broadening and deepening with it as a man. He came West a practical business man, who had made and lost a fortune, who had the essential democracy of the American aristocrat of the latter half of the nineteenth century, who had the ideals of the governing classes, and he came West to grow up with the country.

And every day of his life he did grow up with the country—spiritually. Growth was the motive of his life. He socialized himself as completely as it is possible for a man to socialize himself and live practically in modern civilization. He lived a soldier's life—a soldier of the common good, and he had to be forever casting off unnecessary equipment. His paper dropped whisky advertising. It turned away quacks and clairvoyants. It barred fake land sales and get-rich-quick schemes of all kinds. Many harmful patent medicines went by the board.

Scare headlines never were allowed in the *Star*, nor was appeal ever permitted to the prejudice and passion of the ignorant through red type, flaming letters, and gaudy pictures. The first page of the little four-page sheet issued in 1880 with no box-car letters, and with no screaming heads, is enough like the first page of the *Star* to-day to be the second edition of the same issue. The decent form and the frank statement of the middle-class ideal are the only things in all the *Star's* mental and physical environment that have not changed. And all the while the devil has posted a competitor beside the *Star* who practiced every carnal art known to the yellow trade. One paper after another has entered the evening field with its big scare heads, with its crass appeal to the mob, with dirty advertising, with emotional sob squads like howling dervishes of journalism tearing up the earth around the *Star*; with mud slingers attacking Mr. Nelson savagely, accusing him of personal immorality and sculduggery; calling him a blackmailer, a grafter, a thief—and organizing the criminal section of the community against him. Yet never one word has he replied. Not once in thirty-five years has the *Star* mentioned the name of one of its slanderous competitors, nor replied even by inference to any of their charges.

And the other crowd, the wealthy privilege reapers, have attacked Mr. Nelson and the *Star* in their own way. They have organized advertising boycotts. They have tried to undermine his credit. They have organized with the crooks in politics and have fostered an anti-*Star* party in Kansas City, sometimes operating under one national party name and sometimes under another. They have manned the courts against him, have got behind fake libel suits, have even haled him into court for contempt, and then their weapons bent or blunted, and were ineffective. Once in a libel suit within the last decade or so, when the attorney for the plaintiff was the attorney for one of the great public-service corporations with which the *Star* had been fighting for a bone of privilege, it was announced that they were going to give Mr. Nelson a grilling on the stand and make him tell of all the boodle and graft and corruption he had shared. When he went on the stand he said: "Now I don't want my attorneys to object to any possible questions the plaintiff's attorney may ask. My life is an open book. Go ahead with your questions," and no question was asked outside of the issue, and no attorney ever gave a witness such distinguished consideration as that corporation counsel prosecuting a measly little libel suit gave to Mr. Nelson.

As the years went by he came to know the works and ways of the plunderbund of common interests that preys on every community, large or small; that unites always the very rich and the criminals in a community to maintain the order that is; to stop progress, because progress means a wider distribution of the fruits of civilization. And when the *Star* began a fight it knew its enemies. And for all his wide tolerance of the weaknesses of men, for all his forgiving nature which made him forget easily, no wings of a pale sainthood sprouted under Mr. Nelson's suspenders. He was as proud of his enemies as Cornelia was of her jewels. And he liked to keep them and count them over.

Once the president of a scurrilous newspaper that had dogged Mr. Nelson's heels for years, accusing him of all the crimes of the calendar, became manager of a theatre—the Willis Wood—a beautiful playhouse and popular. The time came for the *Star* to increase its rates. Notice was served on all the *Star*'s patrons, and they agreed to the raise —all but the Willis Wood. It refused to pay its bill. Naturally its advertising was refused. It was told that it could have advertising over the counter at the counter rate. It came in a few times, paid the counter rate, and then formally notified the *Star* that it would use the *Star* no longer as an advertising medium. In a few weeks the manager of the theatre saw that he could not get along without the *Star*. He brought his advertising back. It was refused. Mr. Nelson declared that the Willis Wood had gone out voluntarily; it could stay out.

As the winter grew old it was apparent that the Willis Wood was losing money. Its owners tried to get the *Star* to take the theatre's advertising. Delegations of business men came and pleaded. Mr. Nelson was obdurate. Finally came R. A. Long, one of the most benevolent of the rich men of Kansas City. A kindly, churchly, soft-spoken, meek man was Mr. Long. He sat before the pyramidal hulk of the *Star*'s editor and begged that the *Star* would take the advertising of the failing theatre. He knew, did Mr. Long, that the manager of the theatre, as president of the scurrilous newspaper, had attacked Mr. Nelson unmercifully; had accused him of dastardly crimes; had assailed his honor and integrity, without a word of defense or reply from the *Star*. And Mr. Long recited these things and begged the editor to take a high and charitable view of the man who now was pleading for his financial life. Mr. Nelson's theory was that the community was better off if the manager of the theatre and the newspaper company didn't have any further financial life. Finally Mr. Long said: "Now, Mr. Nelson [he said Colonel, of course, as the world did], now, Colonel, wouldn't you feel better if to-night you could think that in all this town you had not one enemy when you turn on your pillow to rest?"

Quickly as a flash the deep roaring voice came thundering out of the mountainous pyramid with the implacable face at the apex:

"No—no, no, by God. If I thought that I wouldn't sleep a wink."

He loved his enemies—so dearly that he wouldn't part with a real choice one for money. For money had little meaning to Mr. Nelson. He made it easily and valued it lightly. His estate seems to be worth five or six million dollars—perhaps more. He trusteed it for his wife and child for life, and gave it all to the city to found an art gallery for the people. In handling money he invested it, but not upon a speculative basis. When he built a house for rent—and he built many hundreds—he used two by sixes instead of two by fours for the studding and rafters. He put out scores of miles of stone fences around his renting property, and covered the fences with roses and honeysuckles—and kept them growing. He loved beauty. He founded and maintained for twenty years an art gallery, where good copies of famous pictures could be seen seven

days and nights in the week. He sent a shipload of food to the starving
Cubans, not as a newspaper enterprise, but to feed the hungry. The
only newspaper enterprise he knew was to get all of the news and print
it wholesomely. If Providence let unpleasant things happen, it was his
business to tell of it, but not to gloat over it, not to stick a banal snout
in it and whiff it for his readers.

When he bought the old Kansas City *Times,* after one owner following another had been sinking money in it, and the paper mills controlled the property, the first step he took in the trade was to find out
how much money the last owner—a lame man—had sunk in it, and he
made that sum the first consideration in the trade. Thus, when the attorney for the paper mills opened the trade by reciting what good neighbors he and Mr. Nelson had been in the past, the big man listened for
a time and then rumbled from his big chest:

"That's all right—now let's quit being so damn neighborly and make
a trade here that won't rob a cripple."

He did not spell his success in terms of money. He cheapened nothing he did by estimating it in dollars and cents. When he cut liquor
advertising from the *Star* he adjusted no halo on his head. Instead he
laughed and said: "Now I've got that foot loose!" He counted his freedom the gain, and never thought of the hundreds of thousands of dollars he had lost. He saw the need of free swimming pools, playgrounds,
and a convention hall for his town, and they grew out of the columns
of the *Star* like magic palaces. That was in the late years of the last
century.

But it was with the rise of the progressive movement of the first
decade of this century that the *Star's* real power outside of Kansas City
took root and grew and fruited into a slow revolution in the whole idea
of State and city government in the *Star's* territory. In campaign after
campaign in three and four and sometimes five States the *Star* was waging battles for free government. The initiative and referendum came in
Missouri, Arkansas, Oklahoma, Nebraska, and Colorado. Commission
government with the initiative and referendum and recall for city officers came in all these States and Kansas. Direct popular government is
a weapon of the people of the Missouri Valley. So is the primary. The
relation of the State to the citizen has been revolutionized in the *Star's*
territory. Bank deposits are guaranteed. Investments are certified by the
State. The issues of stocks and bonds of public utilities are supervised
by the State; rates of public utilities are being made by the State for con-
sumers of the products of public utilities. Higher technical and professional education is supplied free by the State; the State schools furnish

expert aid to the State in its scientific activities. Preventive medicine has become a State industry that touches every citizen. The Board of Health has almost as much power as the Governor. Mothers' pensions are provided by the county and the hours and wages of women and children are controlled by the State. And in all the *Star's* territory, excepting half a dozen large cities, the sale of liquor is prohibited either by State-wide prohibition or by local option.

During the dozen years while the fight was active for these revolutionary changes in the State governments of the Missouri Valley, Mr. Nelson's reporters were really lieutenants, emissaries, and proconsuls rather than mere writers. They made the news as they went, and like a general in his tent, the big white-haired, ruddy-faced, bull-voiced old soldier of righteousness sat and swore sweetly in mellow joy at the news from the front. He knew every politician in half a dozen States in every party who was true; and the *Star* branded the traitors and the crooks—not by calling names but by printing roll calls. And slowly the firing ceased, and at the beginning of the second decade of the century it was evident that the campaign was over—and won. But the fighting blood still pumped in the brave old heart. He mapped out a new campaign.

When the Progressive party was organized Mr. Nelson followed Colonel Roosevelt, and accepted the Progressive platform as good so far as it went. But he was going farther. Mr. Nelson believed that the courts are bulwarks of privilege, and that high-priced lawyers are the big guns of privilege behind the bulwarks. So he started his campaign for socialized justice. For a public defender, for a commission to throw out vicious litigation, and merely technical causes. If the rich and the poor were real equals in court, had exactly the same kinds of attorneys, as they have the same kinds of judges, or outside of the courts, have the same kinds of school teachers, or the same kinds of preachers, Mr. Nelson believed that privilege would be forced out of the courts. He was perfectly willing to recall judges and decisions if the Bull Moosers desired to recall them to put the fear of the Lord, which is the beginning of wisdom, into the courts. But the recall was a popgun, he thought. The 42-centimeter gun was free justice. Of course it is revolutionary. When it comes, as it will, it will destroy the vicious power of the dollar in the courts, as corrupt practices acts are destroying the vicious power of the dollar in elections and in legislatures, and as the free public schools and universities are destroying the vicious power of caste in social life.

A great vision that for a daily newspaper; for a man to begin striving for at seventy. And yet he rose and went to battle as gayly and as vigorously as he began his first newspaper contest for a modern theatre building in Kansas City. He had come a long, long way in those thirty years, and always in the flush of youth; always with a great laugh that sounded like a cataclysm, always with belief that the particular segment of the millennium he sought was just around the corner. Life never hardened the arteries of his faith, never bleached his hope, never sterilized his wide, humorous charity. For he had never cheapened life by using it for sordid ends nor selfish purposes. His human meannesses and hates and foibles—and never was a man further from anemic sainthood than Mr. Nelson—were not the meannesses and hates and foibles of a prig or an academician or a maiden aunt. When he admitted a person to the intimacy of his enmity, he admitted him as a public nuisance, not in private spite. Mr. Nelson socialized even his enemies. He loved and hated as a public spirit, and with high voltage.

So when he was stricken in death, he met death as an incident of life. For ten days or such a matter his doctor had been sustaining Mr. Nelson's life by an artificial stimulant; by a saline solution. He found it out, and his scorn at living as a sham roused his rage. He called the doctor into the room, and when they were alone, got the truth. He was an old man, as men go—seventy-four years and more. And life was full and fresh and joyous as he was living it. But he would have no life that was not genuine.

"So," he demanded, "I should have been dead the fifth of March?"

The doctor acknowledged the truth.

"And you have kept life going by this—this saline solution, when I had no physical life in me—no real right to live?" he asked.

That also was declared to be about the truth.

"Doctor," cried the patient angrily, "I have taken you into my family; I have given you my confidence as a personal friend; I have trusted you as a square man—and now—this is the way you treat me—this is my reward—that you cheat death from day to day and keep me lying here a dead man by rights." And then came the last cussing out that ever rose from that hearty old breast.

When the doctor had left, Mr. Nelson said very gently to those about him whom he loved: "Well—if this is the end, I am willing to go!"

But he stalked up to death a gentleman unafraid, like his "peers, the heroes of old." He went girding up his loins, alone and with the courage a man feels alone, to enlist for the next battle of the eternal war!

THE SLEIGH RIDE

ARTHUR GRISSOM

Arthur Grissom, at the time of his death in 1901, had acquired a considerable reputation as a writer of romantic short stories and what used to be called vers de société.

His father was an Independence, Missouri, minister, and Arthur went to the public schools and Woodland College in that town. Having sold some of his pieces to leading periodicals, he set off for New York to make his fortune as a freelance writer. He had his troubles getting started, if he did not, in classic fashion, precisely starve in an attic. But one day, on Fifth Avenue, he met an old Kansas City flame of his, who had come to New York to buy a trousseau. A marriage had been arranged for her with a promising young banker at Hannibal; she herself, incidentally, was the daughter of a millionaire banker in Kansas City. Before that day on which Arthur met Julia Woods on Fifth Avenue ended, the two were taking the vows of holy matrimony in the Little Church Around the Corner. Shortly after the daughter of this marriage was born, the father-in-law persuaded the Grissoms to return to Kansas City, where Arthur had a go at banking, which he detested. So Julia went home with the baby, and her father settled a suit for alienation of affections out of court for $18,000.

In the meantime Grissom had brought George Creel, old friend of his freelancing days, back to Kansas City to found the Independent, *one of those urban weeklies common in all growing cities in those days, devoted to society news, amusements, and sometimes literature and politics. The* Independent *had an exciting time fighting the Pendergast organization for a few years; then Creel went west to Denver and Grissom east to New York again; and the* Independent *settled down to the quieter existence which it has since enjoyed. Grissom became first editor of the new* Smart Set, *later made famous by Henry Mencken and George Jean Nathan; but he died after somewhat less than two years of that editorship, at the age of thirty-one.*

The following characteristic poem is especially interesting in that it tells of another kind of "runaway match" than his own, and also celebrates a type of social diversion common in Kansas City (and most other cities, and country towns too, for that matter) in the winter season. It is reprinted from Grissom's Beaux and Belles.

> When all the world is robed in white,
>   And merry night
> By moon and stars is rendered bright,

And everywhere the sleighing bell
　　Rings out to tell
The tale that lovers love so well,

With joy I capture pretty Flo,
　　And off we go
Across the glittering fields of snow,

Our sleigh just large enough for two
　　Who want to woo,
And keep unfrozen while they do.

I place my arm, in comic haste,
　　About her waist,
And find her lips just to my taste.

She shows no traces of alarm,
　　For what's the harm?
Thus on we speed past cot and farm.

How swiftly now the moments fly!
　　The miles go by;
We notice not the darkening sky.

Heigho! what now? 'Mid laugh and shout
　　We're tumbled out!
The snow *is* cool, beyond a doubt!

We climb again into the sleigh;
　　Then in dismay
We quickly learn we've lost our way!

Yes, lost our way—alas, alack,
　　We can't go back—
Down comes a storm upon our track!

In yonder cottage shines a light—
　　It's hardly right,
But there we'll have to spend the night.

And who should answer at the door
　　But Parson Bore,
Who's oft seen runaways before.

And—well, I don't know what is said,
　　But all turn red,
And Flo and I, we—just get wed!

SAM ARRIVES IN CENTROPOLIS

John Selby

John Selby was born in Gallatin, Missouri, in 1897 and attended Park College 1915–1916, the University of Missouri 1916–1918, and Columbia University in 1927. He was on the staff of the Kansas City Star *1918–1929 and was literary editor and book reviewer for the Associated Press 1932–1936. His first novel,* Sam, *from which the following passage is taken, was published in 1930 and won the All-Nations Prize Novel Competition. Since that time Selby has published several other successful books, and was editor-in-chief of Rinehart & Company, book publishers, 1945–1953.*

"Centropolis" is, of course, early Kansas City. It is interesting to compare William Allen White's description of the Kansas City of 1891 in his Autobiography *(p. 205) with that here presented.*

Sam arrived late one afternoon in the cupolaed and stinking Union Depot at Centropolis. The Bottoms had been unexpectedly flooded the week before, and underneath the wooden boards of the platforms in the train shed there was cindery black mud which squashed up between the cracks when baggage trucks were pushed over them. The flood had left a subtle odor of decay over everything. Although it did not occur to Sam that the odor had to do with his depressed morale, he was conscious of a gone feeling in his midriff. Gentlemen drank for that feeling, but now even liquor would have to be bought gingerly—there were seven silver dollars and a little small change lying loose in Sam's pocket, and when this little pile was gone, there would be hunger looking up at him.

"Huh," he grunted. "I ain't busted yet."

He pushed his one satchel before him over the legs of the people on the rattan benches, over the brass cuspidors. He ignored the black hackmen in front of the depot, and turned down Independence Avenue toward a tall five-story hotel that looked promising. It looked even better close up; the name was The Planters, although the lobby was full of cattlemen, and there was no colonel, not even a major in sight. Sam registered, washed up, and descended once more into the lobby. The men who were not on their way to or from the bar were sitting in enormous leather chairs, a brass spittoon on a rubber pad between each pair. Sam sat down, pushed back his round black hat, pulled out a cigar, and smoked. His legs dangled freely before him, for they could not reach the floor. It annoyed him, but it wasn't his fault.

Presently he was arguing about Grover Cleveland with the man next to him, and shortly after that the man was buying Sam a drink. Sam pulled himself up, but still was only a head above the bar. They had a drink, and another and supper and another drink. Then the cattleman suggested a little stud. He had sold a load of steers, and had nothing to do. His name was Martin.

"Sure," said Sam, "sure thing. Come up to my room, Martin." Which used quite a bit of Sam's nerve, because the seven dollars were now four, and stud with a cattleman might be pretty expensive. Sam peeled his coat and played in a stiffly starched dickey and his long-sleeved gray undershirt. Martin shed his coat too; he wore a heavy blue flannel shirt under it, and Sam noted, a man-sized revolver in a hip holster. They had picked up two more cattlemen, both of whom remained vague in the minds of Sam and Martin. Sam won a fifteen dollar pot on a pair of jacks in the first deal; the three cattlemen flung their Stetsons admiringly into a corner, ordered up a bottle, and settled.

Breakfast was sent in at six in the morning, but before it arrived the two strangers had been carried out horizontally, about even financially, and happily insensible otherwise. Sam and Martin ate flannelly wheat cakes, sausage, a small steak with potatoes, and kept on.

It was well past noon before they stopped. They parted good friends; Sam lent Martin enough to get back to Abilene. Then he lay down on the bed because he couldn't stand, and emptied his pockets. He found a little more than four hundred dollars in money, a cashier's check duly indorsed for $3750, and a gold hunting-case watch with a bell-stacked locomotive on one side, horribly intertwined initials reading T. O. M. on the other, the whole attached to a gold chain heavy enough to hang a St. Bernard dog.

Sam, still stretched across the bed, raised himself on one elbow and surveyed his wealth. He swung the watch to and fro by the chain, admiring its weight and thinking how prosperous he would look with the chain stretched across his vest. He pushed himself up to the head of the bed, and put a pillow behind his head. Then he strung the watch and chain across his front and carefully put away the money. He closed his eyes for a minute, waiting to see whether the images before them would whirl or be quiet. They were quiet and he slid his feet to the floor and stood up. He was worried about Martin.

Presently he and a shiny black boy found Martin sitting quietly on the top stair of the flight leading to the lobby, eating peanuts and carefully stuffing the shells under the turkey-red carpet. They took him back to Sam's room, washed him carefully in cold water. Then the two of them loaded him into a cab, and Sam drove him to the Union Depot and helped him aboard the Abilene train. He watched the train pull out, a grin on his face.

"Thanks," he muttered. He had a drink in a bar across from the station, ate some more cakes and sausage in the station restaurant, bought the largest and most expensive cigar the dough-faced female at the cashier's desk could find for him, and walked to the cab rank.

"What's the busiest part of town?" he asked. "Most people?"

"The Junction," answered the man.

"Sure," said Sam, and seated himself in the exact middle of the faded black broadcloth seat. "I'll get out at the Junction." They drove by a necessarily circuitous route up Independence Avenue, around the foot of the bluff, and then up a long slow incline which infuriated Sam because it was not steep enough for a hard pull, and too steep for the horse to do more than walk. "What is the Junction," he finally bellowed at the driver, jumping him off the seat six inches. "Junction o' what?"

"Junction of three streets," said the cabby, after he had quieted himself and his horse. "Makes a Y-shape, kind of."

Sam said nothing until he paid the man. Then he looked up into the driver's face, and demanded in the same awful voice, "Where's a saloon?"

The driver pointed up a side street with his stubby whip. "See that sign, says Hancock and Bang?"

"Yes," said Sam, "I do."

"Well, almost across the street is Joe Ray's Red Plush. Best barroom in the Middle West, by God."

"You don't say," Sam answered, and for once in his life he turned his back on a saloon. He was interested in Centropolis, and for an hour or more he walked up one street and down another, past wooden dwellings nudging the fat sides of brick business blocks, streets in which most of the lots were losing an old building to gain a new one. The town was green, lanky, and rather ugly when you analyzed it. But it had the attractiveness of late adolescence in spite of itself. It had an engaging quality which even Sam felt—better yet, it looked to Sam like a place in which he could make money. He was beginning to wonder just how he could make money when, to his surprise, he found himself in front of Joe Ray's Red Plush. He was tired, thirsty, he needed an audience.

It was dark inside the Red Plush, and because it was not yet late enough to catch the early quitters, there was only one man in the place besides the three bull-necked bartenders. The one customer was a jowled and rather thick young man, engaged as Sam hove alongside in trying to fill the jigger a little above the top with rye whisky. One bartender and Sam watched nervously; finally Sam could stand it no longer.

"T'won't hold any more," he declared. The young man jumped, and the whisky spilled.

Both men were temporarily stunned. Then the thick young man looked down at Sam. "Guess you're right. Have a drink?"

"No," said Sam positively. "Have one with me. Hell, don't hold back. I just made a pile I didn't expect. Goddam lucky, too. Down to my last four dollars."

They had a couple of drinks, and settled the weather and national politics. Sam liked the young man, whose name was Wells Fort. Fort liked Sam. The bartender chuckled at the two of them and finally slipped away to talk with the man at the front station.

"Jeez," said he, "jever see two such cards? The little one sounds like an election crowd bawling all together, and the big one sounds like a bull fiddle in a closet. Jeez, they're funny."

Sam and Fort adjourned from the bar to one of the plush-lined booths against the opposite wall. "What line you in?" Sam demanded suddenly.

"I'm city editor of the Centropolis *Sun*," said Fort, "until Saturday. Two more days."

"What d'you mean? Speak so's I can hear you. Paper folding?"

"Yeah. It's a ratty little sheet anyhow, and the boss is tired of the struggle."

"How many papers here?" Sam went on.

"Three, if you count *The Sun*." Fort turned his glass slowly, looking sidewise at Sam. "There's a business for you," he finally got out. "I think a live guy could make a pot of money here. Need a little work, maybe."

Sam was taken with the idea, but nervous about it. "Sure. Guess you're right. But what the hell do I know about running a newspaper?"

"You couldn't know less than Charlie Frey knows. He's the town's prize sap."

"Yes," said Sam. "But I still don't see how that'd help me."

Fort said nothing for a moment. "Well—I guess this will sound like trying to make a job for myself. But I know a good deal about running a paper."

"Finish your liquor," Sam decided things with speed. "Let's look up Frey."

"Sure."

"But I ain't goin' to pay him all the cash I got. He'll have to give me time and lots of it."

"Listen, Mr. Larson," Fort was serious indeed. "The only thing Frey's got that's worth anything is that new press. It's pretty good, but you might remember that there isn't anything in the world harder to sell than a second hand newspaper press. He'll take anything in reason."

He did. Weeks later Martha was sent for. She looked apprehensively at the sooty Depot, smelled the sour smell of the inescapable creamery cans, and saluted her husband.

"Sam," she began, "where in the world did you get enough money to buy a newspaper?"

"Won it playin' poker, honey. Played all one night and then some."

"Good heavens. The poor man—"

"Poor man hell. He lost honest and I won honest. He's still got plenty o' cows out in Abilene. Look, Martha, I won this watch too."

He lifted the heavy chain and ran it fondly through his fingers, and took out the watch itself and popped open the case.

"Pretty," said Martha. "But Sam, what do you know about running a newspaper?"

"More'n I did last week, honey," said Sam. He drove her around the bluff in a two-horse cab, and past the Junction, and up the hill past the Orpheus Theater. The cab stopped at a four-family flat in Quincy Street, on the edge of the high bluff. Martha looked out over the Bottoms, the Depot far below her in the foreground, and in the blue distance the smoking chimneys of Centropolis' embryo packing district. A half mile away on the right the river swung gently along.

"It's a nice place, Sam, and I hope we stay settled a while."

"Damn' right we stay. This here's my town, now."

BALLAD OF KANSAS CITY

C. L. EDSON

C. L. Edson, born in Nebraska, educated at the University of Kansas, was a columnist for the Kansas City Star *from 1904 to 1912. It was in his column of March 31, 1908, for that paper that the "ballad" of which we reprint the opening stanzas first appeared.*

Edson was the author of The Gentle Art of Columning *(1922) and* The Great American Ass *(1926).*

Grain built Babylon, war raised Rome.
Films built Hollywood, as gold built Nome.
Hogs made Chicago with their dying squeal;
Up popped Pittsburgh with the birth of steel.
Come, Kansas City, make your story brief:
"Here stands a city built o' bread and beef."

The streamlined *Hummer* with its ears pinned back,
Races through the city on the Belt Line track,
Sees the Union Station, and the brakes buck down,
And we tarry twenty minutes in the Big Beef town.

The Pioneer Yankees who had nine lives
Built this City where the race survives.
The sod-corn planter, when the world was new—
And the herders and the traders and the stock yards crew;
They planted Kansas City, and the darn thing grew.
A Mid-West Main Street with cow-town capers
Is hidden from the eye by the high skyscrapers.

The planters and the hunters from the buffalo chase
Had to have a city for a market place.
The bear-cat killers and the Dan Boone clan,
The boys who taught the panther his respect for man,
Had planted Kansas City where the bull trails ran.

The log cabin builder found himself "Out West;"
He built a soddy dug-out like a ground squirrel's nest.
The ax, and the chopper, and his woods were done;
He had to shed his ax and get a buffalo gun.
The Dan Boone tribe then traipsed across the grass,
Eating buffalo beef but nary garden sass!
The St. Louis steamboats stopped at this land,
Their nozzles high and dry in the Kaw River sand.
Kansas City "landing" was a plainsman's retreat
That grew into a Capital of Beef-and-Wheat! . . .

OTHER CITIES AND
TOWNS OF MISSOURI

THE "ST. JO GAZETTE"

Eugene Field

Eugene Field was born in St. Louis, attended the University of Missouri for one hilarious year, and worked on newspapers in St. Joseph, St. Louis, and Kansas City. When he was thirty-three years old (1883) he settled down in Chicago to work for the Daily News *during the remainder of his life. His "Sharps and Flats" in that paper set the pattern for the miscellaneous columns (often called "colyums") of amusing and literary materials that enlivened the editorial pages of many metropolitan newspapers for several decades.*

Field's verse was facile, and often topical; he is best remembered for his poems about and for children, and for his translations, or rather adaptations, of Horace.

It was in 1875 that Field was a member of the staff of the "St. Jo Gazette." By the word "local" in these verses from his Second Book of Verse *he means the department of local news.*

When I helped 'em run the local on the "St. Jo Gazette,"
I was upon familiar terms with every one I met;
For "items" were my stock in trade in that my callow time,
Before the muses tempted me to try my hand at rhyme,—
    Before I found in verses
    Those soothing, gracious mercies,
Less practical, but much more glorious than a well-filled purse is.
A votary of Mammon, I hustled round and sweat,
And helped 'em run the local on the "St. Jo Gazette."

The labors of the day began at half-past eight A. M.,
For the farmers came in early, and I had to tackle them;
And many a noble bit of news I managed to acquire
By those discreet attentions which all farmer-folk admire,
    With my daily commentary
    On affairs of farm and dairy,
The tone of which anon with subtle pufferies I'd vary,—
Oh, many a peck of apples and of peaches did I get
When I helped 'em run the local on the "St. Jo Gazette."

Dramatic news was scarce, but when a minstrel show was due,
Why, Milton Tootle's opera house was then my rendezvous;
Judge Grubb would give me points about the latest legal case,

And Dr. Runcie let me print his sermons when I'd space;
    Of fevers, fractures, humors,
    Contusions, fits, and tumors,
Would Dr. Hall or Dr. Baines confirm or nail the rumors;
From Colonel Dawes what railroad news there was I used to get,—
When I helped 'em run the local on the "St. Jo Gazette."

For "personals" the old Pacific House was just the place,—
Pap Abell knew the pedigrees of all the human race;
And when he 'd gi'n up all he had, he'd drop a subtle wink,
And lead the way where one might wet one's whistle with a drink.
    Those drinks at the Pacific,
    When days were sudorific,
Were what Parisians (pray excuse my French!) would call "magni-
fique;"
And frequently an invitation to a meal I'd get
When I helped 'em run the local on the "St. Jo Gazette."

And when in rainy weather news was scarce as well as slow,
To Saxton's bank or Hopkins' store for items would I go.
The jokes which Colonel Saxton told were old, but good enough
For local application in lieu of better stuff;
    And when the ducks were flying,
    Or the fishing well worth trying—
Gosh! but those "sports" at Hopkins' store could beat the world at lying!
And I—I printed all their yarns, though not without regret,
When I helped 'em run the local on the "St. Jo Gazette."

For squibs political I'd go to Colonel Waller Young,
Or Colonel James N. Burnes, the "statesman with the silver tongue;"
Should some old pioneer take sick and die, why, then I'd call
On Frank M. Posegate for the "life," and Posegate knew 'em all.
    Lon Tullar used to pony
    Up descriptions that were tony
Of toilets worn at party, ball, or conversazione;
For the ladies were addicted to the style called "deckolett"
When I helped 'em run the local on the "St. Jo Gazette."

So was I wont my daily round of labor to pursue;
And when came night I found that there was still more work to do,—
The telegraph to edit, yards and yards of proof to read,
And reprint to be gathered to supply the printers' greed.
    Oh, but it takes agility,
    Combined with versatility,
To run a country daily with appropriate ability!

There never were a smarter lot of editors, I'll bet,
Than we who whooped up local on the "St. Jo Gazette."

Yes, maybe it was irksome; may be a discontent
Rebellious rose amid the toil I daily underwent.
If so, I don't remember; this only do I know,—
My thoughts turn ever fondly to that time in old St. Jo.
      The years that speed so fleetly
      Have blotted out completely
All else than that which still remains to solace me so sweetly;
The friendships of that time,—ah, me! they are as precious yet
As when I was a local on the "St. Jo Gazette."

AT THE CROSS-ROADS OF THE NATION

Minnie M. Brashear

*Minnie M. Brashear came from a pioneer family in the Kirksville re-
gion of Missouri. The village of Brashear was named after her father.
She received her A.B. and A.M. degrees from the University of Missouri and her Ph.D. from the University of North Carolina. She was a
member of Missouri's English faculty for twenty-five years, retiring in
1944. She died in April, 1963; one of the last letters she wrote was the
one giving us permission to reprint the final chapter of her book* Mark
Twain, Son of Missouri—*a work which was accepted immediately upon
its publication in 1934 as an important contribution to Mark Twain
criticism.*

      These chapters have been, first of all, an essay at presenting
some neglected aspects of the region out of which Mark Twain came—
a small region, a backwater, if you will, of the fabulous forties; and
that is not to say that it is to be discredited. "All that goes to make the
me in me was in a Missourian village, on the other side of the globe,"
Mark Twain wrote in India, looking back through the vista of three-
score years. Sam Clemens's region had too vivid and too highly idealized
a life of its own to be drawn authentically by a satirical pen, by any
historian who cannot catch the spirit of what it tried for. More nearly

Reprinted from *Mark Twain, Son of Missouri* by Minnie M. Brashear. By permission of the author and of The University of North Carolina Press. Copyright 1934 by The University of North Carolina Press.

approached today in some parts of Texas, perhaps, than elsewhere in
America, the Missouri of Mark Twain's boyhood is not accounted for
by any of the attempts so far made to describe the American frontier—
partly in that it developed a culture that was favorable for the nurture
of a literary ambition.

In religion Sam Clemens's habitat was, by and large, puritanical,
whether of the Church of England, brought from Virginia, as in early
Pike County country communities, or, more commonly, of the evangelical churches, especially the Presbyterian. Because the church had
been trusted from the first to lift border society out of ruffianism, its
interests were enthusiastically supported, though professional men in
the district were likely, in a silent kind of way, to be free-thinkers of
the Jefferson type. If their beliefs came from Tom Paine, they did not
much acknowledge it.

On its worse side, the obvious paradoxes of the social structure, as
well as the futility of being committed to unattainable ideals, made for
hypocrisy and errors of the flesh. The aristocratic, Church-of-England
woman knew that her husband's western, hail-fellow-well-met manners
and easy conscience furthered his political ambitions. Free-thinking political leaders knew that the religious sanction made for the success of
their enterprises—for the founding of colleges as well as the securing
of votes for congressmen. Senator Dillworthy in *The Gilded Age* made
his religion pay. The appraising glance could always detect the equivo-
cation, which, when the prosperous days after the Civil War came, made
so rich a harvest for satire. But the life of the country before the Civil
War was lived on such a generous scale and tried so genuinely for the
noble way of life necessary for the success of the American social experiment, that its insincerities were not the most real thing about it.
The big thing about it as a culture, in contrast to the industrial society
that has grown out of it, was that, because every man in that broad
expanse might have his own domain, however small, whereon his individuality could express itself, it did not lend itself readily to standard-
ization. And this fostering of individual gifts was due as much to the
influence of early evangelical churches as to an agrarian economy.

The region was western—western in its belief in "honest toil" for
all men, in its undivided adherence to the progressive doctrines of
agrarian democracy, with a belief in its own perfectibility, and a trust
in the Manifest Destiny of the West. To its citizens as to their contemporary, Emerson, whom they may have heard lecture in St. Louis, there
was "virtue yet in the hoe and spade." "The dignity and necessity of
labor to every citizen," if less transcendentally interpreted, was a more
fully developed principle with them than with him. The year before
Orion Clemens took over the *Hannibal Journal,* that newspaper voiced

this spirit for the West: "The cultivation of the soil, in a free country, is the highest and noblest profession in which man can be engaged—as it is the foundation of all true wealth." The *Western Journal and Civilian,* published in St. Louis (1848-1855), found a deeper significance in this favorite doctrine of the region: No pursuit of man, it declared, is "so free from vicious contamination"; none "requires closer observation of natural facts, more rigid analysis of cause and effects . . . ; none better calculated to impress on man the duties of this life and lift him to the habitual contemplation of another." The development of an early culture in Missouri was possible because the rich new lands brought in quick returns for all labor bestowed upon them. Waterways offered a means of reaching St. Louis markets. In less than a generation people had money for securing the merchandise of civilization which makes for better living and better thinking. This quick turn-over, with the hope that went with it, gave a hearty trust to life there that was western more than it was southern.

To say that the region was agrarian, however, is not to say that it was of peasant quality—as a recent foreign visitor to the Valley characterized its descendants of the present generation. The poorest of its citizens had often a spirit and social grace that lifted them out of the common-place. The truly homespun among them were objects of amusement. Society did not exclude them, though where it was southern rather than western it was likely to give them a rope to hang themselves with. Mark Twain's story of Nicodemus Dodge in *A Tramp Abroad* concerns a Hannibal rustic of this sort.

The region was both southern and western in that it was a man's world. The men spurred forth to California to seek a fortune, Joe Bowers fashion, to lay at the feet of the women they left behind. They rode off to the Seminole and the Mexican wars, rationalizing their thirst for adventure as the call of honor. In general, they were sporting men, whose ideals of integrity and ethical standards came from giving authority to their passions: at its best, it was the disciplined and trusted impulses of the southern gentleman that actuated its men, with something of the solid substance of the British squire riding to the hounds. Men engaged in hot debates over political issues. They might be aided and abetted by the wit of their wives, but the women themselves had no aspiration to such public preëminence as Mrs. Emily Newell Blair's "Courageous Woman" attained to. They would have disapproved of her aspiration heartily.

But this was not because either the women themselves or their men doubted their importance in the general social economy. The chief glory of the region, in fact, in both its southern and its western aspects, was its women. Mariolatry, one of Mark Twain's American critics dubs the

regard for women represented in his life and writings. It was as queens
of earth rather than of heaven, however, that he viewed them; Sam
Clemens touched off their harmless vanities and peccadilloes in his
Assistant's Column. But the place assigned to women in his region was
an element in the epic of the West. The wives and daughters of the
men who built up the economic substructure of its society were of
charming purity, at the same time that they were gay, and often witty.
Their social functions had something of formality and unusual charm.
The principle on which society was maintained was of the simplest
kind. Men trusted women to keep society on the ideal plane to which
they desired the new community to attain. Theoretically social intrigue
did not exist, and the "fallen woman" was not in the picture. Her
existence was ignored. In the newspapers of the time France is often
referred to acidulously as the country of social irregularities—an attitude which finds an unfortunate echo in "What Paul Bourget Thinks
of Us." Becky Thatcher is typical of the small daughters of the region.
Mark Twain's lifelong delight in the society of young girls is a trail-
over from the attitude he naturally felt to be ideal. His own three daughters were considered, by highly bred strangers who met them, to be
lovely in a flower-like way, an impression confirmed in his poem "In
Memoriam," written after the death of Susie Clemens, and in "The
Death of Jean." Laura Hawkins of *The Gilded Age,* who stepped outside the pale, was an adopted daughter. She did not properly "belong,"
was not typical of the women whom the men there delighted to honor.
Mark Twain's description of an acquaintance out of the "beautiful past,
the dear and lamented past," whom he happened upon in Calcutta, is
typical of his memory of the women of his home town: "Mary Wilson,"
as he recalls her, "was dainty and sweet, peachblooming and exquisite,
gracious and lovely in character." His attitude found its supreme expression in his knightly story of Joan of Arc, dedicated to his wife. Of
no small significance in the present study is the fact that it was in Hannibal that the story of "the maid" first touched his imagination.

Above all else, the region was proudly southern—but southern with
a difference. Instead of large plantations with swarms of slaves to support its social fabric, it had a simpler—at best, an idyllic—type of farm
life, where slaves lived for the most part happily, their only fear being
that a turn of fortune might make it necessary for them to be "sold
down the river." These farms supported country towns as centers of
the social life of the region. Their social traditions came down mainly
from Virginia by way of Kentucky. The robust taste for life, as well as
its pride and vanity and curiosity, was indirectly out of Renaissance England, from which Virginia got her name. These are seen in the news-

papers of the section, in the tall language of the political speech, in the large enterprises proposed to the state legislature, and in comments, often satirical, on the social, political, and literary affairs of the world. A Renaissance taste for life at high pitch is seen in the hold-over of the duel for settling the private quarrel, satirized by Mark Twain in *Pudd'n-head Wilson,* and in the gusto with which wives and sweethearts, with patriotic suppers, sent their men forth to the wars. The region was southern in that the amenities of social life and the call of honor took precedence over business interests—an attitude made possible by slave labor. While their capacity for a vivid leisure saved them from becoming bound down to business, their taste for good living made them intensely practical. The small thrift of the Yankee they had no ability for. This transplanted, new South avoided many of the tyrannies of the old. Its newspapers reveal an undercurrent of distrust of the institution of slavery—a distrust felt in Jefferson's Virginia, out of which it came.

Finally, although its citizens were intelligent rather than intellectual, the region was "literary"—literary, that is, in an amateur, southern way; it consistently encouraged an interest in the safe and reliable classics. And the young women of the Hannibal Female Seminary were just as eager to get their verses into print in the early fifties as college sophomores are to-day. The newspapers printed at county-seats and larger towns contained much quotation from classics and anecdotes and squibs about their authors. Even though in its practical ambitions the region looked forward to after-the-war baroque achievements, in its most approved sentiments it looked backward to eighteenth-century writers. The speeches of professional men were impressively ornamented with flowers of rhetoric from the classics—if Greek and Latin, so much the better. Champ Clark, of the later period, was its favorite son.

Sam Clemens started on his career as writer with this kind of oratory ringing in his ears, but from his genuinely high-minded father and his keen-witted mother he had somehow inherited a reaching spirit that could not be contented with commonplace performance. All his life he tried for something that eluded him. His tremendous curiosity about life kept him turning to new situations. As printer's apprentice, as sub-editor, as journeyman-printer, as river-pilot in the Middle West, he paralleled his excursions into life with experiments at writing down the materials of life. The necessity that Joseph Conrad saw for the artist to render justice to his materials themselves, and to his own temperamental angle of vision, was Mark Twain's necessity. Writing late in life of the need of each man to have his own pattern of patriotism, he phrased what would have been his creed. The artist must *labor it out* in

his own "head and heart, and in the privacy and independence" of his
own temperament. What he writes must be "fire-assayed and tested and
proved in his own conscience."

The culture that produced Mark Twain gave the trend to both his
earlier and his later work. *Roughing It* is a realization of travels into
Nevada and California which he had already experienced vicariously
through many stories of earlier argonauts, set up in print in the Hannibal papers. His own is of larger proportions than any that preceded it.
The epic character of *Huckleberry Finn* and *Life on the Mississippi* is
attributable to the glowing, vigorous life of the Mid-West setting
which Mark Twain knew. His submerged consciousness of the dangers
that lurked under the fine ideals of his Missouri world was more real
to a young newspaper man than to most men, because it was his part
"to castigate the times." It got the better of the artist in him only gradually, however, as life failed to fulfil his vision of what it might be.
Then he went about with a lantern in his hand peering into men's faces,
scanning his own face in the mirror, to discover whether man could
ever show himself trustworthy to act an uncalculating and noble part.
His passionate hatred of meanness and cruelty and sham was the hatred
felt by a community where life was young and was trusted to perfect
itself. To say that he remained a youth till his death is to say that something from that early time lingered in his spirit till the last. He devoted
his life to its hope. In his rôle as ideal husband, ideal father, ideal
friend, he made his own little world a glorious dwelling-place. But the
dreams that his youth had cherished, in the brave new frontier world,
miscarried. The transition in America to an industrial economy left him
hopeless about man's future. He was one of the first writers to realize
whither America was drifting, and because he could see nothing but
inescapable doom in the vista ahead, his heart broke. He had had such
a glorious vision of the ideals by which America had formed itself that
he was glad his own passing would be with their passing. Stimulating
as the social and ethical teaching of his later period was, the real significance of his last years lies not primarily in anything that he said or
wrote, but in the fight that he fought to the last. His defiance of the
powers that ruled the cosmos, as he conceived them, is of heroic proportions. At the end he was an American Prometheus, but the American
masses he wrote for were a highly idealized, mythical citizenry, not a
congeries of humanity turning daily to the leaders that could promise
the largest rewards—"scrambling at the shearer's feast." And because
to him the hope of the world lay in America, his despair was for all
mankind.

And this is not to say that he betrayed his region in *The Gilded Age*.
Looking back from the vantage ground of after-the-war abuses, he saw

what had grown logically out of the inconsistencies of the early time. Some unconscious feeling however, that he had failed to get the whole truth about his home country written down, must have caused him to turn to his boys' books. As a boy's world the region had been full of charm. And thus it was by doing the smaller thing that he did the larger thing. Because he was so authentically of Marion and Monroe and Pike counties, he was authentically of Missouri, and authentically of America—for Missouri lies at the cross-roads of the nation.

In whatever Mark Twain was, in his vanity, his curiosity, his ambition to secure what was first-rate, along with his need to keep his spirit clear from the taint of self-interest; in whatever he did: on the lecture platform, in the drawing-room, by the banquet table, at his desk, "beguiling all of the people all of the time," his hope for social justice, for the *raison d'être* of America, was a passion larger than that of ordinary men. In that passion he called to account the very gods of the universe. In his rôle as the supreme apologist for the American experiment he defies final analysis; he will ever be a figure of legend.

FAIRVIEW

E. W. HOWE

Edgar Watson Howe was born in Indiana and spent most of his life in Atchison, Kansas, editing the Daily Globe *(1877–1911) and* E. W. Howe's Monthly *(1911 until his death in 1937). He was brought to Missouri in 1856, when he was three years old, and he spent his boyhood in the northern Missouri towns of Fairview, Bethany, Gallatin, and St. Joseph. He learned to set type when he was eleven years old, worked as a printer in various cities, and eventually became famous for his clever aphoristic paragraphs in the* Atchison Globe, *which were widely clipped as "fillers" by other editors. His famous novel,* The Story of a Country Town, *was published in 1883 and was the forerunner of the school of "realistic" interpretations of town and village life. Chapter I of that work is here presented.*

Ours was the prairie district out West, where we had gone to grow up with the country.

I believe that nearly every farmer for miles around moved to the neighborhood at the same time, and that my father's wagons headed the procession. I have heard that most of them gathered about him on the way, and as he preached from his wagon wherever night overtook him, and held camp-meetings on Sundays, he attracted a following of men travelling the same road who did not know themselves where they were going, although a few of the number started with him, among them my mother's father and his family. When he came to a place that suited him, he picked out the land he wanted—which any man was free to do at that time—and the others settled about him.

In the dusty tramp of civilization westward—which seems to have always been justified by a tradition that men grow up by reason of it—our section was not a favorite, and remained new and unsettled after counties and States farther west had grown old. Every one who came there seemed favorably impressed with the steady fertility of the soil, and expressed surprise that the lands were not all occupied; but no one in the great outside world talked about it, and no one wrote about it, so that those who were looking for homes went to the west or the north, where others were going.

There were cheap lands farther on, where the people raised a crop one year, and were supported by charity the next; where towns sprang up on credit, and farms were opened with borrowed money; where the people were apparently content, for our locality did not seem to be far enough west, nor far enough north, to suit them; where no sooner was one stranger's money exhausted than another arrived to take his place; where men mortgaged their possessions at full value, and thought themselves rich, notwithstanding, so great was their faith in the country; where he who was deepest in debt was the leading citizen, and where bankruptcy caught them all at last. On these lands the dusty travellers settled, where there were churches, school-houses, and bridges—but little rain—and railroads to carry out the crops should any be raised; and when any one stopped in our neighborhood, he was too poor and tired to follow the others.

I became early impressed with the fact that our people seemed to be miserable and discontented, and frequently wondered that they did not load their effects on wagons again, and move away from a place which made all the men surly and rough, and the women pale and fretful. Although I had never been to the country they had left, except as a baby in arms, I was unfavorably impressed with it, thinking it must have been a very poor one that such a lot of people left it and considered their condition bettered by the change, for they never talked of going back, and were therefore probably better satisfied than they had ever been before. A road ran by our house, and when I first began to think about it at all, I thought that the covered wagons travelling it carried people moving from the country from which those in our neighborhood came, and the wagons were so numerous that I was led to believe that at least half the people of the world had tried to live there, and moved away after an unfortunate experience.

On the highest and bleakest point in the county, where the winds were plenty in winter because they were not needed, and scarce in summer for an opposite reason, the meeting-house was built, in a corner of my father's field. This was called Fairview, and so the neighborhood was known. There was a graveyard around it, and cornfields next to that, but not a tree or shrub attempted its ornament, and as the building stood on the main road where the movers' wagons passed, I thought that, next to their ambition to get away from the country which had been left by those in Fairview, the movers were anxious to get away from Fairview church, and avoid the possibility of being buried in its ugly shadow, for they always seemed to drive faster after passing it.

High up in a steeple which rocked with every wind was a great bell, the gift of a missionary society, and when there was a storm this tolled with fitful and uncertain strokes, as if the ghosts from the grave lot had crawled up there, and were counting the number to be buried the coming year, keeping the people awake for miles around. Sometimes, when the wind was particularly high, there were a great number of strokes on the bell in quick succession, which the pious said was an alarm to the wicked, sounded by the devil, a warning relating to the conflagration which could never be put out, else Fairview would never have been built.

When any one died it was the custom to toll the bell once for every year of the deceased's age, and as deaths usually occur at night, we were frequently awakened from sleep by its deep and solemn tones. When I was yet a very little boy I occasionally went with my father to toll the bell when news came that some one was dead, for we lived nearer the place than any of the others, and when the strokes ran up to forty and fifty it was very dreary work, and I sat alone in the church wondering who would ring for me, and how many strokes could be counted by those who were shivering at home in their beds.

The house was built the first year of the settlement, and the understanding was that my father contributed the little money necessary, and superintended the work, in which he was assisted by any one who volunteered his labor. It was his original intention to build it alone, and the little help he received only irritated him, as it was not worth the boast that he had raised a temple to the Lord single-handed. All the carpenter's work, and all the plasterer's work, he performed without assistance except from members of his own household, but I believe the people turned out to the raising, and helped put up the frames.

Regularly after its completion he occupied the rough pulpit (which he built with especial reference to his own size), and every Lord's Day morning and evening preached a religion to the people which I think added to their other discomforts, for it was hard and unforgiving. There were two or three kinds of Baptists among the people of Fairview when the house was completed, and a few Presbyterians, but they all became Methodists without revolt or question when my father announced in his first preaching that Fairview would be of that denomination.

He did not solicit them to join him, though he probably intimated in a way which admitted of no discussion that the few heretics yet remaining out in the world had better save themselves before it was too late. It did not seem to occur to him that men and women who had grown up in a certain faith renounced it with difficulty; it was enough that they were wrong, and that he was forgiving enough to throw open the doors of the accepted church. If they were humiliated, he was glad of it, for that was necessary to condone their transgressions; if they had arguments to excuse it, he did not care to hear them, as he had taken God into partnership, and built Fairview, and people who worshipped there would be expected to throw aside all doctrinal nonsense.

As I shall have something to do with this narrative, there may be a curiosity on the part of the reader to know who I am. I state, then, that I am the only son of the Rev. John Westlock—and the only child, unless a little girl born a year before me, and whom I have heard my mother speak of tenderly as pretty and blue-eyed, is to be called up from her grave and counted; and I have the best of reason for believing (the evidence being my father's word, a man whose integrity was never doubted) that he moved to the place where my recollection begins, to do good and grow up with the country. Whether my father remarked it in my presence—he seldom said anything to me—I do not now remember, but I believe to this day, in the absence of anything to the contrary, that the circuit he rode in the country which he had left was poor, and paid him but rarely for his services, which induced him to quit preaching as a business, and resolve to evangelize in the West on his own account, at the same time putting himself in the way of growing up with the country, an idea probably new at that time, and very significant.

In the great Bible which was always lying open on a table in our house, between the Old and the New Testament, my name and the date of my birth were recorded in bold handwriting, immediately following the information that Helen Elizabeth Westlock arrived by the mercy of

God on the 19th of July, and departed in like manner on the 3d of April; and I did not know, until I was old enough to read for myself, that I had been christened Abram Nedrow Westlock, as I had always been called Ned, and had often wondered if any of the prophets were of that name, for my father, and my mother, and my uncle Jo (my mother's only brother, who had lived at our house most of his life), and my grandmother, and my grandfather, were all named for some of the people I had heard referred to when the big Bible was read. But when I found Abram before the Nedrow, I knew that I had not been neglected. This discovery caused me to ask my mother so many questions that I learned in addition that the Nedrow part of the name referred to a preacher of my father's denomination, and not to a prophet, and that my father admired him and named me for him because he had once preached all day at a camp-meeting, and then spent most of the following night in prayer. I therefore concluded that it was intended that I should be pious, and early began to search the Scriptures for the name of Abram, that I might know in what manner he had distinguished himself.

The first thing I can remember, and this only indistinctly, was concerned with the removal of our effects from an old house to a new one, and that the book on which I usually sat at the table was mislaid during the day, which made it necessary for me to stand during the progress of the evening meal. I began to cry when this announcement was made, whereupon my father said in a stern way that I was now too old to cry, and that I must never do it again. I remarked it that day, if I never did before, that he was a large, fierce-looking man, whom it would likely be dangerous to trifle with, and that a full set of black whiskers, and a blacker frown, completely covered his face; from that time I began to remember events, and they will appear as this narrative progresses.

Of my youth before this time I have little knowledge except that my mother said once in my presence that I was a very pretty baby, but that I had now got bravely over it, and that as a child I was known in all the country round as a great baby to cry, being possessed of a stout pair of lungs, which I used on the slightest occasion. This, coupled with an observation from my uncle Jo that when he first saw me, an hour or two after birth, I looked like a fish-worm, was all I could find out about my earlier history, and the investigation was so unsatisfactory that I gave it up.

Once I heard my father say, when he was in a good humor, that when the nurse employed for my arrival announced that I was a boy, my mother cried hysterically for half an hour, as she desired a blue-eyed girl to replace the one she had buried, and when I heard my mother tell a few weeks afterwards, in a burst of confidence, to a number of women who happened to be there, that my father stormed for an hour because I was born at all, I concluded that I had never been very welcome, and regretted that I had ever come into the world. They both wanted a girl —when the event was inevitable—to help about the house, as Jo was thought to be all the help necessary in the field, and in the earlier days of my life I remember feeling that I was out of place because I did not wear dresses, and wash dishes, thus saving the pittance paid a farmer's daughter during the busy season.

The only remarkable thing I ever did in my life—I may as well mention it here, and be rid of it—was to learn to read letters when I was five years old, and as the ability to read even print was by no means a common accomplishment in Fairview, the circumstance gave me great notoriety. I no doubt learned to read from curiosity as to what the books and papers scattered about were for, as no one took the pains to teach me, for I remember that they were all greatly surprised when I began to spell words, and pronounce them, and I am certain I was never encouraged in it.

It was the custom when my father went to the nearest post-office to bring back with him the mail of the entire neighborhood, and it was my business to deliver the letters and papers at the different houses. If I carried letters, I was requested to read them, and the surprise which I created in this direction was so pronounced that it was generally said that in time I should certainly become a great man, and be invited to teach school. If I came to a word which I did not understand I invented one to take its place, or an entire sentence, for but few of the people could read the letters themselves, and never detected the deception. This occupation gave me my first impression of the country where the people had lived before they came to Fairview, and as there was much in the letters of hard work and pinching poverty, I believed that the writers lived in a heavily timbered country, where it was necessary to dig up trees to get room for planting. Another thing I noticed was that they all seemed to be dissatisfied and anxious to get away, and when in course of time I began to write answers to the letters I was surprised to learn that the people of Fairview were satisfied, and that they were well pleased with the change.

I had never thought this before, for they all seemed as miserable as was possible, and wondered about it a great deal. This gave me fresh reason for believing that the country which our people had left was a very unfavored one, and when I saw the wagons in the road I thought that at last the writers of the letters I had been reading had arrived and would settle on some of the great tracts of prairie which could be seen in every direction, but they turned the bend in the road and went on as if a look at Fairview had frightened them, and they were going back another way.

It seems to me now that between the time I began to remember and the time I went out with my father and Jo to work, or went alone through the field to attend the school in the church, about a year elapsed, and that I was very much alone during the interval, for ours was a busy family, and none of them had time to look after me. My father and Jo went to the fields, or away with the teams, at a very early hour in the morning, and usually did not return until night, and my mother was always busy about the house, so that if I kept out of mischief no more was expected of me. I think it was during this year (it may have been two years, but certainly not a longer period) that I learned to read, for I had nothing else to do and no companions, and from looking at the pictures in the books I began to wonder what the little characters surrounding them meant.

In this I was assisted by Jo, who seemed to know everything, and by slow degrees I put the letters together to make words, and understood them. Sometimes in the middle of the day I slipped out into the field to ask him the meaning of something mysterious I had encountered, and although he would good-naturedly inform me, I noticed that he and my father worked without speaking, and that I seemed to be an annoyance, so I scampered back to my loneliness again.

During this time, too, I first noticed that my father was not like other men who came to our house, for he was always grave and quiet, and had little to say at any time. It was a relief to me to hear him ask blessings at the table and pray morning and evening, for I seldom heard his voice at any other time. I believe I regarded his quiet manner only as an evidence that he was more pious than others of his class, for I could make nothing else out of it, but often regretted that his religion did not permit him to notice me more, or to take me with him when he went away in the wagon. Once I asked my mother why he was always so stern and silent, and if it was because we had offended him, to which she replied all in a tremble that she did not know herself, and I thought that she studied a great deal about him, too. My mother was as timid in his presence as I was, and during the day, if I came upon her suddenly, she looked frightened, thinking it was he, but when she found it was not, her composure returned again. Neither of us had reason to be afraid of him, I am certain of that, but as we never seemed able to please him (though he never said so), we were in constant dread of displeasing him more than ever, or of causing him to become more silent and dissatisfied, and to give up the short prayers in which we were graciously mentioned for a blessing.

The house where we lived, and into which we moved on the day when my recollection begins, was the largest in the settlement; a square house of two stories, painted so white that after night it looked like a ghost. It was built on lower ground than Fairview church, though the location was sightly, and not far away ran a stream fringed with thickets of brush, where I found the panting cattle and sheep on hot days, and thought they gave me more of a welcome than my father and Jo did in the field; for they were not busy, but idle like me, and I hoped it was rather a relief to them to look at me in mild-eyed wonder.

Beyond the little stream and the pasture was the great dusty road, and in my loneliness I often sat on the high fence beside it to watch for the coming of the movers' wagons, and to look curiously at those stowed away under the cover bows, tumbled together with luggage and effects of every kind. If one of the drivers asked me how far it was to the country town I supposed he had heard of my wonderful learning, and took great pains to describe the road, as I had heard my father do a hundred times in response to similar inquiries from movers. Sometimes I climbed up to the driver's seat, and drove with him out to the prairie, and I always noticed that the women and children riding behind were poorly dressed, and tired looking, and I wondered if only the unfortunate travelled our way, for only that kind of people lived in Fairview, and I had never seen any other kind in the road.

When I think of the years I lived in Fairview, I imagine that the sun was never bright there (although I am certain that it was), and I cannot relieve my mind of the impression that the cold, changing shadow of the gray church has spread during my long absence and enveloped all the houses where the people lived. When I see Fairview in my fancy now, it is always from a high place, and looking down upon it the shadow is denser around the house where I lived than anywhere else, so that I feel to this day that should I visit it, and receive permission from the new owners to walk through the rooms, I should find the walls damp and mouldy because the bright sun and the free air of Heaven had deserted them as a curse.

BOYHOOD IN A COAL TOWN

JACK CONROY

Jack Conroy was born in 1899 in Monkey Nest coal camp near Moberly, a locality described in the following article taken from the American

Reprinted from the *American Mercury,* May, 1931, by permission of the author.

Mercury *of May, 1931, and later in Conroy's most famous novel,* The Disinherited. *Leaving the University of Missouri in his freshman year, "partly," as he says, "because I found the military training too onerous," he traveled as a free-riding boxcar passenger all over the country, picking up material for the novels he was to write later, and working at odd jobs to keep alive. Incidentally,* The Disinherited *has recently been republished in paper covers in Hill and Wang's American Century Series; it is a strong and honest story of the Depression Thirties.*

Conroy is remembered (or should be) also for his editorship of the "little magazines," The Anvil *and* The Rebel Poet. *Presently he is senior associate editor of the Standard Education Society and teaches creative writing at Columbia College.*

The Monkey Nest coal-mine tipple stood twenty years; its dirt dump grew from a diminutive hillock among the scrub oaks to the height of a young mountain. Stubborn shrubs, wiry grasses, and persistent dewberries struggled for a roothold on it, but the leprous soapstone resists all vegetable growth, even in decay. White and cold like the belly of some deep sea monster incongruously cast out of the depths, the dump dominated Monkey Nest camp like an Old World cathedral towering over peasants' huts. To begin with, Mr. Stacpoole, the owner, had christened the mine the Eagle, but the miners had decided otherwise. Somebody had dubbed it the Monkey Nest, and so it remained—so it is yet in the memory of those who recall it or its history.

I first saw the Monkey Nest's shaft when it was only head-high to Old Man Vaughan. Father led me to the brink and I peered over fearsomely, clinging to his legs. Old Vaughan caught me under the armpits and swung me down; then he threatened to keep me there indefinitely, but I knew better. I was used to miners' joshing. Three taciturn Italians were slicing the tough white clay with keen tile spades and throwing it clear of the edge, grunting "hah!" at each spadeful.

"Looky here, Jacky!" said Vaughan. "A dad-blamed crawdad's hole and a crawpappy hisself at the bottom of it. I've follered that scoundrel from the grass roots and here's the bottom of his hole finally. You know, when I've been digging a ditch or something, lots of times I strike a crawdad's hole, and wonder just how far it runs in the ground. But I never *did* see the *bottom* of one before, did you?"

The crawfish, a small lobster-like creature, angered and bewildered at this rude violation of his retreat, waved furious and menacing pincers. Vaughan was delighted, having realized a long cherished ambition; and I was tickled, too, because I had often wondered just how far a crawfish burrowed into the soil. I have felt that thrill of accomplishment only a few times since.

The shaft bored past the clay, past the blue hardpan, blasted through the rock and into the coal. The Monkey Nest's tipple rose; its hoisting engine vibrated the heaps of slag and soapstone, oftentimes starting miniature avalanches down the dump. Cages shot up and down the shaft like office-building elevators. A mine tipple is like a gallows, especially if you chance to see its black timbers etched against a setting sun; and the cage cable dangles from the cathead like a hangman's rope. I have thought whimsically when a miner's head has appeared out of the shaft, apparently supported by the cable only, that his tongue should protrude and his legs kick spasmodically.

My brother Dan went to work in the mine when he was only twelve. There were nine children at home, and Father had more than he could do to feed us. It was against the law for a boy under sixteen to work in the pit unless he was with his father. But even with his father, the boy miner's cheeks blanch just the same; his shoulders stoop, apparently trying to fold in front of him like an angel's wings; and the hollow asthmatic cough begins before he is twenty—if he dodges rocks that long.

Expert miners thump the roof inquiringly with a pick handle before they venture into their "rooms" of a morning. They learn the meaning of a whole octave of sounds indicating the solidity or lack of solidity in the ceiling, but pot rocks slip out as though they were well greased. They give no warning rattle. And bell rocks spring like panthers, leaving a smooth, cup-like cavity. Always the rocks hang overhead like the fabled Damoclean sword, except that the sword was not too wide to allow some chance of jumping from beneath it.

When the cage delivered him up to the world of sun and daylight, Dan walked a quarter-mile bowed double before he could straighten his cramped spine. Evenings he lay on his back in the yard, staring at the stars. But he wasn't wondering where the Great Dipper or the Pleiades were located or whether there were people on Mars, as we used to do together. He never said a word, but only chewed the end of a timothy stalk. At nine o'clock, the very latest, he would limp into the house to bed, and when I came in from playing he would be snoring loudly with his mouth hanging wide open. I never snored that way till ten years later, when I shovelled gravel all day on the highway gang.

Our house wasn't a camp house. It had a neatly painted porch, and was a story and a half high. A barbed wire fence surrounded it and kept cows out of the yard. Below it the camp houses extended in a rough semi-circle at the foot of the hill. The hillside was our commons, and on it we played wild horse, leap-frog, cowboy and Indian. Diamond Dick rode valorously to rescue his sweetheart Nell from scalping at the hands of redskins just in the nick of time; while Handsome Harry, the old sarpint of Siiskiyou, proclaimed to the world that he was an extremely pisen rattler possessing sixteen rattles and a button; moreover, he was not a bit averse to biting viciously if he were provoked sufficiently.

The farmer boys were our natural enemies, and because of our communal life we easily triumphed in every combat. The isolated farm houses prevented any kind of defense organization, so we ambushed the rustics singly and collectively. Smarting under the implication—and, alas, the conviction—of social inferiority, we battled with extraordinary ferocity, fashioning spears out of horse weeds that grew rank in the creek bottoms, and charging the fleeing hinds with all the fervor of King Arthur in the lists at Camelot. We raided their school-house and even hunted the teacher far away through the brush, stuffing the chimney with rags, and overturning the privy, which backed up to and squatted over a crick.

The older boys carried on the tradition, roaming the woods like satyrs, leaning against tree trunks and pumping doleful accordions, or sitting on fallen logs tootling merry flutes. They shot craps in the forest, and to the dour farmer youths they were mad and unholy. But the faunish farm girls giggled behind the buck bushes and squealed with mingled terror and delight when the miners chased them home. If one were imaginative enough one might fancy goat hooves and jaunty horns as the miners pursued their quarry through the second growth of oak saplings. Once a hired hand caught my brother Dick in a wild cherry tree where he had climbed after the fruit, and pelted him with Osage orange hedgeapples, as large as a small grapefruit and as hard as a cocoanut.

Father came from Montreal. He wore a long and curly chestnut mane like that of a *fin de siècle* matinée idol and a most romantic mustache. Somehow he was always the Man from Mars among the miners. You could catch him muttering strange words to himself. He often sat stark still on the doorstep, thinking for hours.

It didn't take him long to win leadership of the miners' local union— or rather he had it thrust on him. When he spoke in lodge he used a deep rolling voice so much different from his ordinary tone that we called it his meeting voice. It was years before anyone discovered that he had been a priest in Canada, and it came out accidentally. He never liked to talk about *that*. At intervals, newspapers came from Canada, but they were printed in French. Certain items would be marked heavily in blue pencil. Father would sit and read them, then he would crumple the paper in his clenched fist and stare stonily across the fields.

My sister Madge and I were exploring his desk and found a faded velvet jewelbox containing a rosary and a crucifix. I took them to father to ask him what they were.

"Beads! Nothing but beads!" he said harshly, "and this is a bit of gold, nothing else."

Then he spoke more kindly: "But your grandmother gave them to me long ago. Put them back where you got them."

We were starved for print. Our schoolbooks were worn threadbare, and this was before the Paper Trust began educating the masses with *Western Tales* and *Love Confessions*. I have never overcome the habit of stooping to capture every vagrant circular or stray newspaper that I encounter abroad. It is atavism from Monkey Nest days.

Then Rodney Millbank began delivering the Indianapolis *News* every morning. This was before rural free delivery had begun functioning. Rodney made a whistle of hickory bark when the sap was running, and shrilled like a postman as the paper thudded against the weatherboarding. We pounced on the *News* with shrieks of delight and devoured it from the front page to the last editorial, even the advertisements. I recall a favorite comic strip labelled "The Terrors of the Tiny Tads," in which the unfortunate principals were constantly harassed by hyphenated beasts such as the camelephant and the panthermine. Abe Martin sat on his sagging barbwire and expectorated the *bon mots* that continued for twenty-five years until death silenced him. I shall always be grateful to the Indianapolis *News*. Wherever it may be or whatever it has grown to, it was to me a window and a door.

Such a transaction as buying a ton of coal would have seemed incredible to us. We bagged it in gunny sacks from the tipple, shifting the load continually in an endeavor to ease our smarting backs with a flat-surfaced chunk. We sank puffing to the sward half way home, and the surrounding terrain detached itself from the general landscape as though under a microscope. Maybe a busy tumble-bug patiently trundling his malodorous pellet, or a tribe of ants bearing a dead grasshopper. One had only to smash down with a stick or stone to feel like God loosing an earthquake or a tidal wave. We halted by a decayed log and placed our mouths against the ground, chanting: "Doodle, up! Doodle, up! Doodle, up!" If we waited long enough a small black bug would squirm energetically out of the loam, and we were always sure that the doodle-bug came in obedience to our command, though tardy. It was a childhood legend.

Huge lumps of coal bounded down the chutes and into flat cars, side by side. A screen divided the rough from the fine, coal dust fouling the air like a thunder cloud. We spat black for hours. Often chunks rebounded to the ground, and these were our legitimate prey. My brother

Tim stood back and watched, warning us when the top men were about to dump; but he frequently became negligent or mischievous and we darted from between the cars under a shrapnel of fine and a heavy artillery of larger lumps.

The hoisting engine was a perpetual marvel to us. Its steel cable wound around a glistening drum, and had cut grooves in it. The cable extended through a hole in the wall and across the cathead of the tipple. The engineer was proud of his job, and handled the levers like the pilot of the Cannon Ball Express, never deigning a glance toward the boys peering through the doorway. Behind his shack an exhaust soughed softly out of a rusty pipe from which condensed steam trickled in rust-yellow drops. Tim said if you held your hand over the end of the pipe, the boiler would blow up. When the spiffy engineer took notice of us long enough to chase us away, Tim hinted darkly that he would encompass the ruin of the whole shebang even if, like Samson, he brought down the fragments about his own ears. But he always relented before actual perpetration of the deed.

One day as we stood silently admiring the hoist, a miraculous contraption clattered down the slag road leading to the main highway. A revolving chain like that of a bicycle whirled over sprockets at the side, and its one-lunged motor coughed cacophonously. The proud possessor of this marvel, none other than the mine owner, Edward Stacpoole, leaped to the ground and extended a hand to his wife, who had been holding on grimly as the vehicle jounced along. As the lady descended, I caught a glimpse of an elaborately frilled garter, the first I had ever seen. Coal miners' wives and daughters held up their stockings with rags tied just tight enough to support the weight without stopping the circulation.

My sister Madge had a fashion of rotating her tongue madly in a small circle when she was excited, and she approached this curious object with her tongue agitated like a snake's. A Little Lord Fauntleroy of eight had descended, and now darted from behind his mother and pushed Madge into a mud puddle, jeering meanwhile:

"Coal miner's brat! Coal miner's brat! Catch and eat a rat, eat lean and eat fat!"

Tim was standing close to the exhaust pipe, and darted behind the building. I was sure he would carry out his threat to blow the works to kingdom come, and awaited the explosion apprehensively. Mr. Stacpoole had disappeared in the engine-room, and Mrs. Stacpoole, attracted by Madge's wails, looked back, mildly reproving:

"Oh, Elvin! You *shouldn't* do that! Tell the little girl you're sorry. You hear mother? Tell her you're sorry, like a little gentleman!"

Madge was crying bitterly and smudging her already grimy face with muddy fists. Tim reappeared with both hands full of the greasy slush and filth that accumulates around all steam engines. Plop! Horrific and odoriferous gooey splattered over Elvin's straw hat and matted his golden curls. Splash! The second fistful completed the wreckage by polluting his lace collar and oozing down his virginal blouse. It was the nativity of a bit of business which has since made Hollywood rich.

Tim fled, whooping derisively: "Now go home and wash *your* black face, smart aleck." I helped Madge to her feet and we cut and ran, but not as the vanquished decamp; for we felt that whatever glory hovered over the ghastly field was ours.

Mother was frying salt pork when Jimmy Kerns came to tell her about Dan. You have to parboil it to get the salt out, and roll it in flour before even a strong stomach can hold it down, but it was cheap. That's the reason we ate it. Mother was tossing the white puckered slices into the skillet when Jimmy knocked.

"Aha! Mrs. Conroy, hard at it, I see," he blurted out with a feeble attempt at jocosity. It was a full hour before the quitting whistle should blow. Jimmy's beady eyes flew about the room, and mother couldn't catch and hold them.

"Tell me, Jimmy! Is it Tom?" she cried, grasping both lapels. Miners' wives and mothers sense bad news intuitively.

"Why Missus Conroy, no! I . . . I just . . . y'see. . . ."

"Then it's Dan. It must be Danny! I dreamed of black cold water last night."

She sank to a chair, her eyes dry and aching. She never knew the relief of tears. Four miners carried Dan in on a stretcher and eased him on to the couch; but when they had to pull the stretcher from under him, blood gushed from his mouth. He breathed in short jerks, his eyelids fluttering. Mother knelt beside him and held his hand; the palms were just beginning to callus. He was fourteen, but since he went into the mine at twelve his time had been mostly divided between the pit and his bed.

"Where does it hurt you most, Danny?" mother asked.

He couldn't get the answer out, and in the night I sprang out of bed when Mike Crumley's wife began keening piercingly and our collie howled mournfully and melodiously, as they are said to do always when there is dead in the house. Dan had drawn the sheet off his feet in a final agony, and his toes stood apart like the fingers of a hand. A hemorrhage had finished him. Tim took his place in the mine, for he was already twelve and strong for his age.

Everybody agreed that father was a funny man. For one thing, his best friend was a Frenchman and a Catholic. There were not many Catholics in that neighborhood, and less Frenchmen. The sons of these miners readily joined the Ku-Klux-Klan when the fiery cross was burned twenty years later. People said that Frenchy Barbour ate cats and snakes, and that he prayed to the Virgin Mary to make his shots roll out another ton of coal. His shack was so close to the dump that soapstone and empty powder kegs had rolled right into his front yard.

Every Sunday he walked seven miles to the Catholic church in town, and on the way back he stopped at our house. Father waited for him on the back doorstep, a big slab of rough stone. The earth around the back door was black and sour because mother poured dish water there. Frenchy would appear around the corner smirking and twirling his waxed mustache. His blue serge suit was often grey with dust, and his cuffs a little soiled where his wrists had sweated. Coal dust will come out no matter how many times you wash.

"*Bon jour,* Monsieur Tom," he would chirrup blithely, "how goes it everyt'ing?"

"Hullo, Marcel!" father would say. "Squat down and tell me something."

Then Frenchy would jerk a perfumed handkerchief from his vest pocket, dust off the step, hitch up his trousers to save the crease, and sit down. They talked, gouging in the ground with twigs blown off the maple tree in our yard and tracing geometrical designs in the walk. They laughed uproariously and sometimes seemed to argue heatedly. Then Frenchy would go home in a huff.

Frenchy would come into father's room in the mine at noon, and maybe give him a little home-made wine out of the water deck in his dinner pail. He would sit with his back against a prop, his legs extended stiffly before him, and draw pictures on soapstone with the smoke of his lard-oil lamp. Often they conversed in French, and this made the other miners sore because they fancied they were being discussed in a derogatory manner. I had to see the French section of Quebec, with voluble citizens gesticulating on the street corners, before I realized that Frenchy had supplied something in father's life that phlegmatic and practical miners could never give.

Madge and I waited for father at the pit-head. As the haughty engineer shuttled cages up and down, we speculated as to which would contain father and our brothers. The lard-oil torches appeared first, gleaming like smoky stars, then a coal-blackened face, then the torso with a dinner pail clamped under its arm, and the full body was resurrected from the depths.

We had been warned about going too close to the open shaft, so we contented ourselves with standing back and watching. We were a little early when they brought Frenchy Barbour screaming off the cage, but so far away that we saw him first only when John O'Toole stumbled with his corner of the stretcher, draining the blood that had collected in the sagging middle. Frenchy almost rolled off, and the other miners gave John a mean look for his awkwardness. They laid Frenchy on the engine-room floor. He was panting like a rabbit. There was no telephone, but one of the miners rode like Paul Revere for the doctor. Frenchy swept the faces around him with a glance.

"Tom Conroy! Tom Conroy! Where is he?" he whimpered.

Father shouldered his way through the knot of men and knelt by his friend's side.

"Marcel! Marcel! Here I am!" he called out.

Frenchy gripped father's arm till white spots blossomed on his finger nails.

"Tom, *mon cher ami!* I die! I am dying—finished, I know. No priest, *sacre Dieu,* no priest here!"

"Now! Now! Marcel, you know what I told you about superstition. Don't you worry any. I thought you said . . . ."

"Yes! Yes! I know, but it seems different now. Afraid! Yes, I *am* afraid! Soon it will be too late to be afraid."

He was going fast, gasping like a fish on a sunny bank. He chewed the ends of his mustache.

"Marcel!" father spoke again. "You remember what I told you about the monastery?"

"Ah, yes! O Mother of God! But quickly."

He began to mumble feverishly: *"Confiteor Deo omnipotente . . . beatae Mariae semper Virgini . . ."*

Father's "meeting" voice sounded clear and sonorous. I heard some of the words years afterward and remembered most of them. *"Dominus vobiscum et cum spiritu tuo . . . in nomine Patris . . . et Filii . . . et Spiritus Sancti. . . ."*

Frenchy was about gone, but he heard and it seemed to do him good. His hand dropped across his chest before he had finished the cross. When his face set, I absurdly noticed that his lower lip fell in a snarling grimace, exposing squirrel-like teeth stained at the roots by tobacco. Father faced the astonished miners with a challenging look. I was grown before I read Balzac's story of how Bianchon marvelled at Desplein's inexplicable devotions. I comprehended then a little of the affection father must have had for the volatile Frenchman.

There were no conversational amenities at a miner's table. We ate seriously and wolfishly, scorning sprightly banter. But we would halt momentarily when father would vouchsafe:

"Looks like another strike the first of the month. We'll have to live on blackberries and sowbelly for a while."

And mother would scour the woods for the wild sweet blackberries, canning them against the days of famine, for it always settled down to an endurance contest. The mine-owners depended upon the miners' starving into submission; the miners upon the owners' cupidity dictating that it was cheaper to capitulate than to maintain the luxury of armed guards and inefficient workers who would themselves eventually organize.

The first days of a strike were always gay and exciting. Enthusiastic meetings, brave resolutions. Wagonettes loaded with strike-breakers appeared, guarded by detectives with menacing rifles. Each morning and evening the camp's population lined the road and the scabs had to run a gauntlet of taunts and epithets, and on occasion an impulsive striker threw a stone and the guards clicked their rifles ominously:

"Scab! Scab! Scab!" shouted the men.

"Scab! Scab! Scab!" the women shrieked, shaking their fists.

"Scab! Scab! Scab!" howled the children with lusty hate.

Toddlers waddled from the camp houses and piped "Scab! Scab!" They drew it in with their mothers' milk.

The wagonettes hurried by, the drivers whipping up the horses; and the scabs kept their eyes on the ruts ahead, but flushed purple and scarlet even under the coal-dust.

Mother counted the ebbing cans of blackberries and began slicing the last flitch of bacon. Father sat about moodily, and my brothers lay in the sunny yard with their hats over faces, for want of something better to do. Mr. Stacpoole sent word that he wanted to see father in his office in town; and I went along. Father took a flour sack, because he thought he might possibly get credit at some of the grocery stores. Miners used flour sacks and gunny sacks for shopping bags.

Mr. Stacpoole's lady clerk was a dazzling creature. She penned letters on elaborate letterheads bearing a more or less fanciful representation of the Monkey Nest, only it was always called the Eagle in this place. She wrote in a delicate Spencerian hand and her balloon sleeves drifted gently to and fro like miniature dirigibles. I thought they must have been blown up by a bicycle pump. Her heavy bust bulged above a waspish waist, but she was a baby doll in those days. The pen scratched and spluttered when it hit a flaw in the paper, and Mr. Stacpoole looked up.

"Oh, Conroy, I'm glad to see you here. I reckon you fellows know by now that the Eagle can run without you just the same. But I ain't no hand to hold grudges—believe in live and let live. I'll have to let the wage cut stand, of course, because I've contracted all my coal out on that basis, but I'll take all the old men back, and I just been thinking if you wouldn't make a dandy pit boss. . . . That's a fine boy you got there; and I'll bet you he's a big help to you right now. . . . Miss Lotter has wrote out a contract, and if you'll just step around here by the desk. . . ."

"Yes, he is a fine boy, and this long trip *for nothing* has tuckered him out. We must be home by dark, and I got some groceries to pack, too." There was only mild reproof in father's voice, but Mr. Stacpoole was champing his cigar venomously.

Phelps, the grocer, who had known our family for a long time, was sorry but the strike had run him pretty close, too. The wholesalers were crowding him for their money.

Storms had a good chance at our house, but father loved a tempest. He liked to stand in the back door and let the wind whistle through his hair. He liked to hear "heaven's artillery crash," as he called it, and he thrilled to the lightning's swift zigzag. He often seemed to resemble Ajax defying the Jovian thunderbolts as he declaimed:

> "Thy spirit, Independence, let me share.
>   Lord of the lion heart and eagle eye,
> Along thy steps I follow, bosom bare,
>   Nor heed the storm that howls along the sky."

We thought this sounded grand, and we often repeated it ourselves.

Wind worried our house until its ancient timbers snapped like rifle shots. Rats milled through the attic, stampeding like wild horses when it stormed. Supple catalpas flayed the warped cedar shingles like a mule driver's lash. You notice a storm more at night, too, I guess. Anyway, we didn't hear the man knocking for a while. When father opened the door, he stepped quickly inside, shivering. Rain drops dribbled down his pit clothes on to the floor, and bubbles squirted out of his soggy shoes. Father stood aghast and undecided; the door swung to and fro, sucked by the wind. Mother was trying to shield the kerosene lamp with her body.

"I'm workin' at the Monkey Nest," he chattered, his teeth clicking like castanets. "I must have went to sleep in my room, and nobody missed me. I found the shaft and climbed up the buntings. I don't know the way to town, and if you'll show me. . . ."

Before he finished father emerged from his trance and plugged him a resounding smack on the jaw. For a minute he lay with his feet in the door and his body outside. Then he scrambled to his feet and sloshed off in the night before father could wrench his shotgun from its antlers above the door.

"You scab! You damned scab!" he roared, the shotgun booming and a red flash momentarily lighting the doorway for the wind had extinguished the coal-oil flame when mother had whirled to see what was happening. The room was in darkness and the air was pungent with powder fumes. Mother groped for the lamp and dropped the chimney with a sharp exclamation when it burned her fingers. She ignited the wick with a trembling hand.

My older brothers and sisters were swarming down the stairs. Tim and I were goggle-eyed. Father grasped each of us by an arm, crying with passion:

"Boys! Boys! Listen to me! If you must be one, be a thief, a murderer, anything, but don't ever be a scab! You hear me? Don't ever be a scab!"

"We won't never, pappy," we promised solemnly.

The Monkey Nest never gave Tim a chance to stray from his vow, because he cushioned the fall of a bell rock before he was sixteen. But I have never forgotten that night or the promise exacted.

The strike came to an end somehow. Reminiscing about it, it is hard to say definitely just how it did end or whether it was won or lost. Somehow the miners seemed to lose the individual strike, but steadily progress along the far-flung battle line of their goal. The history of the miners' union of that period is punctuated with strikes. Each faction battled doggedly, but it had to surrender something finally.

Years crowded in on the Monkey Nest. A mine dies young in the sparse croppings of Missouri; twenty years is a hoary old age. But the Monkey Nest left monuments to its memory in many cemeteries, particularly Sugar Creek graveyard, where the pine headboards bristle among wild blackberry vines and rampant tiger lilies that long ago burst the borders of prim beds and sent their progeny adventuring across the mounds. Frenchy Barbour's grave has caved in, for his coffin was cheap and not made to withstand much weight. Sand and gumbo must fill his skull, and stain his squirrel-teeth browner than tobacco did. Father and my three brothers are side by side.

When the time came to dig Tim's grave it was raining and the ground was treacherous with Spring thaw. The clay kept slipping as the men dug and they had to pause frequently to clean off their spades with a discarded table knife. The sides crumbled so that Dan's coffin projected into the new-made grave, after five years. Somebody got the idea of

masking it with canvas so that mother couldn't see it. I had been told
that in the casket a man's hair and beard keeps on growing just the same,
that his toenails and fingernails do not die. I wondered about this.
Familiarity may breed a large contempt for death; but this morbid curiosity about it is also a typical characteristic of the mid-Western mind.

Worked-out mines marked only by a hummock of vegetation-defying
soapstone or a rusty boiler tilted on one end, its flue holes resembling
a great Swiss cheese, hedged the Monkey Nest in. Tunnels that radiated
in all directions from the shaft were always breaking into abandoned
works. Deadly black damp and water seeped in. Incombustible sulphur
rock gleamed in the coal like gold, and the dwindling veins faded until
a man must crawl on his belly like a snake to pick out the sparse coal.

Then the tipple fell in a whirlwind, and the stiff legs stuck ludicrous-
ly in the air like those of an overturned wooden horse. Time has had
its way with the Monkey Nest. In its quiet grottos crumbling rails and
phosphorescent ties are sinking in pallid slime, while flabby fungi cling
to the rotting timbers. Bats scream and fight. A venturesome boy climbed
down the shaft, but fled in terror when he was covered from head to foot
with pulsing, furry bodies, before he could travel twenty feet into the
main entry. It was lucky for him at that, because the black damp knocks
you out without any warning.

To keep cows from falling in the open shaft, it was decided to fill it.
The assorted urchins of a superannuated miner volunteered to perform
this incredible feat, more stupendous than any storied Herculean labor.
In casting about for a comparative peg on which to hang their undertaking, I must mention the persistent Mr. Beers of the poem who, amidst
his neighbor's jeers, had been resolutely digging in his garden, with
China as a goal, for forty-seven years. Think also of that prodigious rock
in Svithjod land, a hundred miles high and a hundred miles wide. To
it every thousand years comes a canary bird to whet his dainty beak.
When that Gargantuan boulder shall have been worn to the level of the
plain, preachers are fond of saying, it will be only breakfast time in
Hell.

But the boys rigged up a coaster wagon that had been discarded by
some more fortunate child, and began wheeling soapstone and slag
to fill the gaping void. At first a faint splash was the only evidence
of their toil, but within six months they could see bottom by throwing
down a kerosene-soaked and ignited cattail. It took them a year to complete the job, but they were paid twenty-five dollars in cash, not in trade
out of a company store.

So the Monkey Nest's mouth is stopped with dust, but in its time it
had its pound of flesh. Yes, I figure it had its tons of flesh, all told, if
laid side by side in Sugar Creek graveyard.

TOWN CHARACTERS

ALBERT EDMUND TROMBLY

The author of the following poems was born in New York, educated at Harvard and at the University of Pennsylvania, and came to the University of Missouri to join its Romance Languages Department in 1922.

Professor Trombly is possibly at his best in such character sketches in verse as we present here, but he has written many short lyrics that show the deep thoughtfulness characteristic of the authentic poet together with the charm and skill in versification that is Trombly's own.

Five small volumes of his poems have been published from time to time over the years. It is from the one entitled Little Dixie *that the following are taken.*

TABITHA

Everybody has a word for Miss Amelia,
A good neighborly word, and calls her "aunt,"
Except Tabitha who snaps she can't abide her;
And when you can't abide a body, you can't.

For years, it must be thirty-odd, Tabitha
Has sung at every funeral in these parts.
Yearly her rusty pipe is cracking wider:
No telling where she'll end from where she starts.

The day it got around that Miss Amelia
Was right smart low and didn't look
Like she could last the week, we heard Tabitha
Rehearsing hymns, the mournfulest in the book.

Likely a strain of it reached Miss Amelia;
Likely she told herself it wouldn't do.
Howsoever that may be and spite of doctor,
She perked right up, she did, and pulled through.

"A right-minded Christian," snorts Tabitha,
"Would have let herself die, seeing the mess
And bother I was put to with hymns to practise
And smartening up my funeral bonnet and dress."

Reprinted from *Little Dixie* by Albert Edmund Trombly. By permission of the author. Copyright 1955 by the Curators of the University of Missouri.

HIRAM TODD

Rare head for reasoning
Had Hiram Todd;
He broke with the family,
He sloughed off God.

He stood in his bare feet
Six foot two,
Reasoning, chawing
His favorite chew.

Once and forever
He toed the taw
And settled women
With one guffaw.

Labor, capital
He would hew
With a damn and
A stolen phrase or two.

The day that Hiram
Was sixty year,
The neighbors reckoned
That he looked queer.

He seen, of a sudden,
Bright as day,
He could reason reason
Clean away!

Three days later
They buried Todd.
Graveyard grasses
Have a cryptic nod.

MELVIN SAPP'S EPITAPH

Not given to abstract thought; nonetheless,
Somewhere in his twenties he had fought
A bout with it and carried off this prize:
*Whiskey was not made for priming pumps
Or rinsing drains.* And henceforth to the day
On which he grounded here—with singleness
Of purpose rarely met this side of genius
He showed his fellows what the stuff was for.

NEGRO LIFE
AND LETTERS

UP FROM SLAVERY

Martha Swearingen

Martha Swearingen was brought to Missouri as a babe in arms when her parents became residents of Liberal. A graduate of State Teachers' College at Springfield, she was a housewife and freelance writer in Kansas City for nearly fifty years. Since she began writing in 1956, she has had more than a hundred articles and children's stories published. She now lives at Hemet, California.

She wrote this feature article for the Kansas City Star, *and it was published July 16, 1960, the day before the 100th anniversary of Carver's birth. It was shortly after the death of Dr. Carver that the Missouri Legislature urged upon Congress by a unanimous joint resolution that lands near Diamond, Missouri, be set aside as a national monument in his honor. Leader in that movement was Richard Pliant, of Washington University, St. Louis, who presented to a Congressional committee a petition signed by thousands of names, with these eloquent words:*

We Missourians are determined that the world shall never forget that it was from our Ozark hills Dr. Carver took his origin. We cannot but believe that it was to these faraway hills of his childhood that Dr. Carver looked when he said, as he was wont to do, "look to the hills from whence cometh comfort, lift up thine eyes to the hills!" One born in these hills may become by turns a Kansan, an Iowan, an Alabaman, but he never ceases to be a Missourian. One cannot become a native of these hills by adoption, only by birth, and it is to the place of his birth rather than the color of a man's skin or the fatness of his pocketbook that we look. Like that other great Missourian, Mark Twain, we have no regard for pomp and parade, show and sham —nothing but the essential man matters, and that is all that matters.

We venture to borrow the title of Booker T. Washington's autobiography as the heading of this story because of its special appropriateness to Carver's career.

Tomorrow brings the 100th anniversary of the birth of Dr. George Washington Carver, who rose from slavery to become a world famous educator and scientist at Tuskegee (Alabama) Institute for Negroes.

Known as the "Wizard of Tuskegee" because of his accomplishments in creative chemistry, this tall ebony gentleman with the beak-like nose

Reprinted from the *Kansas City Star*, July 16, 1960. By permission of the author and the *Kansas City Star*.

was all his life dedicated to one purpose. "I must serve my people," he said, "help lift them out of ignorance and poverty."

In so doing he revolutionized the economy of the South, changed the face of American industry, and won for himself countless honors— among them a fellowship in the Royal Society of London.

Born on the farm of Moses Carver near Diamond in Southwest Missouri, puny young George early displayed that intense interest in plants which later made him an outstanding botanist. "Little Plant Doctor," the neighbors called him, noting his skill with sick plants.

Curiosity lay at the very root of this boy's nature. "I must know all about every thing," he told himself. So at the age of 10, he set out to get an education. Trudging into Neosho eight miles away, he found a home with Aunt Mariah Watkins, a respected mid-wife. (It was this same Mariah Watkins who later officiated at the birth of Missouri artist Thomas Hart Benton.)

During his two years with Aunt Mariah, George learned to cook, sew, wash and iron. Thus equipped he went on to Kansas, where for 14 years he worked his way through grade and high school. Rejected for college because of his color he filed on a homestead in Ness County; but after three drought-stricken years, he left for Iowa, where he enrolled at Simpson College in Indianola. Here a childhood talent for art blossomed and his "Yucca Gloriosa" won honorable mention at the Chicago World's Fair. Now an intense longing to be an artist warred with his pledge to serve his people. The conflict finally resolved, he began the study of agriculture at Iowa State College in Ames.

Graduated with honors, he served two years on the staff at Ames as an experimental botanist, and here began that penetrating study of fungi which eventually made him America's most outstanding mycologist.

On field trips Carver often took with him a doting lad, by name Henry A. Wallace, to whom he explained the mysteries of plant fertilization, thus contributing to the development of a famous hybrid corn. Years later, as secretary of agriculture, Wallace came to Tuskegee to consult with his childhood mentor and to lend the might of the federal government to Carver's dream of rehabilitating the South.

Carver was 36 when he left Ames to become head of the agriculture department at Tuskegee Institute, which Booker T. Washington had started 15 years before. Here the young professor found the school farm still in a primitive condition and widespread poverty in the country round about. Immediately he discerned the cause of this poverty. A vicious one-crop system (cotton) had exhausted the soil and victimized the farmer, making him dependent upon a woefully inadequate cash crop.

Setting up an experiment station at Tuskegee, Carver began teaching
his students scientific agriculture. Then on Friday afternoons he would
hitch a mule to his demonstration cart and jog out into the country to
instruct the farmers. "Plant something besides cotton," he urged. "Raise
vegetables." Studying the local fungi, Carver showed the farmers how to
save their crops from disease. Scientific journals printed his brilliant
mycological discoveries, and in 1935 he was appointed a collaborator to
the U. S. Department of Agriculture.

In his popular but thoroughly scientific "Professor Carver's Column"
in the papers he instructed the farmers, too, in animal husbandry; and
by letter and in person hundreds of them sought his help for their ailing
livestock.

Bulletin after bulletin poured from Dr. Carver's pen. *The Ladies'
Home Journal* reprinted the one on the sweet potato. His articles appeared in the *Literary Digest* and *Review of Reviews*. He wrote a text-
book on botany and one on nature study for the Boy Scouts, and he filed
with the government exhaustive reports on medicinal plants. He was
frequently called to Washington for consultation, and in 1932 he came
to Kansas City to receive from the attorney general of Kansas the
Spingarn Medal for distinguished research in agriculture.

But it was chiefly as a creative chemist that Dr. Carver won acclaim.
"God's Little Workshop" he called his laboratory at Tuskegee. "Because," he said, "here Mr. Creator tells me what I am to do, and shows
me how to do it."

From the peanut alone he created 300 useful products, including
printer's ink and milk. "And it's not blue boarding house milk either,"
he would chuckle. "Mr. Creator showed me how to make rich Jersey
milk." From the sweet potato he made 118 products including egg yolk
and alcohol.

From hillside clay he recreated the lost purple dye of ancient Egypt,
and one of his paintings, "Peaches," done with paints also made from
clay, was requested for hanging by the Luxembourg galleries in Paris.

Pioneering in the use of waste products, he made marble from saw-
dust, wallboard from peanut shells, and paving blocks from surplus cotton. As a result of his creations new industries sprang up all over the
country.

His most valuable discoveries Dr. Carver gave to anyone who asked.
As his fame spread, he received fabulous offers for his services, but he
refused them all, even one of $175,000 a year from Thomas A. Edison.

Although prominent men like Henry Ford cherished his friendship,
Dr. Carver of course suffered many indignities in the South of his day.
On lecture tours he must ride in the drafty "Jim Crow" cars. Invited to
address a luncheon meeting of the Peanut Growers' Association, he must

enter by the back door and eat alone in his room. Once threatened with lynching, he fled all night in the rain. But he had no time for resentment.

He had no time either, his friends complained, to dress properly. He insisted on making his own ties. "I want to try out my dyes on them," he explained. Year after year he wore the same old black suit, keeping it spotless with cleaning compounds of his own concoction. But lacking in style though he might be, Dr. Carver always wore a flower in his buttonhole—a flower that strangely enough never seemed to wilt.

Nor did his sense of humor ever fade. Once when a reporter described him as a "stooped and toothless old man" he protested with a twinkle in his deepset hazel eyes. "It's not true. I may be stooped, but I'm not toothless. If the young man had asked me I could have shown him my teeth; I had them in my pocket all the time."

Dr. Carver never married. He died at Tuskegee on January 5, 1943, and is buried there. In that same year Congress authorized the George Washington Carver National Monument—210 acres surrounding his birthplace in the foothills of the Ozarks. This monument was dedicated in 1953.

I REMEMBER THE BLUES

LANGSTON HUGHES

Accident of birth (in Joplin) made Langston Hughes a native Missourian, but he is essentially a cosmopolitan, having traveled widely and lived in many places. He has also written widely, both in verse and prose. Perhaps his most distinctive work has been done in ballads and in a special verse form which he devised and calls "blues songs." The latter are found chiefly in his volumes Weary Blues *and* Fine Clothes for the Jew.

The article here presented was printed in the Panorama *supplement of the* Chicago Daily News *of January 26, 1963; it was derived from Mr. Hughes's contribution to "Trio," produced by Martin Levin for the National Educational Television and Radio Center.*

All my life I've heard the blues. In Kansas City as a child fifty years ago on a Charlotte Street corner near my uncle's barber shop, I remember a blind guitar player moaning to the long eerie sliding notes of his guitar.

> I'm goin' down to de river,
> Take my rockin' chair,
> Yes, down to de river,
> Rock in my rockin' chair,
> If de blues overcome me
> I'm gonna rock on away from here.

And in Chicago in my teens, all up and down State Street there were blues, indoors and out, at the Grand and the old Monogram theaters where Ma Rainey sang, in the night clubs, in the dance halls, on phonographs.

Shortly thereafter the three great Smiths—Mamie, Bessie and Clara —began to come to fame. No relation, only sisters in the blues.

It was during the summer of the great Mississippi flood of 1927, about which Bessie Smith sang her famous "Backwater Blues," that I met Bessie Smith in person.

> It rained forty days
> And the winds began to blow . . .

She was staying at the same colored hotel as I was, next door to the colored theater in Macon, Georgia. I made a beeline to the theater to hear her sing, not realizing that I could sit right in my room in the hotel (which I did the rest of the week) and hear just as well her great booming voice right through the walls. She never needed a microphone in her life, and at that time, in that place, there was none.

The last time I saw Bessie was on the screen at a private showing of her film, "The St. Louis Blues," after her tragic automobile collision when she bled to death at the door of a white Southern hospital that refused to admit Negroes. To the showing of this film in New York came many of Bessie's friends and admirers. Everybody cried so during the screening that the film had to be run again so folks could see it clearly.

> I hate to see
> That evenin' sun go down,
> Yes, I hate to see that
> Evenin' sun go down.
> The one I love's done
> Gone and left this town.

Bessie gone, Mamie gone, Clara gone, the great Ma Rainey, all long-gone—but their blues live after them. Contemporary singers recreate them—Dinah Washington, Claire Austin, LaVern Baker, Barbara Dane, Juanita Hall. There's a long-time echo to the blues, that catch the ache—and the hope—in everybody's heart. The blues sometimes define themselves in their own verses.

> They tell me that the blues ain't nothin'
> But the dog-gone heart's disease.
> They tell me that the blues ain't nothin'
> But a good man been done wrong.
> They tell me that the blues is when you wonder
> Will a match box hold your clothes.
> They tell me that the blues
> Is how long, how long, how long?
> How long will it be before you
> Ever learn to quit mistreatin' me?

They tell me that the blues is longing for somebody so bad that you are willing to say:

> Let me be your rag doll
> Until your china doll comes.
> Baby, let me be your oil stove
> Till your big gas range arrives.

The first of all blues to be written down was W. C. Handy's "Memphis Blues"—and into it Handy wrote the first jazz break ever to be put down on paper.

Two years later, in 1914, Handy published his famous "St. Louis Blues," which was destined to become America's best known popular song all around the world. I have heard "The St. Louis Blues" on Japanese jukeboxes sung in Japanese, in Russia sung in Russian, and in the various languages of Europe. In French provincial cafes with their little orchestras, almost every time a party of American tourists walks in, they play "The St. Louis Blues" evidently under the impression that it is the American National Anthem.

Toward the close of the war there was a story to the effect that when the American troops entered Paris as the Hitlerite occupation was withdrawing, over the public loudspeakers came the "St. Louis Blues." This song, like all Negro and Jewish music, had been banned by the Vichy regime under Hitler. One American reporter was so curious as to how "The St. Louis Blues" had remained a part of Parisian radio programs that he went to the radio station to ask. He was told that the French loved "The St. Louis Blues" so well that they managed to play it all during the Nazi occupation by telling the German censors that it really was an old French folk song—that St. Louis was actually King Louis XIV, and the woman with the diamond rings was Marie Antoinette.

> Saint Louis Woman with your diamond rings,
> If it wasn't for your powder
> And your store-bought hair,
> The man I love would not have
> Gone nowhere, nowhere!
> Oh, that man's got a heart
> Like a rock cast in the sea,
> Else he never would have gone
> So far from me.

They all stem, all blues, from the old-time basic anonymous 12-bar, 3-line lyric, deep South blues that nobody knows who made up, nobody knows who added what line where. They grew into jazz, America's great music, whose heartbeat is those sad old, bad old, glad old blues, crying, laughing—laughing maybe to keep from crying. And that's the way it is with the blues. They are often very sad songs. But there is almost always in the blues something to make you smile, and in their music a kind of marching-on syncopation, a gonna-make-it-somehow determination in spite of all, that ever-present laughter-under-sorrow that indicates a love of life too precious to let it go.

> I'm going down to the railroad,
> Lay my head on the track.
> Going down to the railroad,
> Lay my head on the track.
> But if I see that train a-coming,
> I'll jerk it back.

That's the Blues.

HONEY'S WEDDING

Fannie Cook

Fannie Cook was born in St. Charles, Missouri, was graduated from the University of Missouri, and taught English at Washington University in St. Louis. In her four novels she used chiefly Missouri backgrounds.

Mrs. Palmer's Honey received the first George Washington Carver Novel Award; it is a sympathetic and understanding story of a Negro servant girl in St. Louis and her friends.

Reprinted from *Mrs. Palmer's Honey,* by Fannie Cook. By permission of Jerome E. Cook.

The Boston household was as hushed and beflowered as if a funeral instead of a wedding were about to occur. Big Mama in a new blue dress and Papa in his country-club frock coat were sitting stiff and silent next to Mrs. Boston, who didn't bother to talk to them. She was at the end of the second row of chairs bearing on their backs the inscription: BOSTON DECEASEMENT HOME. She leaned against the highly polished inlaid table, bare today of cards. She leaned with the triumph of a winner who has unexpectedly scooped up all, for Ben was to be married and happy, yet she would not have to become either an outcast from his home or an intruder within it. She and Honey had talked it out. Honey was a girl who could talk straight and stay polite too.

A tinkle of laughter escaped from the kitchen. Mrs. Boston rose and tiptoed around the lace-trimmed dining-room table with its tiered cake topped by paper bride and groom. The door to the pantry squeaked; then the laughter ceased and was not resumed.

When she returned she saw that Honey's sisters had come. Carmen, as white as powder and net ruffles and cotton gloves could make her, sat stiffly alone on the davenport, which had been pushed back against the wall. From Eulatha's ears jangled long red earrings. Her costume was savagely expensive and her hands were bossy as she ushered eight uninvited small Hoops into the back row. Her own had wailed to come. Secretly, chuckling, Eulatha got all the children ready. She knew Honey wouldn't mind; she hoped Big Mama and those *dicktee* Bostons would.

The children struggled up into the chairs. One of Big Mama's wore pigtails, but the rest of the little girls wore straight, polished bobs topped by artificial flowers. The little boys' heads were shaved except for a sudden upstanding narrow fan of hair above their foreheads. Mrs. Boston approved the gleaming cleanliness. Her quick eye traveled the row of percale blues and reds and greens, observing all the Hoop economies: the dress trimmed from the left-overs of a shirt, the man-size neckties, the mended jumper. Satisfied, she nodded. These were respectable people. With a swoop of her arms she commanded the wrigglers to move into the front row where they could see.

Loraine, shapely in yellow chiffon, was keeping the door, opening it before the bell could be rung, whispering what she had to say. She was using her funeral-parlor habits. Following her example, all the household was hushed and reverent.

When at last Ben arrived, he walked between two men. The tan, plump one was the Methodist minister whose church the Bostons attended. The little man with the dark, pocked skin was the Baptist minister who had baptized Lamb. He was known as a shouter.

Lamb was looking at him as if at his own past. The minister dropped

his eyes. Then he lifted them again, and he and Lamb nodded like old
friends. Gloria's pop-eyed glance kept searching the wide staircase for
Honey. Ben, a white boutonniere on his coat, had gone up two at a time.

When Honey appeared it was not down the handsome stairway but
as if from nowhere. Suddenly she was in the room facing the minister,
her hands clasped lightly against each other.

Upstairs Ben had told her why there were two ministers: he couldn't
slight either one. Both had performed many services for him, dozens
and dozens of free ones for the poor.

"It's all right," Honey said. "Just so it ain't Episcopalian. I ain't high-
up enough for that. And not Church of God. That's too new for Mama.
She's Methodist, and Papa was Baptist, so I reckon it's about right to
have both."

"You're a pretty bride, Honey, mighty pretty," Ben said thickly.

Honey's eyes rolled toward Mrs. Boston's long mirror. "I reckon so,"
she said appraisingly.

"You didn't want a white dress? Because if you did—"

"I didn't, Ben," Honey said hastily. "I done wore a heap of white
in my day. Maid's uniforms, they was. I didn't want nothing like that.
Colors was too bold. And black too sad. So I picked gray. It looks right
nice with your orchid. I ain't never had an orchid before. I had one offered once, but that was all. . . . My dress, it's good, I reckon."

"It's pretty, mighty pretty."

"It's made plain, and it ain't long like some, but it don't make me
look none like Mrs. Palmer's Honey. It looks like I'm my own."

"And mine."

"And yours, Ben. Yours. I'm mighty proud I'm yours too."

Rev. Topaz, Methodist, prayed before and after Rev. Higginton, Baptist. At first they prayed for show, in defense of their own craftsmanship;
then they prayed in reply to Honey's wide-eyed searching for their
meaning. Their prayers became admonition and well-wishing and social
comment. The admonition and well-wishing wove lightly around and
around, like the circles of a spider's web. The social comment was the
spread of sturdy spokes upon which they dared to rest their weight.

Closing his eyes and rippling out his full lips, Rev. Topaz spoke intimately to his God, reminding Him of black loyalty despite the unchris-
tian behavior of white Christians, yet why, oh why was it that only dark
Christians held to the doctrine of the brotherhood of man, held to it in
deeds as well as words? Surely the All-Powerful had some divine motive for the sinfulness of white children. Rev. Topaz did not doubt the
wisdom of the motive or that someday the white man would really catch
religion and cease his sinning, but in the meantime colored men and
women had to stagger forward, bearing terrific burdens on aching shoul-

ders. He described the ache much as a union leader might have described it. It was college graduates working as porters—and slights everywhere. Honey, chin high, earnestly awaited his impending advice. To ease the ache—the ministerial bass scolded—colored men and colored women and colored children must practice Christian humility, must learn it and practice it!

Startled, Honey turned to look at Ben. How was he taking this unforeseen betrayal? She saw that Ben, masked by polite inattention, was adream with love of her. He had not heard.

The shouting of Rev. Higginton was louder and crisper, yet also self-righteous with condemnation of the ways of white folks. Remembering how he had stayed dry while his hired men immersed Lamb, Honey knew in advance all the talk would come to nothing.

Me and Ben, she thought, come we're going to be one, we got to make us one ourselves. All this here talk ain't going to do it. I reckon we got to do it every day. It can't be love and hate both, like it was with Snake. It's got to be love and taking care of each other. The sins of white folks got to be fought off so as we can be people, brave enough to know Honey and Ben is as good as we is good inside, and that skin ain't where evil lives.

She began to be sorry she had let the salesgirl who sold her the gray dress talk her into having the short gray wedding veil too. It was becoming, yes, it was; but why must a brown girl copy white folks even when she was getting married?

Out yonder in the kitchen there was a cateress putting tiny sandwiches on platters. She had her chicken salad made and her coffee, the sherbet ready to be put into the tall blocks of ice. She had the white satin bow on the knife for cutting the wedding cake. She had champagne on ice. She had everything ready just as Honey would have had it ready for Dotty Jane.

I reckon we ain't got nobody to learn it from except white folks, Honey lamented. Only difference is that come Ben and me don't stick to each other and love each other and do for each other, the world, it's going to bear down harder on us than on white folks. I reckon I'm right lucky marrying Ben, because Ben, he's got nothing in him but goodness. Ben, he's for true.

She slipped her hand through his arm, the way she had been too shy to do at first. His elbow pressed it exultantly against his heart. Later, they agreed that was the moment which pronounced them man and wife. What the minister said was only a distant echo vaguely heard, vaguely remembered.

COUNTRY LIFE

QUILTING PARTY

HOMER CROY

Homer Croy was born near Maysville, Missouri, and attended the University of Missouri. He was one of a group of boys whom Walter Williams sent to St. Louis to get out one number of the Post-Dispatch, *a kind of preview of the School of Journalism soon to be organized. A writer from boyhood, Croy made his first great success with a realistic novel,* West of the Water Tower; *it was screened for movie audiences, as were many of his later books. Much of his early work was fiction, often with a humorous phase; but in later years he has turned to the field of popular biography, in which he has been very successful. In 1958 the University of Missouri conferred upon him the honorary degree of Doctor of Letters.*

When the writer of this headnote informed him of the plans for this volume, Doctor Croy wrote, "You can use anything of mine you want." He did not add "without fee," but it was so understood; if we were wrong it is just too bad. We have been generous with ourselves by enriching our anthology with two pieces from his writings—the following selection from his autobiography Country Cured *and a passage that will be found later in this volume about Jesse James.*

In November Phebe would say, "Aunt, don't you think it is about time to have the quilting party?" She would never say *a* because we had one each year.

My mother would say, "Yes, I think it is. Go ahead and get things ready."

My mother always had charge of the Sunday dinners, swimming parties, sausage making, and so on, but Phebe was the quilter in our family and Quilting Day belonged to her. She was the best quilter in the neighborhood and was immensely proud of her ability.

A thousand things had to be done. Cloth and thread and cotton had to be bought. "Homer, will you bring home some chalk?" she would say.

Word would be sent to the neighbors we were to have our quilting on a certain day, and, as the time approached, our house would get busier and busier. There would be rolls of batten and piles of cloth, and out would come the rag bag we had been keeping all year, and Phebe would hunt through it and lay out in little piles the odds and ends for the crazy quilt.

Reprinted from *Country Cured* by Homer Croy. By permission of the author.

She would come to a piece and show it to my mother and their voices would fall. My mother would sit a moment, thinking, then go to the bureau in the spare room and get the wooden box that held Pa's wedding gloves and take out a piece of dress goods.

"I believe I'll put it in," she would say, her voice very low now, because the piece was part of a dress that had belonged to my sister who had died before I was born.

"Do you want to embroider her name?" Phebe would ask, and my mother would nod.

"I'll chalk it for you," Phebe would say and would go and get her style book and take the piece of chalk I had brought home from school and make a fancy capital *A,* and the rest of the name Alice in small letters. Ma would take her silk thread and begin to stitch along the chalk marks.

After a while Pa would come in and Ma would hold it up and he would say, "I'm glad it's going in."

In going through the rag bag, Phebe would bring out a piece, "It's part of Homer's dress. Do you want it to go in, Aunt?"

I could hardly believe I had ever been so little I had to wear a dress. But there it was.

"I want it to go in," my mother would say and in it would go, because our crazy quilt was an album of the Croy family.

The rag bag was a turning point. All year things had been going into it; if they went into it there was never any doubt about them. They were headed straight for the crazy quilt. But some things hung in the balance, still good enough to wear, but just on the verge of going into the crazy quilt.

Phebe would go to the closet in her room and bring back a dress and hold it up and say, "Aunt, do you think it ought to go in?" Ma would examine it and say, "I expect it better. Styles change so fast these days you probably can't ever use it again."

"It's the one I wore to Sister Mary's wedding," Phebe would say a little choked, because Mary had married and Phebe hadn't.

She would spread the dress on the table and cut out a piece under a pocket where it hadn't faded. "Do you want to put in anything of Blanche's?" she would say as the scissors made grating noises on the table.

"Yes," Mother would say.

"I've got something," Ma said and went to her own private box and came back with a campaign ribbon with PIERCE AND BRECKENRIDGE printed on it, and smoothed it with her fingers.

"Do you think it's strong enough?"

"I'll stitch a back on it," Phebe said.

"Then I'd like it to go in."

The day before the quilting, Phebe would say, "Homer, I want you to wash off the frames." More work for me. Always more work for me. That's the way it seemed.

I would go to the smokehouse and get out the wooden frames. Two X's made the end pieces; when set up they were held together by two poles which were two or three feet longer than the average quilt. I would get a bucket of soap and water and begin to scrub the frames, but no sooner would I start than Phebe would come trotting out. "Now don't you go and wet the edging." The "edging" was a piece of ducking about twice as wide as my hand which ran the length of each pole; to this the quilt was sewed while it was in process of construction. I would have to scrub the poles carefully so as not to get the edging wet. More work. I didn't have to be so careful with the X's. I could give them a slosh of water and a few quick rubs and be through. "Now you can lean them against the fence and let 'em dry." I would lean them promptly.

We'd be up early on the day of the quilting, and a kind of excitement would vibrate over the house. I liked it, even if it meant extra work.

"Homer, I want you to get the stove going," Phebe would say. More work.

Sometimes the parlor wouldn't be used all winter. But it was on Quilting Day. If a woman had her quilting in her everyday living room, she'd have to have a pretty good excuse or be talked about.

By nine o'clock the first buggy would show up, then a surrey would appear, because it wouldn't do to go in a wagon on a stylish day like a quilting; pretty soon, Mrs. Gerilda Knabb would come over the brow of the hill in her sidesaddle, and I would have to dash out and hold her horse close to a surrey step so she could get down.

Haying and threshing and clover-seed hulling and road-work day belonged to the men. But Quilting Day belonged to the women. It was all right for a man to deliver his wife at a quilting, but he had to get away as fast as he could. If he went to the house and sat down with the womenfolks and tried to be sociable, they'd have run him out with brooms. No man in his right mind would go *near* the house.

It wasn't proper for the women to sit around and visit; get right down to work, because work was more important than manners. It was a tremendous honor to be the first woman at the frames.

There, in the middle of the floor, would be the frames with the quilt-to-be strung between them, and with cotton batten between the two lengths of cloth. The cloth would be stitched to the edging, but the quilt hadn't been tightened. When all was ready, one woman would take hold of one ratchet wheel and another woman would take hold of the

other ratchet wheel and Phebe would dash up and down the frames
giving the cotton the last smoothing out, then she would say, "Tighten!"
and the women would begin twisting the ratchet wheels. A wooden
tongue fitted into the teeth of a wheel and each time the tongue fell it
gave a click. It was a hard job to get the quilt started just right, because if it was slewed, the whole thing would be collywobbled and no
amount of work would ever get it straight. So Phebe would dash up and
down the frames, tightening pins and loosening threads, and having
one woman tighten and another loosen until the quilt was finally squared
on exactly right. "Fasten!" she would order, and the women would push
the wooden tongues down so they wouldn't fly loose and cause no end
of trouble.

Phebe would take the advertising yardstick from Eversole's and get
ready to "lay off" the quilt in diagonals. Two women would take hold
of the yardstick to steady it and everybody would grow hushed, for a
ticklish moment had come. Taking the chalk, Phebe would draw it
along the yardstick, making a straight white line on the cloth. This was
for the women to sew along and so that the quilt, when finished, would
have fine, even diamonds.

As soon as enough white lines were down, the women would take up
their needles, put on their thimbles, and begin to quilt, four women on
one side, the same number on the other. Up and down would go the
needles, snip-snip would go the scissors. Then the women would visit,
the neighborhood news now.

Phebe was the leader. They all asked her how she wanted this done,
or how she wanted that. She would tell them, now and then stopping to
show how she turned a corner, or put in a rabbit ear. Ma wasn't important today.

When the row of white lines was finished, Phebe would say, "I guess
we can turn now." The women would go to the ratchet wheels and
Phebe would say, "Roll," and the ratchet wheels would move and the
little wooden tongues click; then the women would go back and take up
their needles.

The other women would be in the sitting room visiting, or helping
Ma in the kitchen. But that was only until the quilters got tired. Now
and then one of the women from the sitting room would get up and go
to the frames and say, "I expect you're tired, Mrs. Kennedy. I'll take
your place for a while."

Mrs. Kennedy would say she wasn't in the least tired, but in a minute the new woman would be at the frames and Mrs. Kennedy would
be in the sitting room visiting.

On other days the polite thing was for everybody to sit down to dinner at the same time, but not on Quilting Day. The frames must be kept turning. The women who were not quilting would eat, then go to the frames; those who had been quilting, would go to the table. Not much to eat, but no one expected fancy things, because today was workday. Get as much done as possible.

After while we'd see Pa coming through the yard; then we'd hear him on the back porch taking off his overshoes. He'd sit down at the table, but there'd be no grace. He'd gulp down his food and get out of the house as fast as a tramp.

After dinner the women would get sleepy and the chatter would fall off; now and then one would hold her hand, with a thimble on the middle finger, up to her mouth and try to hide a yawn. Then she'd say, "I was up with a calf last night," and everybody'd understand.

Now and then one of the women, without a word, would get up and leave the frames and put a fascinator over her head. We'd all know what that meant. When she came back in she'd hold her hands over the stove and say, "It's getting real chilly outside."

Finally the quilt would be done and Phebe would say, "We can take it off now." Back the other way the ratchet wheels would go and the quilt would sag in the middle from its weight, then it would be unstitched and unpinned from the edging. Phebe would hold it up and all would examine it to see who had made the best diamonds. "Now the crazy quilt."

It took experts for this, for a crazy quilt is twice as hard as an ordinary quilt. But Phebe knew how and would go from one to another, arranging patches and making suggestions. And now, as the day's quilting drew to a climax, there would be a great hubbub as they tried to decide which color of thread went with which patch and what kind of stitch to use. But Phebe knew. She wouldn't fancy stitch at all herself, because she would be too busy showing others. Ma would come in and stand in the background handing out patches and picking up the chalk when it rolled off on the floor.

Phebe would lower her voice. "Aunt, where do you want the campaign ribbon to go?"

"In the middle," Ma would say.

The women's voices would fall away to a hush, because they all knew what the campaign ribbon meant.

It could not be finished in a day; sometimes it took a woman years, working alone winter evenings, to complete her crazy quilt. But it was helped along, and the women all wanted to say they'd had a part in the quilt.

They would begin looking out the window to see if the men were coming. "There's Newt," Mrs. Kennedy would say. One by one the men would arrive and stand in the lot talking to Pa, never dreaming to go to the house.

One by one the carts and buggies would leave. Mrs. Gerilda Knabb would come out, but there would be no surrey now, so I would have to go to the granary and get two sawhorses. I would try to maneuver her horse up, but he had been standing all day and wanted to get home. Mrs. Knabb, standing on top of the sawhorses, would shout, "Whoa! Whoa! Stand still now!" and I would shout, too, to the prancing horse. Ma and Phebe would hear us shouting and would come to the door and begin calling warnings to Mrs. Knabb and instructions to me. And now, with everybody shouting, the horse would prance more than ever. Finally Pa would come up through the hog lot and take hold of the bit, and I would help Mrs. Knabb and pretty soon she would be on and going toward the main road, pulling and sawing at the frisky, snorting animal.

"Homer, take down the frames," Ma would say, once more coming into charge.

The parlor floor would be littered with thread and scraps from the crazy quilt and pieces of chalk and a thimble someone had stepped on. Ma would begin gathering these up and I would take the frames and lean them against the parlor wall. During the winter, they would be moved into the sitting room where Ma and Phebe would quilt alone.

But when Ma said, "Take down the frames," Quilting Day was over.

THE LONG DROUTH

JOSEPHINE JOHNSON

Josephine Johnson (Mrs. Grant C. Cannon) was born in Kirkwood, Missouri, attended Washington University, and lived on a farm in St. Louis County for many years. She is novelist, short-story writer, poet, and artist; and she has long been active in social causes. Her short, beautifully written novel Now in November *won a Pulitzer Prize in 1934. It is from that work that we take the following moving story of an incident of farm life.*

The drouth went on. Trees withered, the grass turned hay, even the weeds dried into ashes, even the great trees with their roots fifty years under ground. Burdock and cockle were green near the empty creek-bed, but the giant elms began to die. The limas died, lice on their blossoms, convolvulus strangling the string-bean bushes, and the carrots so bound in earth that nothing could budge them from the ground.

I walked some nights in the hay fields hoping to find a cooler air, and the desire for rain came to be almost a physical hurt. I could not feel any more the immensity of night and space, that littleness we speak of feeling before the stretching of fields and stars. I felt always too big and clumsy and achingly present. I could not shrink.

And then one noon when it seemed that we could not stand it any longer, that we should dry and crack open like the earth, there was a sudden blast of cold air and in the north we saw an enormous bank of rising clouds. The air had been hot and still, storm-quiet and dark; but for a week clouds ominous and storm-surfed had been covering the sky and dissolving into nothing. The sunsets were clear and crystal as after a great rain, but not one drop had fallen. Now we saw the clouds tower up and reach forward like great waves, and there was the bull-mumbling of thunder. It had come up fast and still, no warning except the quiet, and we stood there staring like blocks of stone. Then Merle shouted, "It's here!" and ran out fast like a crazy person, and we saw stabs of lightning all through the black upboiling mass. Dad looked at Mother, and I saw the awful unmasking of his face, as if all the underground terror and despair were brought to the surface by his hope, and I felt a jab of pity and love for him stronger than I'd ever known before. Mother snatched up a bucket and put it out on the stones, half-wild to think that a drop might escape or go where it wasn't needed. We dragged out buckets and saucepans, even grabbed up bowls and put them out on the window-sill, and Merle pulled Grant's drinking-cup down from the nail. It got darker and a fierce wind whipped our clothes, and Merle was wild with excitement and the cold rushing of air. We saw Kerrin running up from the barn, lashed back and forth like a willow switch, and the sheep poured down along the road in a lumpy flood, baaing and crying toward the barn. I wanted to run and shriek, get wings and flap like the swooping crows. Grant looked ten years younger, shouted and called like a boy. We all looked at each other and felt burst free, poured out like rain. "Bring up the tubs," Father shouted. "She's coming, all right! She's here, I tell you!" He ran toward the cellar steps just as the first drops fell, hard-splashing and wide apart. He staggered back up with the wash-tubs, and the drops struck down like a noise of hammers on hollow tin. There was a wonderful brightness on Mother's face, a sort of light shining from it, almost a rapt and mystic look as she stood there with flower-pots dangling from her hand.

Those first few drops scattered a few dead leaves on the vine and sank out of sight in earth. In the north a rift of blue widened and spread with terrible swiftness. The storm clouds loomed high and went on south. No more drops fell, and a long pole of sunlight came down through the clouds. A burnt and ragged hole in the clouds with the sun's eye coming through. We could feel the wind dying already, leaving only a cooler air. No rain.

Father's knees seemed to crumple up under him and he sat down heavy on the steps.

"God's will be done!" Kerrin said, and burst out laughing. "What're the barrels for, Grant?"

"Tubs to catch sunlight in," he answered her, "—storing up sweet light for the dark!" He looked fierce and haggard, sweat dry on his face from the wind, and a wire-cut ragged across his cheek like a lightning mark. Kerrin started to laugh again and threw up her arms. She looked queer and ridiculous, and I saw how thin she'd gotten, her neck like a twist of wire, and the wind seemed to blow through her bones. It made my heart sick to look at her. Grant turned away and shaded his eyes toward the sun. "Damned old Cyclopean eye!" he muttered. Stared up hating and helpless at the sky.

The clouds moved out and apart. Enormous stretches of sky were clean as glass. The thunder sounded a long way off, almost unheard. . . . Nothing was changed at all.

MAY IN MISSOURI

LEONARD HALL

Leonard Hall was born in Seneca, Missouri, in 1899. He spent part of his boyhood at Potosi. He now lives at Possom Trot Farm, not far from there; the name of his place has become well known to Missourians through Hall's letters to the St. Louis Post-Dispatch *and through his books and lectures.*

Hall was educated at Washington University and the University of Wisconsin. He holds an honorary degree from Westminster College.

Every year at about this time I find myself thinking how much pleasure can be added to country living—or to city living, for that mat-

Reprinted from *Country Year. Journal of the Seasons at Possum Trot Farm.* Copyright 1957 by Leonard Hall. By permission of the author.

ter—by an interest in natural history. Life today is so full of gadgets and the many kinds of salesmanship which create a desire for these gadgets that we finally arrive at the point where we feel our very existence depends on them. The truth is, of course, that their existence depends on us. We become convinced that life would hardly be possible without the motors, radios, grocery stores, beauty shops, gasoline stations, and the manufacturers of a thousand articles that are always at our fingertips. We forget that, pleasant and useful and convenient as these things are, they are no more than services that we support. And in the final analysis, both they and we are altogether dependent upon certain very basic earth relationships. Today, as when the first sentient man walked upon earth, it is the same energy from the same sun, carried up to us through the food chains of the soil-water-plant-animal cycle, which makes human life possible.

Even we who live on the land, now that we have become production specialists with lockers, refrigerators, and deep-freezes, are prone to forget where our food comes from. We roar across our fields on the seat of the tractor with our heads enveloped in exhaust fumes. No longer do we walk in the furrow with the sun on our backs, conscious of each plant the plow turns under, of the rich life that exists in good soil, of the blackbird following along behind us to pick up his morning meal. If we don't watch out, we are apt to find ourselves believing that it is the noise of our passage which makes the corn grow; and this is a conceit in which farming loses its real meaning.

It is impossible for the man or woman with an interest in natural history to fall into such errors as these. Such a person, be he countryman or bank teller, has a firm grasp upon the realities of life. He need not be a scientist, a trained botanist, ornithologist, or agricultural expert to develop that perception which gives meaning to the wonders of nature. He needs only curiosity and a keen eye. The bird life in a city park, the weedy growth on a vacant lot, the earthworms in a garden, the plant and animal life processes in a cow pasture—all of these have meaning. In all of them we may study the means by which nature achieves her ends of form and existence. Thus it is that an occasional farmer, though not nearly enough farmers, can contribute as much to agricultural science as the most-skilled technician working in the laboratory.

There are no limits set for the amateur naturalist; fascinating fields for study lie no farther away than one's own dooryard. Nor do I mean by this a mere re-cataloguing or verification of fact already established by professional authority, for in the whole area of the natural sciences are a thousand fields that have barely been glimpsed through gates that some amateur may swing wide open.

Most of the wildflowers that we write about each spring grow out in

the woodland along the limestone bluff above our creek. There are perhaps four hundred kinds of them, from March until frost, growing
in constant succession or in direct competition. There are, in addition,
perhaps a hundred species of shrubs and forty kinds of trees. Here is,
obviously, the type of life community toward which nature builds when
man does not interfere. The animal life in this area is as rich as the plant
life and consists of many kinds of songbirds, rabbits, squirrels, foxes,
raccoon, opossum—not to mention the insects, small rodents, and rep-
tiles such as frogs, lizards, skinks, turtles, and snakes. Deer browse
the area from time to time and now and then we permit a small amount
of carefully managed grazing. There is a thick layer of humus on the
ground, rich and moist and filled with a hundred life forms too small
for the eye to see.

Here is the life cycle at its best. Here is a "biotic community" created by nature to make maximum use of organic and inorganic materials
from the soil and of the energy of the sun to support a rich and complex life structure. Might not a farmer draw some interesting conclusions
from such a landscape? Not far away from this woodland are many ex-
amples of how man uses the land with an almost absolute lack of com-
prehension of its life-producing potential. Here is a field planted to
wheat, as it has been for many years past. It was plowed up and down
the hill, sowed up and down the hill. Last winter the drill rows turned
to small gullies which joined to make larger gullies. How many tons
of the thin remaining topsoil left that field to go down the creek, I
would not venture to say. Certainly there is no richness of humus here,
nor of life within the soil.

A sense of real husbandry has as yet been grasped by far too few
Americans, and this is something that goes beyond the crop we produce.
We must develop a perceptive faculty to read the lessons of nature.
When we do this, the whole vast accumulation of knowledge that is
science takes on new meaning and we begin to understand the world
we live in.

The other day a neighbor stopped by to look at a buck rake we have
for sale and we fell to talking about this strange and fascinating business
of farming. He was experimenting with the new ladino clover that is
just making a start in our country, and spoke of his wife's somewhat
caustic comment when he appeared with a small sack containing twenty
pounds of seed and admitted that it had cost forty dollars. "But you
know how it gets hold of a fellow," he said, "this business of planting
some new kind of seed and then watching for it to grow."

A farmer must have this feeling for the land bred in his bones. He must like his animals, too, if he is going to succeed with them. One of the most successful poultrymen I have ever known was showing me through his laying houses one day when I spotted an old rocking chair. We had seen a number of interesting pieces of improvised equipment on this farm, but I never knew a hen that preferred a rocking chair and said as much. My friend explained that whenever he had a half hour to spare, he came out and sat in this chair and watched the hens. He did this often, and there is little doubt that the intimate knowledge gained in this manner had much to do with his success. He had found, among other things, that certain hens which were potentially high producers were also very timid. Other hens crowded them away from the feeders. So he had invented a feeder that gave every hen an equal chance, and the egg production went up. The rocking-chair technique paid off.

One would hardly think that there would be much individuality in a herd of a hundred beef cattle, which look pretty much alike to begin with and are out on pasture a good part of the year. Yet there is. A good cattleman soon comes to know each head of stock, whether it is an easy keeper, a good mother, a heavy milker, a fence jumper. We have just been through one of those experiences that mean little to some farmers and a lot to some others. A cow took sick. Very often, when this happens, she will mope for a day or two and then turn up her toes with no effort whatever to keep on living. Sheep are even worse on this score than cows. But we doctored the old girl and she did everything she could to help us. Dr. Sheets came regularly each week, and we fed her glucose and tried every treatment we could think of.

As with a lot of seriously sick patients, one day she'd be better and the next day worse. Now and then she would try to eat, but mostly what food we got down her we poured down. That meant mixing and straining and feeding two or three quarts of gruel four or five times a day. Once or twice the old cow managed a bit of grass or we would see her chewing her cud. Never once did her ears droop, the sure sign of a losing battle with a sick cow. She was a game one, and Matt and Ginnie and I grew increasingly fond of her. We hated to lose her, moreover, for she was carrying a June calf. But finally, she knew she couldn't make it and we knew it, too. An animal has this sense of mortality, like some old settler when he asks "the women" to straighten the quilts and, turning his face to the wall, makes ready for the end. I have seen it happen enough times to make one wonder whether "dumb brute" is a good description for an animal. At any rate, I believe you have to like animals to do well with them.

It is interesting to see how the season pushes ahead regardless of weather. Now the last of the buckeye trees are in bloom and the bees seem to prefer these blossoms to any other. Only the grass is slow, so that we must shift the cattle from one pasture to another to keep it from being eaten down too close. But during the past week, the comeback has been fast.

Last week Matt and I tackled a job that I had been dreading for three years, and we find it not too bad. We have a forty-acre pasture, over on the east side of the farm, which is overgrown with hickory sprouts. Big fellows they are, and tough, for they had not been cut out in sixteen years before we came here. But we cleared and mowed a couple of acres last autumn and the bluegrass came up thick and green this spring, so we decided to tackle at least another strip. Brush clearing is a chore that once was turned over to some old fellow in the neighborhood who liked to work alone at a job where he was not pushed, and he demanded a modest wage accordingly. Today most farmers turn pale at the sight of a double-bitted ax and tackle the brush clearing with 2-4-5T or similar chemicals. But sixteen-year-old sprouts take a long time to die and a lot of spray equipment, and farming is a business where you frequently find yourself substituting muscle for machinery.

To date we have cleared probably eight acres, piled the brush, disked the cleared land, and fertilized it. If corn planting and haying do not overtake us, we hope to finish the job before hot weather. It is not easy work, but it is good work, and, as Matt puts it, "a fellow sure appreciates his beans" after a day of cutting brush.

You have a chance to observe a lot of things at a task like this. The steers come grazing past and you get them well sorted out in your mind as to quality. Here are the "good doers," as the cattlemen say, and here the ones that are cut too high in the flank and will have a hard time grading "good" at the market. We see the ducks come in to the pond and the band of a dozen jacksnipe that frequent the marshy land. There have been greater and lesser yellowlegs and a half-dozen kinds of sandpipers, and a pair of great blue herons work back and forth along the creek. The quail have paired off and there seem to be more of them than last season, with plenty of cover in which to raise their broods. A pair of sora rails have nested for the past three years at the Big Pond and we have seen the young ones, now almost full grown.

Now and then when we are both well winded, Matt and I walk over to see how the oats are coming along, or the bicolor lespedeza that we planted in the wildlife area. The preacher from Caledonia comes to fish for perch in the pond and pulls out several bluegills and a good bass while we watch with a twinge of envy.

CHRISTMAS COOKING

JEAN BELL MOSLEY

Jean Bell Mosley was born in Elvins, Missouri, and was graduated from the Flat River Junior College and Southeast Missouri State College. She has contributed short fiction to many leading American magazines, and has been president of the Missouri Writers' Guild. Her home is now in Cape Girardeau.

The following is a chapter from her book Wide Meadows.

The kitchen was the hub of our lives. From it we went forth, and to it we returned. The front door was used only by strangers—or when it was known that Mama and Grandma were having Ladies Aid. The kitchen was big enough (once it had been a single-room log-cabin home) for one to carry on an industry of dressmaking, or reading, at one end, completely undisturbed by the rest of the activity going on, yet be pleasantly aware of the nearness of loved ones and the hum of homey occupations.

How pleasant it was on gloomy, dark winter days after the long, cold walk home from school to come into its warmth! Rain dripped off the low eaves and made a cozy patter on the pantry roof. Old Tabby, curled up on the hearth, purred loudly, loving the stir of our homecoming and the good smells emanating from the oven. The teakettle on the back of the stove sang gaily and every once in a while a log in the fireplace would break in two, causing a busy sputtering of sparks.

Many of our treasures were concentrated in this one room where we could look around and see them all at once. There was the clock on the mantel with its exquisite jewel-like pendulum, the big hunk of many-faceted green glass that was used as a doorstop, the colorful Mexican basket hanging on the wall, and the Blue Willow bean jar on the cabinet. The walls were decorated with such necessary items as the almanac, the shaving mirror and comb rack, and a map of Europe. The continent of Europe was changing. Mama had marked with a pencil the location of the Marne River where her Cousin Jim had recently been killed. There was a huge bird chart we'd gotten with carefully saved Arm and Hammer baking soda cards. Winter birds, summer birds, meadow birds, mountain birds were all assembled in one setting, and the purple grackle had an insect in its mouth.

The big square table in the center of the room wasn't merely a place

Reprinted from *Wide Meadows* by Jean Bell Mosley. By permission of the author. Published by The Caxton Printers, Ltd.

to eat. It doubled as Mama's cutting board when she sewed. It was our study table. There we played checkers and dominoes and a most peculiar game that I have never seen repeated by other children. It originated in the fertile brain of Lou, and had it been named it would probably have been called "Salting the Heifers." This game was best indulged in when Mama and Grandma and all other adults were outside. A small pile of salt was spooned onto the corners of the table. Then we pursued each other around the table, having to stop at each corner and take a lick at the salt with our tongues. What hilarious fun to see the pained expressions on each other's faces when we had reached the saturation point of salt consumption. Of course the floor became good and crunchy, too, and ofttimes, if it were summer when we played barefooted and there happened to be a raw, sore toe, one participant might be sent yelling for the wash pan, where the offended member was quickly dipped.

But it was at Christmas time that the kitchen really came into its own. Although there was much good cooking going on at other seasons throughout the year, especially at threshing time or any summer Sunday when company was expected, still it was at Christmas that it was most enjoyed, for the heat from the old black range was welcome and comforting then.

We seldom had company for Christmas dinner on account of the roads. By this time frozen ruts were so deep and continuous that it was a cold, hazardous journey for the aunts and uncles and cousins. If the neighbors dropped in, they walked, and we would serve them hot buttered popcorn or a plate of molasses candy. But still we baked and fried and stewed and boiled from a week before Christmas clear up through New Year's, experimenting with new recipes and perfecting the old ones.

Throughout the holidays, everyone's favorite cake, cookie, or pie would be served, so the route to the cellar, the smokehouse, and pantry, that great triumvirate for the garnishment of our table, was kept well traversed. There was a constant warm smell of vanilla, cinnamon, nutmeg, rising dough, roasting meat, baking bread, and boiling cranberries. We picked out quarts of hickory nuts and walnut kernels and shelled gallons of popcorn.

Starting off early in the holidays with the plebeian gingerbread, butter, molasses, and ginger cookies, we progressed through raisin, mincemeat, and pumpkin pies; raised doughnuts fried in the deep leaf lard in the old three-legged kettle; pound cake, devil's cake, hickory-nut cake, divinity, and fudge, to wind up with the glorious queens of all, Grandma's five-layer cocoanut cake and Mama's peach custard pudding.

Of course, in and out and round about all these sweetenings were the rosy, pink slices of baked ham; the pungent brown sausages replete with salt, pepper, and plenty of sage; golden, bubbly chicken pie, butter beans, green beans, pinto beans; fried, baked, boiled and scalloped potatoes; cole slaw, and a roster of pickles and jellies that would reach from one end of the valley to the other.

But on Christmas Day, there for dinner, centering the table on the glass-stemmed stand, was the high, light, creamy, five-layer, becocoa-nutted cake, and for supper the golden-studded, meringue-covered peach custard pudding.

Grandma had three, little, thin, tin cake pans which she kept on top of the pantry shelves for her cake-baking alone. Woe be to anyone who dared to use them for anything else. In preparation for her cake-baking she washed and dried these carefully, greased and floured them lightly, and distributed them equally distant along the top of the cook table. There was nothing slipshod or bang-up about this culinary concoction.

Lou and I, who have seen to it that the wood box is filled and spilling over with good dry split wood, pulled from underneath the pile, are allowed to lean our elbows on the table and watch the proceedings.

Into the big blue crock Grandma drops a cup of butter, and over this she sifts a cup of sugar. Then, with the big cooking spoon, she whips and beats, mashes, spins and cajoles it into a light, fluffy mass, the color of the creamy white honeysuckles on the summer porch. At this point on lesser occasions she would poke a spoonful of the sugary concoction into two drooling mouths, but not today!

Then come the eggs, five or six, broken deftly on the edge of the crock and spilled over the contents. Then again the beating process, even more vigorous than before. The withered skin at Grandma's throat flaps back and forth, and her old hand, gnarled from too much rheumatism, goes round so fast it is just a blur. The rickrack on her dust cap quivers and the batter grows lighter and lighter. Grandma does not measure her flour but grabs the sifter, puts in a certain amount of baking powder and salt, just so much flour, and proceeds to raise a fine white mist in, over, and around the cook table. Flour, milk, flour, milk, until the right consistency is reached—and only she knows this—then the vanilla, more beating, and into the three pans. That's all the oven will hold at one time. After the first baking, two of the pans are pressed into the second shift.

How the cake eventually comes out even and well rounded is a feat architectural more than culinary because the layers are invariably higher on one side than the other. This is due to the fact that the whole kitchen slopes a little downhill toward the river. But by alternating the high and low sides, putting a bigger daub of icing here, a smaller amount of cocoanut there, it goes upwards, plumb with the table, pleasing to the eye, and perfect to the palate.

After feasting our eyes on it the remainder of the morning, sitting in all its chaste glory in the center of the white-covered table and coming into even more tantalizing proximity during the meal, finally Grandpa would cross his knife and spoon neatly on his plate, pick up crumbs, real and imaginary, and after an eternity say, "Now, Ma, give me a slice of the riverward side of that cake."

It was inconceivable that when only a third of the ambrosial mass remained, leaning precariously like Pisa, that we would ever again want anything to eat, especially so soon as suppertime. But appetites would be whetted by coasting down the hill back of the house, skating on the frozen river, or merely by taking a long tramp in the snow, to say nothing of the evening chores that would come later.

Taking a long tramp over the farm was Grandpa's favorite way of spending a Christmas afternoon. Sort of a busman's holiday since he had spent a good part of the spring, summer, and fall walking over the farm, but this day he set aside to check up on his little animals, as he called all the furry creatures that made their homes up and down the river valley.

Chances were Lou and I had found some new red knitted mittens and sock caps under the Christmas tree that morning, so, donning these, coats, and galoshes, we accompanied Grandpa on the trip.

He was a stern taskmaster in the matter of local animal lore. You couldn't really get a good grasp on things, he maintained, unless you knew the life that went on about you in the fields and woods. "It'd be just like getting a new suit and never putting your hands in any of the pockets," he explained.

He spat in disgust when we confused the tracks of the possum with those of the coon and, I believe, he would have rapped us on the head had we mistaken the way the rabbit was going from his footprints in the snow.

So we came to look upon the little animals as a part of the farm and felt secretly rich and inordinately proud when we found the hollow-tree home of some smelly skunk or knew where the possum had a nest of young. "You know the possums are no bigger than a pinto bean when they're born, don't you?" Grandpa demanded, which was his way of telling us, and, although we didn't know, we never forgot thereafter.

We knew at what hour to find the muskrat sunning on his sycamore snag, tracked hundreds of rabbits to their briar patches, and even found the mud slide of an otter once.

Adding something tangible to our knowledge, like finding a quail nest or a fox den, was just like having a new possession, and we weren't above bragging about it at school and elsewhere and using it for trading timber. Once I had canceled a debt of twenty-five sheets of slick tablet paper I owed for showing someone a chipmunk's burrow.

We even felt proprietary towards old "P.B.," the terrapin, although it was our neighbor, Paul Britt, who had carved his initials on the shell long ago. But he was found mostly on our place, poking his inquisitive head up among the dewberry vines, giving us a terrible start, or resting under a May apple umbrella. Then maybe in less than a week we'd run across him in the bluebells, way over in the far meadow. Sometimes a year would go by before we'd hear from him, then one night at supper Grandpa would report, "Ran across old P.B. today." It was like hearing from an old friend. We were interested in his perambulations.

So, on such a Christmas Day, if we were blessed with snow, we might find the dainty handprints of the mink, the larger ones of the coon and possum, the triangular tracks of the rabbit, and the delicate embroidery stitches of the field mice.

"Un-huh," Grandpa would say, satisfactorily, when he came across them, and looking on, Lou and I had the feeling that all was going well. Running ahead to a smooth, snow-deep place in the meadow, we would lie flat on our backs, sweep our arms in semicircles, making "angel" tracks of our own, and wait to see what Grandpa would do when he came across them. "And this," he'd say in heavy reverence, "is where the angels slept last night!"

December twilight came on fast. At the hour of four we began to close the day. Long since the icicles had ceased to drip and begun to grow thick and lengthy again, making a pretty fringe at the barn's eaves and around the roof of the chickenhouse.

There is warmth and life in the barn. Shaggy-haired cows low gently at the sound of milk buckets rattling, and horses make soft throaty sounds through their velvet nostrils. Barn cats crouch close to some convenient mouse hole that leads to hidden rooms within rooms where beady-eyed creatures make noises with favorite old corncobs and leave intricate patterns on the dusty floor. Up in the cavernous region of the rafters are the mud daubers' labyrinthine homes, and woolly spiders hang their winter festoons across the gable windows.

The wind whistles around the corners, sifting snow about, and through it we see the lights from the kitchen where warmth and food await. For supper there are the dinner leftovers, plus the peach custard pudding. For this delectable dessert, Mama has put cookie crumbs in the bottom of the big corn-bread pan, poured on melted butter, and arranged peach halves in symmetrical rows. This is all buried under a cream custard and topped with nubby meringue, browned to golden perfection in the oven, and served generously in the gold-rimmed glass dessert dishes.

After supper we will go over our presents again. Perhaps Uncle Hayden has sent us some new records for the gramaphone—"The Preacher and the Bear," or "Moonlight in Jungleland," and we play them over and over. Lou and I fondle our gifts, a big red ladybug that winds up and crawls across the floor, some doll dresses, a scrapbook Lillian has prepared for us, flannelette and serge to go into winter clothes, and the big, rare oranges we keep laying aside, saving the best for the last.

"Fill'er up again?" Dad asks, lifting the stove lid to one side and peering in.

Grandma yawns and reckons she's ready to turn in. We are not reluctant to follow suit for it has been a good day, and there is tomorrow and tomorrow and tomorrow.

COUNTY FAIR

MARY MARGARET MCBRIDE

Mary Margaret McBride was born in Paris, Missouri, and was graduated from the School of Journalism at the University of Missouri. She held various newspaper positions before she went into radio broadcasting in 1934. Her special show on WEAF and later on the NBC national network brought her pleasing personality into millions of American homes. She has received many awards, and the Governor of Missouri did her the special honor of proclaiming November 22, 1940, "Mary Margaret McBride Day."

Miss McBride is the author of many magazine articles and several books. We present here a chapter from her book of reminiscences entitled How Dear to My Heart.

I wore my best white dotted swiss with my pink sash and the pink hair bow to match when fair time came round.

I had a pass because my Papa was a fair director, and it's a wonder Anna Lois, Sallie Joe, Anna Mae and the other little girls I played with had anything at all to do with me during fair time, the way I was so stuck up about my pass. Even Mr. Brayton, who brought almost the first automobile to our town, a great red monster that you had to have veils

Reprinted from *How Dear to My Heart* by Mary Margaret McBride. By permission of the author.

and linen dusters to ride in, wasn't a fair director, probably because he had lately come to Paris from Illinois. I never thought of that and believed that Papa was more important even than the owner of a great red automobile! It was a wonderful thought, since I was inclined to be self-conscious about my social position from being born on a farm when most of my little friends were born in town! Those were the days when I bolstered up my pride by lording it over my Cousin Mary, who still lived in the country. To prove my superiority I would write letters to her thickly studded with French phrases picked out of the spelling book!

I went to our fair every day and all day as long as it lasted. It was every bit thrilling—first the pass, riding in grandly with Papa and nothing to pay, then the merry-go-round with its galloping horses, and finally the sody-pop, ice cold from the bottle, cotton candy, pink and white, taffy in greased paper, crackerjack and ice cream cones. Trash, my father called all that, and with an indescribable inflection designated as "fair people" the men who guarded the merry-go-round and the refreshment stands under the amphitheater. But in spite of him, to me those men were gods. The minute I got inside the fairgrounds I ran for the merry-go-round—that is, if I had a nickel. Then, if there was any money left after my ride on a prancing yellow steed, I bought first my bottle of sparkling sody-pop, then a balloon, a whip, or a realistic snake of paper that you could blow out at perfect strangers without it being considered rude, because anything went in fair time.

The boys were the ones who especially liked the whips, smart little affairs with green, red or yellow trimmings and sharp lashes on the end that hurt when somebody flicked at your legs and called "Oh, you kid."

It was hard to tell where these young hoodlums sprang from, I heard Papa tell Uncle Milt. Certainly they weren't from round about Paris. There was nothing to do about them, of course, since they had paid their admissions and were entitled to walk about the fairgrounds. If our old marshal caught them hitting at us girls, however, he was likely to give them a good chase but they always outran him. The attractions they liked were the hoochy-coochy dancer's tent and the booth where you threw balls and tried to hit a little grinning, kinky-headed colored boy who ducked when he saw a ball coming but always had great lumps on his head for weeks after the fair.

There were frenzied days in our neighborhood before our county fair opened each year. Show-offs were deplored but it was all right to show off at the fair! Not yourself, to be sure, but your beautiful cakes or light rolls or yellow butter.

Such a flutter! "I don't know what was the matter with that last batch of flour," you'd hear. Or—"My angel food fell flat as a pancake. Must be the stove. I've been telling John for years I can't make cakes in that oven, but he won't listen."

You seldom see such superb food as Floral Hall held on opening days of our fair. Emerald, ruby, topaz and amethyst jellies that had been strained through flour sacks and jelled in clear glass. Loaves of bread with delicate brown crusts, risen until they threatened to leave their pans from lightness. Rolls that were poems of fine-grained perfection, cakes—but the cakes deserve a whole paragraph to themselves since Monroe County undoubtedly held the champion cake bakers of the country—Miss Sade, Miss Kate and Miss Mame (Miss Mame was my aunt).

Auntie was famous for her delicate white layer with rich buttery chocolate icing. Also for a chocolate fruit cake made with coconut, dates, figs, angelica and almonds. How I used to scheme to be at her house when there was a cake pan to be licked! And sometimes she would let me bake a little cake for myself in a small tin she kept just for me.

Miss Sade was best at a luscious hickory nut interior with caramel topping and halves of hickory nuts set thick over it, but her black walnut with fig filling was something else to inspire an epic.

Miss Kate excelled at applesauce cake and I've heard tell that she used pork fat for part of the shortening, which upset some of our more conservative cooks, but little we children cared for that when we got a chance to taste the moist, spicy deliciousness coated deep in butter cream frosting, the secret of which went to the grave with Miss Kate.

I can see them now—angel food with thick cinnamon-colored fudge icing (that was Miss Ruby's); coconut piled six inches high on a dark devil's food crumbling with its own deliciousness; Miss Alice's pink lady cake, made with her famous raspberry preserves in the center, and a mystery to all how she kept it there, a squishy surprise like the liqueur in foreign chocolates.

It wasn't quite nice to admit you wanted to win. You had to pretend a sort of polite indifference even after the blue ribbon was pinned securely on your offering for all the world to see and marvel at. But the winner was her own best audience. I used to think that anybody who showed anything at the fair really went there just to look at his or her exhibit.

Rivalry ran so high that nobody cared to serve as judges in the Floral Hall. To avoid hard feelings somebody had the happy thought of bringing in men and women from a neighboring county, who wouldn't have to live afterwards among the defeated.

We children would press wistful noses against the glass cases and brag. "My Aunt Clara made it—see, it's got a red ribbon!"

"That's nothing. *My* aunt's cake got a blue ribbon and that's better than a red one," you'd hear another little boaster saying.

What I couldn't understand was the way the judges merely nibbled. I was sure that if *I* had been a judge I would have eaten and eaten until there wasn't a crumb left of any cake.

We had lots of animals at our fair—cows, pigs, mules and horses—kept in especially built stalls some distance from the amphitheater. I hardly ever went down there, though. I could see plenty of animals at home. That was Papa's province.

To Papa the fair meant two things—horses and people. Papa was a chunky, bowlegged little man with a bald spot on the top of his head, and brown twinkling eyes. Men, women and children alike loved him and he was never satisfied until he had shaken the hand of every farmer on the grounds. When he left me at the gate he would begin to circulate, chucking children under the chin, joking with the women, whom he admired extravagantly, talking horses with the men. In a way it was *his* fair—that is until the time he showed his stallion in the judging ring of the amphitheater and got a red ribbon. What a day that was!

Like many men of warm natures, Papa also had black moods when his Irish temper got beyond control. Then we all kept out of his way. He had a reckless streak, too, and horses were his passion. He could ride or handle, break or drive any of them. When he and Mama were first married he drove that pair of black trotting horses we had as fast as the wind. Mama met him first at the fair, and quite typically he was showing off, walking a plank on the top of the amphitheater to the applause of an admiring audience.

Mama fell in love with him there and then, though he was going with another girl at the time. "And she was crazy about him too," Mama always said when she told this story to us. "Suppose Papa had married Miss Alice, would we have been your children or his?" we'd ask Mama in puzzled tones and she would answer quickly, "Mine!"

Feeling as he did about horses, Papa held out for a long time against automobiles. Finally, however, he bought a second-hand car and had it delivered to the house. He wasn't at home when it came and so there was no chance for anything to be explained to him. When he got back, he stood in front of the automobile for a little while, looking. Then to the terrified astonishment of his family, he got into the driver's seat and remarking, "I know about machinery—I guess I can make this thing go!" put it into second and drove off.

Sometime later, after a tour of the countryside, he rattled back into the barnyard, still in second. He drove like that all his life—not in second literally, but casually, taking an interest in the landscape and leaning out the window to wave genially to friends, rather to the consternation of passengers who expected the worst and sometimes got it. The automobile never took the place of the horse in his affections, and we kept a horse long after we had no use for one.

Best of all the horses that he owned when I was a child Papa loved Lyle, a fine-looking black stallion and one of the meanest animals that ever lived. Mama was deathly afraid for us children to go near him. She said sometimes that she felt in her bones Lyle would bring Papa bad luck.

The day he showed Lyle, Papa started off for the fair full of confidence and pride. He simply knew that Lyle was the best of his kind in the county. When the time for judging came the whole family was in the amphitheater watching while Papa led Lyle out into the ring where the horses were shown. The judges went over all the stallions carefully. They made the owners parade them again and again. Finally they gave Lyle a red ribbon. I think that ribbon made Papa actually *see* red for he grabbed it off, threw it into the ring and stamped on it. Then he thumped out of the arena with Lyle gamboling after. Papa never showed a horse at the fair again and nobody ever dared mention the incident to him. But Mama and Tommy and I were so ashamed that we got into the surrey and went home with our dinner uneaten.

I cried a little, partly at the disgrace and partly because I had looked forward to sitting under the great oak tree on the fairgrounds and having the picnic dinner we'd brought in a shoebox from home—salmon and potato salad, boiled ham, dressed eggs, hazel nut cupcakes.

LITTLE BROWN JUG

This play-party song is found in many collections of ballads. Professor Belden states in his Ballads and Songs Collected by the Missouri Folk-Lore Society *that the tune was the work of R. A. Eastburn, and he had been told that one J. E. Winner was the author of the words. There are different versions of both words and music.*

> My wife and I lived all alone
> In a little log hut we called our own;
> She loved gin and I loved rum,
> I tell you what we had lots of fun.

Chorus:

> Ha, ha, ha, you and me,
> Little brown jug, don't I love thee!
> Ha ha, ha, you and me,
> Little brown jug, don't I love thee!

'Tis you who makes my friends my foes,
'Tis you who makes me wear old clothes.
Here you are, so near my nose,
So tip her up, and down she goes!

When I go toiling to my farm
I take little brown jug under my arm;
Place it under a shady tree—
Little brown jug, 'tis you and me!

If all the folks in Adam's race
Were gathered together in one place,
Then I'd prepare to shed a tear
Before I'd part from you, my dear.

If I had a cow that gave such milk
I'd clothe her in the finest silk,
I'd feed her on the choicest hay
And milk her forty times a day.

The rose is red, my nose is too,
The violet blue, and so are you;
And yet I guess, before I stop,
We'd better take another drop.

RIVERS

JOURNEY UP THE MISSOURI

H. M. BRACKENRIDGE

Henry Marie Brackenridge was born in Pittsburgh, Pennsylvania, in 1786, the son of Hugh Henry Brackenridge, pioneer jurist and politician, and author of a once famous picaresque and satirical novel entitled Modern Chivalry. *Young Henry was sent out to a school at Ste. Genevieve, in "Upper Louisiana," when he was seven years old to receive special instruction in French, though he later found more use for his Spanish.*

H. M. Brackenridge became a lawyer, traveler, and writer. He practiced law for a short time in St. Louis, and there became acquainted with Manuel Lisa, chief owner and director of the Missouri Fur Company. Lisa was in charge of the expedition the beginning of which is described in the following narrative. This particular venture of Manuel Lisa's happened to be in competition in its early phases with an Astor (Columbian) Fur Company expedition which started up the river in four boats a few days ahead of Lisa's one-boat operation. When the two groups reached the Sioux country at the same time, Brackenridge had all he could do to prevent a duel between Lisa and Wilson Price Hunt, the captain of the Astorians; but eventually all went on up the river to the Mandan country amicably. There Lisa traded horses he had obtained on an earlier visit from his Indian friends for boats, and the Astorians set off across country for the West. A little later, Brackenridge returned to St. Louis in charge of two boatloads of valuable beaver pelts.

The account presented here is taken from Brackenridge's Journal of a Voyage Up the River Missouri, Performed in 1811, *which is an 1816 reprint of part of a work published two years earlier entitled* Views of Louisiana, Together With a Journal of a Voyage Up the Missouri River.

In later years, Brackenridge served the federal government in various capacities and devoted much of his time to writing. His best known book is Recollections of Persons and Places in the West *(1834).*

With respect to myself, I must own to the reader, that I had no other motive for undertaking a tour of several thousand miles, through regions but seldom marked even by the wandering footsteps of the savage, than what he will term an idle curiosity: and I must confess that I might have employed my time more beneficially to myself, and more usefully to the community. Would that I were able to make some amends, by describing the many interesting objects which I witnessed, in such a manner, as to enable the reader to participate in the agreeable parts of my peregrinations.

We set off from the village of St. Charles, on Tuesday, the 2d of April, 1811, with delightful weather. The flood of March, which immediately succeeds the breaking up of the ice, had begun to subside, yet the water was still high. Our barge was the best that ever ascended this river, and manned with twenty stout oars-men. Mr. Lisa, who had been a sea-captain, took much pains in rigging his boat with a good mast, and main and top-sail; these being great helps in the navigation of this river. Our equipage is chiefly composed of young men, though several have already made a voyage to the upper Missouri, of which they are exceedingly proud, and on that account claim a kind of precedence over the rest of the crew. We are in all, twenty-five men, and completely prepared for defence. There is, besides, a swivel on the bow of the boat, which, in case of attack, would make a formidable appearance; we have also two brass blunderbusses in the cabin, one over my berth, and the other over that of Mr. Lisa. These precautions were absolutely necessary from the hostility of the Sioux bands, who, of late had committed several murders and robberies on the whites, and manifested such a disposition that it was believed impossible for us to pass through their country. The greater part of the merchandise, which consisted of strouding, blankets, lead, tobacco, knives, guns, beads, &c., was concealed in a false cabin, ingeniously contrived for the purpose; in this way presenting as little as possible to tempt the savages. But we hoped, that as this was not the season for the wandering tribes to come on the river, the autumn being the usual time, we might pass by unnoticed. Mr. Wilson P. Hunt had set off with a large party about twenty-three days before us, on his way to the Columbia. We anxiously hoped to overtake him before he entered the Sioux nation; for this purpose it was resolved to strain every nerve, as upon it, in a great measure depended the safety of our voyage.

Having proceeded a few miles above St. Charles, we put to shore, some of our men still remaining at the village. It is exceedingly difficult to make a start on these voyages, from the reluctance of the men to terminate the frolic with their friends, which usually precedes their departure. They set in to drinking and carousing, and it is impossible to collect them on board. Sometimes they make their carousals at the expense of the Bourgeois: they are credited by the tavern keeper, who knows that their employer will be compelled to pay, to prevent the delay of the voyage. Many vexatious abuses are practised in these cases. It was found impossible to proceed any farther this evening—the men in high glee from the liquor they had drank before starting: they were therefore permitted to take their swing.

We had on board a Frenchman named Charboneau, with his wife, an Indian woman of the Snake nation, both of whom had accompanied Lewis and Clark to the Pacific, and were of great service. The woman, a good creature, of a mild and gentle disposition, greatly attached to the whites, whose manners and dress she tries to imitate, but she had become sickly, and longed to revisit her native country; her husband, also, who had spent many years among the Indians, had become weary of a civilized life. So true it is, that the attachment to the savage state, or the state of nature (with which appellation it has commonly been dignified), is much stronger than to that of civilization, with all its comforts, its refinements, and its security.

The next day, about two o'clock in the afternoon, having at length succeeded in getting all hands on board, we proceeded on our voyage. Found an excessive current, augmented by the state of the waters. Having come about six miles encamped. In the course of this evening had as much cause to admire the dexterity of our Canadians and Creoles, as I had before to condemn their frivolity. I believe an American could not be brought to support with patience the fatiguing labors and submission which these men endure. At this season, when the water is exceedingly cold, they leap in without a moment's hesitation. Their food consists of lied corn homony for breakfast, a slice of fat pork and biscuit for dinner, and a pot of mush, with a pound of tallow in it, for supper. Yet this is better than the common fare; but we were about to make an extraordinary voyage, and the additional expense was not regarded.

During the night we were completely drenched with the rain; the bark itself in a bad condition in the morning. Weather somewhat cloudy —clearing up. A short distance from our encampment, the hills approach the river N. E. side; they are not high, but rocky, and do not continue more than a mile, when the alluvion again commences. About eight a fine breeze S. E. sailed until twelve—passed several plantations S. W. side. The bottoms are very extensive on the lower part of this river, the banks high, far above the reach of inundation. Timber, principally cotton wood; a few of the trees intermixed with it are beginning to vegetate. The red-bud, the tree which blooms earliest in our woods, and so much admired by those who descend the Ohio, early in the spring, appear, in a few places. Passed an island, where the river widens considerably; the current rapid, obliged to abandon oars and poles, and take the towing line. Above the island the bluffs again approach the river; there is a brownish colored rock, with a few dwarf cedars growing on the top and in the clefts. In going too near the shore, we had the misfortune to have our top-mast broken by the projecting limb of a tree. Encamped some distance above.

This evening one of the most serene and beautiful I ever beheld, and the calmness of the water in unison with the cloudless sky. Several deer, which I descried at a great distance, stepping through the shoals which separated the smooth sand bars, seemed to move across this stilly scene,

like the shadows of the phantasmagoria, or Ossian's deer made of mist.
I now felt that we had entered on our voyage in earnest. He that has
not experienced something of these solitary voyages, far removed from
the haunts of civilization, can scarcely imagine the heaviness which at
the moment of departure weighs upon the heart. We all looked serious.
I could see that some of our poor fellows heaved a sigh at the prospect
before them, and at the recollection of the pleasant homes which they
had left behind in the hopes of gaining a little money; perhaps to support a wife and children. A fire was kindled on the bank, the pot of
mush and homony were prepared: and after their frugal repast, wrap-
ping themselves up in their buffaloe robes and blankets, they soon forgot their woes in sleep.—I observed on the sand bars, a kind of scaffold,
ten or fifteen feet in height, which I was informed was erected by the
neighbouring settlers for the purpose of shooting the deer by moonlight; these usually come out of the thickets at this time, to avoid the
moschetoes and to sport on the smooth beach: the hunter ascends the
scaffold, and remains until the deer approaches. Came this day about
twenty miles; navigation comparatively easy.

  Friday 5th. Wind S. E. this morning, enabling us to set off under sail
—continued until ten, when it forsook us. Passed several plantations,
and two islands. The bluffs disappear on the N. E. side, and are seen
on the S. W. for the first time since our leaving St. Charles. They rise
about two hundred feet, and are faced with rock, in masses separated
by soil and vegetation. These are called the *Tavern rocks,* from the circumstance of a cave in one of them affording a stopping place for voy-
agers ascending, or on returning to their homes after a long absence.
The Indians seem to have had some veneration for the spot, as it is
tolerably well scratched over with their rude attempts at representing
birds and beasts. From this place, through a *long reach,* or straight part
of the river, we have a distant view of the terminating bluffs N. E. side.
A violent storm of rain, wind, and thunder, compelled us to put to
shore, having passed a very dangerous and difficult place. The number
of trees which had lately fallen into the river, and the danger to be
apprehended from others, which seemed to have but a slender hold,
rendered our situation extremely disagreeable. Towards evening a canoe
with six or seven men passed on the other side, but we were unable
to distinguish them. At this place I measured a cotton-wood tree, which
was thirty-six inches in circumference; they grow larger on the lower
parts of this river than perhaps any where else in America. The bluffs,
in the course of this day appeared higher, but not so abrupt or rocky.

  Saturday 6th. Having passed a small willow island, we found ourselves beyond the hills on the S. W. side. At 11 o'clock the wind became
so high that we were compelled to stop, as it blew directly down the

river. This is Boon's settlement—about sixty miles from St. Charles. A number of plantations at the edge of the bottom. [This was the settlement known as the Femme Osage, made by the sons and several friends of Daniel Boone, upon land granted to the latter (1795) by the Spanish governor, Don Trudeau. The plantations extended for several miles along the Femme Osage Creek.] The wind abated in the evening, we proceeded a few miles further and encamped.

Sunday 7th. Water rising. Crossed to the S. W. side, and encountered a very swift current, at the head of a willow island. The difficulty of this navigation is not easily described. Made Point Labadie, so called from a French trader, who formerly wintered here. Forty years ago this was thought a distant point on the Missouri, at present there are tolerable plantations every where through the bottom. The carcasses of several drowned buffaloes passed by us; it is said that an unusual number of them have been drowned this year—some have been seen floating on the river at St. Louis. Upwards of forty were counted on the head of an island, by a gentleman who lately descended the river from Fort Osage. In the spring of the year great numbers of these animals perish in attempting to pass the river on the ice, which at this season is easily broken. Immediately below the Point Labadie the river contracts its breadth, and is confined to a channel of three or four hundred yards wide. Passed between an island and the main shore; a very narrow channel, but the current and distance less. A channel of this sort is often taken in preference, and it is one of the means facilitating the ascending of this uncommonly rapid river: but there is sometimes danger of the upper end being closed with logs and billets of wood matted together, as it turned out in the present instance; fortunately for us after the labor of an hour we were able to remove the obstacles, else we should have been compelled to return. Opposite the head of the island there is a tolerable loghouse, and some land cleared; the tenant, a new-comer, with a wife and six children, had nothing to give or sell. Here the banks fall in very much: the river more than a mile wide. A great impediment in opening lands on this river is the dilapidation of the banks, which immediately ensue when the trees are cut away, from the current acting upon a soil of a texture so extremely loose. It will be found absolutely necessary to leave the trees standing on the borders of the river. The river exceedingly crooked in the course of this day. A number of plantations on both sides. These usually consist of a few acres cleared, on the borders of the river, with a small log hut or cabin, and stables for horses, &c. They raise a little Indian corn, pumpions, potatoes, and a few vegetables. But they have abundance of hogs and horned cattle. Having made about fourteen miles, we put to shore, after passing a very difficult *embarras.* This word requires some explanation. Independently of the current of that vast volume of water rolling with great impetuosity, the navigation is obstructed by various other impediments. At the distance of every mile or two, and frequently at smaller intervals, there are *embarras,* or rafts, formed by the collection of trees closely matted, and extending from twenty to thirty yards. The current vexed by these interruptions, rushes round them with great violence and force. We may now judge what a boat encounters in grappling round these rafts. When the oars and grappling hooks were found insufficient, the towing line was usually resorted to with success. There is not only difficulty here, but considerable danger, in case the boat should swing round. In bends where the banks fall in, as in the Mississippi, trees lie for some distance out in the river. In doubling points, in passing sawyers, difficulties are encountered. The water is generally too deep to admit of poling; it would be absolutely impossible to stem the current further out than a few yards; the boat usually passes about this distance from the bank. Where the bank has not been washed steep, which is most usually the case, and the ground newly formed, the young tree, of the willow, cotton-wood, &c., which overhang the stream, afford much assistance in pulling the boat along with the hands.

Monday 8th. The water fell last night as much as it had risen. About ten, came in sight of a little village N. E. side called Charette. There are about thirty families here, who hunt, and raise a little corn. A very long island lies in the bend in which this village is situated. About this island, passed under a gentle breeze, some very handsome bluffs, S. W. side to the *isle aux Boeufs;* they are about one hundred feet high, and excepting a few places where rocks appear, covered with oak and other timber. At this place the river makes a considerable bend. Instead of taking the main channel, we entered a small one between the island and the shore, which will shorten the distance; the current not so strong. The channel is about fifty yards wide, and very handsome, having clean even banks, and resembling a small river. It is about four miles in length.

Through all these islands, and on the Missouri bottoms, there are great quantities of rushes, commonly called scrub grass. They grow four or five feet high, and so close, as to render it very disagreeable, as well as difficult, to pass through the woods. The cattle feed upon them in the winter, answering the same purpose as the cane on the Mississippi.

At the upper end of the *isle aux Boeufs,* we were compelled about five o'clock in the evening to put to shore, on account of a violent storm, which continued until after dark. In the badly constructed cabin of our boat, we were wet to the skin: the men were better off in their tents, made by a blanket stretched over twigs.

We have been accompanied for these two days past, by a man and two lads; ascending in a canoe. This evening they encamped close by us, placing the canoe under cover of our boat. Unsheltered, except by the trees on the bank, and a ragged quilt drawn over a couple of forks, they abode the "pelting of the pitiless storm," with apparent indifference. These people are well dressed in handsome home-made cotton cloth. The man seemed to possess no small share of pride and self importance, which, as I afterwards discovered, arose from his being a captain of militia. He borrowed a kettle from us, and gave it to one of his boys. When we were about to sit down to supper he retired, but returned when it was over; when asked, why he had not staid to do us the honor of supping with us; "I thank you gentlemen," said he, licking his lips with satisfaction, "I have just been eating an excellent supper." He had scarcely spoken, when the patron came to inform Mr. Lisa, the boys were begging him for a biscuit, as they had eaten nothing for two days! our visitant was somewhat disconcerted, but passed it off with "poh! I'm sure they can't be suffering!"

He resides on the Gasconade; his was the second family which settled in that quarter about three years ago. He has at present about two hundred and fifty men on his muster roll. We were entertained by him with a long story of his having pursued some Pottawatomies, who had committed robberies on the settlements some time last summer; he made a narrow escape, the Indians having attacked his party in the night time, and killed four of his men after a desperate resistance. The captain had on board a barrel of whiskey to set up tavern with, a bag of cotton for his wife to spin, and a couple of kittens, for the purpose of augmenting his family: these kept up such *doleful serenades* during the night that I was scarcely able to close my eyes.

STEAMBOATS AT HANNIBAL

MARK TWAIN

Missouri's leading contribution to American literature, one is always proud to note, is Mark Twain.

Samuel Langhorne Clemens was born in Florida, Missouri, and reared in Hannibal, on the Mississippi—the great river that was so important in his early life and figured so largely in some of his best books. Hannibal was the setting of Tom Sawyer *and of the early chapters of* Huckleberry Finn.

Our selection from Mark Twain appeared first in the Atlantic

Monthly *in 1875, in a series entitled "Old Times on the Mississippi," and nine years later was included (with some changes) in the volume* Life on the Mississippi.

When I was a boy, there was but one permanent ambition among my comrades in our village* on the west bank of the Mississippi River. That was, to be a steamboatman. We had transient ambitions of other sorts, but they were only transient. When a circus came and went, it left us all burning to become clowns; the first negro minstrel show that ever came to our section left us all suffering to try that kind of life; now and then we had a hope that, if we lived and were good, God would permit us to be pirates. These ambitions faded out, each in its turn; but the ambition to be a steamboatman always remained.

Once a day a cheap, gaudy packet arrived upward from St. Louis, and another downward from Keokuk. Before these events, the day was glorious with expectancy; after them, the day was a dead and empty thing. Not only the boys, but the whole village, felt this. After all these years I can picture that old time to myself now, just as it was then: the white town drowsing in the sunshine of a summer's morning; the streets empty, or pretty nearly so; one or two clerks sitting in front of the Water Street stores, with their splint-bottomed chairs tilted back against the walls, chins on breasts, hats slouched over their faces, asleep—with shingle-shavings enough around to show what broke them down; a sow and a litter of pigs loafing along the sidewalk, doing a good business in watermelon rinds and seeds; two or three lonely little freight piles scattered about the "levee"; a pile of "skids" on the slope of the stone-paved wharf, and the fragrant town drunkard asleep in the shadow of them; two or three wood flats at the head of the wharf, but nobody to listen to the peaceful lapping of the wavelets against them; the great Mississippi, the majestic, the magnificent Mississippi, rolling its mile-wide tide along, shining in the sun; the dense forest away on the other side; the "point" above the town, and the "point" below, bounding the river-glimpse and turning it into a sort of sea, and withal a very still and brilliant and lonely one. Presently a film of dark smoke appears above one of these remote "points"; instantly a negro drayman, famous for his quick eye and prodigious voice, lifts up the cry, "S-t-e-a-m-boat a-comin'!" and the scene changes! The town drunkard stirs, the clerks wake up, a furious clatter of drays follows, every house and store pours out a human contribution, and all in a twinkling the dead town is alive and moving. Drays, carts, men, boys, all go hurrying from many quarters to a common center, the wharf.

* Hannibal, Missouri.

Assembled there, the people fasten their eyes upon the coming boat as upon a wonder they are seeing for the first time. And the boat *is* rather a handsome sight, too. She is long and sharp and trim and pretty; she has two tall, fancy-topped chimneys, with a gilded device of some kind swung between them; a fanciful pilot-house, all glass and "gingerbread," perched on top of the "texas" deck behind them; the paddle-boxes are gorgeous with a picture or with gilded rays above the boat's name; the boiler-deck, the hurricane-deck, and the texas deck are fenced and ornamented with clean white railings; there is a flag gallantly flying from the jack-staff; the furnace doors are open and the fires glaring bravely; the upper decks are black with passengers; the captain stands by the big bell, calm, imposing, the envy of all; great volumes of the blackest smoke are rolling and tumbling out of the chimneys—a husbanded grandeur created with a bit of pitch-pine just before arriving at a town; the crew are grouped on the forecastle; the broad stage is run far out over the port bow, and an envied deck-hand stands picturesquely on the end of it with a coil of rope in his hand; the pent steam is screaming through the gauge-cocks; the captain lifts his hand, a bell rings, the wheels stop; then they turn back, churning the water to foam, and the steamer is at rest.

Then such a scramble as there is to get aboard, and to get ashore, and to take in freight and to discharge freight, all at one and the same time; and such a yelling and cursing as the mates facilitate it all with! Ten minutes later the steamer is under way again, with no flag on the jack-staff and no black smoke issuing from the chimneys. After ten more minutes the town is dead again, and the town drunkard asleep by the skids once more.

My father was a justice of the peace, and I supposed he possessed the power of life and death over all men, and could hang anybody that offended him. This was distinction enough for me as a general thing; but the desire to be a steamboatman kept intruding, nevertheless. I first wanted to be a cabin-boy, so that I could come out with a white apron on and shake a table-cloth over the side, where all my old comrades could see me; later I thought I would rather be the deck-hand who stood on the end of the stage-plank with the coil of rope in his hand, because he was particularly conspicuous. But these were only day-dreams—they were too heavenly to be contemplated as real possibilities.

By and by one of our boys went away. He was not heard of for a long time. At last he turned up as apprentice engineer or "striker" on a steamboat. This thing shook the bottom out of all my Sunday-school teachings. That boy had been notoriously worldly, and I just the reverse; yet he was exalted to this eminence, and I left in obscurity and misery. There was nothing generous about this fellow in his greatness. He would always manage to have a rusty bolt to scrub while his boat tarried at our town, and he would sit on the inside guard and scrub it, where we all could see him and envy him and loathe him. And whenever his boat was laid up he would come home and swell around the town in his blackest and greasiest clothes, so that nobody could help remembering that he was a steamboatman; and he used all sorts of steamboat technicalities in his talk, as if he were so used to them that he forgot common people could not understand them. He would speak of the "labboard" side of a horse in an easy, natural way that would make one wish he was dead. And he was always talking about "St. Looy" like an old citizen; he would refer casually to occasions when he was "coming down Fourth Street," or when he was "passing by the Planter's House," or when there was a fire and he took a turn on the brakes of "the old Big Missouri"; and then he would go on and lie about how many towns the size of ours were burned down there that day. . . . This fellow had money, too, and hair-oil. Also an ignorant silver watch and a showy brass watch-chain. He wore a leather belt and used no suspenders. If ever a youth was cordially admired and hated by his comrades, this one was. No girl could withstand his charms. He "cut out" every boy in the village. When his boat blew up at last, it diffused a tranquil contentment among us such as we had not known for months. But when he came home the next week, alive, renowned, and appeared in church all battered up and bandaged, a shining hero, stared at and wondered over by everybody, it seemed to us that the partiality of Providence for an undeserving reptile had reached a point where it was open to criticism.

This creature's career could produce but one result, and it speedily followed. Boy after boy managed to get on the river. The minister's son became an engineer. The doctor's and the postmaster's sons became "mud clerks"; the wholesale liquor dealer's son became a barkeeper on a boat; four sons of the chief merchant, and two sons of the county judge, became pilots. Pilot was the grandest position of all. The pilot, even in those days of trivial wages, had a princely salary—from a hundred and fifty to two hundred and fifty dollars a month, and no board to pay. Two months of his wages would pay a preacher's salary for a year. Now some of us were left disconsolate. We could not get on the river—at least our parents would not let us.

So, by and by, I ran away. I said I would never come home again till I was a pilot and could come in glory. But somehow I could not manage it. I went meekly aboard a few of the boats that lay packed together like sardines at the long St. Louis wharf, and humbly inquired for the pilots, but got only a cold shoulder and short words from mates and clerks. I had to make the best of this sort of treatment for the time

being, but I had comforting day-dreams of a future when I should be
a great and honored pilot, with plenty of money, and could kill some
of these mates and clerks and pay for them.

THE BUTTING FIGHT

ROBERT A. HEREFORD

*Robert A. Hereford spent most of his life as a newspaperman and teach-
er in St. Louis. His one book, called* Old Man River, *was an informal,
slightly fictionalized biography of Captain Louis Rosché, a famous Mississippi River steamboat captain. Following is Chapter I of that book,
which was published in 1942.*

I crouched in my hiding place behind the wheat stacks in the
dark, dusty hold of the steamboat. I had found a spot as far away as
possible from the white square of daylight above me, the hatchway opening, and from the two flickering oil lanterns which sent weird, dancing
shadows.

Soon the square of light would fade, and I would know it was night.
Then the big engines would start, shaking the frame of the boat with
their throbbings. The mate would call, "All aboard, A-l-l a-b-o-a-r-d!";
the "nigger engine" would go "chug, chug, chug" as it spun the spool-
like capstan and wound the ropes hoisting the staging.

The deck hands would cast off the lines, and, while the roustabouts
yelled and the passengers cheered, the boat would back away from the
St. Louis levee, swing out into the channel of the Mississippi, and head
toward her destination.

And this time I would be aboard!

Often I had stood on the St. Louis levee, an excited youngster, and
watched that wonderful event—a steamboat departure. Each time I
would imagine that I was on the boat, a member of the crew. I had not
stopped at imagining, either. I kept pestering the gruff mates who did
the hiring, but it was not easy for a twelve-year-old to get a job on a
steamboat even if he was large for his age and boats were in need of
cabin boys and decksweeps.

It was 1864. The Civil War was in its final year, and, although

Vicksburg had fallen and the North was getting boats through to New Orleans, the river traffic was far from normal, and steamboat jobs were scarce.

The mates laughed at me as I stood before them asking for a job.

"Go on home to your mother, boy, and get weaned."

"We ain't hiring babies today."

"Here, you—cook—fix up a sugar-tit for the new hand."

While the crew guffawed at these remarks and I stood there with my cheeks very red, the mates said other things not fit for a twelve-year-old's ears.

So I had finally decided that the only way I could become a steamboatman—and later be a captain and wear one of those white silk caps and own my own boat, or maybe a pilot and sit up in the glass-enclosed pilot-house and steer big boats through the Mississippi's dangerous channels, or a mate and growl gruff orders out of the side of my mouth and watch the black roustabouts jump at my commands—was to stow away.

Here I was. Once the boat left the levee, I would find the mate and tell him what I'd done. He'd be mad, I knew, and curse me soundly and maybe beat me, but they wouldn't turn the boat back, and it would end with my working out my passage. So, early on this bright spring morning, I had watched my chance and slipped by the watchman to my hide-out in the hold.

I thought I had stowed away in a part of the hold that was fully loaded, but suddenly I heard the voices of the negro roustabouts growing louder, and I knew they were approaching the hatchway opening. They were singing at their work, their rhymed songs that they made up as they went along, and, even though I was afraid that they might find my hiding place, I was enjoying their singing.

"Willie had a gal in New O'leans," boomed a big bass.

"A high yaller gal, and in her teens," answered a piping tenor.

"Had prettiest little shape you ever seen."

"But Willie didn't have no money in his jeans."

"And she ran away with a man of means."

"Now Willie ain't got a gal no mo', it seems."

There was a roar of yells from the roustabout gang over this ending line, and the boat fairly shook as all the blacks joined in the chorus:

"Now Willie ain't got a gal no mo', it seems."

The hatchway opening suddenly went dark. Peeping from behind a sack of wheat, I saw a giant black man coming down the hold ladder. I had never seen a man so big. I smelled the heavy odor of sweat and became weak and sick at my stomach. I had been crouching in my hiding place for nearly twelve hours and hadn't had any breakfast or lunch.

The Negro wore a soiled blue shirt, the sleeves cut off short and the neck open. His trousers, made of a rough cloth, were held up by a piece of twine which served as a belt not too dependable in appearance. The toes of his huge feet showed through a pair of ancient shoes. He balanced a heavy sack of wheat on his right shoulder, handling it as easily as though the sack were filled with feathers.

Behind him came a second Negro, a fat roly-poly man whose skin was as black as the unlighted corners of the hold. He had a kind face that seemed to be set in a constant smile. I liked him right away.

The big black dropped his sack of wheat to the floor with a thump, and a cloud of dust arose. I felt the sneeze coming and I was frantic, for I couldn't do anything about it. I clapped my hand to my nose, but it came like a muffled explosion.

"Who back thar?" It was the booming voice of the giant. I recognized it as the bass of the roustabout singing.

"Reckon hit's a rat." It was the piping tenor.

"G'wan, Snowball. Rats don't sneeze. I gwine see what it is."

I was trembling all over, and I guess my teeth were chattering too as the black giant walked straight toward where I was crouching. I went weak with fright as I looked upward and saw that his eyes seemed to be shining at me in the dark like the eyes of a cat.

The big black man walked straight up to me, clamped a huge hand around my neck, and lifted me struggling into the air as though I were a rabbit he was getting ready to kill. I could see he was grinning, a horrible grin.

" 'Tain't a rat, Snowball. Hit's a mouse, a sneaking white river mouse, what was trying to hide away in de wheat."

He tightened his hold on my neck until I had to gasp to get my breath and dragged me up the hatchway to the main deck. My heart stood still as he grabbed me by the seat of my trousers with his free hand and swung me back and forth over the bullrail as though he were getting ready to toss me into the water. The shore was only fifteen or twenty feet away, but I couldn't swim a stroke.

"Le's see can a white mouse swim," the big fellow said.

"No, no, I can't swim! I'll drown sure!" I gasped out.

I noticed that the fat Negro, who had been called Snowball, had lost his smile for the first time. "Big Jake," he said, and his words were sweet music, "you let that white boy be. You should know better'n lay you' hand on a white man."

Big Jake scowled and walked over toward Snowball, dragging me with him. He was choking me, but it was a big relief to know that I wasn't going to be drowned right away and that I had a friend aboard.

"This hain't a white man. This is trash, just a little piece of white

trash. Besides we's in Missouri, a free state. You know dat General
Lyon done win St. Louis fo' de Yankees and free all de niggers. We's
good as white folks now."

Big Jake emphasized his remarks by tightening his hold on my neck.
I tried with all my might to break loose, but I was growing weaker
every second. My eyes felt as though they were going to pop right out
on the deck, and I guess they must have been getting glassy too.

I saw Snowball reach down swiftly, pick up a big stick of wood from
the fuel pile on the deck, and swing it sharply against the shins of Big
Jake. With a howl the giant Negro loosed his hold on me and grabbed
his injured shins. I guess that's what Snowball wanted, and he acted
just in time. In another moment I must have passed out.

Suddenly Big Jake, forgetting all about me, turned on Snowball. He
flexed the muscles of his arms until they stood out in bulges like knotted
ropes. Then he beat his hairy chest with his huge hands. I had once seen
a picture of a gorilla, and I thought of it now. Quickly I crawled behind
Snowball.

Big Jake's peculiar eyes seemed to be spitting fire. In a voice like a
bull he was bellowing, "Nigger, you just committed suicide. Dat's zactly
what you just done. Look at me, black boy! Look at me! I'm forty times
deadlier than the wildest jungle beast; I got rattlesnake poison in my
veins 'stead o' blood; my teeth is wolf fangs, and I eats my meat raw
and bloody. My grandfather on my mother's side was a cross between
an alligator and a crocodile; my great uncle was a rogue elephant; and all
de womans in my family are she panthers that eats fat babies for breakfast. And me, I'se de o-riginal, maneatin', sabre-tooth tiger, and I'se
gwine tear you limb from limb. My uncle was a billy goat, and my
grandpappy was a bull, and my pappy was a rocky cliff——"

Here I saw Big Jake suddenly shift his position so as to be squarely
in front of Snowball and lower his head as though he were a bull, about
to charge.

"Put yo' haid down, nigger. I'se gwine butt it wide—wide open," he
shouted.

I had now forgotten all about my aching neck and my recent danger.
I was going to see a butting fight. I had watched many bloody river
fights on the levee where the rough and rugged deckhands and roustabouts talked and fought violently, but I had never seen a butting fight.
By this time a crowd of roustabouts had gathered in a ring about Snowball and Big Jake and were shouting delightedly, "Buttin' fight, buttin'
fight!"

But I also noticed that the disturbance had attracted the attention of
the mate, a tall wiry man, whose nose was twisted as though it once
had been broken and then set crookedly. The mate grabbed a small axe

from its hook on one of the boat stanchions and waded through the crowd of Negroes. My interest in the feat of the mate was less than my disappointment that the butting fight was to be stopped.

The blacks melted away before the swinging axe. The mate faced Big Jake and Snowball, and he was scowling. "What the devil you think we are paying you niggers for? To break each other's bones? First thing you know one of you will get killed, and we're already shorthanded as it is."

"That's all right. If those boys have a difference to settle, let them fight it out."

I turned, as did the others, to see from whom the quiet authoritative voice was coming. The speaker was dressed like a swell, with a high hat, a coat with flowing tails, and a vest made of costly, bright material. His white linen shirt was spotless, and he carried a gold-headed cane.

He continued, "However, if there's going to be a butting fight, we'll conduct it properly and according to the rules."

"Yes, sir. As you say, sir," said the mate.

I suspected right away from the mate's way of acting that the well-dressed man must be one of the owners of the boat. A companion of the dandy turned to him and said, "You can't let that butting fight go on. The big fellow will kill the fat boy!"

The dandy reached in his pocket and opened his wallet, and I saw him take out a one-hundred-dollar bill.

"I'll just bet you this hundred, even, that the fat one wins. He may not look as strong, but I'll wager he's the smarter of the two. I favor brains over brawn in a fight any time."

The other man shrugged. "Well, you've got a bet," he said, "and I'll never win money easier. The fat one's brains won't do him any good spattered all over the deck."

I watched excitedly while the mate, acting as a referee, quickly made preparations for the butting fight. He first measured off ten paces on the deck. Then he obtained from a roustabout a piece of twine of the kind used for sewing up torn sacks, and, pulling a tobacco sack out of his pocket, he emptied it and tied it in the center of the string. Then he gave either end of the string to one of the roustabouts and directed them to stand at a point in the middle of the imaginary ten-pace line and on either side of it, so that the tobacco sack hung about waist high right over the line.

"I'll count five," said the mate. "At the count of five, you boys charge. Keep your hands behind your backs and aim at the sack with your heads."

I was trembling as I watched the two black men prepare for the fight, and it was not altogether with excitement. I wanted to see the fight go on, but I began to feel sorry for Snowball. I didn't have the dandy's confidence in him. I seemed still to feel Big Jake's fingers around my neck, and I knew how strong he was.

Big Jake's face wore a murderous scowl as he bent his great body over at the waist and tensed himself like a steel spring. His head looked as big as a tobacco barrel.

Snowball, smiling and seeming quite unafraid, was bent over, ten paces away. I wanted to shut out the sight I felt sure I was going to see, but I couldn't take my eyes away.

"One—two—three—four—*five!*" counted the mate, and, at the word "five," the bodies of the two Negroes seemed to hurtle through the air like stones from slings. I heard a sharp cracking sound like the report of an axe striking dry wood.

I scarcely could believe what my eyes saw. The deck seemed to shake as the body of Big Jake crashed onto it and lay there still, little streams of blood starting from his mouth and nose.

Snowball, standing erect, was still smiling. One of the roustabouts fetched a bucket of cold water and doused it on Big Jake, and several others grabbed Snowball and began slapping him on the back, shouting their congratulations.

The dandy who had bet on Snowball pocketed his hundred-dollar bill and another to match it, walked over to the smiling Snowball, and handed him a five-dollar bill.

"You earned it, boy," he said, "as I knew you would. Now tell me how you knocked that big man out. He's twice your size."

"Thank you, suh. Thank you, suh. Now bout'n that buttin' trick. I learned long time ago they was mo' ways than one o' usin' yo' haid. Ef ah'd a met dat nigger haid on he'd split my skull right in two. But I got him with the hard part of my haid—the top—on the soft part of hisn—the temple. I hit him a glancin' blow, ah guess yo' might say, and I reckon it sort of made him *indisposed.*"

Everybody laughed at Snowball's explanation of his success. Then, all at once, I saw that the dandy was looking at me.

"Well, young man," he said, "you seem to have been the cause of all this excitement. What have you to say for yourself?"

I was trembling, but I tried to hide it. I took a couple of deep breaths and managed to say, "I'm sorry, mister, but I didn't mean to do anything wrong. I stowed away because I wanted to get a job on the boat."

The dandy laughed, and I was relieved to see that he wasn't angry with me.

"Well, boy," he said, "you needn't be frightened. There's nothing wrong about wanting to work—although I never have been partial to work myself." Here he winked slyly at his companion.

He turned again toward me and looked at me for a long time until I began to get embarrassed.

"Well," he finally said, "maybe I do owe you something for this sporting entertainment. What's your name, young man?"

"Louis Rosché, sir. Folks generally call me Lou for short."

"Well, Lou, how old are you?"

I looked at the deck when I next answered. I couldn't look my questioner in the face, because I was lying. "Fourteen, going on fifteen, sir."

He gave me another one of those long searching looks. "Well, Lou," he said finally, "I don't think you're that old, but you are a fine, sturdily built lad, and you will be a big man someday. I notice you seem to be neat, too, although Big Jake has mussed you up a bit. You are not a bad-looking boy, either."

I guess I must have reddened at this, because he said, "Oh, there's no need to blush, Lou. Good looks are an asset to a man." Here I saw him wink at his companion again as he continued, "With that curly brown hair and those hazel eyes, I'll bet you'll be playing the very devil with the women before long."

"Now," he went on, "why anybody would be so eager for work that he'd stow away to get it is a complete mystery to me, but, if you're so hell-bent on getting a job on the river, maybe I can help you."

Here he turned to the mate. "Do you suppose you could use this fellow as a cabin boy or decksweep?" And I knew from his voice that he was not asking a question but was giving a command.

"Yes, sir, we could make a place for him, sir," said the mate.

The well-dressed man turned on his heel and walked away.

The mate fixed me with a none too friendly eye. "We're casting off at twelve, midnight, promptly," he said sourly. "If you really want a job, be here on time."

THE CURRENT RIVER

WARD DORRANCE

Ward Dorrance is Missouri born (of Southern lineage) and a graduate of the University of Missouri; he was a member of the French faculty of that institution for many years. Since his retirement from academic life he has lived in the East and in England.

Reprinted from *Three Ozark Streams* by Ward Dorrance. By permission of Martin Mayes. Copyright 1936 by Martin Mayes.

Dorrance is the author of many short stories of distinction. The vivid and sensitive sketch here offered first appeared in his book, Three Ozark Streams.

At its junction with Jack's Fork.

With clamor of wings and of confluent waters we wheel as the inflowing stream gives way, as the new river catches us turning us downstream to the right. Like the two travelers of the *Divina Commedia* we are moved from realm to realm in excitement so tense that the way of our transport is not clear.

Should we see no more of this river now, we should go saying: "It is powerful, it is swift!" The sound of these words has been drowned by these waters times without number and long ago. After the redmen the French said *La Rivière Courante;* after them the Spanish *Corrente;* the English *Current.* And on this day as then the water rings out on the rock its claim to the name.

The width, depth, and speed of the Current are fairly constant. It moves steadily and grandly, flanked by camel-backed mountains whose forests close down to the water in neatly drawn arcs. It seldom forks into separate passages, but turns rather along its whole breadth upon the rapids. To feel the boat settle into the long v-shaped approach, viscous, silent, eager; to paddle vigorously an instant along the inside bank where the water is sharp-toothed, hissing; to shoot down a lane of whitecaps (standing erect in the prow, my field of vision filled by the rush, by the foam of the broken river); this is to experience a moment of absolute and exquisite excitement—joy by which afterwards I may gauge the importance of much else.

After the little pools of the Black, the blue pools mirroring roses; after the jocular intimacy of the Fork, we are pleased at every turn by the grand scale of the Current. We have come down to a spot with a tempting name—Powder Mill. Suddenly, very suddenly, we cross a bar of mist lying, we know not why, across the water. Out of it, on the left, amethyst under its foam, tumbles a spring-stream. We can not know, but we are fairly sure that a god lies close, that shortly there is to come one of those moments which we shall have in mind at eighty, if at that age we are good enough to look back, regretting life.

Beyond this place we camp in a cove, looking back frequently as we pitch the tent, as we eat. Upstream sits the sugar-loaf hill which marks the valley of the spring-stream, the valley of the mist. On either side of the river, in one of those "stereoptican" intervals which play such tricks in the Ozarks, are rich woods. Now at dusk the bar of mist lies as we saw it, covering the breadth of the stream, dense along its center line, feathery at the edges. Now it widens, momentarily concealing a boat that comes through. Again it concentrates, throwing up plumes which the wind scatters, silver against the hill. Now it grows thicker still, uniting with the usual evening mist, until only the mountain's crest is visible. It can not be over a thousand feet high, yet now it seems an inaccessible peak remote and cold, a dark untrodden rim of the globe.

George has gone fishing. He sits under the mists, his weight in the back of the boat, the prow high out of the mirror of the water. He returns with a fat jack salmon. Walking to meet him I am surprised to find light streaming from over my shoulders. Behind me, above the serrated candle-flame shapes of the young sycamore leaves, a crescent moon is high.

At sunrise, starting the herons from the shore, we row back to the bar of mist where the coloured stream shoots out, chilling the air. Up its narrow valley, our feet in spray, we follow around two bends through frigid mists that all but veil the trunks of trees. Somewhere in the dimness (cleft obliquely by beams of light) there are scores of cardinals. Except for one which cuts through the mist between us they are unseen. But over the wild song of the stream they sing wildly, earnestly, as if in response to a leader's exhortation.

In this real *scala sancta* we feel that we should be on our knees. We are not wrong. Presently we stand before a holy of holies—a pool some hundred feet across. Beyond the hair-line where the water flowing from it crashes on the rock, it is gem-like, still. And this is what excites us most: it is purple!

Moving to the right of it (wordless, shoulder to shoulder as if for protection) we find that from this angle it is blue. Blue it is. That is its name: Blue Spring of the Current River. But our lips will never move to define that blue. It is the hue of poetry, the colour of music.

By now we have eyes for the bluff opposite us, reflected precisely in line, but with violets, roses, jades. Suddenly we draw back, withholding a cry. We stand at the foot of one cliff; yes, but at the crest also of another. Beneath, at our very feet, terrace on terrace, sinks a garden of tall plants, luxurious, motionless, perfect. There—under the sweet cold water—swim fish, dim in shadow, knife-like in light, chasing one another and suddenly still, turning where the sun runs down their flanks.

We turn away. It is not possible or necessary to stay long. This is the very ecstasy of poets and saints. If we could think, if we could find our tongues, we should likely wish to say: *"Non sum dignus, Domine!"*

And this enthusiasm blows like flame in wind until our horizon is aglow with this and kindred moments rekindled. Sonorous words—Latin, French, English, Italian—toll out in my skull. As when at some news the bell-ringer leaps on his rope giving at once to the swing of the bell the full measure of its arc, the great sounds crack about my ears, and with the strength of my first consciousness of them. *Super flumina Babylonis . . . Di lontano conobbi . . . This is that Lady Beauty in whose praise . . . Ton souvenir en moi luit comme un ostensoir . . .*

We leave, two chastened lads, eyes downcast, breath uncertain, as if we had just buried a friend—or rather, seen his resurrection.

Everywhere a fine gracious sweep to their lines as the hills fold to the water. Everywhere a lustiness, a plenitude of forest. Students of the French exploration of the Valley, of the American frontier of 1804, should come here, should sweep round these bends to find the full flavor of their matter, to see not what the explorers did, but how they felt.

We are in the country of great springs. Before many days we shall have seen the largest on this continent. In the meanwhile, the small springs which we find on every hand are charming enough. Like the rapids, they never fail to quicken our spirits.

Some are set back a distance from the shore, approached by criss-crossed paths worn like the ways of mice to a hole in the base-board.

Others tumble over high banks to the river. We hold back the boat, laughing as the water thuds into our bucket.

One we find flowing in fan shape from a terraced gravel bar. There are several basins, the largest lying between the gnarled toes of an oak. But one can make a new basin anywhere. The gravel is evidently a loose, uncertain roof. Everywhere there is a leafy sound of rising, running, flowing. If we should place our ears to the ground we might hear the pulsing of a heart.

We are surprised to hear that we are not far from Van Buren. The hill-folk do not often admit that we are close to any goal. The distance is invariably still great and dotted with dangers. Soon the village is in sight, sprawled beneath its green ranges. Dusk is pulling in. At this point the river is wide and fine. But this is Saturday. So near a town the banks are lined with outing parties. It would be useless to seek a camp site.

We put up therefore at an inn, and, dinner over, we step down to
the village square. However it may appear in impartial daylight, it is
charming in this summer dusk. A public library, but with too many dead
flies and cob-webs to raise hope. An Orpheum Theatre with "players
every Wednesday night"; but it was not last Wednesday or the one before when one might have seen them. Before the jail door we stop to
speak with a boy inside. He does not wish to talk of his reasons for taking up residence here. He has "just got into a little trouble." All in all
he seems "a better lad, if things went right, than most that sleep outside."

This morning we hurry out of town. We have been spoiled by the
river, by the high society of herons. We are shocked by the indecency
of decent clothing, offended by the proximity of people, by the lack of
privacy in a hamlet.

We come to a group of cabins kept for hunters and fishermen by
Leo Anderson. We stop, though we have not gone far, meaning to know
this man and to visit Big Spring, largest of the region.

From a Swedish father Anderson has kept a burr of his speech, a
friendly "Sorr?" which inclines all but the flinty-hearted in his favor.
Physically he has little of the Scandinavian, much of the Indian. He
is dark, slight, sinewy, slow, and deft—having lost, in his woodsman's
living, the habit of futile movement. It is his business to house and to
guide the men who come here from the city for bass and deer. He is
the best of the type, but we have met a few others like him.

These fellows are quiet and modest. They do not have to boast. From
the expression of their eye, from the timbre of their voice, from the
sense and sobriety of their occasional remark comes evidence enough of
their merit, of their simple, intuitive gentlemanliness. They are tactful
from their dealings with "office sportsmen." They are delicately, almost
tenderly patient, as must be those who train hounds, who handle boats,
who live on the strong haughty rivers. Their knowledge of nature (and
especially of human nature) has grown slowly, ring on ring, like the
heartwood of oak and ash. For their match, though they are sometimes
young, one must go to the old doctors, to the old priests.

From Anderson and his brother we learn of the habits of fish and
wild-cats. We hear of the snake-bird (the incredible *anhinga anhinga*)
and are told how many herons may be seen in the largest flocks. We
learn what is happening when the sky "clabbers over" and what the
"he-coon" of a district is. We are shown that the hillfolk have retained

for their dogs the names that are traditional in English packs: Drum and Ring, Lead, Muse, and Trailer. We hear enumerated localities of the Current River: Beaver Pond, Gun Bay, Coot's Chute, Ike's Root, and Coleman's Failure. Of these points the brothers discuss the navigation. At this shoal one of them takes to the right; the other believes the left is safer. Here there is a hidden stump, there a deceitful eddy. To them the surface of water is a legible page. As they talk we think of another Missourian who one day made a book called "Life on the Mississippi." He is not the least of Missourians and we are grateful to feel this degree closer to him.

The brothers are also collectors of Indian relics. They have acquired a store of information, with technical vocabulary surprising in these woods. We have marched down museum aisles and have turned away wearily, thinking the Indian very dull. Now, in the lamplight, with warmth of voices, crossing of glances, with passing about of individual relics, the subject takes on life. We are stirred to have from the hand of our host a stone ceremonial pipe, effigy of bird or gopher, with drill marks plain in the rock, with bowl still caked. We walk off to bed, willing to find in the air a tang of camp fires, the smell of drying hides, the yelp of mongrel puppies.

Education, we reflect, should be caught by contagion of enthusiasm, not conveyed by fact. We have sat to worse professors.

It is not always possible to combine in one morning the sublime and the horrid. Since breakfast, however, we have met them both. We have seen the Big Spring and the crowds which flock to it on Sunday. Honest labouring and mechanical folk, with others neither bourgeois nor workers nor hillmen—the riff-raff who have simply come to see. There are men in undershirts, women in pajamas, twitching their bodies over the dance floor of a "concession." There is a great tangle of guy ropes and tent poles; a changing of diapers; a tossing away of melon rinds. Of it all there is nothing which might not be done as happily on any vacant city lot, with the taller weeds cut down.

I am told that after this summer all this will change. The State will raze the "concession," forbid automobiles beyond a certain point, remove campers and their tents to an almost suitable distance.

This is heartening news. Yet I am glad to have seen things at their worst, to have witnessed the serene unquestioned triumph of Beauty over its opposite. Already over the rumour of the canaille, over the loathesome accents of the radio, I hear a song: "walk toward me, little brother, I am lovely. *Surge et veni!* I am immutable. I am strong!" Already through the crowd I see the spring-stream, see the magic blue which is terse as poetry, which has never failed to lift, to quicken. ("How did you know he was a god? Because the moment I looked at him I was satisfied.")

Picking a spot where no people are, we lean over the rock looking down into the bowl of the spring as it surges from beneath its cliff. It has been impatient in its subterranean ways. Upward it escapes with a last great sigh, in strong waves colourless at first, or leaden blue. At once it dashes over a moss-covered ledge (from which it takes the green hue) to a wider path strewn with rocks. Against these it leaps, white, silver, robin's egg blue, throwing up fingers of foam which fall back whispering over the roar. Immediately now it passes, beaded, into eddies blue and more blue until, after its climax of intensity, that colour trails out as tenuous, as delicate as mist, so that no one may say: "Here it ends."

I have been reared by Southerners to whom *State* meant helmeted goddess. Not able in my generation to worship quite what they adored, I have from them none the less a fund of loyalty to dispense. Their love I have received and kept in flame, though I have transferred it from the State politic to the State of hill-and-field. Now before me lies uncovered the very heart of that State, pulsing fiercely, but generous, but unsullied, but virginal, triumphantly virginal.

A man and his wife have come up behind us. The woman is chewing gum. Her companion drones (from a poster set up by the rangers): ". . . largest single spring in North America . . . maximum recorded flow . . . eight hundred million gallons . . ." (I am lovely, little brother, I am strong!)

Anderson came last night to sit by our fire until late, leaving us too excited for sleep. There was talk of hunting and trapping, of water-witching, of tie-drives and logging. Especially there was talk of treasure tales, with buck-skin maps, pine knots buried in significant positions, arrows scratched on walls. There is no cave, if one listens to some of the hillmen, in which Frenchman or Spaniard, Confederate or Yankee, or simple train robber, did not bury treasure.

A hermit of the vicinity was one day telling Anderson of the presence of gold in the Copper Mine Valley Cave:

"And Leo, I know right whar it's at."

"Why don't you go after it, Martin?"

"Leo, I jist kain't git round to it."

A bystander spoke up: "Leo, mebbe he *kain't* dig treasure!"

"What does he need beside pick and shovel—and more get-up than he'll ever have?"

"Wal, they'se folks that *kain't* dig treasure, I tell ye."

And he relates a tale of old Jake Hepburn, who came to the mouth of a cave hunting gold. At once the wind blew. The day grew dark. The earth beneath him trembled. Hepburn caught his mare and left, but, on reflection, he chose to see in the disturbance a natural phenomenon—just a plain, ordinary, everyday earthquake. He returned to the cave, but before he could dismount he was driven away in the same manner.

"Yessir, Leo, I reckon they'se folks that hadn't better go foolin' around with no treasure diggins."

This camp below Panther Cave is one of the choicest which have fallen to our lot. The tent stands on clean gravel behind a growth of willows. Opposite are two mountains, one scar-faced and precipitous; the other round-shouldered, wooded, with a clearing far up, where cattle graze, giving scale to the scene. To our right are the shoals and "Gun Bay,"an inlet between island and hill. The river, broad and lake-like, quiet, swift, is of a deeper jade than usual. In the last light of dusk it takes on the sheen of polished stone. A little yellow birch leaf falling is mirrored as accurately as the mountain itself. Undulations of the shore are marked with deep beds of willow herb. All is clean and park-like, but with a free, strong, authentic look which parks do not have. Over the spinning-song of the shoals comes the tenor of a spring on the opposite shore, clear, with a fragile, frosty clarity in the night.

"Critter trouble" is manifest in three forms. We have had "hog trouble," "cattle trouble"— now it is "dog trouble."

A great scurrying in the willows as we pitch this camp. Five hounds emerge, one blue-gray like a bird's egg; one salt-and-pepper; three black and tan. They are so lean that our fingers fit into the grooves between their ribs. Their rumps are raw as monkey's rumps, and along their backs (healed or yet raw) are ugly scars. As we stoop to pick up a tent-stake, an axe, all five scatter to cover. All five sit thwacking their tails in the leaves, ducking their heads from side to side, rolling their eyes so that they show the whites. All five creep forward again, fawning.

Tonight they lie circled darkly about us in view of the fire. Occasionally they rise, stalk restlessly about, and sink again to the noisy leaves. At moonrise, seeing them too near the supplies, I reach from my cot for a stone. A prompt scramble. At a distance on the whitened beach the five sit in a semi-circle watching me. From time to time one throws back his ears to bay—a sound in which there is the very quality, the grave wild beauty, of moonlight. From far away here and far away there come answering cries, like the chain of an Indian signal. Out of the "draws," the hollows, from the dark high ridges, comes a message riding the moonlight.

Today we are half angry, half amused and touched. The five are still with us. Every morsel of food must be kept from their reach. They are quick as light behind our backs. Yet how strike creatures with such eyes? How deal with bandits of love and of bacon?

At mealtime the smoke has not risen an inch from the fire when all have appeared to lie with front paws extended, with tails thumping furiously, throwing their red tongues about their chaps, making little anguished noises.

Bit by bit they advance, making much of a gentle rebuff; retreating hastily, but never quite to the original point; returning with the same hypocritical play (as an actor repeats a difficult entry) until their muzzles lie within sniffing range, eyes raised the while to see and dodge a blow. A bite thrown to them is met with a click which seems to precede the landing of the bite, as one sees the smoke of a gun before one hears the report. There is no visible effort of swallowing.

Having given the last morsel we can spare, seeing that even in the sight of dogs we are tourists succumbing to easy charm, we begin to deal out real blows. They are instantly forgiven. They may sicken us, but they are light in comparison with those which left the scars.

We should, as we know now, have made fresh wounds. We return from the beach this evening to find a strong smell of bacon about the tent. Nearly all our meat is gone, all our bread, every cracker, every egg. Presently arrives the hound which we have reason to suspect. He tries to swagger out of it, but under our glance his art breaks down. He is soundly whipped, and through the brush he crashes yelping, half a mile.

But it is we who are sick at heart, we who are guilty. We have struck a thing whose great eyes plead: "Give me a little food and a great deal of love. Let me make you a haven of affection. Let me light your way with adoration." And like all who prefer goods to love, we stand clutching our silver, ruefully considering the small currency of coin.

Because our beach faces east we are driven off by the sun soon after breakfast. We take to the boat, shivering a little as we meet the wind from over the water, and come to the spring at the foot of the mountain opposite. Here noon will pass before the cool of the night will yield.

This spring, below a steep forested drop, a little way back from the water's edge, has made a cavern into which a child might creep. Its roof is formed of the moss-covered loops of an elm root. Brilliant, cold, and sweet-smelling, its water ripples to the river, threading the wild roses, the equisetum, the cane with its bamboo look and its crushed satin sound.

From my chill green bay I look out at the hot bar across the river, at the willows with cardinals swaying on their tips. At my elbow, around and under my feet, the water flows, lighted by a slanting beam which picks out the pebbles, yellow, salmon, jade. Dragonflies play about me, bright as newly varnished toys. A hummingbird comes within reach of my fingers to drink.

In the willow herb of the spring's bay sits George in the white boat, fishing. He is motionless, but the line in the water is nervous. It hisses, it bends. It yields a bass, a brilliant sun-fish, a "goggle-eye."

A native comes up for a drink. On his way from home he has seen a mink, and, more important, a wild-cat. He was at the foot of Kelly's Holler, sharpening a pole for his boat. "I heared my old bitch hound a-barkin' and never paid her no heed till I looked up, and about as fur as from hyar to that rock, hyar come a bobcat a-scrunchin' along on its belly like a house cat. And me 'thout no kind of gun!" On his trot line this morning he found a twelve pound carp. "I thowed a sack over that feller and he nearly knocked me out of the boat." He is deeply interested in George's bait-casting. "Seems like I couldn't get no sport out of that, nohow!" "Well I'll be dawged," he exclaims at every catch, "I'd a thought in common sense he wouldn't kill nothin'!" He nods apprecia-tively at our story of "dog trouble." He has had vexations of his own. "These yur range cattle . . . people neglects to salt 'em, and if they gits on to yer camp they're liable to chaw up anything—a rope, a strap. Why them critturs 'd eat up a man's shirt fer salt!" Of his own this danger may have been real.

At Tucker Bay we camp where the river wrinkles off the shoals, where it spreads into a deep pool beneath the cliff. A spring stream enters at the bend.

Up this we paddle, seeing at once that we are dealing with no slug-gish bayou, with no ordinary spring. Partially dammed by gravel thrown up across its mouth by the river, this stream is wide and smartly moving. Paddle-and-arm length will not touch bottom. Moving up the channel between beds of cress we reach a wide pool of pure blue in which stands another of those miraculous gardens, with sun fish flashing orange and violet from among the antlers of the plants.

A native standing in a pathway along the bank motions us to shore. He is lean but well built, naked except for overalls, black-bearded, blue-eyed. He is pathetically hungry for talk. He wishes to know if we are acquainted with others who have come by in past years, leaving him their names. Especially do we know his landlord, a "tooth-dentist" in Saint Louis—a Mr. Green? He has forgot the "given name" but he will go home to ask his wife if we should like to know and if we promise not to go away.

He tells us that along the path in which he stands once ran a narrow-gauge railroad carrying logs from the hills to this point where the current could float them out. Here indeed was the unloading dock. Pointing to the blue pool he shows us far below a score of tremendous logs criss-crossed, graying, ghostly. These, he says, are a part of the last cutting—some thirty years ago.

Now that the ugly work of destroying the forests is over (at least on such grand scale) why are the Ozark logging days less romantic than those of the fur trade and the steamboat traffic? Does not the sudden cessation of this pioneer industry (replaced by no other) explain in part the homesick bewilderment of the hillmen in these modern times?

Less than fifty miles of river remain for us. We drift down in the shade of the hills, having little work to do because of the fulsome speed of the stream. A musical touch of the paddle keeps us straight. Before it is dipped again we have watched a turtle off a log, exclaimed to see a fish head and tail out of the water, pointed out a redstart, a chat.

We spend an afternoon at Coleman's Failure. Here, so the story runs, a man of that name—having spent the last of his money for a raft of timber to float to market—overturned on a snag and was drowned. Well might he strike a snag here and well might drown.

Tonight we are camped on a bar behind a loose screen of birch and of sycamore in whose branches are balls of the mistletoe which at Christmas yield green boatloads for the hillfolk. We lie under an arch of birch talking by moonlight. Now and then a fish slaps on the water with a sound to make one think, as the natives say, that a hog has fallen from the bank. Our own stringer of bass thrashes the shallows beside the moored boat. The catch was large today. Several pretty fellows were turned back—which was pleasing to me. It is fine to see the line cut to an arch, hissing, to see the fish fight his way to the boat inch by inch.

But once in sight he is so alive, so graceful of fin and tail, his eye is so round, his gills so red, he is so much a part of the foam in which he is brought to a stop, that I am always relieved to see him make off.

There are no shoals opposite us today. But the water is deep to our waists, flat as a floor and as smooth, smouldering with mist. In its quiet there is speed. To walk against it is difficult, to swim any distance impossible. This morning being very hot I wade out, gasping as the cold current takes hold of me, find a rock for a foot brace, and "sit down" against the water. With slight movements of my elbows to keep balance it is possible to remain so indefinitely. Throwing out my arms I make "angels" in the foam as I once made "snow angels" years ago. Another pleasure I had lost.

Below nearly every shoal, on the hard side of the current as it sweeps to the foot of its bluff, is found a bay. On this river there is enough movement in their water that they do not all resemble the sloughs or bayous of the Black. Some are wide at the mouth so that their breadth, joined to that of the stream proper, gives the look and the dignity of a lake. Others are tiny, so tiny that it is amusing to find that each has a name and that its lily-pads are numbered in the minds of the hill people.

The smallest of them merits its name. In their depths fish lurk. On the gravel of their shallows the young white herons love to wade. From the tangle of their foliage the gangling adults rise. From their sweet-gum and pawpaw comes a vast deal of fluted talk from the smaller birds. Moccasins striate the water. Behind a log a muskrat "plops."

We have come down what the fishermen call "mighty pretty water" —the most that Saxon manhood may risk before superlative beauty. We are camped tonight within sight and sound of Pig Ankle Shoal. There has been a shower. Dusk is sweet with the smell of wet bark. The frantic pennant of our flame is doubled in the water. Dripping leaves break the dark with refracted firelight as from the planes of a crystal cave wall. We look out on the night as from the center of a faceted stone.

This is the last time we sleep with you, Current River!

Goodnight! Tomorrow you turn the bend without us, leaving us still with questioning eyes. Until the day we die we shall ask: "What was its beauty after that? How was it, running to meet the Mississippi; merging with the Osage, the Missouri; joining the Fox, the Ohio; mingling with Cumberland and Illinois, and with the great Red River of the Arkansas? How did *La Rivière Courante,* did *Rio Corrente,* ring out among these names of home?

Goodnight, this ultimate time goodnight, green and amiable river!

Now we have heard silence over the halted oar. We have seen coloured birds cut singing through the mist and lilies bobbing where the water panted, lapping the elbow of a curve. We have walked where the stream laid a music on the hills. We have worked to the heart of the wood where the young birds learn their song, and have seen the river where it was young.

Are two men the same, having witnessed mystery together? When spring comes again and youth looks out from the shade, when the flame of redbud flushes the limestone ledges, if we meet will it not be as islanders on a mainland, each abashed, each mutely asking: "What of home? How go the mists? How go the waters, they the honey-coloured, they the jade, and the two of them keening over rock?"

To our surprise there is no sick regret. Seeds of gratitude and hope have been dropped for the first warm rain in our heart. These are not mean emotions. Will not our chins stay high all winter, our eyes alight? Will not men who have the right ears turn in the street hearing the ring of our heels behind them? Having reached the State Poetic need we fear the State Politic? Shall we not be the best of all possible citizens being ecstatic?

Today we pass under Doniphan Bridge, coming to our last landing place. Here is a pleasing collection of craft, a pretty bobbing and bumping of boats at the foot of the road which leads to town.

It is a pity that because of spring floods no settlement of this region dares to take advantage of its water front. What would not the tiniest hamlet of France, of Holland, of Italy, do with this chance. There would be a sturdy parapet, houses rising from the water's edge, the cat's back of a bridge, a quickening union of shore and river life. To be sure the Ozark town would not have the same kind of prettiness, but it would have its own kind, and even if it were ugly it would take on the look of an old elm scar which is part of the tree's attraction.

Doniphan is not without charm—a court house begun loosely in

French renaissance style (but completed in a way to escape charge of slavish emulation); a square from which slopes a main street of stores with high balconies slenderly propped. Here and in all such towns there lingers an acrid, but faintly agreeable, frontier smell.

We drive out over the hills with the *Wilma* swaying mournfully behind us on a trailer. She to whose side the fierce proud bass fought inch by inch; she who thrust her white nose to the spray, who sundered the mirrored clouds and like a wild goose entered the stillness of coves, she has lost her grace. She plunges like a frightened cow. She looks surprised and grieved. No less are we.

Tonight we shall have come back to Mountain View, our point of departure. At least we shall be resting in one of the most gracious of country inns, one of those exceptions in which the voice can not be lifted in praise too loud. Its name—the *Commercial*—is a quaint misfit. Nothing is farther removed from trade. The building is a collection of wings which come together in casual meeting as three people who step under a doorway during a shower—the whole somehow surmounted by a pepper-box tower. The style is unimportant. Under so much honeysuckle a Christopher Wren would show no finer shape.

Moreover it is of the hostess and her fare that we are thinking. We know that we shall be met by a quiet soft-voiced woman, one of those dear souls who is filled with satisfaction at the sight of hungry men eating, one who never in her life has been surprised at any hour without supply of cold chicken, biscuits, of butter still sweating beads of milk from the churn.

We shall be led along the bright rag-rugs of the corridor (over a floor as uneven as the stones of Saint Mark's) to a room in the tower. There, we know, will be the "hand-painted picture"—an American primitive overlooked by collectors. A stream which disappears suddenly in its own perspective (as if embarrassed by its role in the foreground), its rude flood arched by a gingerly bridge, like a "measuring worm." A row of trees receiving a curiously local shower from a cloud which the hasty might take for a block of ice.

There we shall lie in the moonlight, high in the honey-suckle tower. And as the village blades go home, stumbling, calling from group to group, we shall have time to think of how we came home to Mother Missouri, and of how she took in her two boys.

Now to get back while the spray is still wet upon us, and the charm! Now to rally those whose throats need help to carry the native tune. Now to get news of this to those who walked with us to the wharf, but did not sail!

LAZY RIVER HITS HARD

ELSTON ·J. MELTON

Elston J. Melton was born in Jefferson City in 1891. He has been a newspaperman virtually all his life, and for the last thirty-five years he has been editor and publisher of the Cooper County Record *at Boonville, Missouri. He is a past president of the Missouri Press Association.*

The following pages reproduce Chapter XX of his novel Towboat Pilot. *In 1960 he published a second novel,* Quick Darkness, *dealing realistically with a murder trial and hanging. It is interesting to note that Mr. Melton once studied at the Chicago Art Institute, and that his books are illustrated by his own pen drawings.*

Tom arrived at his new job the first week in November, aboard the *Major Louis,* which was the largest of its type on the Missouri. Its steel hull drew five feet of water. The river now was dead low, and between Council Bluffs and Gasconade ran six hundred miles of sprawling stream in no fixed channel.

Tom heard veteran pilots voice what Captain Young had said. "Desk men in the War Department don't understand. If they did they'd never send young Franklin out with her."

There was much activity aboard the *Major Louis.* Steel drums, chains, timbers, fuel—all things movable—were hauled to an attached barge, and for two days all hands kept an endless procession of wheelbarrows transferring coal. The boat's draft was lightened about six inches, but she still needed four and one-half feet of water. Many shoal crossings now were covered by less than four feet.

Captain and crew scanned the skies, hoping for a late fall rain, but the days remained clear and crisp, and weather reports printed in the *Nonpareil* said it was good hunting weather in the Rockies. Tom hoped the sign would hold no better along the continental divide than that night on the Gasconade when he and Johnny Sanders tried to sleep while the storm beat on the bottom of their upturned jo-boat.

With the Missouri still falling, the *Louis* steamed away from Council Bluffs, but she hadn't gone far when she grounded on a crossing. They laid lines and tugged and tugged, trying for hours to pull off. They backed, raced the engines, churning waves over the crossing; then with spars and long pulls on the lines they finally eased her over. Their calloused hands were blistered and their muscles ached, but it was good to be in deeper water again.

Captain Franklin was a tireless worker and he took no unnecessary chances. When two or more chutes appeared he sent Tom rowing ahead in a skiff to sound water, directing him with a whistle. If Tom found enough depth he raised an oar. If not, he pulled over to the mouth of the next chute.

On bad stretches Tom spent practically all day in the yawl. Sometimes he was a mile ahead when the *Louis* ran aground. Then he rowed back against a three-mile current to help all hands.

Time and again they stuck on the shallow crossings. Occasionally they were lucky and got off within an hour; but usually it took most of a morning or an afternoon, waiting while set spars held the hull in position to trap enough water to get her over with engines turning steam capstans and all hands tugging on the lines.

Night running was out of the question; at dark the crew turned in, shaky from exhaustion. Days in pale sunshine and breathing frosty air through the forced draft of exertion left Tom with no spare energy for study. He went to bed early and promptly sank into deep sleep, but by next morning he would be refreshed and would eagerly accept the challenge of the new day. In every bend, and often on straight stretches, they encountered new problems. Every few miles the boat buried her nose in sand or clay. Weeks dragged into a month, and still they were above Kansas City.

What first had been adventure now was tedious repetition and painful monotony. The fair, cool weather held, with hardly a break, and what little rain there was didn't reach the river; it was sucked down by the thirsty earth—sickly wheat in dusty bottoms had a bare chance of growing into winter pasture.

If there should come a long cold spell and freeze over the Missouri, the *Major Louis* could not reach Gasconade. Captain and crew redoubled their efforts at the thought. They forged on toward the bigger river, but gain in distance was offset by the stream's shrinkage from drought. They kept grounding, and getting free.

One afternoon they tied up alongside woods west of Waverly as a slate-gray sky and a slow drizzle brought darkness early, even for December.

Next morning Tom was first at breakfast, and finished while the others were still at the table. A bad stretch lay ahead, so he would set out at once with the yawl to plumb for the channel. He was thankful for heavy clothing, for the wind on deck was sharp, and mist had frozen during the night, leaving a thin coating of ice.

He made a round of inspection before starting for his skiff, which was tied to starboard. Near the head of the *Louis* he took a misstep that sent him sailing through space.

He shot out feet first, clear of the deck on the offshore side. His back struck the water flat. It stung through his woolens and the blow slapped the air out of his lungs.

He went under, but soon floundered to the surface, gasping from shock, cold, and lack of breath. In a river too low for safe navigation he was in depth enough to drown—and everybody else still at breakfast! With windows and doors closed against the weather, and with table clatter and conversation, nobody would hear his calls for help.

He sputtered and blinked as he was being swept past the *Louis*. He tried to swim back, but his heavy clothing prevented. It was only with effort he kept afloat.

A line drooped amidships of the barge. Maybe he could fight his way over to it as he was swept along.

His legs were becoming numb, almost useless, so he struck out the harder with his hands. The sagging rope was several feet beyond his finger tips, and he was moving downstream faster than toward it.

He rallied his failing strength, working his legs despite the feel of needles being driven into them and closer and closer he bobbed toward the hawser. It hung so low here that it dripped back from the waves he was churning up, but as he clawed at it, the greasy hemp began arching upward just out of reach. After several tries his outstretched hand took a firm grasp on the tightly bound strands. He was saved!

But the line began paying out. Loose! It hadn't been made fast. Sliding off into the water with a soft splash, it gave no more anchorage than a floating reed.

Now Tom would be joining Johnny Sanders beyond that other river. The thought was pleasant. But Johnny always had fought to the last, and Tom must strive on and on. He must live and become a pilot.

He thrust his fingertips into seams in the side of the barge, but the current was too strong for the slender hold. It washed him down again and again. He was nearing the end of the barge.

Some carriage boltheads protruded the least bit and he hooked the ends of his fingernails between them and the wood. The nails broke off, his fingers began bleeding.

It didn't matter. The cramps had left his legs, now dead of feeling. The numbness crept up his body, but his lungs were hot and raw. His mind seemed detached; he was not sharply aware of anything, not even of a voice crying, "Hold up a little longer; here's a line." A loop sailed toward Tom and he caught it. Captain Franklin was at its other end.

After a moment's rest Tom tried to raise his right leg to put it through the noose, but it wouldn't move. He tried the left. It was paralyzed, too.

Holding the line with raised left hand, he put his right forearm under the knees and tilted his body backward in the water. As his feet lifted to the surface he dropped them through the rope, then with both hands high he hoisted himself laboriously and wiggled farther into the loop until his body in the chill wind and his lifeless legs in the water were balanced.

Captain Franklin strained against Tom's weight and shouted for help. Nobody answered him. He yelled again. Tom felt the line slip. Captain Gerald called louder, waited. Then everybody seemed to get out at once. They hauled Tom up, put him on his feet, but his legs buckled. They caught him as he fell.

They carried him gingerly the length of the barge's slick deck, on to the *Louis* and up to his cabin, where they ripped off his clothing, chafed his benumbed legs, and put him to bed. They poured a pot of hot tea between his chattering teeth. Soon he got up and hobbled to the bath, where he lay for a long time in the hot water.

He got out feeling fine. In dry clothing again, he was back in the yawl alone two hours after he was rescued.

The *Louis* crept on down the river, feeling its way like a blind man. People waved gaily from bluffs in a mood reflecting what they thought was a carefree life aboard.

Only fishermen and squatters waved solemnly. They knew this constant struggle against heavy odds: the river and the wilderness of her islands, bluffs, and ravines. They knew lazy days in the sunshine, and rain lashing across skiffs miles from home while wind put white teeth on the gray surge of a mile-wide flood. They knew the ways of wild creatures in woods and waters; discipline from gaunt hunger; and of waiting quiet and cold in snowy duckblinds.

In houseboats and shanties of tar paper and tin, these people, removed from the main current of life, lived much like the pioneers who first used the river as the road to bring civilization into the wilderness. They were as free as the frontiersmen, and as self-reliant. Most of them had gathered their winter fuel—driftwood caught from the current or picked up ashore after a runout.

The *Louis* pushed on past Waverly and Miami, Arrow Rock and her historic tavern with a dinner bell that once was on a steamboat. They slipped by Glasgow and past the mouth of the sluggish Lamine River that flows from the rolling prairies of western Missouri.

They churned by mouths of creeks that had become sunken, leaf-strewn passageways through forests, with here and there a stagnant puddle. Small streams no longer fed the river or watered stock. Occasionally a farmer was seen driving a herd down the mud slopes from the Missouri's bank.

Through the swinging span of the railroad bridge at Boonville they gazed up at a town that now had stood on those hills for more than a century. Tom had learned some of its history that winter he had spent cooking on the *Manuel Lisa;* that it had been the first seat of government for the Boon's Lick Country in Indian times, and across the river and a few miles up the bottoms. Daniel Boone, while hunting had discovered a salt lick and built a cabin near by. He had made it head-quarters for several winters while hunting and trapping alone in the territory, and later his sons boiled salt there, which they rafted down to St. Louis.

While in Boonville Tom had learned that the first steamboat to ascend the Missouri, the *Independence,* had as its far west stop Franklin, just across the stream. Franklin! Its few brief years were brilliant. It was the biggest town between St. Louis and Santa Fe. Fact was, the Santa Fe Trail started originally from Franklin. Four future governors of Missouri lived in the town at the same time; while Kit Carson, destined to be a great scout, was a home-town boy apprenticed to a saddler there.

But Franklin, like the lost state for which it was named, was to vanish, washed away by the river's changing course after most of its business had moved to the high hills opposite. Pioneer steamboats arrived in increasing numbers, and Boonville became the outfitting point for the Santa Fe Trail that twisted for nearly a thousand miles from "civilization to sundown." The river had mothered travel to the West. The Santa Fe Trail was one of the great highways of the world, and from the old Boon's Lick trace between St. Charles and Franklin extended the Salt Lake and Oregon trails.

Throughout its history Boonville had produced many rivermen, and old-timers and scholars agreed that the stream had played a big part in the life of our country. The first battle of Boonville, on the bluffs east of town, was the first land battle of the Civil War. It clinched Missouri, a slave state, for the Union, and kept the river open to the West to enable all that territory to send gold, lead, wheat, cattle, and men to help the government in Washington keep the United States one nation.

The *Louis* passed Wooldridge, Lupus, and Sandy Hook villages. Often darkness caught the boat in the woods or open country and the crew tied in under the best point available. Backed by hard work, their luck held, along with the fair weather, and when they passed under the shining dome of the state capitol on a south bluff at Jefferson City, Tom felt they had about outmaneuvered the sullen stream's passive resistance.

Later, as they pulsed by the mouth of the Osage, he felt growing assurance. And a few days before Christmas they brought her shipshape into Gasconade after about seven weeks spent covering six hundred miles. The boat was laid up and the crew paid off. All hands shared with young Captain Franklin the exultation of victory that follows a hard battle. They had done the impossible.

THE OZARKS

THE CHAMPION

HAROLD BELL WRIGHT

The greatest best seller ever written about life in the Ozarks was Harold Bell Wright's The Shepherd of the Hills. *Wright was born in New York, and he came to the Ozarks seeking a cure in that region for a tubercular ailment. While there he became interested in the people around him and, like his own "Shepherd," began preaching in a schoolhouse and giving religious instruction. He later spent nearly twelve years in the ministry of the Church of the Disciples, occupying pulpits successively in Pierce City, Lebanon, and Kansas City in Missouri, one in Pittsburg, Kansas, and finally one in Redlands, California.*

It was at Pittsburg that he wrote his first novel, That Printer of Udell's. *Before that book was quite finished, Wright met Elsberry W. Reynolds, head of the Book Supply Company, of Chicago, and the greatest mail-order bookseller of his times. Reynolds had been reared in Missouri and Kansas and had much in common with Wright, including strong religious interests.* That Printer of Udell's *sold a surprising 450,000 with Reynolds' strong advertising behind it; and this encouraged the author to do a story with a setting of Ozark scenery and people.* The Shepherd of the Hills *was finished during his pastorate at Lebanon. It eventually sold about 1,250,000 copies in hard covers.*

"The Shepherd of the Hills Country" lies north and west of Lake Taneycomo. "Matt's Cabin" is a little over seven miles out of Branson; it overlooks "Mutton Hollow," "Sammy's Lookout," and other landscape features described in the novel.

Our selection is Chapter XXVII of The Shepherd of the Hills.

A big wagon, with two men on the seat, appeared coming up the valley road. It was Wash Gibbs and a crony from the river. They had stopped at the distillery on their way, and were just enough under the influence of drink to be funny and reckless.

When they caught sight of Ollie Stewart and Miss Lane, Wash said something to his companion, at which both laughed uproariously. Upon reaching the couple, the wagon came to a stop, and after looking at Ollie for some moments, with the silent gravity of an owl, Gibbs turned to the young lady, "Howdy, honey. Where did you git that there? Did your paw give hit to you fer a doll baby?"

Young Stewart's face grew scarlet, but he said nothing.

"Can't hit talk?" continued Gibbs with mock interest.

Glancing at her frightened escort, the girl replied, "You drive on, Wash Gibbs. You're in no condition to talk to anyone."

An ugly leer came over the brutal face of the giant; "Oh, I ain't, ain't I? You think I'm drunk. But I ain't, not so mighty much. Jest enough t' perten me up a pepper grain." Then, turning to his companion, who was grinning in appreciation of the scene, he continued, "Here, Bill; you hold th' ribbens, an' watch me tend t' that little job I told you I laid out t' do first chance I got." At this, Ollie grew as pale as death. Once he started as if to escape, but he could not under Sammy's eyes.

As Wash was climbing down from the wagon, he caught sight of Young Matt standing in the door of the mill shed. "Hello, Matt," he called cheerfully; "I ain't a lookin' fer you t' day; 'tend t' you some other time. Got more important business jest now."

Young Matt made no reply, nor did he move to interfere. In the backwoods every man must fight his own battles, so long as he fights with men. When Stewart was in danger from the panther, it was different. This was man to man. Sammy, too, reared in the mountains, and knowing the code, waited quietly to see what her lover would do.

Coming to Ollie's side, Gibbs said, "Git down, young feller, an' look at yer saddle."

"You go on, and let me alone, Wash Gibbs. I've never hurt you." Ollie's naturally high pitched voice was shrill with fear.

Wash paused, looked back at his companion in the wagon; then to Young Matt, and then to the girl on the horse. "That's right," he said, shaking his head with ponderous gravity. "You all hear him. He ain't never hurted me, nary a bit. Nary a bit, ladies an' gentlemen. But, good Lord! look at him! Hain't hit awful?" Suddenly he reached out one great arm, and jerked the young man from his horse, catching him with the other hand as he fell, and setting him on his feet in the middle of the road.

Ollie was like a child in the grasp of his huge tormentor, and, in spite of her indignation, a look of admiration flashed over Sammy's face at the exhibition of the bully's wonderful physical strength; an admiration, that only heightened the feeling of shame for her lover's weakness.

Gibbs addressed his victim, "Now, dolly, you an' me's goin' t' play a little. Come on, let's see you dance." The other struggled feebly a moment and attempted to draw a pistol, whereupon Wash promptly captured the weapon, remarking in a sad tone as he did so, "You hadn't ought t' tote such a gun as that, sonny; hit might go off. Hit's a right pretty little thing, ain't hit?" he continued, holding his victim with one hand, and examining the pearl handled, nickel plated weapon with great interest. "Hit sure is. But say, dolly, if you was ever t' shoot me with that there, an' I found hit out, I'd sure be powerful mad. You hear me, now, an' don't you pack that gun no more; not in these mountains. Hit ain't safe."

The fellow in the wagon roared with delight at these witticisms, and looked from Young Matt to Sammy to see if they also appreciated the joke.

"Got any more pretties?" asked Gibbs of his victim. "No? Let's see." Catching the young man by the waist, he lifted him bodily, and, holding him head downward, shook him roughly. Again Sammy felt her blood tingle at the feat of strength.

Next holding Ollie with one huge hand at the back of his neck, Wash said, "See that feller in th' wagon there? He's a mighty fine gentleman; friend o' mine. Make a bow t' him." As he finished, with his free hand he struck the young man a sharp blow in the stomach, with the result that Stewart did make a bow, very low, but rather too suddenly to be graceful.

The fellow in the wagon jumped up and bowed again and again; "Howdy, Mr. City Man; howdy. Mighty proud t' meet up with you; mighty proud, you bet!"

The giant whirled his captive toward the mill. "See that feller yonder? I'm goin' t' lick him some day. Make a face at him." Catching Ollie by the nose and chin, he tried to force his bidding, while the man in the wagon made the valley ring with his laughter. Then Wash suddenly faced the helpless young man toward Sammy. "Now ladies and gentle-men," he said in the tones of a showman addressing an audience, "this here pretty little feller from th' city's goin' t' show us Hill-Billies how t' spark a gal."

The bully's friend applauded loudly, roaring at the top of his voice, "Marry 'em, Wash. Marry 'em. You can do hit as good as a parson! You'd make a good parson. Let's see how'd you go at hit."

The notion tickled the fancy of the giant, for it offered a way to make Sammy share the humiliation more fully. "Git down an' come here t' yer honey," he said to the girl. "Git down, I say," he repeated, when the young woman made no motion to obey.

"Indeed, I will not," replied Sammy shortly.

Her tone and manner angered Gibbs, and dropping Ollie he started toward the girl to take her from the horse by force. As he reached the pony's side, Sammy raised her whip and with all her strength struck him full across the face. The big ruffian drew back with a bellow of pain and anger. Then he started toward her again. "I'll tame you, you wild cat," he yelled. And Sammy raised her whip again.

But before Gibbs could touch the girl, a powerful hand caught him by the shoulder. "I reckon you've had fun enough, Wash Gibbs," remarked Young Matt in his slow way. "I ain't interfering between man and man, but you'd best keep your dirty hands off that lady."

The young woman's heart leaped at the sound of that deep calm voice that carried such a suggestion of power. And she saw that the blue eyes under the tumbled red brown locks were shining now like points of polished steel. The strong man's soul was rejoicing with the fierce joy of battle.

The big bully drew back a step, and glared at the man who had come between him and his victim; the man whom, for every reason, he hated. Lifting his huge paws, he said in a voice hoarse with deadly menace, "Dirty, be they? By hell, I'll wash 'em. An' hit won't be water that'll clean 'em, neither. Don't you know that no man ever crosses my trail an' lives?"

The other returned easily, "Oh, shucks! Get into your wagon and drive on. You ain't on Roark now. You're on Fall Creek, and over here you ain't no bigger'n anybody else."

While Young Matt was speaking, Gibbs backed slowly away, and, as the young man finished, suddenly drew the pistol he had taken from Ollie. With a quickness and lightness astonishing in one of his bulk and usually slow movements, the mountaineer leaped upon his big enemy. There was a short, sharp struggle, and Wash staggered backward, leaving the shining weapon in Young Matt's hand. "It might go off, you know," said the young fellow quietly, as he tossed the gun on the ground at Ollie's feet.

With a mad roar, Gibbs recovered himself and rushed at his antagonist. It was a terrific struggle; not the skillful sparring of trained fighters, but the rough and tumble battling of primitive giants. It was the climax of long months of hatred; the meeting of two who were by every instinct mortal enemies. Ollie shrank back in terror, but Sammy leaned forward in the saddle, her beautiful figure tense, her lips parted, and her face flushed with excitement.

It was soon evident that the big champion of the hills had at last met his match. As he realized this, a look of devilish cunning crept into the animal face of Gibbs, and he maneuvered carefully to bring his enemy's back toward the wagon.

Catching a look from his friend, over Young Matt's shoulder, the man in the wagon slipped quickly to the ground, and Sammy saw with horror a naked knife in his hand. She glanced toward Ollie appealingly, but that gentleman was helpless. The man with the knife began creeping cautiously toward the fighting men, keeping always behind Young Matt. The young woman felt as though an iron band held her fast. She could not move. She could not speak. Then Gibbs went down, and the girl's scream rang out, *"Behind you, Matt! Look quick!"*

As he recovered his balance from the effort that had thrown Wash, Young Matt heard her cry, saw the girl's look of horror, and her outstretched hand pointing. Like a flash he whirled just as the knife was was lifted high for the murderous blow. It was over in an instant. Sammy saw him catch the wrist of the uplifted arm, heard a dull snap and a groan, saw the knife fall from the helpless hand, and then saw the man lifted bodily and thrown clear over the wagon, to fall helpless on the rocky ground. The woman gave a low cry, "Oh, *what a man!"*

Wash Gibbs, too, opened his eyes, just in time to witness the unheard-of feat, and to see the bare-armed young giant who performed it turn again, breathing heavily with his great exertion, but still ready to meet his big antagonist.

The defeated bully rose from the ground. The other stepped forward to meet him. But without a word, Gibbs climbed into the wagon and took up the reins. Before they could move, Young Matt had the mules by their heads. "You have forgotten something," he said quietly, pointing to the man on the ground, who was still unconscious from his terrible fall. "That there's your property. Take it along. We ain't got no use for such as that on Fall Creek."

Sullenly Wash climbed down and lifted his companion into the wagon. As Young Matt stood aside to let him go, the bully said, "I'll see you agin fer this."

The strong man only answered, "I reckon you'd better stay on Roark, Wash Gibbs. You got more room there."

PLAINSVILLE'S FIRST HOSSLESS KERRIDGE

Amos R. Harlin

Amos R. Harlin was taken by his family to West Plains, Missouri, in childhood, and was educated in the high school there, and in St. Louis University. His father was mayor of West Plains for thirty-two years. The following narrative is from his book For Here Is My Fortune *(1946).*

The first mistake in judgment father ever made was, in the light of his usual foresight, the most incredible mistake he could have possibly made.

Father was a successful businessman. Which is another way of saying he possessed a talent for assimilating facts, seeing those facts in their true perspective and thus reaching a correct reckoning of things to come.

Yet when he saw the invention which was to give Plainsville more than all else, more than his own efforts, and the efforts of those like him, more than the railroad would ever give, he could not foresee its future.

By the first law of economics the railroad could bring Plainsville little more than it took away. Plainsville could only send away what it took from its trade territory, and vast as was that territory, this was very little. This territory extended back through miles and miles of hills, but what strength it had was dissipated through a hundred crossroads stores with but comparatively little reaching Plainsville. A good team could lug no more than half a load over the existing mountain wagon trails, so the farmer produced but little more than he used, usually no more than enough to cover his staples. This surplus he would not haul a mile further than necessary.

The invention which was to change all this was to encourage the farmer and stock man to produce enough not only for his needs, but also for luxuries and a comfortable bank account. That which was to bring all this surplus flowing into Plainsville and give it a degree of wealth, stability and security, stood before Father's eyes.

Yet Father, like all the businessmen of the town, with the exception of Jess Erickson, who saw it in the light of advertising value, found this worker of miracles only very amusing. And it was funny that day. There had been few days when we had known such hilarious fun.

They unloaded this new wonder onto the railroad freight platform one morning in early spring. Two men came from the factory to demonstrate it to Jess Erickson with the hope he would add it to the line of buggies, wagons and farm machinery he carried in his big hardware store.

Standing black and shiny on the freight platform, it might have been a rather heavily built rubber-tired hack, without a top, shafts, or a tongue. Otherwise it was a high-wheeled hack, complete to patent leather dashboard and mud guards. As Stub Fletcher said, being a little on the happy side again:

"Be thet all of hit? 'Pears a mite bobtailed, lookin' from yhere."

The factory men worked over the machine, stopping to look inside, squatting to peer underneath, followed by every boy who could duck school. We pushed and shoved to look just where they had looked, squatting to peer up underneath, following their gaze, just as if we knew what we were looking at. Businessmen and town loafers alike stood about the platform, lounged on packing boxes and freight trucks, wearing all-wise expressions of tolerant amusement. They smoked a lot, chewed and spit a lot and talked loud and knowingly. Beyond the fact that it was an "auteemobile" or, what was more easily said, a "hossless ker-ridge," they knew no more of what they were looking at than we boys, but they had no doubt as to its future.

"They'll niver git hit to the squarr," said Ned Hill.

Cousin Lew Conway spat bravely off the platform and called out, "Mought jist as well load her back on the kivvered kyars, fellers; thim featherbed tars won't last out halfway up river hill."

"Gawd a'mighty," said Will Sterling, "I opine I'd hafta hawg-tie, blindfold and back my woman and our young'uns into thet thang."

The factory men gave no attention to these remarks other than to grin when the men laughed loudly at what they considered a good one. Finally they brought out a crank and inserted one end in a hole on the right side of the machine just under the front seat. One man climbed into the seat and arranged himself under a bar which, when he was seated, was within easy reach of his hands when held about a foot above his lap. He pushed the bar away, then drew it toward him and the front wheels moved slightly from right to left. We kids drew back and the town men fell silent.

The man in the seat braced himself, adjusted a small lever on the bar and called, "Watch you arm, Fred. All right, twist her tail."

Fred heaved on the crank. There was a clicking sound. The body of the machine rocked a trifle on its springs, then jerked back into place. Fred repeated his twist a dozen times. Sweat trickled down into his eyes. He wiped it away and threw off his coat and said, "Sure your spark's retarded, Harry? I'll spin her."

He grasped the crank in both hands, set his feet wide apart and heaved the crank around and around. The machine trembled under the force of his efforts.

Suddenly there was a loud pop. The machine leaped upward like a spurred horse and a cloud of sooty smoke was exploded from the back end. Then silence.

The man in the seat jiggled the little lever.

"Try her again, Fred. She'll go this time."

Fred spun the crank. There was a loud pop, then, pop-pop-pop. The machine, its four wheels planted firmly on the platform, shook its body exactly as a dog coming out of water stops, plants his feet and shakes his body . . . then, silence.

Fred spat, flipped off the sweat, adjusted his galluses and spun again.

The pops came in rapid staccato. The machine shook violently, jiggled the man in the seat up and down like a man on a wagon seat with his team in a dead run down a rocky hillside. After a moment, the man adjusted the little lever and the pop and clatter softened to a somewhat regular put-put-put.

The four wheels settled firmly on the platform but the body of the machine continued to undulate back and forth, from side to side, in a tremulous rhythmic swing.

Stub Fletcher began to shout in time with the rhythm and wriggle his hips. "Tata-tah-tah-tah-tee-dee-ah-tah-tah-tah-tah-tah. There, fellers," he yelled, "is a hootchy-kootchy fer ye."

Uncle Johnnie became the barker for Stub and the undulating hossless kerridge. He held a length of white pine for a cane and his hat tipped over one eye at a rakish angle. His voice low, his tones persuasive, he chanted:

"See Zubelda. See her dance. You have seen your mother make jelly . . . you have seen it quivvah . . . see Zubelda . . . how she dances . . . how she quivvahs."

The factory men were surprised and a bit puzzled by these monkeyshines but they laughed with everybody else. Then Fred shouted, "You ready, Harry? Run her down the ramp."

Everybody stepped back a step or two. Fred cleared the way to the ramp. Harry pulled down the little lever, the popping became louder and the sway of the body increased to a bounding jiggle. His foot pressed a pedal and the chains tightened on the sprockets inside the back wheels. The machine jerked, leaped forward, settled back on the wheels then rolled down the ramp. Harry brought it to a stop in the middle of the street.

The crowd rushed down to gather round. Until they had seen with their own eyes, none could believe it would move under its own power. Talk was rapid and excited. We stood looking up in awe at Harry on the high seat. How did a man learn to control such power?

Fred called to Jess Erickson, "Come on, Mr. Erickson, climb in."

Jess Erickson hesitated, not because he was afraid of the machine, but he dreaded being conspicuous as he would be up there in the back seat with all eyes upon him. He searched the crowd until he spotted Uncle Johnnie.

"Come on, Johnnie," he called, "what ye say?"

Uncle Johnnie, who would have mounted a loco mustang in front of the crowned heads of Europe if it promised to be fun, climbed in, tipped hat, white pine stick and all. Jess Erickson followed him.

Fred climbed into the front seat beside Harry. There were shouts of caution and advice, and with a steady pop-popping they rolled forward up Ozark Avenue.

Kids whooped, dogs barked and everybody trotted along beside the machine.

Somebody called to mind the town's favorite story of Newt Riley and his brother Phil trying to ride a wild colt in the barn lot and there came shouts of:

"Hold her, Newt, she's a-rarin'."—And from across the street— "Hold her, hold her! She's a-headin' fer the barn. Circle her, Newt, circle her—she'll kill us both!"

Up the street, farmers were battling teams and wagons into alleys and side streets while women, children and old men risked life and limb to scramble out between wheels and over tail gates to run back to the street and stand bug-eyed along the curb.

As the street made a gradual climb, the speed was never more than a comfortable trot, so where the grade became steeper as it neared the square, men ran ahead to free horses from the hitching rack around the courthouse fence. Even so, two horses snapped their reins, galloped to the far side of the square where they stood, heads and tails high, snorting defiance at this weird hossless hack that rolled uphill, popping and shooting smoke out of its tail as it came.

With a gay put-putting the machine rounded the square gathering an ever-increasing crowd, and turned into South Street to come to a triumphant stop before Erickson's Hardware and Farm Implements Store. The men stepped down to go into the store.

Jess Erickson called to Moon, telling him to get into the seat and not let anybody climb over the machine. Moon made the seat in a single leap and motioned me to follow. He then told Jug and Pook-eye to get in the back seat, as "it looked like hit was goin' to take a heap of watchin'."

At first folks kept their distance, but gradually came closer until they were touching the wheels, crouching down to peer up underneath, testing the slickness of the patent leather mud guards and dashboard.

Moon discovered a large rubber bulb fastened to the side of the seat. Inserted in the bulb was the end of a brass horn, the bell pointing to the ground. He gave the bulb a quick squeeze. The resultant honk produced four bruised heads, started babies crying and dogs barking. Thereafter we waited until a group of newcomers had gathered around; we even urged them to get down low and view the wonders underneath, then we took turns blowing the horn. Everybody had a fine time.

By evening it was known that Jess Erickson had agreed to buy the machine providing it climbed to his house, high on the side of Hobart's

Hill, under its own power. As no such important news could be kept secret, every detail was discussed by young and old. The factory men had agreed not only to drive up to Jess's house, but to back the machine all the way up the steep climb. As everybody knew how difficult it was to back a wagon up even a slight slope, all agreed that Jess's money would stay right where it was in the bank. The trial was set for the next morning.

South Street, leaving the square, climbs a gentle slope for a block or two, then drops sharply to cross a deep wash on a high fill before starting its long steep climb to the top of Hobart's Hill. The road is level on the fill, so Fred and Harry turned the machine around here and made their preparations for backing up the hill.

The footbridge crossing the wash was crowded to the breaking point but not a person went more than a block up the hill. All said that outsiders just didn't know Ozark Hills. Why, a good team had to stop as many as ten times dragging any kind of load up Hobart's Hill.

Jess Erickson stood alone, far up the hill where he had drawn a line across the street in front of his house. He held an Erickson Hardware and Farm Implement Company check in his hand. Everyone knew when a wheel crossed that line the check was Harry's and it was a closed deal.

Father sat on the rail of the bridge. He spoke low to Cousin Matt.

"Jess sure knows how to play to the grandstand. It's good business even if he gets the damned thing. Everybody in the country is talking Erickson's Hardware. But a contraption like that will never get anywhere in this country."

On the fill the machine stood shimmying in rhythm with a soft put-put from the pipe sticking out of the back. Fred and Harry took a last look around and climbed into the front seat. The put-put increased its tempo to a vicious popping and the machine started backing. It moved slowly but steadily upward.

There were no shouts, no calls. Folks walked slowly, in silence, keeping pace with the machine. There was something awe-inspiring, something unbelievable in the sight of that bobtailed hack backing steadily up the steep grade. The steering bar jerked frantically back and forth in Harry's hands as the wheels dropped into a rut or fell off a rock, but the machine continued to climb.

A freckle-faced boy walking in his sock feet beside me, carrying a pair of new store-bought shoes in his hands, said, "Hit'll stop whar thet shelf of rock goes antegogglin' acrost the road."

But the machine twisted over the six-inch shelf of rock and went on. Folks were looking from one to the other now, and measuring by eye the narrowing distance between the machine and Jess Erickson.

Strange how people will shout over small things yet in the face of a real wonder remain silent. There was hardly a word spoken, only the heavy breathing as they, straining forward, hurried to keep abreast of the machine. All eyes were on Jess Erickson, standing on the line, holding aloft the check.

A wheel crossed the line and Harry reached out a hand and gathered in the check. He waved it high above his head. There was an awed cheer, then those who still had wind enough started to run, for it was evident that the machine was going on to try for the crest of the hill.

The grade lessened above Jess Erickson's line until it was nearly flat on the crest where earth had been cut away to make the fill at the bottom of the hill. The machine gathered some speed and was rolling backward over the comparative level with a gay triumphant popping when, with the hilltop a scant ten yards away, Monk Watson's mule team came over the crest.

Monk was bringing a load of stove wood to town; his woman, kids and grandpap were strung out, sitting on the wood behind him. His team, half-blind with age and weary after pulling a load up the far side of the hill, would not have noticed a lesser apparition; but a shiny hack backing at them, shooting as it came, was too much for even a pair of aged mules.

They reared straight into the air, whirled around until a front wheel cramped against the wagon. The wagon groaned, reeled, and threatened to come apart, but slid around and went bumping away behind the mules as they galloped down the far side of the hill.

The mules were too stiff-jointed to attain any speed, even down hill, and all would have been well had not Grandpap attempted to stand upright to shout, "Gawd damn hit, hit's a thang—tain't man ner beast!"

He had a wooden leg so he stood none too firm on the stacked wood. A roll of the wagon sent him head first over a back wheel, but by some miracle of agility he landed upright. His wooden leg, which supplied the missing member from the knee down, plunged into soft earth and snapped off half its length.

Grandpap lay flat on his back, waving the remnant of his wooden leg in the air, while his shouts called upon the Lord to witness that he had "met the workin's of the Devil plumb squarr in the middle of the big road; and hit warr all the fault of Mattie [his oldest grandchild!] who warr a-runnin' the brash with thet Gawd-defyin' Homer Hawkins."

But his tune changed when Monk brought his team to a stop, turned around and came back to pick him up. Monk believed lawin' beat work any day. A few words in Grandpap's ear, and by the time they lifted him back on to the wagon he had discovered pains from the top of his head to the bottom of his one foot. Come evening, Jess Erickson owned an automobile complete with suit for damages and attachment.

The factory men were in town for two days teaching Ed Hawks, who assembled plows and wagons for Erickson's Hardware, to operate the machine. They didn't try Hobart's Hill again. When they had gone Ed practiced a few days, keeping to fairly level ground. Then he and Jess tried for a solid week to get up the hill, but they never got more than a quarter of the way. A month passed before Ed Hawks' brother, who worked in an automobile plant in Detroit, came home for a visit and solved the mystery. He explained how the machine, being geared so much lower in reverse, would of course climb a much steeper hill backward than it would forward.

Jess Erickson didn't care. He laughed more at himself than anybody dared laugh at him. The machine was polished and set just inside the big window of his warehouse where his wagons and farm implements were on display. Few there were who came to town without dropping in to see the hossless kerridge. In turn they looked at the new wagons and plows. Far more new wagons appeared on the roads, far more new plows broke the earth than ever before. You had to get up early in the morning to beat Jess Erickson.

So it was that our first automobile, standing bright and shiny in the window, though it never saw a hundred miles of road, brought its own change, as if predicting the vast changes its descendants would one day bring even to the farthest hills.

WHO BLOWED UP THE CHURCH HOUSE?

VANCE RANDOLPH

Vance Randolph lived for some ten years in Pineville, Missouri, and for about the same length of time in Galena; thus we freely claim him as a Missourian, though he was born in Kansas and is now a resident of Fayetteville, Arkansas. He has attained fame by his researches in the folklore of the Ozarks, and the State Historical Society of Missouri published his great collection, Ozark Folk Songs, *in four volumes. The story here offered is the title piece in a volume of short tales; its setting is in the Missouri Ozarks.*

One time there was an old bachelor named Longstreet and he did not do no work, because he drawed a big pension every month.

After while he got so fat he wouldn't even chop his own kindling, and he hired some fellow to haul wood into town and rick it up right by the back door. The old man kept a fishpole in the house, and it was just eight feet long, with a notch cut in the middle. He used to bring out the fishpole and measure the wood careful, and if the woodpile was eight foot long and four foot high, he would give the fellow seventy-five cents. But if it measured even one inch short, old man Longstreet says it ain't a full rick, and he would not pay nothing till the fellow put on some more wood.

The fellows that cut wood and sold it did not like old man Longstreet much. He did not get along very good with his neighbors, neither. Every time a little cold spell come along, old man Longstreet would be up town grumbling how somebody was stealing his wood in the night. "There's folks in this town that ain't got no woodpile at all," says he, "but there's smoke coming out of their chimney just the same, and you can smell meat a-frying." Finally he put up KEEP OUT signs in his back yard, and he says he is going to shoot anybody that come around there of a night. The sheriff told him he better get a big dog to watch the woodpile. But old man Longstreet says it would cost too much to feed the critter, and the goddam neighbors is mean enough to poison a dog anyhow.

The Baptist church set right across the lane from old man Longstreet's place, and one Sunday they had got a new preacher down from Springfield. It was pretty cold, and the preacher wanted to build a little fire to take the chill off the pews. Old man Longstreet was not home, as he had went fishing somewheres, so the new preacher went into the back yard and got an armload of wood. He says surely nobody will begrudge a few little sticks for the worship of God, but he didn't know old man Longstreet. The preacher got the fire going good, and then he walked out to the door of the church, a-thinking about his sermon.

All of a sudden the stove blowed up KER-WHAM! It knocked the pulpit down, and broke most of the windows, and scattered live coals all over the church house. The whole place was full of smoke, and the preacher was hollering like a scalded bird dog. He wasn't hurt none, but he was scared witless. Some folks come along and pumped water, and carried it round in their hats, or else the church house would have burnt plumb down. And if that stove had blowed up after the meeting got started, it might have killed half the Baptists in the settlement.

The folks thought old man Longstreet had fixed a stick of wood with powder to blast out the scoundrels he claimed was stealing his wood in the night. But the old man swore he never done it, and he figured the neighbors must have loaded up a stick and put it in the woodpile to murder him, as they are a low-down thieving lot and he would not put anything past them. The neighbors says they never done no such a thing, and who would want to kill a crazy old fool like that, which he has got one foot in the grave already? One fellow says old man Longstreet is always having trouble with the woodcutters because he claims they don't give him a full rick for his money, and maybe the woodcutters put the powder in to get even with old man Longstreet. The fellows that hauled the wood says it is a outrageous lie, and people better be goddam careful who they are accusing of things like that. And one woodcutter says everybody would like to get rid of old man Longstreet and the neighbors too, but he can't afford to buy powder so long as them tightwads only pay seventy-five cents a rick. "If they will give me a dollar and a quarter," says he, "I'll put free dynamite in every woodpile, and them damn fools can blow each other up all over town for all I care."

We never did find out which one done it, or who they was trying to blow up. Some says one thing, and some says another. There was a piece in the Durgenville paper about how the folks down our way is against religion, but the home folks all knowed better. There ain't nobody in this county would blow up a church house on purpose, and run the risk of killing a lot of good Christian people. It was just one of these here unfortunate accidents, and you can't make nothing else out of it.

BAD MEN

THE BALLAD OF JESSE JAMES

*There are various versions of this famous ballad, as there are bound to
be of verses that come down to us by word of mouth and are recorded
from memories of different persons. The one here presented is taken
from* Ballads and Songs Collected by the Missouri Folk-Lore Society, *edited by Professor H. M. Belden. Belden was a member for many years
of the English faculty at the University of Missouri and a nationally
known figure in the field of balladry.*

> Jesse James was a lad that killed many a man.
> He robbed the Danville train.
> But that dirty little coward that shot Mr. Howard
> Has laid poor Jesse in the grave.
>
> It was Robert Ford, that dirty little coward,
> I wonder how he does feel;
> For he ate of Jesse's bread and slept in Jesse's bed
> And laid poor Jesse in the grave.
>
> *Chorus:*
> Poor Jesse had a wife to mourn for his life,
> His children they were brave;
> But that dirty little coward that shot Mr. Howard
> And laid poor Jesse in the grave!
>
> It was his brother Frank who robbed the Gallatin bank
> And carried the money from the town.
> It was at this very place they had a little chase,
> For they shot Capt. Sheets to the ground.
>
> They went to the crossing not very far from here,
> And there they did the same;
> With the agent on his knees he delivered up the keys
> To the outlaws Frank and Jesse James.
>
> It was on Wednesday night, the moon was shining bright,
> They robbed the Glenville train.
> The people they did say, for many miles away,
> It was robbed by Frank and Jesse James.
>
> It was on Saturday night, Jesse was at home,
> Talking with his family brave.
> Robert Ford came along like a thief in the night
> And laid poor Jesse in his grave.

The people held their breath when they heard of Jesse's death
And wondered how he ever came to die.
It was one of the gang called little Robert Ford,
He shot poor Jesse on the sly.

This song was made by Billy Gashade
As soon as the news did arrive.
He said there is no man with the law in his hand
Can take Jesse James when alive.

THE DUAL NATURE OF JESSE JAMES

HOMER CROY

Many books have been published about Jesse James, most famous of Missouri outlaws; certainly one of the best of them is Jesse James Was My Neighbor, *by Missouri born and bred Homer Croy. We are privileged to reprint here Chapter IV of that book—an interesting and discriminating study of the young Jesse, with something about the Younger brothers.*

There is a story told about Jesse James by General Jo Shelby, the famous Confederate leader. Jesse was going to Lafayette County to buy horses for his stepfather; on the way he stopped at Jo Shelby's, but Shelby was away. Jesse said he would like to feed his horse and rest awhile, himself. Mrs. Shelby was pleased to have him there and made him feel at home.

She had a colored houseboy named Joe Miller. She sent him to a small town named Aullville, and while he was in town he got into a fight with a white boy of his own age, which was about fifteen. The white boy was named Catron. As the two fought, a crowd collected, most of them taking sides with the white boy.

Joe Miller started home.

The white boy then ran to his own home, got a gun, mounted a horse, and started to follow the colored boy. He began to gain, and as he came closer Joe ran and got behind the gatepost at the Shelby home. Catron fired his shotgun, but none of the shot struck the colored boy. Before he could reload, Joe rushed at him, pulled him from the horse, and began

Reprinted from *Jesse James Was My Neighbor* by Homer Croy. By permission of the author.

to belabor him. Just then Joe looked up and saw a mob coming down the road from town. Knowing what would happen to him, he rushed in and implored Mrs. Shelby to protect him.

Jesse James said, "I'd be pleased to take care of that for you, ma'am."

He made a quick survey. The mob, to get to the house, would have to cross the Davis Creek bridge nearby. So he hurried out and got to the bridge first. There he drew his two pistols, and when the mob came up he said, "This is as far as you go. Turn around and go back."

The mob debated, studying the man with the cold-blue eyes, with the two pistols in his hand. Finally they thought better of it, and went back down the road in the direction whence they had come.

This story illustrates the dual quality of Jesse James's nature. He was as quick to defend life as to take it; something had intervened here that was stronger than his natural feelings as a Southerner under the Reconstruction. But on another occasion he was to shoot a defenceless man without consideration and without qualm.

As he approached his twentieth birthday, the time when the course of his life would begin to take a permanent direction one way or another, the two natures in Jesse were struggling against each other. He had been taught honesty by his mother and stepfather; no more honest a person ever lived than his mother, and his stepfather was scrupulously upright. He had ridden and shared life with some of the lowest, thievingest, most blasphemous rascals and cutthroats in the War Between the States. But he did not swear, he did not thieve, he had not (so far as is known) had any adventures with women, he did not even smoke. The name 'Dingus' still clung to him, with all that it connoted of gentlemanly manners under stress. On top of all this was his interest in religion, inherited from his father and furthered by his mother.

Jesse had a deep and abiding affection for his mother. In July, 1864, Jesse and two other guerrillas were near Fayette, in Howard County, Missouri, when they heard that a Union soldier named Allen Bysfield had come home on a furlough. A Union soldier! They surrounded the house, then demanded the door be opened. It was, but the young Union soldier had got word and had escaped.

The men surmised that he must have rowed across the river; going down to the Missouri, they succeeded in finding a rowboat and managed to get across into Cooper County. There was an old shanty near the landing; they went to it—and there was the Union boy.

They decided to shoot him, then and there.

The boy began to beg for his life, but they paid hardly any attention; then he said he had come back to see his mother. Jesse knew this but now, with the boy saying it, it made an impression. Jesse looked at the piteously begging boy with renewed interest, then began to ask questions. Finally he turned to the others and said: "He's come back to see his old mother. Any man ought to be willing to go through hell to see his mother, and that's what this boy has done. Let him live. He deserves it."

There was a short conference between the three. What Jesse said carried weight and in a few minutes the three walked out, leaving the young Union soldier, who could hardly believe his good fortune. The three men rowed back across the river and disappeared.

Frank was never the complicated character Jesse was. When he was asked to go on an 'expedition,' he went and that was all there was to it. He would never have dreamed of getting up in church and praying out loud for Jesse. If Jesse wanted to go to Heaven, he would have to do it on his own. No help from brother.

The days of moods and meditations continued for Jesse. God wanted him. Perhaps; but so did his bold friends. He was an expert shot, he was a fine horseman, and he was fearless. He was an addition to any band. And, young as he was, he was beginning to show qualities of leadership. It seemed easier to make a living robbing a bank now and then than it did farming. There is a good deal of evidence—too detailed to go into here—to indicate that Jesse was violently pulled between the requirements of a religious life and the demands of banditry. He became moody; his mother complained that he would no longer 'talk' to her. She had lost his confidence. Once she told her husband, "I don't understand him any more."

Not far away was another powerful influence. The Youngers. Big, portly Cole Younger also had a great interest in religion (sometimes the others called him 'Bishop'), but he didn't allow it to confuse the issue; the issue with Cole was banditry. He had been in the Richmond raid, although he always said he hadn't been. But then, he was the most sanctimonious liar in three counties.

Cole Younger had ridden with Quantrill in Kentucky and thought he knew all about it. He began to talk up Kentucky as a land overflowing with gold and banknotes, and finally convinced the others this was true. In his whole bandit career Cole never did anything above and beyond the intelligence of a sheep dog. Sometimes, it would seem, the dog had it on him a little.

He said that Russellville, Kentucky, was just waiting to be plucked, so he was sent down to scout it. He used the method that had, almost unconsciously, been adopted by the gang. He went to the window and said, "Can you change this $100 note for me?"

The cashier looked Cole over and smelled something.

"I'm a cattle buyer from Louisville," said Cole.

He looked about as much like a cattle buyer as he did like a musk-ox.

"No," said the cashier, "I'm afraid I can't."

The cattle buyer returned his $100 note to his pocket and left.

A week later, on March 20, 1868, Cole led the gang back; among the six was Jesse James.

By a streak of good luck, the gang galloped out of town with $14,000 in the faithful grain sack, and without killing a single man. They didn't even give the inevitable posse a chance not to get too close to them.

But the Russellville bankers were not satisfied with halfhearted pursuit and a hue and cry that quickly died down. They wired to Louisville and engaged a detective to get on the trail—D. T. Bligh. He began to work with an assistant, William Gallagher, and they soon discovered that Jesse James was suspected but that nothing had been done about it. Bligh and his man decided to do something. And now, for the first time, Jesse had detectives to deal with.

Jesse was accustomed to outdistancing posses. He didn't know about the kind that came in the silence of the night and listened at keyholes. But some way or other he found out that they were on his trail, and he realized that he had to do something and do it fast. He had plenty of money, so he did a surprising thing. He went to New York, saw the sights, got on a boat and went to Panama. He crossed the Isthmus, got on a steamship, landed in San Francisco, then, his trail well confused, he headed for Paso Robles, California, the place where he had intended to go all the time.

Paso Robles was thirty miles south of San Luis Obispo, and the reason Jesse went there was his uncle, Drury Woodson James, the one whom he was named after. 'Mr. D. W.,' as he was called, had been one of the founders of the present incorporated city of Paso Robles, at that time called El Paso de Robles. In 1860, with John D. Thompson, he had bought 10,000 acres of government land on La Panza Rancho and stocked it with 2500 head of cattle. D. W. realized the value of the mineral springs. He and Thompson built a wooden hotel and cottages, and the place soon became famous for its hot sulphur springs and mud baths. On September 15, 1866, D. W. James had married, and now, to visit his uncle and pay his respects to his new aunt, came Jesse James.

Jesse was driven twice a week to take the baths, and soon looked less like a hunted man. He then began to ride the range with the cowboys; sometimes he would be gone with them for days. The men noticed that he had a couple of peculiar traits, but at the time they did not think what might be behind them. When the men rode in a group, Jesse always rode on the outside. At night, when the men rolled up in their blankets, Jesse always went off and slept by himself.

One of the cowboys was a boy younger than Jesse, named Charles Morehouse. Jesse took a fancy to him. The young boy had an inferior lariat, made out of horsehair interwoven with grass fiber. The best lariats were made of rawhide. Jesse had one of these.

One day Jesse said to the boy, "Is that your best lariat?"

"Yes."

"Here's mine. You keep it. I won't need it any more."

The next day he disappeared.

Some time during 1868 Jesse and Frank were back on the James farm. They thought things had blown over. There is indication that they wanted to settle down, for they began to farm again. Jesse began once more to attend church regularly, singing in the choir, and was 'converted' and baptized in the Kearney Baptist Church. (By a strange irony the church was located on the spot which later became a graveyard, the place where Jesse lies buried today.) His mother, according to local legend, is reported to have said, "This is the happiest day of my life."

The year that followed must have been a happy one for Jesse as well. He was twenty-one, a husky young man an inch under six feet, friendly and more approachable than his brother Frank. He had the solace of religion, and he was still courting his cousin. In addition, the times were settling down. The bitterness of the Border Warfare days was partially subsiding. Now and then the rebel yell was heard, but for the most part Clay County was more peaceful than it had been in fifteen years.

However, a new phase in local feelings had come along: the dislike of *both* banks and railroads. The banks squeezed the farmer till he bled. When a train killed a farmer's cow, he had to wait years to be paid. Sometimes sparks from the engine set farmers' haystacks on fire. The farmer would write a handful of letters, and not even get a reply. The feelings the railroads aroused were soon to be reflected in the career of Jesse James, a career which—despite the calm and promise of a change for the better—was soon to be resumed.

Just a little over a year after Jesse had returned from California seemingly finished with 'road work' and persuaded to life on the farm, he mounted his horse and, together with Frank and Cole Younger, rode off toward Gallatin, Missouri, about forty miles from the James farm. They appeared in the town on December 7, 1869. Cole and Jesse went in, leaving Frank outside to hold the horses. Cole used his old dodge—

could the cashier change a $100 bill? The cashier said he could and started to count out the change. As he was doing so, Cole drew his pistol and said, "Don't make a move or I kill you."

Out came the grain sack and Jesse began to toss in all the money he could see, which, goodness knows, wasn't much—$700.

Two or three persons had started to enter the bank, but Frank warned them off. Suddenly the people realized what was happening and scurried away after their guns. Frank yelled to Cole and Jesse to hurry.

A characteristic of Jesse's was his loyalty to friends. Now, as he was filling the sack, his attention was suddenly caught. Where had he seen that cashier before? Stepping over to Cole, he talked in a low undertone, both of them looking intently at the cashier. And then suddenly Jesse shot him. The cashier fell dead in as cold and cruel a murder as Jesse ever committed.

By this time Frank was popping away right and left. The other two rushed out, but in attempting to mount Jesse was thrown. He was in a pickle. He had no horse and the citizens were beginning to come up with their hardware. The tricky situation was solved by Frank, who pulled Jesse up behind him and out of town they galloped, Jesse clinging to the sack.

Luck was with them. In fact, luck was with Jesse all his life, until the last. The two met a man on a horse. In no time at all Jesse had a horse and an honest farmer had none.

As they approached the next town they met another man and made him pilot them safely around it. Something was on Jesse's mind; finally he said: "We were just up to the Gallatin bank. I killed a man there. I think it was S. P. Cox. He killed Bill Anderson and I always said I'd get that man if I could."

The Anderson he referred to was Bloody Bill. But Jesse hadn't killed S. P. Cox; he had killed Captain John W. Sheets, a local man.

A posse rode out to no avail. But something else happened. The riderless horse was caught and was identified as belonging to Jesse James. The local talk about the 'tough James Boys' boiled up again with a vengeance, and became more than just talk, for the Gallatin men went to Captain Thomason, the sheriff of Clay County, gave their proof, and asked the sheriff to 'bring 'em in.'

The sheriff knew Jesse's and Frank's courage and their ability to take care of themselves and didn't hanker after the job. But he had to do it. So he swore in three deputies and rode over to get the Boys. They turned in from the main highway and advanced toward the house.

Frank and Jesse saw them coming, but instead of trying to get out the back side of the farm, they rode out to meet them. This was more than the deputies were counting on.

"You boys've got to go to town with us," called Captain Thomason.

"We don't want to go to town with you," said Jesse with complete logic.

The four deputies glanced at one another, then one said, "You boys think it over."

"We've thought it over," said the Boys.

"I'll count ten," announced the sheriff.

"You can count all you want to, but it won't do you any good. We don't figger to change our minds."

Frank glanced at his brother. Jesse's pistol flashed out, and, taking careful aim, he shot the horse the sheriff was on. The animal reeled to the ground, Thomason managing to keep from being entangled with it.

Whirling, Frank and Jesse dashed away. The deputies fired a few shots, hitting nothing but the wind.

The humiliating part came when the sheriff had to go to the house and get Mrs. James's permission to borrow a horse. She gave him her permission and something he hadn't asked for—a piece of her mind. She was very liberal with this; it steamed a little around the edges.

The deputies started back to Liberty, pretty well ashamed of themselves. They had gone out to bring in the James Boys. All they were bringing in was one of their horses. And *he* would have to go back.

There is a footnote to this story which illustrates Jesse's sense of fair play. He was honest except when he went out to rob (there was no paradox in that to him). Captain Thomason's term as sheriff of Clay County expired, and his son Oscar was elected. In 1872, after Oscar too had served out his term, he started to Texas with a friend to buy cattle. They traveled by covered wagon, with a fringe of horses to take care of the cattle on the way back.

As they were jogging along in northern Texas, they saw two men on horseback coming toward them. After they had passed, Oscar Thomason exclaimed, "Why, that's Jesse and Frank James!"

They looked back and saw that the two men seemed to be puzzled and quite a bit disturbed, for they had halted and were conferring. One of the men got off his horse and went behind a tree with his rifle at ready; the other rode slowly back displaying a white handkerchief. When he came up he called, "Are you looking for us?"

The man who called was Jesse James.

"No, we're not," Oscar shouted in return. "I'm not sheriff now. We're on our way through Texas to buy cattle."

"Oh!" exclaimed Jesse, relieved.

He came closer and waved Frank out from behind the tree; all four caucused a while.

Then Oscar Thomason invited them to have dinner. A fire was started beside the road and a meal cooked, the men still talking in a friendly way. At the end of the meal, Jesse said, "I've had it on my conscience about shooting that horse from under your pa that day, Oscar. How much did he value that animal at?"

"Well I would say he was worth fifty dollars."

"I would say about the same thing," replied Jesse. "I'd like to square that off here and now." Pulling out his purse he counted fifty dollars.

The men continued to visit, then Jesse and Frank rode off in one direction, and Oscar and his friend in the other. Jesse had squared his conscience.

There was so much feeling from the Gallatin raid and the murder of Sheets that the Boys had to clear out—this for the second time. And although they didn't know it, D. T. Bligh and his man were still on the trail.

It is not established where they went; the early writers said they went to Kentucky to their mother's folks and that would seem to be as good a guess as any.

The deacons, who had welcomed him in less than a year before, called a hasty meeting and read Jesse out of the church. They didn't want that kind of member, even if he could sing in the choir.

And now Jesse was twenty-two years and four months old. He had seen a great deal of life. He was to see more.

FRANKIE AND JOHNNIE

This famous ballad is probably very old. It doubtless is based upon a real crime, supposed by some scholars to have been committed in St. Louis. (See Tyrrel Williams, Missouri Historical Review, *January, 1940, pp. 292–293.) Orrick Johns, in his autobiographical* Time of Our Lives, *says that there is a tradition in St. Louis that the song originated with "Mammy Lou," who sang it at Babe Connors' "high-brown bawdy-house" in that city in the early 1890's. The Belden version (H. M.*

Belden, Ballads and Songs Collected by the Missouri Folk-Lore Society)
uses the name Albert instead of Johnnie; it is believed that vaudeville
singers changed the name from Albert to Johnnie.

John Huston wrote a play called "Frankie and Johnnie," produced
on Broadway in 1930; Huston said it was based on the killing of Al
Britt by Frankie Baker in 1899, though early forms of the ballad prob-
ably antedate that crime by as much as half a century. The motion pic-
ture "Frankie and Johnnie," starring Helen Morgan, was produced by
Republic Pictures in 1939; this was the basis for a $200,000 defamation
of character suit brought by Frankie Baker, who was then proprietress of
a shoe-shining parlor in Portland, Oregon. Frankie lost her suit.

Frankie and Johnnie were lovers,
Oh Lordy how they could love,
They swore to be true to each other
Just as true as the stars up above,
He was her man, but he done her wrong.

Frankie and Johnnie went walking,
Johnnie had on a new suit,
Frankie paid a hundred dollars
Just to make her man look cute,
He was her man, but he done her wrong.

Johnnie says I've got to leave you,
But I won't be very long,
Don't you wait for me honey,
Or worry while I'm gone,
He was her man, but he done her wrong.

Frankie went down to the station,
Stopped in to buy her some beer,
Says to the fat bartender
Has my lovin' Johnnie been here?
He was her man, but he done her wrong.

Now I aint going to tell you no story,
Aint going to tell you no lie,
I saw him pass about an hour ago
With a gal named Nellie Bly,
He was her man, but he done her wrong.

Frankie took a cab at the corner,
Says driver step on this can,
She was just a desperate woman

Getting two-timed by her man,
He was her man, but he done her wrong.

Frankie got off on South Clark street,
Looked in at a window so high,
Saw her Johnnie man a-lovin' up
That gay haired Nellie Bly,
He was her man, but he done her wrong.

Johnnie saw Frankie a-coming,
Out the back door he did scoot,
But Frankie took aim with her pistol
And the gun went root-a-too-toot,
He was her man, but he done her wrong.

Oh roll me over so easy,
Roll me over so slow,
Roll me over easy, boys,
Cause me wounds they hurt me so,
I was her man, but I done her wrong.

Bring out the long black coffin,
Bring out the funeral clothes,
Johnnie's gone and cashed his checks,
To the graveyard Johnnie goes,
He was her man, but he done her wrong.

Drive out the rubber-tired carriage,
Drive out the rubber-tired hack,
There's twelve men going to the graveyard
And eleven men coming back,
He was her man, but he done her wrong.

The sheriff arrested poor Frankie,
Took her to jail the same day,
He locked her up in the dungeon cell
And threw the key away,
She shot her man, but he done her wrong.

This story has no moral,
This story has no end,
It only goes to show you
That there aint no good in men,
He was her man, but he done her wrong.

BELLE STARR

Bartlett Boder

Bartlett Boder is president of the St. Joseph Historical Society and of the Board of Directors of the St. Joseph Museum. He has been president of the Missouri Valley Trust Company since 1931. In his younger days, Mr. Boder worked on St. Joseph newspapers, and he continues his writing by contributions to the Museum Graphic, *the always interesting organ of the St. Joseph Museum, from the Spring, 1953, number of which the following article is taken.*

This is a little history of Belle Starr and her times. She could correctly be called the feminine Jesse James. At gun's point she robbed banks, stores and stagecoaches. In a similar way Jesse James had held up banks and planned Missiouri's first peace time train robbery. They provide an example where environment has outweighed heredity.

They were both reared in Missouri and both were Southern sympathizers. They both served with or for Confederate guerrilla bands during the Civil War where shooting and robbing Northern sympathizers was regarded as a patriotic necessity. Both served with or for William Clarke Quantrill, the noted guerrilla leader. There are too many other parallels to mention all. They were about the same age. Belle Starr was born between 1846 and 1848. Jesse James was born in 1847. After "Judge" and Eliza Shirley moved from Carthage, Missouri, to Texas, near the close of the Civil War, taking along their daughter, Myra Belle Shirley, she had her first love affair. It was with Cole Younger, formerly a member of Quantrill's band. Cole Younger was with Jesse James in 1875 in the attempt to rob the Northfield, Minnesota, bank.

Jesse James had come of a good Kentucky family. His mother Zeralda Cole was attending school at Saint Catherine's Catholic convent in Lexington, Kentucky, when at sixteen she married Robert James who was studying at Georgetown college for the Baptist ministry. When he graduated they came to Clay County, Missouri, where Jesse James was born in 1847. There Jesse's father, Robert James, organized two neighborhood Baptist churches, but made his living by farming. He was one of the organizers of William Jewell College at Liberty.

Belle Starr's father, "Judge" John Shirley, of Carthage, was described by a neighbor of Civil War days: "As pleasant a man as you could find." He owned most of the city block on the north side of the square in

Reprinted from the *Museum Graphic,* courtesy of the St. Joseph Museum, St. Joseph, Missouri.

Carthage, including the large Shirley House. His young daughter, Myra Belle Shirley, received her education at the brick Carthage Female Academy which was incorporated by an act of the legislature in 1855, and was situated on the south side of the square opposite the Shirley House. The bell of the Academy is still preserved as a historical relic. The title "Judge" which John Shirley bore was perhaps a courtesy title, a tribute to his personality and prominence. He might at one time have been a justice of the peace.

Myra Belle was spoken of as being about sixteen, small for her age, "a rather pretty girl and everybody liked her." Her brother Bud was spoken of as "a good companion, and as brave a man as you could find anywhere." He was then about twenty-two.

A further parallel: Belle Starr was shot in the back in 1889 on her ranch on Younger's Bend of the South Canadian River in the Indian Territory. The whole world knows that Jesse James was also shot from behind, in St. Joseph. No one, it seems, dared to shoot it out with either of them face to face as was required by the code of frontier ethics of the old gun-fighting west.

The Civil War in western Missouri was a succession of bloody killings of neighbors by neighbors. Confederate guerrillas would shoot a Northern sympathizer and burn his home. The Missouri State Militia and its irregular followers would be revenged by similar action against Southerners. Each side thought the other had started the whole business, but short of extermination of one side or the other, there seemed no way of stopping it. Such intense hates and passions were not engendered by the bigger War Between the States, where the rules of civilized warfare were generally observed and where the lives of prisoners were reasonably safe.

Myra Belle's beloved brother Bud had been quite successful as a scout and raider during the earlier days of the war, and remained in the Carthage region most of the time. He sometimes slipped into town to visit his parents and Myra Belle. In 1864 he was trapped by a small Union group at the home of the Stewart family near Sarcoxie, 13 miles southeast of Carthage. He and his companion, Milt Norris, were scaling a fence in flight as he was killed. Milt Norris, though slightly wounded, escaped and hurried to Carthage and told the Shirleys of their son's death. Bud's mother rode over the next day and little Myra Belle went along, smarting for revenge. She wore two cap-and-ball revolvers in holsters on her belt. After they had gone home, Union men returned and burned the house for harboring the two young guerrillas. During this terrible period Union families were also being evacuated from the region by the state militia.

The previous October, 1863, Confederate guerrillas had burned the courthouse at Carthage. It had been temporarily deserted by its Union garrison which had gone in pursuit of General Jo Shelby's raiders.

Then there appeared from the north an unbelievable and portentous sight. It was Quantrill's well-mounted men to the number of five hundred. They were fresh from their raid on Lawrence, Kansas, and were heavy with the loot of the town. At their head rode William Clarke Quantrill himself, the outstanding guerrilla leader of the war. It must have been pleasant news for Myra Belle and Bud Shirley, and for their more discreet parents, still operating the Shirley House for all comers. Most amazing was the fact that most of Quantrill's men were wearing captured Union blue uniforms; others wore civilian garb, while still others wore guerrilla overshirts of scarlet or butternut color with a V-shaped collar ending in a rosette. Butternut was supposed to be the official color for Confederate guerrillas.

Quantrill was born in Ohio and went to Kansas with a party of free state homesteaders from that state and took up a farm. He found life too dull and in 1858 travelled with an army wagon train bound for Utah with supplies for troops stationed at Camp Floyd. At Salt Lake he became a gambler under the name of Charlie Hart. He returned to Kansas and taught school in 1859–60. During the latter part of 1860 he lived near Lawrence with Indians or renegade whites, again under the name of Charlie Hart. Several thefts were traced to him, and a warrant was issued for him for horse stealing, and he left for Missouri. He later returned to Kansas as a proslavery man and was arrested on the horse stealing charge. He escaped again to Missouri and joined the Confederate army as an irregular and fought at the battle of Lexington, Missouri, in 1861, and became chief of a large band of guerrillas. They were mustered into Confederate service and he was made a captain.

According to Ward L. Schrantz, border history writer, they galloped into Lawrence, Kansas, at dawn August 26, 1863, and between 150 and 175 men were killed, most of them unarmed. Many men of Quantrill's command became sickened by the carnage during the four hours of pillage. They showed their clean revolvers to the weeping women to reveal that they had not taken part in the killing of their husbands and brothers, fathers and sons. Quantrill had ordered that women and children be spared, but not men. Cole Younger and Frank James probably belonged to the moderate group. The latter to his dying day, though a bandit, conducted himself with moderation and dignity. He was a student, as was his preacher father, and was an ardent reader of Shakespeare.

Quantrill's band had not entered Carthage that October fifth, 1863, but had passed twelve miles to the west, heading south. Perhaps because of the Lawrence raid, Quantrill soon lost control of his followers and they divided into small groups. Like most of the men who played a part in Belle Starr's life he was shot to death. It was toward the end of the war in Kentucky. Her first husband, Jim Reed, and her second, Sam Starr, both former guerrillas, met the same fate much later. According to the author, Homer Croy, Cole Younger who was Myra Belle's first love interest, after spending twenty-five years in prison following the North-field, Minnesota, bank robbery attempt, was pardoned in 1890 and returned to his old home in Missouri with "seventeen bullets still reposing in him." Had Belle Starr lived one year longer, they could have renewed their friendship of many years before.

In Texas at the war's end "Judge" John Shirley owned a ranch near Dallas. They had left Carthage after Bud Shirley was killed. For a time Myra Belle with her boarding school accomplishments and her superb ability as a horsewoman became a social favorite in frontier Dallas.

Ex-Senator Allen McReynolds of Carthage and Ward L. Schrantz, editor of the *Carthage News,* have generously contributed information to us concerning the earlier Myra Belle Shirley and the later Belle Starr. Senator McReynolds is former president of the State Historical Society of Missouri, and Mr. Schrantz is well known for his outstanding articles on Missouri history in both book form and in newspaper articles. He is probably the greatest living authority on Civil War guerrilla warfare.

Senator McReynolds tells us that little Myra Belle Shirley first attracted general attention as follows:

Myra Belle Shirley lived in Carthage at the beginning of the Civil War. She was the daughter of a tavern keeper here. Taverns in those days were hotels and did not have the same connotation that they do at the present time.

As far as I can determine Shirley was a respected citizen of the community. He had two children; the daughter and a son who was perhaps a couple of years older than Myra Belle.

When the Civil War broke out this whole country was in turmoil (before it was over the whole town of Carthage was burned). Of course sentiment was divided. The Shirleys were Southern sympathizers. The son was connected with an organization, guerrilla or otherwise. They had headquarters at Newtonia, Newton County. Some of the Federal troops came to Carthage and by reason of the situation in the hotel Myra Belle learned that they planned to capture the Confederate sympathizers located at Newtonia. In fact a squadron of Federal cavalry started for Newtonia. She immediately jumped on her riding horse and at breakneck speed cut across country to Newtonia and warned her brother and his group, thereby permitting them to escape. Naturally this incident attached more or less glamour to the girl's name at that time.

Though not so stated by Senator McReynolds, Newtonia is about 23 miles southeast of Carthage and by following a circuitous route through the woods Myra Belle must have ridden a much greater distance.

After the Shirley family moved to Texas, the people of Carthage lost knowledge of Myra Belle and did not connect her with the famous Belle Starr, the bank and stagecoach robber, and cattle and horse rustler.

Ward L. Schrantz has sent us his newspaper account of Belle Starr which he published in his January 29 edition of the *Carthage* (Missouri) *News* of this year. We quote from that:

Carthage in May 1886 apparently heard for the first time that there was any connection between this city and Belle Starr, the Indian Territory character who was soon to become the most widely chronicled daughter of Carthage in history. . . . Myra Belle was the fiery little daughter of old John Shirley who had run a hotel on the north side of the square at the beginning of the Civil War and for years prior thereto. She had gone to Carthage schools, including the Female Seminary where she along with others acquired such culture as that institution had to offer, including music, art and that sort of thing. Quite a girl, Myra, in those days, pretty, dark and dashing. A fearless horseback rider too, and an excellent shot.

Writing further of Belle Starr, Ward L. Schrantz quotes from his newspaper as of 1886. It tells of the return of the Carthage Light Guard Band from Fort Smith with $400 in prize money:

While in Fort Smith the Carthage bandsmen saw the noted Belle Starr. . . . Belle was one of the performers at the fair. The talk was that though she was under a sentence for outlawry as a result of a recent trial; being deemed trustworthy, was permitted to give a riding and shooting exhibition just the same. . . . Riding a horse bareback at full gallop, she broke clay pigeons and glass balls with rifle fire while in motion, varying the performance by leaping from the animal while moving at full speed, breaking more glass balls or clay pigeons from the ground with her rifle, then leaping back on her animal as it galloped past her again, still at full speed and continuing her firing.

Though Mr. Schrantz's *Carthage News* of 1886 did not mention it, the Fort Smith fair came near to being still more dramatic. St. Joseph's former citizen, Federal Judge Isaac C. Parker, through his court commissioner, had just discharged Belle Starr on a second or highway robbery charge. On the first charge in 1882 she had been found guilty along with her husband Sam Starr of horse lifting and she seemed grateful for the light sentence of one year in the Detroit Michigan House of Correction. She bore Judge Parker no ill will, but hated the prosecutor for his bitter personal attacks on her husband during the hearings and the earlier trial. At Detroit in 1883 she had been a model prisoner and was given light work in the prison chair factory, doubtless often thinking of her former confederates among the St. Joseph ex-guerrillas then busy making the buffalo horn furniture for her, pictures and descriptions of which accompany this article.

Judge Parker, the famous hanging judge, was more lenient with women than with men, and was president of the Fort Smith Fair of 1886, and agreed to ride in a stagecoach which was to be the object of a mock holdup by Belle Starr leading some Indians. Another passenger in the stagecoach was to have been the prosecuting attorney at her hearing, but he failed to appear. The story is that she carried a loaded cartridge among the blank cartridges she was to use, and was planning to shoot the prosecutor and to excuse herself by claiming the loaded cartridge got into her revolver by mistake.

After their return from Detroit, where they received three months' credit for good behavior, the Starrs had been living again on their 1,000-acre ranch at Younger's Bend, Indian Territory. Judge Parker had originally gone to Fort Smith, as a Federal Judge in 1874, from St. Joseph which he had represented in Congress for two terms. It was he in 1861 who, as city attorney of St. Joseph, had prepared the famous ordinance which prohibited the flying of any flags, including the United States flag. It is known as the ordinance which dethroned a city, as told in the 1952 fall issue of the *Museum Graphic*. The Indian Territory west of Fort Smith was within his jurisdiction, and had been a refuge for ex-guerrillas after the Civil War. When Lee surrendered to Grant at Appomattox some of these guerrillas refused to surrender, or weren't allowed to, and carried on private wars of their own. The Cherokee Indians had brought negro slaves with them from the Carolinas, so sided with the South in the war. The Starr ranch became a haven of refuge for fugitives from justice. In 1885, twenty years later, Sam Starr, still at war with the government, fled to New Mexico for a while after a post office had been robbed. When Myra Belle married Sam Starr, who was half Cherokee, she gave her age to the Indian agent as thirty-two and the date of her birth as 1848. Before she married Starr, Myra Belle Reed was, as a widow (Jim Reed had been shot in Texas), a member of a hard-riding band of outlaws, cattle and horse rustlers, bank and store robbers, and had ranged from the Texas panhandle to Nebraska. She herself may have taken refuge at the Starr ranch more than once before she decided to marry again.

After this marriage she sometimes went to St. Louis to buy wardrobes at the fashionable stores there. She was fond of side-saddle riding habits of the type approved for gentlewomen of Europe and America, a style now limited to British royalty.

In the June, 1886, hearing before the commissioner of Judge Parker's court, mentioned above, the witness said Belle Starr looked smaller than any of the bandits who robbed him. Soon afterward Sam Starr shot it out with the officers who were arresting him on the old post office robbery charge and he was wounded and captured, but soon escaped.

Probably on the advice of Belle Starr who trusted Judge Parker, he rode into Fort Smith and surrendered. While he was free on bond awaiting trial he was killed in a gun-fighting mixup. Early in 1889 on returning horseback from Fort Smith someone in hiding at her ranch shot Belle Starr off her horse from behind with a charge of turkey shot. While she was unconscious the assassin took her revolver from its holster and shot her through the head as she lay face down in the mud. She, by her own gun, died as Jesse James had, for his assassin, Bob Ford, had used the revolver given him by his victim.

A PREFACE FOR "IN MIZZOURA"

AUGUSTUS THOMAS

Augustus Thomas was one of the country's leading playwrights for some three decades at the turn of the century. Perhaps "The Witching Hour" (1907) and "The Copperhead" (1917) were his two most successful plays. In the latter, Lionel Barrymore gave one of the greatest performances of his career.

Thomas was born in St. Louis in 1857, was a page in the Missouri House of Representatives in the winter of 1868, a member of a St. Louis stock company for a short time, and a reporter and cartoonist for the Post-Dispatch.

The story of "In Mizzoura" was based on a local express robbery which Thomas had helped to cover for his paper, as he tells us in the following "preface" written for the printed version of the play; but the main interest is the sheriff's love story. The play was first staged in 1893.

This preface is one of a number* trying to show each for its particular play, the manner of the play's conception, whether starting from a theme, a character, or a situation; the difficulty of the start and the larger problems of the story's development, together with the ways considered and chosen to answer them. It has been thought that such accounts might be of interest, and in some instances, perhaps, helpful to others beginning on the same kind of work.

In the spring of 1891 Mr. Nat Goodwin was one of the most popular and successful, as well as one of the most skillful, of American actors. He had played lively and slight farces almost exclusively; but having

* The Witching Hour; Mrs. Leffingwell's Boots; The Earl of Pawtucket, The Harvest Moon; Oliver Goldsmith.

the ability for serious work as well, he was ambitious to try it. In a comedy by Brander Matthews and George H. Jessop, called "A Gold Mine" he had given one or two dramatic scenes most convincingly; and one sentimental soliloquy with a rose in exquisite tenderness. In person he is under the average height; and then, was slight, graceful, and with a face capable of conveying the subtlest shades of feeling. The forehead was ample; the eyes were large and blue, clear and steady. The nose was mildly Roman; the hair was the color of new hay. His voice was rich and modulated. These points are reported because they helped form the equipment of the star, who wanted a serious play in which he should be the hero. The order was without other conditions; the play might be of any period and of any land.

My own ignorance fixed certain limitations. At that time I had acquaintance with no other countries than the United States and Canada. These I knew fairly well. I had traveled them with one night theatrical companies; and also in newspaper assignments; and over restricted districts I had worked in the employment of a railroad company. I didn't care to write from books; so my Goodwin hero was to be perforce an American. It seemed best to make him an American of 1891. Other times and places were excluded and dismissed from mind.

Now, a blond hero five feet seven inches tall and weighing under one hundred and fifty-pounds—a Roman nose, and a steady, steel blue gaze!

I stood the Goodwin photograph on my table and looked at it until it talked to me. The slight physique couldn't explain the solid confidence of that look except there was behind it a gun. We were doing more man to man shooting in the country then than now; and my Western friendships made me more tolerant of the gun than some others were. Goodwin and a gun sent me searching mentally over the West from Colorado to the Coast, and through all occupations from bandit to fighting parson; and then my potential gallery, quite apart from any conscious effort of my own, divided itself into two kinds of gunpackers; the authorized and the others. I concluded that there would be less trouble, less "lost motion"—that was a phrase learned, and an idea applied in the old-fashioned composing room—less lost motion, in portraying a lawful gun toter than in justifying an outlaw; and the Goodwin part was therefore to be either a soldier or a sheriff. I have said that he was thin, graceful—and he was, but he wasn't particularly erect. He was especially free from any suggestion of "setting-up": sheriff was the way of least resistance.

My hero was a sheriff. You see how that clears the atmosphere. When you must, or may, write for a star, it is a big start to have the character agreeably and definitely chosen.

There must be love interest, of course.

A sheriff would presumably be a bit of the rough diamond; *contrast* wherein "lieth love's delight" prompted a girl apparently of a finer strain than himself; and *conflict* necessitated a rival. The girl should be delicate and educated, the *rival* should be attractive but unworthy; and to make him doubly opposed to Goodwin I decided to have him an outlaw—someone whom it would be the sheriff's duty and business—*business* used in the stage sense—to arrest.

Four or five years before the Goodwin contract I had been one of the *Post-Dispatch* reporters on the "Jim Cummings" express robbery. That celebrated and picturesque case was of a man who presented to an Express messenger at the side door of his express car, just as the train was pulling from the St. Louis station, a forged order to carry the bearer, dead-head, to a certain distant point on the run. The messenger helped the dead-head into his car and chummed with him, until about an hour later, when, as he was on his knees arranging some of his cargo, he found a pistol muzzle against his cheek, and his smiling visitor prepared to bind and gag him. Having done this, the stranger packed one hundred and twenty thousand dollars into a valise; and dropped off into the dark, when the train made its accustomed stop at a water-tank. The whole enterprise was so gentle, that the messenger was arrested and held as an accomplice, while the Pinkertons looked for the man with the money.

The robber was a kind-hearted person; and being really grieved over the detention of an innocent man, wrote several exculpating letters to the papers enclosing rifled express envelopes to prove his peripatetic identity. These letters were signed "Jim Cummings," a *nom de guerre* borrowed from an older and an abler offender of the Jesse James vintage.

After he was arrested and in his cell in the St. Louis jail, "Jim Cummings" and I became friends as criminals and newspaper men sometimes do, and as criminals and I always have done, everywhere, most easily. The details of his arrangements, both before and after his draft on the company were minutely in my mind, and were so very vital that with the first need for a drama criminal I took him. Goodwin's rival should be Jim Cummings; a glorified and beautiful and matinée Cummings, but substantially he.

This adoption rescued the girl and the sheriff from the hazy geography of the mining camps, and fixed the trio in Missouri.

After Cummings had dropped from the express car, he had walked some fifteen miles to the Missouri River near St. Charles, and had then gone north on a train through Pike County. I had more than once made the same trip on freight trains; and I had a liking for the county as the home district of Champ Clark, a politico-newspaper comrade of several legislative sessions and conventions. Newspaper experience in those days before the "flimsy" and the "rewrite" emphasized the value of going to the place in order to report the occurrence; and I knew that, aside from these three characters and their official and sentimental relationships, the rest of my people and my play were waiting for me in Bowling Green.

In those days Mrs. Thomas and I used to hold hands on our evening promenades; but I think it was really our foolish New York clothes that made the blacksmith smile. At any rate, we stopped at his door and talked with him. He knew Champ Clark and Dave Ball—another Missouri statesman—and had the keenest interest in the coming convention for the legislative nomination. It was fine to hear him pronounce the state name *Mizzoura,* as it was originally spelt on many territorial charts, and as we were permitted to call it in the public schools until we reached the grades where imported culture ruled. The blacksmith's helper, who was finishing a wagon shaft with a draw knife, was younger and less intelligent and preferred to talk to Mrs. Thomas. It is distracting to listen at the same time to three persons; but I learned that "You kin make anything that's made out o' wood with a draw knife"; and over the bench was the frame for an upholstered chair. A driver brought in a two-horse, side seated, depot wagon on three wheels and a fence rail. The fourth wheel and its broken tire were in the wagon; and the blacksmith said he'd weld the tire at five-thirty the next morning.

We went without breakfast to see him do it. He was my heroine's father by that time; a candidate for the legislature; and I was devising for him a second comedy daughter, to play opposite to the boy with a draw knife. That day I also found the drugstore window and the "lickerish" boxes that Cummings should break through in his attempted escape; and I recovered the niggers, the "dog fannell," the linen dusters, and the paper collars which, in my recent prosperity, I'd forgotten. I also nominated Goodwin for the legislature, which increased his importance and gave him something to sacrifice for the girl's father. But it was all so poverty stricken as I glimpsed it through the blacksmith shop and the little house I'd chosen for its consort. I yearned for some money, not much, but enough to afford "a hired girl," and for some means of bringing the money into the story. When we left Bowling Green I had given Goodwin a substantial reward for the robber's capture; but he wouldn't accept it. That was a mere dramatist's device; and my quiet sheriff was already above it; besides, he wasn't sure that he'd hold the fellow. His wish to please the girl was already debating the matter with his duty.

On the way back to St. Louis, the conductor, who took our tickets, recognized me. Charlie Church had been a freight brakeman when I was in the St. Louis yards. He was proud of his advancement to a passenger conductorship—proud of his train—proud of the new Wabash road-bed on the single track line. This road-bed was made of macadam-looking metal, clean and red as the painted bricks in the local Dutch women's gardens and hard as flint. When we gave the right-of-way and ran in on a siding, Church brought us up a few pieces to the back platform; and with one of them scratched my initials on the glass window. "What was it, iron ore?—no, that mud that the river leaves when it rises —'Gumbo' the people call it. Some fellow found by accident that it became red flint when fired and was making a fortune selling it to the railroad." To burn it, he used the slack coal from the Jonesburg mines nearby, which until then had also been waste. I put a handful of the stuff in my pocket; and after the Conductor left us, I turned the whole enterprise over to the Goodwin part. When the play ended, the audience should feel sure that he and Kate need never want for a dollar. I knew also where he had accidentally burnt his first sample, and made his discovery; in the blacksmith shop.

But what accident brought the raw gumbo there? Perhaps the wheels of the stage coach; but that wasn't definitely Goodwin. The soft gumbo is not unlike putty; it would make a fair cushion for a broken limb: but I didn't want to halt my story with anybody crippled to that extent; and then I remembered the yellow dog drinking from the blacksmith's tub. I broke *his* leg and had Goodwin carry him miles in the stage, with his poor paw in a poultice of gumbo. It was a counter-pointing touch to a sheriff with two guns; it gave him an effective entrance; and it coupled in a continuous train, the sheriff, the bad man who sneered at it, the blacksmith and his motherly wife who sympathized and helped in a better dressing, the forge where a piece of the discarded gumbo should fall amongst the coke, the helper who should pump the bellows for another and verifying bake: and last, and best of all, it gave me a "curtain" for a second act; when perturbed and adrift after being temporarily rejected by the girl, Goodwin should turn in an undefined but natural sympathy to the crippled dog in his box under the helper's bench.

That illustrates one of a dramatist's discovered rules: "if you use a *property* once use it again and again if you can." It is a *visual* thing that binds together your stuff of speech like a dowel in a mission table.

There are few better places than a railroad train for building stories; the rhythmic click of the wheels past the fish-plates makes your thoughts march as a drum urges a column of soldiers. A tentative layout of the story established in the first act, the educated Kate, discontented in her blacksmith father's surroundings; the flash fascination of our transient robber; the robber's distinct lead over Goodwin's accustomed and older

blandishments. The second act saw Goodwin turned down and the robber preferred. The third act should see the robber's apprehension and
arrest. I milled around the question of his identification as Illinois and
Indiana went past the Pullman window; and then the one sure and unfailing witness for that purpose volunteered—the express messenger
himself. There was no reason why this young man shouldn't be a native
of Bowling Green and come home from St. Louis at the end of certain
runs. He would know Goodwin and the blacksmith's family; but to put
him nearer to them, more "into the story" sentimentally, I gave Goodwin a little sister and made the messenger her accepted lover, with his
arrest and detention postponing the wedding. This need to free his
sister's fiance gave the sheriff hero a third reason for getting the real
robber; the other two being his official duty and the rivalry for Kate.
The messenger and the sheriff's sister, the helper and the comedy daughter, and Goodwin and Kate, made three pairs of young lovers. This number might easily lead to a disastrous diffusion of interest unless the playwright were careful always to make the work of each couple, even when
apparently about their own personal affairs, really to the forward trend
of the story.

I doubt if the production of novels, even to the writer temperamental-
ly disposed to that form of expression, is as absorbing as play making.
The difference between the novel and the play is the difference between
was and *is*. Something has happened for the writer of the novel and for
his people. He describes it as it was; and them as they were. In the play
something *is happening*. Its form is controversial—and the playwright,
by force of this controversy, is in turn each one of his characters, and
not merely a witness of their doings. When they begin to take hold of
him, their possession is more and more insistent—all interests in real
life become more and more secondary and remote until the questions in
dispute are not only decided, but there is also a written record of the
debates and the decision.

By the time our train pulled into New York, I was impatient to make
a running transcript of speeches of my contending people. But that is
a relief that must be deferred. Like over-anxious litigants, the characters
are disposed to talk too much and must be controlled and kept in bounds
by a proportioned scenario, assigning order, and respective and progressive values to them. That was the work of a day by that time and
then, with the material gathered, and the intimacy with the people and
the places, the play was one that wrote itself.

MISSOURI ARTISTS

BINGHAM, THE MAN AND THE PAINTER

JOHN FRANCIS MCDERMOTT

John Francis McDermott was born in St. Louis in 1902 and became a member of the Washington University faculty in 1924. He has edited such works as Irving's Western Journals *and Edward Harris'* Up the Missouri With Audubon, *as well as writing the biography* George Caleb Bingham, River Portraitist, *the last chapter of which is presented here.*

To this admirable summary we may be permitted to append the note that Bingham was a strong partisan and capable of bitter hatreds; of this his "Order No. 11," followed by his long feud with General Thomas Ewing, is an illustration. He served a term in the Missouri legislature in 1849.

How Bingham learned to paint so brilliantly and originally remains a very deep mystery. Some understanding, nevertheless, can be reached through the man, for between his life and his work there is a notable accord. Partisanly active as he was in politics, pressed as he was to make a living by his art, Bingham remained at ease with his world. Neither an optimist nor a pessimist, he accepted life as he found it. He was not an artist standing aloof, immersed in his own emotions and reactions, but a man well rooted among people, responding to life. Tranquillity, assurance, a sense of belonging are everywhere seen and felt in his work. The tall man leaning on his setting pole in *The Wood Boat*, the fisherman baiting his hook in *Fishing on the Mississippi*, the gentlemen in the political scenes, the farmers shooting for a prize, the checker players considering their moves, the returning trappers, the loafers and the hangers-on—all have an air of calm acceptance: this is the way life is, they seem to say, and why not? They are not whining or whimpering, beating their breasts, complaining of ill-usage, bewailing the morrow, or exhorting their fellows to action and great deeds. A simple, open, natural, serene man, Bingham has created a world filled with people natural and at their ease before the universe. It is this unity of tone pervading his work that is one of its most marked characteristics. Wherever we turn—throughout the genre pictures, in the landscapes, in the portraits painted over forty-five years—there is everywhere this same quality of being at one with the world.

Critics have placed Bingham among the romantics presumably because he painted the common man and nature, but he was, in fact, a classicist. His intention was not to elevate or glorify the common man. It was to study man. Late in life he made this clear by asserting to Rollins that his purpose had been to record "our social and political characteristics as daily and annually exhibited." To Bingham men were not high or low, aristocratic or common. They were men, behaving as men behave. The likeness that has been seen in his work to that of Poussin and Claude Lorrain was no chance development that happened because the earliest pictures falling into his hands were engravings after these masters or their followers. It is the expression of Bingham's spirit, his controlling force. He painted the world as he saw it—who can do otherwise? —and he saw it with the moderation, the sense of proportion, the restraint of emotion, the good humor and good sense that characterize the true classical tradition. He is a conservative in the best sense—a tolerant observer able to look on his fellows without personal passion or prejudice.

In *Stump Speaking,* for instance, we see the stupid fellow—his back is turned to us, but we know his vacant face—asking a pointless question with earnest importance. We see the speaker, wishing to be all things to all voters, striving to make a reply that will not cause another "sovereign" to ask an opposing question. Bingham is not savage with this self-important dull clod; he expresses no sympathy with or antipathy to the office seeker. He does not turn with disgust from the grinning drunk. Each man in this crowd is a man living his own life. Bingham only looks at them with knowledge and understanding, with geniality, humor, and a certain kindliness. He calls this mixed lot of humanity "the sovereigns of the people," but he is not mocking them or sneering at them any more than he is holding them up to admiration as the representation of the institution of democracy. It is his concern to present and not to judge.

Bingham's paintings are a direct result of his own naturalness and simplicity, of his tolerant understanding, of his honesty of observation and sincerity, of his controlling sense of balance and proportion in life. But beyond all this, they are pervaded by another quality of which Bingham would not have been aware. That quite real and actual world which he painted so objectively—and this is particularly true of the river scenes—was at the same time a world remembered; it was the world of his boyhood, of his youth, a world slipping away from him. Without his knowing it, a nostalgic glow of boyhood remembered is diffused over all his marvelously accurate delineations of western life. He has not merely recorded magnificently his place and his people, but he has evoked life itself. He is not merely a reporter: he is a poet.

BACK TO MISSOURI

THOMAS HART BENTON

Thomas Hart Benton, foremost Missouri painter of the twentieth century, is a grandnephew of the man of the same name who served Missouri in the United States Senate 1821–1850. He was born in Neosho in 1889. He studied art at the Chicago Art Institute and the Académie Julien in Paris. He is best known as a muralist, and had painted three distinguished murals (Whitney Museum of Art, New School for Social Research, Indiana Building at the 1933 Chicago World's Fair) before the time described in the passage from the final chapter of his autobiographical An Artist in America, *here reproduced.*

Since that time, Benton has served as director of painting in the Kansas City Art Institute and has painted a large mural for the Truman Library in Independence. He was awarded an honorary doctorate of Fine Arts by the University of Missouri in 1949. He was given a grand homecoming ovation on May 12, 1962, when Former President Truman unveiled a portrait of him in the City Hall auditorium in Neosho.

In the early winter of 1935, I came into the Middle West on a lecture tour. I went to Iowa and saw Grant Wood. Grant said, "Why don't you come out here and live where you belong?" I thought about that but didn't see how I could do it. Later I gave a lecture in Kansas City and my brother, Nat, then prosecutor in Greene County, Missouri, came up and induced me to take a trip to Jefferson City, the capital, to meet some of the Democratic boys. In Jefferson City I ran into some old Missouri acquaintances and we had one of those regular hotel room parties where you pour liquids down you and stories out of you until the world begins to spin. When the world was spinning pretty well for me, Ed Barbour, the senatorial incumbent from Greene County and an old friend, said with his good Missouri drawl:

"Sa-ay, Tom, you did a picture there for Indiana. Why don't you do one for your home state?"

I replied that I was willing and Ed said that he'd get up a bill on the matter for the legislature.

Now the world was spinning for me and I took Ed's proposition just to be a part of the spinning and forgot about it. I went back to New York and fell into a lot of wordy controversies again. But it seems that Ed and my brother Nat had talked over the business of a Missouri mural before the hotel party, that they had made rather extensive plans which I knew nothing about, and that Ed's question to me was no mere party question but one that had substance to back it. Anyhow, in a month or so, I got a copy of a bill that was up before the Missouri legislature which recommended that I be hired to do a painting for the state capitol on the history of Missouri. There was an awful lot of whereases in the bill but I managed to understand it and sent a telegram of approval to Ed and my brother Nat. A few weeks later I heard the bill had passed and that I had another mural commission. On the very day I received this information, I opened a letter from Ross Howard, director of the Kansas City Art Institute, asking me to teach there. I made up my mind suddenly to leave New York and go home to Missouri for good.

I said in the beginning of this chapter that there were other reasons besides that of the Missouri mural which caused me to leave New York and return home. These reasons grew slowly over a number of years and prepared the ground for a decisive move. In my travels, both for pictorial subjects and for lectures, I had come to see that since the financial collapse of 1929 there had grown throughout the United States a sort of distrust of our great cities which coincided with something I felt within myself about them. I saw that the potentates who owned the towering skyscrapers of the big towns and who ran the country in the days of mounting prosperity and boom had lost their reputations for infallibility. Their immense practicality had turned out to be not so practical after all, and throughout the country, from backwoods stores to the halls of legislatures, derisive jokes about "their majesties" were becoming more and more frequent. I saw that political affairs were taking precedence over those of business and that ideas were beginning to dominate the reports of stockjobbers' moves.

Though politics remains in practice a trading game directed to the shrewd balance of economic interests and the maintenance of the status quo, it has been, nevertheless, making theoretical excursions into what a few years ago was considered the realm of impractical professors. This is a significant matter, for ideas held by professors are just ideas, but when they get into the heads of politicians, they have the potentialities of sticks of dynamite. They may be dropped accidentally and they may explode in extremely crucial places. Such explosions, quite against the conscious wills of those responsible, may generate changes of unpredictable magnitude. Things of this sort happen. Lincoln was not an abolitionist when he came to the defense of the Union. He had no notion of clearing the land of chattel slaves to the end that wage slavery might progress more freely. He was not a revolutionist. There are no revolutionists among our political powers today, but in the body of ideas with which they are flirting there are notions far more menacing to our present social structure than were those of the abolitionists for theirs.

Seeing the country's ferment and prospects of immense changes in its allegiances, I had the desire to escape the narrow intellectualism of the New York people with whom I associated and to get more closely acquainted with the actual temper of the common people of America. I had no way of doing this in any permanent manner and at the same time be sure of making a living, but I considered the matter extensively. I lived much with those who under the illusory sway of their own logical structures ventured to predict our American future. I didn't believe them. I didn't believe they knew what they were talking about. I had myself no certitudes about our future. I could foresee nothing. I was aware, however, of the changes coming over the political psychology of our country, and I hankered to be close to the soil on which these would be most clearly operative.

In addition to politics, other things were taking my mind away from New York and toward the West. In my lecture tours I had seen that along with what appeared to be a reaction against metropolitan economic dominance, there was rising in our smaller cities a marked sort of cultural consciousness. I had large and friendly audiences in my western talks and while I did not lack hecklers, the majority of these seemed to be better informed and to be more sincerely interested in getting at my meanings than did those of the big cities. Everywhere I found what appeared to be a genuine interest in the expressive arts. Some of this was pretty naive, but it was strong enough to make me think that perhaps the end had come to that peculiarly brittle, dry, and empty psychology which had grown up with the great exploitative possibilities of the Reconstruction period, where all effort was directed to immediate monetary profit. I felt that whatever forces were at work, there was growing, particularly in the Middle West, a belief that values could exist in things beyond immediate usage and that these values should be nursed and cultivated. Looking about I saw museums, big and little, springing up all over the land. I saw that universities were inaugurating extensive art courses and that small-town newspapers were commenting on these projects without satirical intentions. This was a revolutionary change from my boyhood days in the West when the word "art" was mentioned only self-consciously in the obscurity of ladies' clubs, and when the few art schools that existed away from the big cities were regarded as the resorts of nuts and cranks.

With all this I began to feel that I, a western artist, the better part of whose work was motivated by western subject matter, should find a

way of being part of the change that was coming in my homeland. When
the opportunity came to return to Missouri with some prospects of
making a living there, I jumped at it. . . .

I have been now two years in my home country.

Working in temperatures that ran from way below zero during the
months of preparation to as much as 118 above during those of execution, I have fulfilled the contract which was primarily instrumental in
bringing me here. My *Social History of Missouri* is finished. Like my
other murals it has received its full share of adverse comment. I have
been put on the mat to defend it time after time. I have talked to
Rotary Club, chamber of commerce, Junior League, church, school, legislative, and barroom audiences.

Although I expected criticism, I must confess that the character of
some of that occasioned by my Missouri mural came to me as a surprise.
I was not in the least hurt by it and have really profited by the advertising it gave me. I have had as well a lot of fun pitting my wits against
those who objected to my ways of seeing and doing. Just the same when
the storm of critical comment came I was not prepared for its astonish-
ingly conventional and often vindictive character. I expected my legislative friends to have their little jokes and I expected a few moralists
and conservative art lovers to express their distaste for my performance.
But that was all. I did not expect any extensive objections. I did not expect that anybody would think that I was trying to degrade or make a
joke of my state when I treated its society in a realistic manner.

During the period in which I was actually painting, thousands of
people from all over Missouri came to see me. I left open the door of
the room where I was working. I tacked a few warning signs about to
keep the hands of visitors off my sketches and materials and to keep
them from bothering me when I was painting, but I let them come in
and look as long as they wanted to. At noon when I rested, and in the
evening when I was through, I would talk to people. During all those
days of work I never heard a seriously intended criticism. Everyone was
friendly. Occasionally a farmer would object to some detail of farm
life. When his criticism was valid, I would change the detail which offended and which might stand in the way of his appreciation of my
work. I wanted plain Missouri people like the farmers to like my painting, and when my total design was not affected by their objections to
some detail of fact I remedied the matter for them. I had all the evidence
necessary to make me believe that my realistic conceptions of Missouri's
social history and life were in line with the reputedly realistic psychology
of the state's people. Missouri is the commonwealth whose motto is

"You've got to show me." I was pretty sure that what I was showing was taken favorably.

When, however, my work was done and I was gone from Jefferson City a storm broke over me, and my illusions about a good many Missouri things were broken with it. I saw that realism was not by any means a completely shared Missouri virtue, and that the habit of calling things by their right names and representing them in their factual character was not wholly agreeable to so many people as I supposed. I awoke to the fact that many of those who came to see me accepted my attitudes simply because of the strangeness and perhaps the fascination of my unusual activities which made them restrain for the moment the actual mushiness and vulgarity of their own views. But in the end they let it out to me, and I found that my basic attitudes were entirely incomprehensible to many people and that my realism and intention to be faithful to my actual Missouri experiences were regarded somewhat as pretensions or poses. The idea that I could be sincere in my attitudes and performances was beyond the reach of a lot of Missouri minds.

One gentlemanly heckler, as I was giving an explanatory talk on my mural, rose from his seat with a sheaf of prepared questions. After reciting my family background in Missouri, he asked me if I was not proud of my state. Now I suppose the average person under the circumstances would have said yes, but I knew I was not proud of my state, and I told him that I was simply interested in it. He had to throw away a lot of his questions then. He lost the opportunity he had anticipated of getting me into a logical trap of words. I am certain that that man was in his way sincere, but the mere statement of his question indicated that he was without the slightest understanding of the sort of thing I stood for. He could not see or believe that I really meant what I said when I told him that I judged the world and the people in it by what they did rather than by what they said. He could not understand any more than could my Communist friends of New York that I did not believe in patterns of words and that such a pattern as "Are you proud of Missouri?" was utterly without meaning for me. Like the New York radicals, he saw my kind of realism as cynicism, as something beyond even a touch of nobility or beauty. Time and time again as I talked about my mural people would rise with questions or statements that indicated plainly that they could not get the connection between beauty, sincerity, or honesty of purpose and the ordinary straight recognition of things *as they were and are* that is behind my work.

However, after three months' arguing, or rather telling, I think Missouri has got used to me. With my basic realism and perfect willingness to call a spade a spade, I have considerable advantages over my hecklers. I have got away with my stuff. I have answered every question and every objection put to me about my mural and because I answered these straight, without any beating about the bush, I think most real Missourians are beginning to like me and have come to the conclusion that I intended and made a pretty fair picture of my state. There are diehards from the young Communists' nests of St. Louis up (or down if you will) to the strongholds of Missouri conservatism who still maintain that because I painted no "idealisms" my work is a disgrace. There are people even among the Democrats of the legislature who sponsored my job and paid me my money, who seem to feel that I should have done better had I painted a sweeter picture of my home state—something a little more delicate, a little more violet-scented. This seems to me a bit odd because in my whole experience of Missouri Democrats, I've never run across any little woodland flowers (among the bucks, anyhow) and I don't believe I've ever seen a single Missouri Democratic politician, drunk or sober, who wouldn't bust you if he thought you mistook him for a violet. A great many of the objectors to the morality of my picture have been the saltiest kind of fellows in actual fact, perfect vindications by their appearance and language of the factual truth of my work. Seeing that most men are quite satisfied with themselves as they are in actuality, I expect that the attitudes of these fellows will change when they become familiar with the form of my picture and are able to look past its unfamiliar conventions to the Missouri people and life it represents. Their Sunday school horrors and resuscitated copybook maxims will be forgotten and they will come over to me and see that the value called "beauty" may reside just as well in the common, ordinary things of life as in idealistic dreams.

During the making of my Missouri mural I traveled all over the state. I met all kinds of people. I played the harmonica and wore a pink shirt to country dances. I went on hunting and fishing parties. I attended an uproarious three-day, old settlers' drunk, in the depths of the Ozarks. I went to political barbecues and church picnics. I took in the honkytonks of the country and night clubs of Kansas City and St. Louis. I went to businessmen's parties and to meetings of art lovers' associations. I went down in the mines and out in the cornfields. I chased Missouri society up and down from the shacks of the Ozark hillbillies to the country club firesides of the ultimately respectable. From this it would seem that I should know my Missouri—and in a sense I think I do. But it is not quite the Missouri I envisaged when I wrote my farewell essay to New York. Somehow or other I had come to believe that I should find a relatively simple and transparent society in my home country, a society which, while it might have its modern prejudices and taboos, would at the same time retain a good deal of pioneer experimentalism and be free of the vulgarity of cultivated affectations and borrowed manners. All of my late notions of Missouri were formed while on bumming trips in extremely rural sections of the state. In my summer wanderings from New York I had avoided the cities of the West and dug into back-country life where behavior patterns were uncontaminated by very many metropolitan hang-overs. I saw nothing of the ways of the well-to-do people of the cities who would, by the structure of our society, be responsible for the protection and cultivation of the arts. In my lecture trips I saw that particular society superficially. While I saw that it had an interest in my American localism, I did not take into consideration that as an expatriate Missourian I might more readily extol the interesting aspects of the real Middle West than I could as a permanent inhabitant. I failed to see also that a lot of the people who attended my lectures and were so friendly to me were doing so partly because I appeared to be like something out of Walter Winchell's New York column.

I came back to Missouri with a good many illusory notions. Not all of these notions have been dispelled and some that were have been replaced by equally interesting and entertaining facts of common life. But one illusion has been knocked out for good—that is, that the cultivated people of the Middle West are less intellectually provincial than those of New York or more ready for an art based upon the realities of a native culture. Those who affect art with the big "A" do so with their eyes on Europe just as they do in New York. They lisp the same tiresome, meaningless aesthetic jargon. In their society are to be found the same fairies, the same Marxist fellow travelers, the same "educated" ladies purring linguistic affectations. The same damned bores that you find in the penthouses and studios of Greenwich Village hang onto the skirts of art in the Middle West.

There is, however, a difference between the precious gentility of the West and that of the East. Your western people are very friendly even when the desire to be of a superior quality runs them into affectation and pose. Among the men of well-to-do society, there runs a strain of wholesome good-fellowship which forbids the hauteurs of Boston and Philadelphia and makes them a little self-conscious as they ape the manners of English country gentlemen. The better part of the male gentility of the western cities seems to be secretly aware of the fact that the antics of a pink coat are not exactly in harmony with the substance of western life. They are aware also that in living above the run of life about them they have become somewhat dull. They invariably speak of one another as stuffed shirts, unconsciously mirroring thereby their secret appreciation of themselves. This basic uneasiness keeps them quite human and I must say that, so far, I have not met a really complete ass among them. If they are a little boresome at times, they are at least not contemptible.

What is called society is, of course, like the froth on a glass of beer, of no consequence. I speak of it mainly because it was very much of a discovery for me to find that it had developed in Missouri in the regular stereotyped Long Island-Philadelphia suburb style. I knew there were wealthy groups in the state, but I felt they would somehow keep the flavor of their background and some of its salty originality. I was fooled.

Below the top economic foam of Missouri, the true native life lies. Although I have painted that life as I saw it and felt it, I am not yet ready to analyze it or pass judgment upon it. Taken as a whole, I like the men and women who make the real Missouri. I get along with them.

From where I live I can take my car and in a few minutes run past the junk heaps and gaudy signs of Kansas City into deep country. In a few hours I can be in the utter backwoods.

There is a high rugged bluff above the Missouri River a few miles from Kansas City. I drive out when I get bored and sit on that bluff. The river makes a great curve in the valley below and you can see for miles up and down the running yellow water. Although I was born and raised in the hill country of southwest Missouri, the great river valley appeals to me. I feel very much at home looking down upon it. Either I am just a slobbery sentimentalist or there is something to this stuff about your native land, for when I sit above the waters of the Missouri, I feel they belong to me, and I to them.

As a matter of fact, I feel I belong all over my state. There is about the Missouri landscape something intimate and known to me. While I drive around the curve of a country road, I seem to know what is going to be there, what the creek beds and the sycamores and walnuts lining them will look like, and what the color of the bluffs will be. Feeling so, I don't believe I shall ever . . . go back [to New York].

EDUCATION

MISSOURI RURAL SCHOOLS IN THE 'EIGHTIES

H. J. BLANTON

H. J. Blanton was for many years editor of the Monroe County Appeal, *published in Paris, Missouri, the town of his birth. He served a long term as a member of the Board of Curators of the University of Missouri, and in 1939, some years after his retirement from that post, the University conferred an honorary doctorate upon him. Blanton was the second of a dynasty of Missouri journalists of five generations—with a sixth coming along.*

The following is one of a series of sketches written for the St. Louis Globe-Democrat *and published in 1952 in a book entitled* When I Was a Boy. *That little volume met with so much success that a second series was issued two years later.*

When I was a boy the school teacher had other duties than teaching. She usually walked or rode horseback from her boarding place to the one-room building in which she did her work. According to the terms of her contract, she arrived early enough to have a good fire in the stove when pupils began to arrive. She also kept the water bucket serviced, the floor swept, the woodbox filled, and the ashes carried out.

Most of the schools had at least 50 pupils, which was quite in contrast with the 5 to 12 rural teachers now have. The small enrollments in these later years have been due to two causes. First, the steady drift of families from the farm. Second, steady decrease in the population of rural counties. In the Washington district, six miles north of Paris, for instance, there were more children of school age, 110 years ago, than at present. There are just as many farms and homes now as in 1840, but most of the homes either are childless or have only one or two for the near-by school.

The pay of rural teachers when I was a boy back in the middle eighties was only $20 to $35 a month. The teacher could not go from home every morning, as now is possible with cars and solid roads. She usually paid $8 to $10 a month for room, board and laundry. Money was so scarce among farmers that there was considerable competition for the position of host to the teacher, even at that low charge.

Many men, most of them with long whiskers, taught school during

Reprinted from *When I Was a Boy,* First Series, by H. J. Blanton. By permission of Edgar P. Blanton.

that era. Some of them were university graduates. Most of them were more or less addicted to drink. One of them, who taught one of our rural schools, was on one occasion called on the carpet by the district board and soundly lectured for the liquor habit. When the scolding was over, he calmly remarked:

"Well, gentlemen, you can't expect all the cardinal virtues for $30 a month."

The late Gus Bower of Paris figured in an exciting episode in his home district out in the country. The bewhiskered teacher kept a shotgun in one corner of the school room and would sally forth for a shot or two when game would appear in the nearby woods. On his return, he would creep to a place where chinking had been removed from between two of the logs and scan the interior for evidence, if any, of pupils who were misbehaving. On one occasion, just as his countenance was being pressed against the opening, a boy on the inside hurled into it a shovel full of hot ashes from the near-by fireplace. The outraged teacher, with singed whiskers and agitated voice, dashed into the schoolroom, demanding to know who did it. When nobody confessed, he undertook the job of whipping every boy in the room. A fight ensued when Gus Bower was reached, in the course of which the latter's arm was broken.

School authorities in those days were thoroughly sold on the idea that to spare the rod was to spoil the child. A teacher would no more have thought of equipping her school room without an ample supply of switches than without maps and textbooks.

An established custom in our rural schools until comparatively recent years was the demand by pupils for a treat at Christmas time, the penalty for refusal being a ducking in the nearest pond. Teachers usually prepared for the day by buying a bucket of cheap mixed candy. Many of them would hide it in their buggies or some other inconspicuous place, then pretend that no treat was to be given, only to surrender when shouting students had hustled them almost to the pond's edge. Much merriment followed as they all ran back to the schoolhouse and retrieved the hidden candy. Once in a long time, however, a belligerent male teacher would refuse to give in, whereupon, after a terrific struggle, he would be heaved into the water.

No college training was needed by the man or woman who aspired to be an educator when I was a boy. Practically all who taught rural schools had gone no farther than the nearest high school.

Whether local high schools and the one-room rural schools do a better job is a matter of considerable debate between old-timers like myself and those of the present generation. Here at Paris since I graduated in 1887 there have been added to the high school a Home Economics Department, a Commercial Department, a Music Department, a Vocational

Agriculture Department, athletic coach and other things. These gains, however, have been offset by the removal of courses like psychology, physiology, astronomy, geology, trigonometry, political economy and ancient history from the high school curriculum, all being studies which opened new and broader worlds of thought to the student.

THE BOX SUPPER

JOSEPH NELSON

Joseph Nelson, who prefers to remain anonymous, says that he and his wife Sally came to the "Big Piney" community on foot "some years back." He was looking for a job as a country school teacher, and he obtained it, at sixty dollars a month. But more than monetary reward was the pleasure of gaining a sympathetic insight into the folk-ways of "Big Piney."

The following story of a box supper is taken from Chapter XI of the author's account of his experiences, entitled Backwoods Teacher.

Today, this Friday of the fourth week, I was finishing my report cards as fast as the pupils appeared so I could put their attendance down, for there were to be big doings, come night. We needed all spare time to finish getting ready for our box supper—or box social, as some call it. The news had been "norated around" and we were hopeful that many women and girls would be here with boxes, and as many men and boys with money to buy them. But we had announced that corn and sweet potatoes and eggs or anything else which could readily be sold would be accepted in payment of bids.

Cap'n Jethrow had promised to take this produce off our hands, and with the money we intended buying work books—arithmetic, history, science, geography, art, spelling, music, and a general one of the history, geography, and resources of our state. All of us were fascinated by the samples which publishers had sent me, for they contained pictures to color or complete and blanks to fill in. . . .

The time for tonight's gathering was "early candle light," which is to say good dusk—though of course there were not so many candles burned by Big Piney folks as among an equal number of fashionable people in town. But the hillman's day is divided by light and dark, the way his year is divided by heat and cold, and he clings to this old time-telling expression which to me has a fine and romantic sound.

If he is a thrifty man he begrudges quitting his work in field or timber before dusk; if the women, as well-conducted women should, don't do the milking he may quit a little early or he may milk by lantern light, granting there are no children to perform the chore. But on a special occasion, as for the box supper, he will "take out" of the field early.

And now, when school was out, the children rushed home to do their chores and get ready to come back. People would be here by families— parents, brothers, sisters, grannies. Except for the young blades, and the young ladies who were being courted.

In the hills a boy "carries" his girl somewhere, just as he did in the old days. Once it was in a rig, afoot, or on horseback, she either riding pillion behind the saddle or on her own mount—which he romantically led. Now he may use a car, but if you are either puzzled or amused when he says he carried her he may not know why. At any rate, we were hoping many a girl would be carried to the box supper by her sweetheart, for it was there we stood to make our best money.

This was a happy day in another way for Sally and me—and, in a minor way for Cap'n Jethrow. It was pay day, and we owed him almost ten dollars—sack of feed for the cow and pig, one dollar; the rest for groceries, a strip of bright oil cloth, and a few little odds and ends. We had lived well, too, for we had brought much canned goods, largely the fruit of Sally's labors, with us; and we had our milk, butter, and cream, for the fall rains had made the pasture good so that the cow and calf could graze all they wished.

It was a long walk around to Kincaid's house to get my money. His dogs warned of my coming. I wouldn't have been greatly surprised, when he came out of the house, had he set them on me. He made no move to hush them and meeting me at the gate he spoke above their mighty barking:

"Here's yore pay if that's what you come fer." He handed me the warrant, which I would get countersigned at the box supper.

I mentioned the social and asked him to come to it.

"We ain't havin' no part in that school," he answered, the hardened muscles of his cheeks pushing his eyes half shut. "And I don't like no outsider comin' a-invitin' me to my own school if I was. But even if we come, don't be 'spectin' to get any money out of us. We got another school to put our money into this year."

I left. This was the first time I had seen him since they measured the schoolhouse for bars. I never knew whether those were simply a threat or were seriously intended, but the board finally decided they would look bad, and that a determined housebreaker could pry them off with a pole unless they were extremely heavy and well attached. So they compromised by putting locks on doors and windows. Perhaps Caldwell was back of the matter and was making a gesture to indicate that an eye was open for trouble, with retributive measures waiting.

When I reached home Sally already had the cow milked and the calf given her share, along with a handful of bran stirred into it, and the pig had had his feed and what skim milk was left from yesterday.

Having a baby seemed to be agreeing with Sally. She never looked better than now. She had her box ready for the supper, but she would not let me see how it was wrapped inside the brown paper sack in which she had placed it. That is part of the fun, not letting one's swain see how one's box looks. We feasted our eyes on the warrant, which would not have to be discounted like last year's. It more than matched the list of figures we had made out the night before.

Sally caught up her hoe and I mine; our fall garden was thriving like smoke. If frost held off, we would be well repaid. If it came early, we wouldn't.

Pete Muehlbach wouldn't come to break ground when Sally wanted to plant it: "They'd be talk, was I to come when the man was away from home; an' on Sattidy I allus catch a ride to town." Brother Helms said he would come "in the evenin' when Brother Nelson is around to kind of show me about how he wants it done—soon as I get a new plow point." The time was set for next day. Two days later, when he hadn't arrived, Sally interviewed Mr. Caldwell—careful to suggest that the time she had in mind was after school.

He brought his team and plow after finishing a field. I relayed his question to Sally, who was standing beside me: How much garden did she want? We were almost out of money and a little fearfully she countered: "How much would a quarter's worth be?" After all, you could hire a man and team for a dollar and a quarter a day—but then it was as much trouble to come for five minutes' work as five hours'.

Stiffly he replied: "I don't hire out; this is neighborly work. How much ground do you need turned?"

Chastened, she showed him the plot she had set her heart on, and since then we had been figuring how best we might repay him.

I spotted Sally's box as she and several other women went to put their offerings on the table on the rostrum. Each was wrapped fancily, and jokes were called back and forth to young swains who would burn with jealousy if their girls' boxes were bought by someone else—for, of course, whoever bought a box helped consume its contents in company with the lady who had packed it.

There were two or three cars on the ground, as dark came on. Other people had come in wagons. Many had brought chairs and these were carried in. By day, an iron heat can settle on the hills in September, but the nights are likely to be cool and this night was. The house was packed, the smells of sweat and tobacco were strong, and now and then I caught a whiff of corn whisky. A baby sucked noisily as I rose at the front and extended a hand for silence. I looked all around once more but nowhere did I see Kincaid, nor anyone who might be of his family.

I thanked people for coming. I told them that one evening soon we hoped to have a Friday night "literary" in which they could see how well the pupils were doing so that, at a later one, they could judge for progress. But tonight we had prepared only an entertainment—and with the money we hoped to raise we intended to buy books which would enable us to do more and better work. I could not forbear adding that our attendance record for the school month was almost perfect, and that I believed this indicated a genuine interest in the school by the children and parents.

I could see that I had done enough speechifying, even though I was getting a few agreeing nods. I glanced at the paper in my hand. I said, "Sue Anne Ashton will recite a poem, 'September.' "

It required forty-five seconds for her to do so, after reaching the stage. She was a pretty little thing and she received a big hand, although it is almost certain no one except the pupils and her parents knew what she said, for she forgot all her coaching once she was on her own. With the bit in her teeth she galloped through and ran to her mother, much pleased with herself.

Encores were invariable on the musical numbers; applause was always generous. But at last the speeches all were said and the songs all sung. Amos Masters's fox and hounds, stirringly presented, was as well taken as I gathered it had been for several years past. And, as it happened, Lonnie Haskins, a notable singer and hand with the guitar, had brought his "inster-ment." He was the uncle of Martha Ashton who had taught her the old ballads she knew—and likewise he was the star auctioneer of the district. He had promised the Ashton children (he lived in their home) that he would officiate for us tonight.

Now he sang "Little Mohee" and an encore to the same melody, "Moonlight and Stars." He gave us a "folly" ballad—a song with a nonsense chorus—and ended with, "Oh, I'm a 'roamer' gambler—"

And now— Now it was time for supper. Grinning and preening himself, the florid musician took the rostrum again. He wore a new

blue chambray work shirt with the shelf-creases still in it, rusty blue
serge pants, and mulehide work shoes without socks. He had a fringe of
reddish hair and a large Adam's apple and a look of sly benignity.

"Folks," he said, "you've seen this yere nice entertain-ment the p'fes-
sor an' the scholars has worked up, an' I want to say that I fer one
enjoyed it, an' I know I speak the senti-ments of one and all when I say
that." He spoke slowly and deliberately, gesturing with his right hand.
"The younguns done good an' they can be proud of theirselves. Now
boys, get yore money ready an' when I call fer bids you better not hang
back or somebody else will eat supper with yore girl an' it may be me.
I know who two or three of them there boxes belongs to, an' I reserve
the right to do a little biddin' myself. I come hyere hongry, an' I don't
aim to go home so. . . . Mr. Teacher—have you p'inted yore clerks?"

Amos Masters and Fritz Baily, my two oldest boys, were taking this
job since neither of them was sparking a girl. They were husky and raw-
boned but their awareness of the other sex so far consisted only in teas-
ing. They took their places at my desk, supplied with paper on which to
keep a record of who "bid in" each box, together with its identifying
number which some of the girls had tagged on as the boxes were
brought in at the beginning of the evening.

Successful bidders were to go forward one by one and settle with the
clerks while the next box was being sold, but they could not take their
purchases until the sale was entirely over. At that point they would go
forward again, receive their boxes, claim their ladies—and eat.

I was disturbed to note that no one had come with any produce, unless
it had been left outside, with which to settle bids. But we did have
several strangers, evidently from neighboring communities, and they
looked as if they might have some money.

Haskins took the first box from a clerk. He said, "Boys, that's a perty
piece of doin' up, that there red ribbon, an' I bet what's inside is as
good as the outside. . . . Now, this yere sale is fer a good purpose.
Hit ain't fer foolishness. Ain't nobody give me leave to set ary price,
but what do you say, folks—no bid starts less'n a quarter? Ain't that
fair? If you taken yore girl to the restaurant in town you wouldn't get
her back out fer no quarter, would you now? Boys, I'm workin' up my
appetite, I bid a quarter myself—"

Someone called, "George, you aim to let ol' Lonnie eat with yore girl?
He allus takes home the girl he eats with—"

Laughter.

"Thirty cents!"

"Thank you, Sam," from the auctioneer. "Now George, if'n you think
this is Marthy's box and you hanker to eat with her, you better speak up.
I tell you that was a right good cake she cooked. Speak up—"

."Don't get no chance, all you old gran'paws jawin' so hard." This
was George Appleby who looked to be eighteen and whose folks were
substantial farmers and stockmen. His brother was off at an agriculture
school. His sally turned the laugh, and he said, "Thirty-five cents."

"I'd bid forty—" from another corner—"but I'm afraid George ain't
got but thirty-five cents an' I'd hate to see him not get to eat with that
girl—"

"Me, too," the auctioneer admitted, "but I'd hate worse to let this box
go fer a measly, pindlin' thirty-five."

Silence. No one wanted to risk forty.

"George," Haskins pronounced solemnly, "I'm aimin' to make you a
proposition. If'n you'll say forty I'll knock it down to you."

Sure of himself, George drawled, "What's the matter with you flint-
skinners? If thirty-five don't suit you, give me a scare."

"Skeer 'im, boys!" Lonnie begged. "If'n that girl wasn't my own niece,
so's I *could* spark her home, I'd bid fo'-bits, shore as God made green
apples—"

Some venturesome soul said, "Forty cents," and I put in with forty-
five before George could speak. For a moment I thought we'd more
than emptied his pocket and that I'd bought a box, but then he said,
"Anybody else?" All was silence. "Four-bits," he intoned grandly.

Lonnie Haskins said, "Son, you've bought you a box. Come an' pay
yore bill. . . ."

He had held out for a good bid on the opener to sort of set the pace
for the evening, but now bids went faster. Apparently people had a
little cash put back, or had trimmed their necessities when they took
their eggs and cream to the store this week, for the boxes brought forty-
five and fifty cents right along. One presently brought sixty-five, and
one was run up to a dollar.

When they were about half gone, Haskins said, "Now, ladies an'
gentlemen, before we sell the rest, we got a few little contests to work
off. Votes will be a penny a hunderd, an' you can buy as many as you
want to. An' you can vote fer yoreself if you feel like you ain't bein'
done right by. We got prizes fer the winners. First-off, we're aimin' to
'lect the best-lookin' man, an' the clerks can put me down fer one of the
candidates. Boys, I'll take a hunderd votes, an' there's the cash."

Laughter, as he tossed a penny to them.

Someone put up Cap'n Jethrow, with another penny. This contest
was good mostly for laughs. It netted ten cents and Haskins received, as
prize, a mirror from an old compact in which to view his beauty. A jar
of pickles, furnished by one of the girls, went to "the most love-sick

couple"—Miss Callie Ashton, a good-looking woman of some forty-five years, and Lonnie Haskins, though they did not go together. There was only a distant relationship between Miss Callie and Lonnie's Ashton kin. He called cheerfully, "Callie, me an' you had jist as good to get married and eat these things an' put an end to gettin' 'lected ever' time." Miss Callie turned pink, but she smiled good-naturedly.

A bar of soap went to the man with the dirtiest feet, as indicated by the voting, and then came the *pièce de résistance* of the contest—the thing all had been waiting for: The Prettiest Girl. She would receive the cake, made and donated by Miss Callie, which rested in splendor on the little table usually occupied by the globe.

Apparently the strangers were here to avenge a wrong under which they had smarted for a year since a delegation from Big Piney attended one of their suppers and elected a Big Piney girl as the prettiest at the gathering. They were the object of glances and whisperings.

Two or three Big Piney girls were nominated. George put up Martha and plunked down fifty cents. Her name, with five thousand votes, was duly placed on the blackboard. In the white light of the Aladdin lamps there was quietness.

One of the strangers called, "Miss Mary French. And you better bring them votes down to a penny apiece so's we can keep track. We'll take ten dollars' worth to start."

"Thank you, Homer," Lonnie said equably. "We can use the money an' I don't blame you fer puttin' her up. Fer a gal that wasn't borned and raised at Big Piney, I think she's as perty as you'd find anywhurs. Mary, stand up an' let's see you. . . . Law me, now, she is perty, ain't she, folks? You Big Piney boys better putt your money whur your mouth is if you aim to keep that cake at home!"

The girl was pretty—a brunette, rosy-cheeked at the moment from embarrassment—but overdressed. A few more half-hearted bids were made on our girl, but it was no use. The outlanders took the cake in triumph.

And the one called Homer said, "An' if any of you boys is countin' on lettin' the air out of our tars to get even, don't bother. We got the car right outside the door here an' we're watchin' it—"

There was now an undercurrent of bad feeling, it seemed to me, but things gradually brightened again as the box auction was resumed. Sally had played a trick on me, swapping boxes with another woman in private and then letting me see the one she took to the rostrum, and she grinned as, with four youngsters gathered wistfully around to help, I ate with their mother. The lady's husband was too wise a fox to be so taken in, and he presently sauntered up—a big, jowly man who filled his shirt and overalls to the fullest.

He said, "Reckon we ain't met, Mr. Nelson. . . . How's the ol' lady's box suit you?"

Sally, eating with one of the strangers, was taking this in. Well I don't like cake made with bacon grease and iced with jelly, but I manfully said, "Fine. . . . Here—help yourself."

"Don't mind if I do—"

I accidentally moved my cake where the hound with him nuzzled it, and with loud protestations of regret I gave it to the beast. I have no doubt that this wise and thoughtful creature has at least one star in its crown.

But, over all, it was a fine evening. We took in thirty-one dollars and thirty-one cents, which cabalistic figure exceeded our dreams by at least eleven, thirty-one. We would have books galore, and we would have something else I'd dreamed of—a microscope. A small, toy-like affair, which would enlarge rather clearly to fifty diameters, could be had for six and a half dollars. I had seen such a one brought by Santa Claus to a child last Christmas. It would open up the outer fringes of a world but vaguely wondered about, so far, at Big Piney school.

UNIVERSITAS MISSOURIENSIS

DONALD F. DRUMMOND

Professor Drummond was born in Ohio in 1914, was graduated at Stanford University, and has been a member of the English Department of the University of Missouri since 1949. In 1955 a Fulbright fellowship took him to the Philippines. He has been a contributor of poems to many journals, and his fourth volume of verse was published in 1963 under the title, The Drawbridge. *The following poem is taken from the pages of the* Missouri Alumnus, *April, 1963.*

> There comes time when a man declares his home:
> Not the house in which his mother bore him, nor
> The fine geography in which he grew,
> The great spectacular of Teton country, nor
> The Big Sur, nor the cactus desert in
> The Arizona calm; the twisted conifers
> Of sand Cape Cod, nor harsh Cape Hatteras:

Reprinted by permission of the author.

But where he lives: the visceral almost-knowledge
Of home, of what his life becomes:
The people, institutions, deep affections
Which time affirms and all his senses share.

Once I had thought, seeing elms brought down by ice,
Seeing the mixed, the clash of four traditions,
The humid cold, the humid heat, the mix
Of twenty landscapes, twenty tongues,
Southwest, Northeast, mechanical, agrarian,
All shades and colors, blended, fixed:
I had thought there is no center here:
Nowhere where conflict ever finds repose.

But I have learned. Essences are elements composed.
In this my home, the great traditions blend
Because they must, because they meet head-on
And in the meeting must define themselves.
Land of the Boones, the Bentons, and the Blairs,
The Fremonts and the Joseph Smiths,
The Hermann Germans and the St. Charles French;
The big and snaky rivers, chiggers, trees;
The sparse, the fecund; politic yet sound.

And yet the point, sure symbol and sure act
Lies at this center where all surely meets;
Sometimes composes, strains, rebels;
The nucleus where traditions dwell: an oak,
A pin-oak, durable hickory, or straight pine—
A university which to me is mine.

Not that I donned an academic robe
Which it bequeathed to me, but where I grew
Slowly in surety, learning what I knew:
The grim bronze tablets with the names recorded
Where this state paid the price it always pays
To maintain the great library where
Stare of the autocratic meets the stare
Of the common human turn of a common phrase
And freedom of the academe is air.

The price is great. The tall Ionic six
Mix youth and age;
And in them mix the ideal and the real.
Here is no accident. Here love is resident.
Devotion to the higher mind, to all
Variety and difference can give
To make a university for all:
For all who make a university themselves,
Beyond ambition, politics, or pride.
But what makes home, the comfortable side
Of knowledge, where the symbol finally lies
Deeper in the eyes, and in the free
Concourse of those who study to be free.
For these: this is University.

AN EDUCATIONAL REFORMER AND HIS TROUBLES

FRANK F. STEPHENS

Frank F. Stephens was born in Topeka, Kansas, in 1878. He took advanced work in history at the University of Chicago and University of Pennsylvania, and joined the History faculty at the University of Missouri in 1907. Dr. Stephens became Dean of Students of the College of Arts and Sciences at M.U. Following his retirement in 1948, he devoted more than a decade to the writing of A History of the University of Missouri, *from which the following sketch of the achievements of President A. Ross Hill is taken.*

The choice of a successor to President Jesse was referred by the Curators on December 10, 1907, to a Board committee of which Walter Williams was chairman. At an adjourned meeting December 27, the committee reported that it wished to offer the presidency to Albert Ross Hill, former dean of the Teachers College who had resigned only eight months before to become dean of the College of Arts and Sciences at Cornell University. The members of the Board

Reprinted from *A History of the University of Missouri* by Frank F. Stephens. By permission of the author and University of Missouri Press. Copyright 1962 by the Curators of the University of Missouri.

felt that a conference should be held with Hill before final action was taken, and such a meeting was arranged by wire for January 6 at the home of one of the Curators, former Governor Francis, in St. Louis. At this meeting and after full discussion, the Board offered the presidency to Hill with an annual salary of six thousand dollars and the use of the President's House on the campus, the same salary Jesse had received. Hill accepted the appointment.

This action of the Board may seem to have been rather precipitate, but the Curators had looked up his previous history before he was chosen in 1903 to be Professor of Educational Psychology and Head of the Department of Education. Born in Nova Scotia in 1870, he was a graduate of Dalhousie College, Halifax, in 1892, and later did graduate work in foreign universities and in Cornell University, where he had secured his Doctor of Philosophy degree in 1895. He then became professor of education for two years in a Wisconsin normal school, after which for six years he was a prominent member of the faculty of the University of Nebraska before coming to Missouri. After the resignation of Thilly as Chairman of the Department of Philosophy in 1904, Hill had succeeded rather normally to the leadership formerly exercised by Thilly. He was not only the Dean of the Teachers College but also an influential member of the Academic Faculty and of the Council. His appointment as president, therefore, was universally popular in the Faculty. His modern outlook, his decisiveness, his natural leadership, would infuse new life into all the official activities of the University. Though he had transferred to Cornell in the summer of 1907, he had kept in close touch with his friends in Columbia, and especially after his election in January was often consulted through correspondence by the officials on the campus and by the Curators. The change in the presidency in the summer of 1908 therefore was accomplished smoothly and quietly.

The question of the establishment of a school of journalism, left standing in December, 1906, when no acceptable dean was immediately available, was considered again in the spring of 1908 when President Jesse and President-elect Hill joined in a recommendation for the election of Williams as the first dean, for him to propose to the Board other members of the faculty, and for classes to begin the coming September. With Williams absenting himself from the Board meeting, these recommendations were approved by the other Curators, after which Williams resigned his position on the Board. With him no longer on the Board, there followed the immediate reference to the President's office of many important details previously handled by Williams, with the resulting growth in influence of the office of president and the acceptance by the Curators of Hill's leadership in the direction of University affairs.

Hill's most successful period as President was the first half of his administration, and it was during this period, through his leadership, that much of the later machinery of administration was developed. He was clear in his perception of the place in society of a great state university and as to how its objectives might be fulfilled. No detail was so small as to escape his notice, no member of the Faculty so obscure but that Hill knew his function in the organization, no subject so technical but that he knew where it fitted into the University curriculum. Unless absent on official business, he was faithful in attendance at the general Faculty meetings where he always presided. He made decisions with slight hesitation, and yet his judgments seemed to be the result of thoughtful consideration. He gave the impression of having thought over the questions long before they arose, though upon occasion he might ask the advice of the whole Council; he consulted freely with a few members of the Faculty, those whose opinions he valued most highly. Having once decided, he did not relish opposition. He was high-spirited and outspoken and gave way at times to outbursts against individuals, but he never nursed grudges. He maintained friendly relations with the members of the Board, whom he very frequently entertained in his own home. One who knew Hill intimately thought it not at all strange that many developments in administration were introduced during these evolutionary years. . . .

The Faculty in the University at Columbia at this time above the rank of assistant numbered 138, while at Rolla there were 17. The salaries of full professors ranged from $1,800 to $2,850, the deans receiving about $700 more. The student body was growing rapidly. During the year 1907-1908, including the summer enrollment but excluding duplicates, 2,307 students were registered at Columbia and 229 at Rolla; of the total enrollment at Columbia 1,627 were men and 680 were women. No women students were enrolled at Rolla. . . .

A subject of general interest in college circles during this first decade of the twentieth century was the character of the curriculum for liberal arts colleges, and the related one as to whether any part of this curriculum should be required of students entering the professional schools. Hill had decided opinions on both of these questions, and his influence helped to fix the pattern of the curricula for years to come.

The free elective system of 1900 in the Academic College had followed the pattern set in other leading universities in America, but by the fall of 1905 the members of the Missouri Faculty were coming to the conclusion that the system of unrestricted electives did not produce the best results. The problem was discussed at considerable length in successive meetings of the Faculty, but little progress was made for over a year. Finally, in a special evening meeting of the Faculty in February, 1907, a committee to which the problem had been referred consisting of Hill, Stewart, Manly, and Trenholme presented an elaborate report. It took two long sessions to adopt, reject, or modify the various provisions of the report, but on February 12 the amended report was approved. The new system which went into effect in September, 1907, and for which Hill as the leading member of the committee was to a considerable degree responsible, included in the first two years a number of required introductory courses, representing the different fields of learning taught in the College, but when a student presented a sufficient number of high school units in certain ones of these classified divisions of subjects, he was excused from a part or all of the requirements in that division, though this did not excuse him from the total number of hours required for the degree. Within a division he usually had some choice as to the particular course he would take, for instance as to a language or a science. The whole plan was an ingenious compromise between a fixed curriculum and a free elective system. . . .

An educational reform which Hill wished to introduce was the requirement of two years of general education courses, similar to that for the students in the College of Arts and Science, for the students in all of the professional schools. Previous to 1906 such students entered the professional schools directly from the high schools; indeed, frequently they had not completed much high school work, though gradually, through the preceding eight or ten years, the entrance standards for all the departments had been raised. In 1906, for the first time, the Medical School required for admission thirty semester hours of specified college courses. In 1909, the School of Education prescribed the first two years of work in the College of Arts and Science for entry, making it for a time the most difficult professional school to enter. In 1910, the School of Law for the first time required one year of college work for entrance, while the School of Medicine the same year raised its entrance requirements to sixty semester hours, or two years of Arts and Science work. The next year the schools of Law, Engineering, and Journalism all adopted the same entrance requirements as Education and Medicine —two years of college preprofessional work. . . .

Hill himself was an able defender of University interests, but he had little understanding of the methods of fostering favorable public relations. He had little knowledge of the point of view of the average local politician of Missouri, and he was not the sort of man who could meet and talk with the legislators in a friendly fashion. In addition, Hill had a grievous personal problem all through these years, namely, the severe illness of his wife. Mrs. Hill underwent a major operation in New

York in September, 1909, which apparently was not completely successful, for it was followed in subsequent years by other operations.
After her return from Europe in the fall of 1914 she seemed to become
better, but broke down completely about Christmas and was bedfast
during the spring of 1915 when the legislature was in session. Mrs.
Hill's condition meant that her husband could not be absent at the capital for any length of time to look after University affairs. With no all-
weather highways and with poor train connections, he had to keep
running back and forth between Jefferson City and Columbia. He was
under high nervous tension.

There was another problem which came to a head during this session
of the legislature. This was the unhappy condition of engineering education both in the University at Columbia and at Rolla. The Faculty of
the School of Engineering in Columbia had never been satisfied with
the requirement for students to complete two years of general collegiate
education before entering the engineering curriculum. This admission
requirement had made a five-year curriculum for engineering students
necessary, resulting in a decrease in the number of engineering students;
the School of Engineering Faculty felt that the requirement was unrea-
sonable. The difficulty was resolved in 1915 by permitting that Division
of the University to return to its former admission requirements, namely,
fifteen units from an accredited high school.

The Faculty at Rolla feared action might be taken by the Board to
limit the curriculum to mining engineering alone, or to reorganize the
School into an entirely different type of educational institution. It was
this situation which led friends of the School to introduce into the
General Assembly of 1915 the Buford bill, making it compulsory for
the Curators to offer at Rolla additional curricula in mechanical, elec-
trical, and chemical engineering, and a general course in science leading
to the degrees of Bachelor and Master of Science. Against the opposition of the President and Board this bill was passed, but subsequently
the Curators came to the conclusion that the bill was unconstitutional in
that the legislature was assuming the legal functions of the Board in
determining what courses should be offered. Since no appropriation
was made to put the law into effect, the Curators decided to take no
immediate action. But during the following summer a student at Rolla
brought suit to compel the Curators to establish the courses named by
the Buford law. The Supreme Court of the state eventually decided in
the student's favor.

An incident which increased the enemies of the University occurred
in the late autumn of 1914. The large hog cholera serum plant of the
College of Agriculture was under the control of J. W. Connaway,
noted veterinarian. Owing to an outbreak of the foot-and-mouth dis-

ease in the livestock of the state, the federal government as a means of control had closed all private serum plants in the state. All orders, therefore, for this preventive medicine were coming to the University Veterinary Department. Before the legislature met, Frank H. Lee, representative from Jasper County, had telegraphed that he had ninety-three head of hogs for which he wanted serum at once: "If you are prompt in this matter, I will favor a large appropriation in the next legislature for your department." A few days later Phelps also sent a telegraphic request for serum for seventy-five head of hogs. In both cases Connaway told his clerks to fill the orders as soon as possible but to give no preference to members of the legislature over anybody else. As a result, the serum in both cases was three or four days late, and both men complained bitterly to the Governor in open letters to the press. Hill published the facts in the case with the statement that the orders had been filled as soon as possible, but no more promptly than orders from more humble citizens from Missouri.

An absurd story, believed by gullible members of the legislature, was circulated that the members of the Faculty were living as aristocrats, and were running around over the country in expensive, state-owned automobiles. Hill met this falsehood by a public statement concerning the one low-priced car owned by the University, and the names of the very few members of the Faculty who owned cars. Still another fabrication, originating apparently in the state auditor's office, charged that the Board was unlawfully transferring funds from one account to another. Hill proved its falseness by quoting the report of the auditor's own examiners, showing that all receipts and disbursements had been properly handled. The examiners' only question had arisen from their confusion of the funds from legislative appropriations with other funds, such as student fees and federal grants, not arising from state appropriations. The Board had deposited all of the latter in a separate account and had transferred it from time to time to the items where the money was needed. . . .

The downright unfriendliness of the legislature in 1915 was not so evident in the following session. One disturbing incident occurred when a committee appointed to audit the accounts of state institutions made its report; it had found expenditures in the University accounts for the purchase of a traveling bag, a bathrobe, motor supplies, and a Ford motorcar, and for the repair of a watch. Instead of asking University authorities for an explanation of these items, the committee reported expenditures in violation of law. Hill issued a statement that the car had been purchased from the sale of products from the fruit farm located four miles from the campus, and was bought to transport laborers and members of the agricultural Faculty to their work at the farm. The item

in regard to a watch referred to the repair of a stop watch used in experimental work in a laboratory. The traveling bag and bathrobe had
been purchased for a hospitalized student who found when she was
discharged that similar articles brought with her when she entered the
hospital had been stolen. Hill's explanation satisfied the committee and
the members of the legislature.

An incident which might have led to legislative criticism was the
publication by a student at Columbia of a sheet called "The Research"
which made defamatory charges against the Greek-letter societies. The
author of the sheet was tried by the student senate, and the case was
appealed successively to the University Discipline Committee, the Committee of Deans, and eventually the Board of Curators, and in each case
a unanimous decision against the student was given. He was then dismissed from the University, following which he wrote a letter to the
members of the legislature charging that the fraternities and sororities
had a disgraceful influence over the Faculty and advocating a law to
drive them out; his influence turned out to be negligible. . . .

Congress had declared war upon Germany within a few days after
the legislature of 1917 adjourned. Educational institutions soon found
their enrollments depleted, their curricula modified, their calendars
changed, and their budgets under need of entire reorganization. With
many faculty men entering the federal service, the salary list could be
shortened, though to be sure some other expenses—that for coal, for
instance—were doubled. The Curators authorized the Executive Board
to make such financial arrangements as were necessary for those members of the Faculty entering government services. Usually, leave without
salary was granted. This of itself relieved the maintenance fund to a
considerable extent because, due to decreased enrollments, replacements
for the members of the Faculty on leave were not necessary.

The same meeting of the Board of Curators which authorized the
Executive Board to make the necessary financial arrangements with
members of the Faculty entering government service, also adopted a
new plan for military training in the University. This revised plan for
the military training of college students, known as the Reserve Officers
Training Corps, had been developed in 1916 by the War Department
as a result of President Wilson's emphasis on "preparedness," due to
the war abroad. For the students this plan, allowing more college credit
for military courses than had been allowed previously and including a
commission in the United States Army if the four-year course were
completed, went into effect in the fall of 1917 and continued throughout that school year. University officials had very little trouble in enforc-
ing the military requirement because by September, 1917, the young
men realized that they would soon be called into active military service,

and they wished to be as thoroughly prepared as possible. The R.O.T.C. was not able, however, to provide enough junior officers for the rapidly expanding army, and various training camps for officer candidates were established over the United States.

Even this was not sufficient to provide officer material, and in the summer of 1918 the R.O.T.C. was superseded temporarily by the S.A.T.C. (Student Army Training Corps). This war emergency measure, with the trainees legally enlisted in the United States Army, was an effort to qualify students for more effective service in the military forces, and at the same time, though certainly secondary to the first objective, to allow them to continue with their education. Enrollment was voluntary and was open to men students between the ages of 18 and 45, but if a student subject to military service did not enroll, he was immediately placed in the Army as a private. In order to provide instructors for the hundreds of S.A.T.C. units over the country without calling upon the Army for officers who were needed so desperately in other places, officer training camps were established in various localities. Newspaper advertisements and official letters explained the purpose of the new military organization to young men and urged them, if they had the necessary entrance requirements, to enter college and enlist in the S.A.T.C. Incentives mentioned were the preparation of the students for better service to their country while continuing their college education, and certain emoluments including clothing (uniforms), subsistence, and thirty dollars a month. The whole country was divided into districts over which military and educational directors were placed, Hill being named educational director of a district composed of the states of Missouri, Kansas, Colorado, and Wyoming.

In the University, fraternity and rooming houses were rented and used as barracks, the members of the unit being fed in the University Commons in relays. Reveille sounded at 6:30 in the morning; after breakfast there were two hours of military drill and tactics. The non-military classes for the soldiers were held from 10 to 12 in the forenoon and during the afternoon. Study halls in charge of noncommissioned officers or University instructors were set apart in buildings to which the young soldiers, when not engaged in drills or recitations, were marched in military formation for supervised study. All members of the S.A.T.C. had to take a course on the issues of the war, for which college credit was given. The Army students had little freedom from early morning until lights were out at night. The day of induction had been eagerly anticipated, but as impatient as the students had been to get into the S.A.T.C., they were many times more impatient to get out. The experience with the S.A.T.C. was unsatisfactory to the Army, highly unsatisfactory to the colleges, and a nightmare for the students.

It is noteworthy that just as soon as possible after the armistice, demobilization from the S.A.T.C. was completed, and the R.O.T.C. was re-established at the beginning of the next term.

Not all the relations of the University with the War Department were as distressing as the experience with the S.A.T.C. During the spring of 1918, an agreement was signed with the Army for the training of detachments of men in various forms of mechanics. The detachments consisting of 320 men were to be sent to Columbia for sixty-day periods, and were lodged in the gymnasium. Most of the training at first took place in the stockjudging and farm machinery buildings. The detachments were later increased in size to 500 men and then to 650 men, and barracks were erected for them on the lawn west of the dairy building; shops were built and equipped on a lot at the corner of Maple and Sixth streets with funds advanced as a loan of twenty thousand dollars by Columbia businessmen.

Another military development of a more permanent nature, growing out of the war, was the establishment in 1919 of an artillery unit of the R.O.T.C. Lieutenant Colonel Lloyd E. Jones, son of Dean J. C. Jones, had written a personal letter to Hill in December, 1918, suggesting this expansion and expressing the hope that Missouri would be the first western university to get a battery. Hill discussed the matter with the Executive Board and was authorized to apply to the War Department for the establishment of a field artillery unit; the Department agreed, and later detailed Jones to be the first officer to take charge of the unit. It was organized in the fall with the privilege given to each student enrolling in the R.O.T.C. to work in either infantry or artillery.

The war years, which corresponded to the University biennium of 1917-1918, turned out to be one of the most frustrating periods in University history. The University personnel, including the members of the Board and the President and Faculty, did their best to continue effective work and to run the University as an educational institution of first rank, but they had an insufficient financial income to meet the steadily decreasing purchasing value of the dollar, the length of the University term was unsettled, students through no fault of their own were constantly being enrolled and discharged, courses were disrupted, members of the Faculty were called to do necessary war work, and even disease epidemics interrupted classwork. No one factor was responsible for all of these adverse conditions. All that can be said is that the institution simply muddled through, and that teachers and students were happy when the period was over.

One of the circumstances which made the last few months of the war period excessively hard, not only on college campuses but all over the country and for that matter all over the world, was the epidemic of

Spanish influenza. It was known to be spreading in other parts of the world before it reached America, and steps were taken to insulate America, all to no avail. In August and September of 1918 it appeared among soldiers and private citizens and spread rapidly. In Columbia the doctors forewarned the people and issued statements as to what might be done to avoid the disease. But within a week after the S.A.T.C. went into effect on October 1, there were seventy cases of the disease among the students. On the Monday following the opening of school an order was issued to suspend all University work, but for the students to remain in Columbia. The suspension of classes was continued from day to day, and all Columbia schools, churches, and movies were closed. The University campus was closed to all persons except students; members of the S.A.T.C. were forbidden to use the east campus or the Library Building, while other students were excluded from the west campus. Even members of the Faculty could enter the west campus only by a permit issued through the President's office. After the suspension of classes had been in effect for three weeks, the University was opened again on Monday, October 26, but only for the members of the S.A.T.C. These soldier-students were required to wear masks in the classroom. The reopening of school was postponed for other students, but it was thought that the disease was so well under control that it was safe to allow the soldiers to return to their school work. Finally, all classes except in the University high school and elementary school were resumed on Thursday morning, October 31. All students and Faculty were required to wear masks.

The University, in the meantime, had converted the old Welsh Military Academy, west of the M. K. & T. railroad tracks, the Kappa Sigma fraternity house, and the top floor of Switzler Hall into temporary hospitals. Instructions were issued for making or purchasing the required masks. In the course of the epidemic many students and members of the Faculty died. The first student to be buried was Lawrence Stewart, son of a University professor. The epidemic returned with renewed virulence in the latter part of November, and the University closed for the term on December 6. This epidemic was the worst that had ever visited the University campus and was probably the chief reason why that fall term was so devoid of worthwhile scholastic attainments. Notice was issued through the President's office that classwork for the next term would begin on Wednesday, January 1, with registration on the two preceding days, but that all students would be required to wear masks.

The effect of the war upon Greek-letter fraternities had been crushing. A rule adopted by the Faculty before the war had prohibited pledges from rooming and boarding in organized houses. In the fall of

1917 the "Greeks" were so reduced in numbers that it was difficult for their chapters to meet running expenses. Acting upon a petition from them, the Faculty suspended the freshman rule, but even this was not help enough. In the spring of 1918 the regulations were relaxed so that any student or any person officially connected with the University could room in fraternity houses during the war emergency. Finally, in the fall of 1918, fraternity life practically disappeared from the campus, and the chapter houses were taken over by the University and used as barracks or hospitals. After the war and upon the return of normal conditions, the federal government was under obligation to recondition all these houses.

Social life on the campus gradually disappeared during the war years. As early as May, 1917, the Senior Ball was cancelled because such a large number of the seniors had already departed to enter training camps or to work on farms or in factories. By the fall of 1918 all student dances had ceased, for the men were under military discipline and were not excused to attend social affairs; even if they had been given furloughs for the dances, the doctors would have banned such an assemblage of people that fall. Social gatherings ceased in the churches, and for several Sundays religious services were forbidden by the Board of Health.

The effect of the war upon intercollegiate athletics was interesting. During the years just preceding the war, under the directorship of Chester L. Brewer, Missouri students had brought considerable renown to the University, and some of the greatest athletes in the history of the University had been developed by the various coaches. Missouri teams won a number of conference championships in all the major sports. At the same time Brewer maintained the high standards established by his predecessor, Hetherington, but was far more tactful in dealing with students and with competitive institutions. In 1913 Hill had secured from Michigan Henry F. Schulte who was a great asset in coaching football and track; Schulte resigned in 1919 to accept a position as head coach in the University of Nebraska. Part of the success in athletics had been due to the sympathetic support of Hill, who was a member of the Intercollegiate Athletic Committee for a number of years, and of W. G. Manly, for a long period Faculty representative to the Missouri Valley Conference. Brewer resigned his position at the beginning of the war and was followed for three years by W. E. Meanwell from Wisconsin.

During the war intercollegiate athletics everywhere took a beating. Young men who ordinarily were in the front ranks in athletics were now in the front ranks in the armed services or in agriculture and industry, and the intercollegiate games for the most part were left to the boys under eighteen or to the physically unfit registrants. As happened in other phases of collegiate life, the rules governing athletic contests were relaxed; freshmen were allowed on the teams, and students might compete for four years. Even so, during the fall of 1918 there were no intercollegiate athletics at all for Missouri students, for under the order of the University Board of Health all football games were cancelled. This was one of the reasons why the students thought of that fall as being such a drab term. . . . [Hill resigned the presidency in 1921. He engaged in business in Kansas City until his death in 1943.]

In summary of Hill's administration as President, he had arrested a decline which had set in during the latter years of his predecessor. The standards of admission to every division of the University had been raised, the accreditation of junior colleges organized, the activities of the University expanded, and except during the war years, student attendance had constantly increased. He had carried the University successfully through a very difficult period of its financial history. While some prominent members of the Faculty during his administration had taken positions elsewhere, it was generally due to higher salaries or greater opportunities. On the other hand, he had been able to recruit many who in later years became prominent in the Faculty. Hill was courageous when personal and family troubles were overwhelming. His high standing with educators throughout the country was notable and was shown in many ways. He was given honorary degrees by such institutions as the University of California, the University of Michigan, Cornell University, and many others. He served as president of several national educational organizations. He received frequent and flattering offers for his services elsewhere. He may not have realized all his dreams for the expansion of the activities, influence, and usefulness of the University, but enough were realized to stamp the years of his administration as one of the great periods in the history of the University, and himself as one of the ablest of the presidents who have served the University of Missouri.

RELIGIOUS ASPECTS

OVERALL VIEW OF MISSOURI CHURCHES

LAWRENCE M. HEPPLE

Dr. Hepple was born in Bevier, Missouri, in 1910 and joined the faculty of the Agricultural College of the University of Missouri in 1942, to become a professor of rural sociology. He died in 1960.

The following paragraphs are taken from the introduction of his essay on "The Church" in Missouri: Its Resources, People, and Institutions.

Father Marquette, a Jesuit missionary, was one of the first white men known to have seen the territory of what is now Missouri, in 1673. We do not know how many white men may have seen the territory before 1673, nor do we know their religious affiliations, if any. We do know that the white man brought the Christian religion to Missouri, and, in addition to providing religious services where settlements were formed, began missionary work among the Indian tribes. As the tribes in time were forced to migrate from the State, information concerning their religion, or religions, is limited to what the archeologists have been able to find. At present it is impossible to indicate more than that the Indians did have a religion and that religious artifacts and remains of structures used for religious purposes have been found. We do not know to what extent they accepted Christianity before they left Missouri, but crucifixes have been found among their artifacts. The intermixture of native Indian religions and Christianity, such as took place in Mexico, did not occur in Missouri. The present religious institutions in the State show no signs of having been influenced by the Indian religions.

The dominant church from 1673 to 1804 was the Roman Catholic Church. During this period the territory of the State was the property of first France, then Spain, then France again. When it became a part of the United States in 1804, it was open to Protestant churches as well as the Roman Catholic Church. However, while Missouri was at least nominally Roman Catholic before 1804, there was no persecution of Protestant ministers who had entered the area. Baptist and Methodist ministers had been preaching in Missouri before 1804. By 1820 the Presbyterian, the Protestant Episcopal, and the Christian (Disciples of Christ) churches, as well as the Baptist and Methodist, had been started in the State.

The first Jewish congregation was formed in 1836. Jews comprise today approximately 5 per cent of the church members in Missouri.

They are the only major religious organization besides the Christian in the State. Approximately one-third of all church members are identified with the Roman Catholic Church, while 50 per cent are included in the major Protestant denominations—Baptist, Christian, Episcopal, Evangelical and Reformed, Lutheran, Methodist, and Presbyterian. The membership of all other religious bodies comprises approximately 12 per cent of all church members. One may say, then, that religious institutions in Missouri are primarily of the Hebrew-Christian tradition.

Churches in Missouri may be classified into four categories, according to their characteristics: the Jewish congregations; the Roman Catholic Church; the major Protestant denominations such as the Baptist, Christian, Lutheran, Methodist, Presbyterian, and Episcopal organizations; the smaller religious groups, sometimes referred to as sects, such as the Nazarene, the Holiness, the Pentecostal, and the Latter Day Saints. The line drawn between the last two classes is an arbitrary one because some of the churches in the class of small sects are in the process of becoming denominations, and there is not complete agreement as to the characteristics that distinguish a sect from a denomination. The above classification will be followed because, while there are some trends that apply to all churches, there are others that concern only one or more of the categories. . . .

The Jewish congregations in Missouri have steadily expanded during the century since their founding; their membership now numbers approximately 87,000. As there are no rural synagogues in the State, this growth has been in urban areas, particularly in St. Louis and Kansas City, although there are also Jewish religious organizations in Springfield, Joplin, Sedalia, St. Joseph, Hannibal, Jefferson City, Cape Girardeau, and Columbia.

The Roman Catholic Church has likewise grown steadily, since the visit of Father Marquette, to its present approximate membership of 612,000. While the Catholic membership has increased in both rural and urban areas, most of the growth has been in urban churches because, until recently, the emphasis of that church has been upon the urban rather than the rural church. Immigration and high birth rates among Catholic families account for a great deal of the increase.

During the century and a half that Protestant churches have been in Missouri they have expanded until they had a membership of about one million by 1950. Churches like the Baptist, Methodist, and Christian made a strong appeal to the individualism and democratic ideals of the pioneer. Its democratic form of church government was an important item contributing to the popularity of the Protestant church during the nineteenth century. In order to keep abreast of the westward migration of the population, some of the denominations adopted the circuit rider system, in which the minister preached at three or four different points on successive Sundays, thus managing to organize and keep going several churches. Urban Protestant churches have continued to grow, but rural Protestant churches reached their peak in membership between 1890 and 1900 and have declined since that time.

The small religious organizations, or sects, often started as the result of a dispute within one of the major denominations. While some of them appear early in the history of Missouri, the greatest growth of these groups has been in the last sixty or seventy years. Their increase in membership during the past quarter of a century has been primarily in urban areas, although most of them began as movements in rural areas and small towns. A few small groups have remained strictly rural, but have not shown large increases in membership.

Growth and decline in church membership seem to parallel changes in the number and distribution of population. This does not mean that revivals, home missions, and other strategies employed by churches have had no effect upon membership. Indeed, it is possible that in certain periods the rate of growth of church membership may have been greater than that of the population. In general, however, the parallel holds: just as total population has increased from the beginning of the State to the present time, so has total church membership increased; and just as urban population is still growing, so is the urban church growing. On the other hand, the decline in rural population since 1900 is matched by a like decline in rural church numbers.

THE COUNTRY CHURCH ERA

H. J. BLANTON

This is another of the sketches by Blanton originally published in the St. Louis Globe-Democrat *and later collected into two small volumes each entitled* When I Was a Boy. *Three of these interestingly and simply written sketches appear in this anthology, all of them good social history. This one is from the first of the two volumes (1952).*

When I was a boy every farm was in easy reach of a country church. Real estate men found it next to impossible to find buyers for farms that were inconveniently located with regard to church and school.

Reprinted from *When I Was a Boy*, First Series, by H. J. Blanton. By permission of Edgar P. Blanton.

To serve rural congregations the policy of religious organizations was
to locate preachers on the field. These godly men hardly ever received
more than enough for a bare living. Most of them said they preferred
souls for their hire. On horseback when roads were bad, and in a one-
horse cart when roads were better, they kept in constant touch with families on their field. When there was a wedding to be performed, the old
pastor was at hand. When there was a death in some family, he always
was ready with a long and comforting funeral sermon. From one end
of the year to the other, he was a guide, counselor and friend to all with
whom he came in contact. It was during this period that country churches
reached their zenith in membership and influence. As religious and community centers they were indispensable.

Along in the early days of the present century young men who
wished to enter the ministry became sold on the importance of courses
in theological seminaries. Few of them had money with which to pay
for tuition and board. To make matters easier for them, state denomina-
tional organizations began encouraging rural churches to have student
pastors. Then, instead of having consecrated old preachers constantly
on the field, congregations which had preaching once a month, as most
of them did, would have the preacher on the field only on two days,
which were the Saturday and Sunday of his preaching week. Several
times a year, road conditions would make it impossible for the student
to keep his appointment. Even under the most favorable conditions, he
hardly got acquainted with his congregation in the course of a year.
While most of the decline in rural churches is attributed to widespread
use of cars for Sunday trips, I believe that lack of interest in them dates
from the time they began divorcing themselves from resident preachers
who knew and loved their congregations as they knew and loved their
own families. The student pastor policy was encouraged by the argument
that, without aid of this sort, poor boys could not prepare themselves for
the ministry. Another thing which popularized the practice was the fact
that those poor boys usually were willing to do the preaching for fewer
dollars than the resident preachers had been getting.

After becoming convinced that resident pastors might stem the tide
which seemed to be running against rural churches, I sought with all
the assurance of youth to stem it. Being a member of the Baptist church
I thought to use that denomination as a sort of demonstration agency for
a brilliant idea. When our County Association held its annual meeting
I presented the plan with much vigor and with eager anticipation of an
enthusiastic response. On a county map I showed the location of all the
congregations that were having preaching only once or twice a month,
as a result of which they had a minister on the field only once or twice

a month. By grouping those churches, as I showed from my map, several preachers could be located on the field, each one in constant touch with the families he served. Instead of being greeted with loud applause, however, I earned for myself a place as Public Enemy No. 1. The student pastors led what came near being an indignation meeting against me. One of them demanded to know who made me a pope who could come into a Baptist meeting and tell the folks what to do. The plan, of course, was thrown down the back stairs, and I was lucky to escape the same fate. That was about forty years ago. There are only two resident Baptist pastors in Monroe County. The same thing is true of most of the other Protestant denominations. The rural church problem gets more serious all the time, many churches having been discontinued and their houses of worship sold as scrap lumber. A majority of our rural children, it is safe to say, are being raised without Sunday School and preaching advantages. These things are available in nearby towns, of course, but for some unexplainable reason farmers, as a rule, are unwilling to attend church services in the towns.

My nephew, Dr. Frank M. Powell, until recently vice-president of the Southern Baptist Theological Seminary at Louisville, tells of a neighborly pastoral incident which came near costing two lives. A Methodist preacher friend had a convert who wished to be immersed in a nearby river. Somebody suggested that he should borrow Dr. Powell's baptismal pants for the occasion. Being made of a rubber treated material, they kept the wearer from getting wet. Unfortunately, the inexperienced young minister put the pants on the candidate instead of on himself. Getting beyond his depth, the pants became filled with water, pulling the candidate down. In his struggles he almost overcame the preacher, and a double tragedy was narrowly averted. Here in Paris many years ago a Methodist pastor who sought to borrow the Baptist baptistry for a candidate who wished to be immersed was curtly informed that the Baptists were not taking in washing. Today, however, the Baptists, or any other sect, would lend their pulpits or pews to a neighboring pastor of different faith if he needed them.

Several years ago what used to be one of the foremost rural churches in our locality closed up and quit. After noticing that none of the members attended services in the large Christian church at Paris, I pressed one of the former elders, a very prominent farmer, for a reason, and this is what he said:

"We farm folks just don't feel at home in your town churches."

In former days the best selling point for a farm was that it was located near church and school. Today, the customer seems interested only in whether the farm is on an electric line and a solid highway.

ROVE SEEKS RELIGION

Frances Grinstead

Though born in Nocona, Texas, Miss Grinstead spent most of her life until 1947 in one or another of the "Little Dixie" counties of Missouri, where her forebears had settled in the 1830's. Some of her formative years (1909 to 1918) were spent at Morrisville in Polk County. Miss Grinstead has taught journalism more than thirty years, first at the University of Missouri, her alma mater, and since 1948 at the University of Kansas. Her father, Hugh Fox Grinstead, was for many years a contributor to the Youth's Companion *and to* West, Frontier, Western Story, *and other periodicals at the high point of development of the American "western story."*

The following story of a "protracted meeting" is Chapter III of Miss Grinstead's novel, The High Road.

Box suppers and candy pulls dropped off after the winter revival meetings started, while play parties ceased outright. There were a few who would have defied preachers' warnings, but they couldn't get enough together for a set—with the other young folks praying at some altar. Rove and his girl went to all the meetings, though he didn't like them as well as school speakings.

Since she seemed to have forgot how she cried over her house unfinished, he let well enough alone and went on trapping. At the same time, he knew a woman never forgets a thing for good. Ma would bring up something on Pa that was already over and done when Rove had been a little boy. And Pa would listen in patience and afterward hold it out of mind till someday when she started in again.

If Jubilee's following of the revivals had lulled her to overlook she'd been out of fix with Rove, he himself put little thought on what happened to them beyond craning to see who admitted sin. Most of the time during preaching he sat and thought how pretty Jubilee was with her head bent when she prayed, or he considered the work he must do to his cabin come springtime, while the preacher's words washed around him like wind in the sycamores along the crick. Or, again, he'd grow impatient for it to be over and they on their way home—though, once started, he would let old Bess pick her way slow as she liked.

He and Jubilee heard Brother Bartholomew preach many a sermon at Grundy, Halfway, or Turkey Roost; but it wasn't till along in February, when a protracted meeting started at their own church house of Pinoak, that he really noticed what the man had been saying.

It might have been because there wasn't as much for his eye to stray to or his ear listen for, here where he'd been brought up. Foremost among the "Amens" was Abner, and Sadie with him. Jubilee and Rove and the other young folk sat toward the back of the house, but Dave Holly always let his son help take the collection. Rove watched him poking out his hat toward people with a long face and, when he gathered it in from the last row, giving the money to his pa to count; Abner never was any good at arithmetic.

It was a strange thing, Rove thought, that Abner, just because he was a Holly, should take up collection when he hadn't ever joined the church. Rove himself wouldn't have dared to stand and hold the Lord's money while he was living in unconfessed sin. Abner, though, seemed to think all Hollys were born purified to take collection. But only at Pinoak church did he sit in the "Amen" corner with his pa.

Somebody ought to convert Abner and make it right for him to gather God's money, Rove mulled to himself as the preacher blessed the change Dave held. Why, if Abner went on this way, doing what he didn't have a right, he was liable to be struck dead, like the un-priested men in the Old Testament that had tried to pick up and carry the Ark.

Rove looked for who else had come to the meeting, and who stayed away, but the crowd was about the same he'd seen all winter. Every-body went to meeting, whether he believed on the Lord or not. The most faithful to be in their places every night were the old hardened sinners that wanted to see how long they could hold out against Him. You could tell how much of the spirit a person had by how close he sat to the front. Right under the preacher's nose were the saints in Israel, that said "Amen" to all his words; they were going forward in God's grace unto their great reward, the preacher told. More or less at a stand-still were the ones next back, that didn't speak out and bless His name, but had been baptized and taken into the church and so were safe. Back of them sat the young folk, whispering and giggling and taking it all lightly, without they'd done something mean enough to go sit in the last row with the backsliders or had a sight of glory lately enough to sit up front with the believers. There wouldn't none of them have showed off so much as to crowd amongst the saints or stand up at the back with the real sinners that stayed near the door so they could slip out if preaching got too powerful for them.

He sat through the first of this sermon as usual, with thoughts filling his head of all he must do to his house before he could ask Jubilee to share it. And then he happened to notice what Brother Bartholomew was saying: that here in winter, between the gathering of fall crops and tilling of spring fields, was the Devil's time to work. That's been the trouble, thought Rove; here the Devil all winter has stood between me and my needing to get a house built. Let the ground thaw awhiles and the Lord's season come again, and I'll be able to finish. He was glad to know what hindered him, for the whole winter long he'd been taking the blame on himself.

The preacher dropped his voice and said gently that before folk got too busy again they ought to stop and remember where in the Bible it told how two men shall be working in a field together and one shall be taken and the other left. Suddenly the man's voice rose. "You wouldn't want to be taken that-a-way, and not be ready!" he shouted.

Rove jumped guiltily. Yes, he thought, if I was to go now, the neighbors would find my foundation stones evened up only a part of the way around and most of the logs I felled still untrimmed. They'd see how the spring has commenced to fill up again and how much rock for the fireplace needs still to be brought up. He wished he could have been Abner, without being like Abner. Then he wouldn't need to mull over uncut logs, since his house would be already built. He wouldn't need to think of dead leaves waiting to be raked out of the spring; he'd have a dug well where no leaves could get in. Nor he wouldn't need to sit wondering how long till he could get married; he would be husband to her he sat beside, with the summer coming that would yield him his first-born.

Why did the Devil have to all time pick on him!

Jubilee leaned nearer, so the collar of her dress brushed his ear. "What you thinking about?" she asked him.

"I was just a-listening to preacher," Rove whispered back. He knew it wasn't what she looked for him to say, but he couldn't tell her he was weighted down with how many a swinging of an ax and hammering of a nail lay between her sitting there beside him and his taking of her across a sill to be his bride.

Now that he knew what had been between him and getting more done, he was proud of himself to have caught as many hides as he had despite of the Devil. By this time he'd decided on only one boughten door, and his window lights had grown smaller in his plans, but he'd made a good start toward their buying. It was true he hadn't taken out as many animals as he counted on when he first greased his traps—and he'd have got a higher price for the hides if he'd commenced earlier in the winter while the fur was prime. Still and all, with Abner working hand in hand with the Devil to close the best trapping ground to him, he hadn't done so bad.

He grinned to think how Jubilee would look when he showed her

his money for a door and two windows. She'd change her mind then
about having waited overlong for a house.

Now if God stood by him like the preacher'd been saying, he might
finish up his place to dwell. The singing and shouting after the sermon
wove through his thoughts as he planned to have lemon lilies in his
front yard and a stile block in place of a gate. The house would be
furbished with Jubilee's help, and on the parlor table would be a fine
Bible with their names written in.

It was then he commenced to feel the Lord there in the church house
with him. As clear in Rove's mind as if He had spoke aloud, Jehovah
was talking to him beneath some sinner's praying.

The Lord said to him, Here you're about to marry and take yourself
a wife, and you ought to be one of the rocks on which I found my
church.

Rove answered, I ain't ready yet.

The Lord said, The time is at hand.

Besides, Rove told him, oncet I went down to the altar and got happy,
and I backslid afore I could get to the crick and be baptized.

The Lord said, I will give unto you a new heart. And as for turning
away from me, my hand will uphold you, my right arm strengtheneth
you.

Under cover of the praying and singing, he and the Lord had quite
a talk. But it wasn't till Pee-wee Hooper's wife started toward him that
he knowed how in earnest Jehovah was.

He'd seen Becky Hooper settle to save a sinner, and it was like a
snake charming a bird in the woods. No use to twitter or fly, for she
would gain her way in the end. At every meeting Becky was the chief
handmaiden of the Lord and depended on by all the preachers. There
was only one thing she couldn't do, and that was get Pee-wee to come
in sight of a church house if she was anywheres around. But, failing to
bring her own man to the altar, Becky done the next best. Every revival
time she persuaded with the old hardened sinners he sold his liquor
to; for a while each season the conversions would cut pretty deep into
his business and Pee-wee'd grow discouraged and stay home from his
still.

She had been working amongst the hard-liquor sinners tonight, but
none would go before the Mercy Seat. Rove seen, as well as if the Lord
took him into confidence, what had happened. The Almighty had prevented her having success with Pee-wee's customers in order to make
her turn elsewhere. The Lord had settled on her to take his own soul
from the Devil.

He held onto the seat in front of him with both hands.

When Becky stopped and asked him in a whisper, "Oughtn't you to go down and ask forgiveness?" Jubilee stood back to let the Lord's handmaiden come closer.

Rove looked at his knuckles, gripped on the back of the bench before him. All the people around were the ones that knew him every day of his life. He hated to own up before them he needed to change—especially before Abner, and him taking collection, or even saying "Amen" if he felt like it, though he never yet joined a church.

He knew it was the Devil put such thoughts in his mind. The Evil One was wilier than the Lord and didn't show himself straight out. But Rove was accustomed to his ways. He plucked at Jubilee's arm to leave. Let him once get away from this church house, and maybe God and the Devil both would forget him.

Becky's voice grew so soft her words sank in. "You'd as well to be a power for good as for evil!"

She moved aside to let him go to the altar.

He glanced down at Jubilee, and she made out she didn't notice what went on. It was a matter between him and his God, and his woman wouldn't say anything one way or another.

Yes, it's just between You and me, he said to God, and nobody else's business what I do. He was bound sometime to yield himself, and might as well be now.

All the people turned as Rove took his first step toward that altar. He saw Ma and Pa with faces surprised but glad, the way they'd someday beckon him into Heaven. He saw Hetty, like a freckle-faced angel with a red-gold halo. He saw Mrs. Holly, counting his soul off on her left thumb as the fifth one saved that week, Jubilee with her head bowed in prayer, and Becky stiff in the aisle like a schoolteacher calling him to stand and spell.

He took another step forward as Brother Bartholomew raised his arms in welcome. "I came to seek and to save that which was lost!" the preacher shouted in the midst of the Holly-led singing.

Rove moved toward the beckoning arms, and but for one thing would have been gathered to the fold. It was when Abner turned and cried "Amen" in his face that he caught step and drew back. He snatched Jubilee by the arm and, turning his face in the other direction, in a minute was out the door beneath the distant stars.

How far it was to Heaven! He felt as if a gate had slammed to behind him and shut him away from whatever great thing the Lord had planned to give him. He knew he ought to have gone on like nothing happened and let Becky point Salvation's road. He knew it had been the Lord speaking Becky's words and the Devil that put "Amen" in Abner's mouth. All the same, he couldn't have stood it for one to shout praises over his conversion that himself had never bent the knee. No use to think of might-have-beens! He lifted his head and breathed in the clean smell of night.

But he hadn't escaped by leaving. Throughout that late winter and spring, whilst he set traps or cured a hide, while he drove to a school program or protracted meeting with Jubilee, or helped Pa plant corn or mend a harness, there might come at any minute that still small voice, too soft for mortal woman's, You'd as well to be a power for good as for evil.

Though discouraged now over either marrying or making peace with God, he kept on with his trapping, because Pa always learnt him if a man put one foot before the other all winter long it was bound to net him something by spring. Pa every year had a money order, big or little, from the St. Louis fur company by the time sassafras roots were ready to make tea. The blue of that money order was the color of mid-morning sky in April and as sure to come.

That was to a man's way of thinking. Ma every year predicted they'd starve out before new potatoes could form in the ground. She was as surprised as when Rove had been a baby if she saw money from a man's hunting in the woods.

It was partly to see the same look on Jubilee's face that Rove had held back how he meant to gain his window lights and door. Sometimes his heart smote him that he kept it a secret, especially when she wouldn't go any more of a Sunday to look at their chosen homesite. The last time she had turned away as if she didn't ever expect to see a house rise there.

Always now in Rove's ear there droned the words, You'd as well to be a power for good as for evil. He lay awake and thought about them so much, he felt the need of a chill tonic earlier than usual. Ma brought the bottle from behind the apple barrel, and he took all that was left in it from last fall and then started in on the new bottle Pa got from Will Chandler's ma at the Halfway store.

Watching the men take their draughts, Ma gloomed, "It's going to be a foul summer, with malary up ever' crick branch." The only way they knew to keep off the fever was this here tonic. If they didn't take it, they'd feel more beat out when the weather turned real warm. Rove held back from dosing as long as he could every spring, for the quinine made a whirring in his ears and his feet felt like they were somebody's else.

Still, through the throbbing of his eardrums, it kept up. You'd as well to be a power for good as for evil, and he knew the Lord meant for him to take heed. He dreaded to find religion; but the longer a man put it off the harder it went with him. Everybody agreed on that, both the ones that did it with rolling and talking in tongues and those that prostrated themselves before the Lord at the mourners' bench.

He was in doubt where to yield himself up. He'd rather it not to be in Pinoak church, with Dave Holly to write his name in the book and Abner to stand by looking pious. But it would be a dreadfuller thing to wait and burn in brimstone because he hadn't got into any church at all.

He went about the business of a farm piece in the spring the way he'd always helped Pa about the place as soon as warmth of sun and song of bird contented him more than fireside heat and crackle. Finally, one day when they had been walking around planning where to dig post-holes, he had a sign the Lord was ready for him.

He had come in and taken an extra dose of chill tonic before lying down across his bed. When he dropped off to sleep he seemed to float on the clouds. It was as if he bounded along like a big balloon he'd seen once at the county seat, with a little string tied to him that might break any minute. He was as lightly joined to this earth as if he hadn't lived in any mortal body. The Lord was showing him how easy it was to change from earth to Heaven. Even when he got up off the bed he still felt so light on his feet he knew he could let go and fly if he'd had wings.

When God put it to him that-a-way, he seen how simple a thing it was to join with the saints. Since there was a revival going on at Grundy Crick by then, he concluded that must be the right place and people. Besides, it was a church where Abner wasn't free to say "Amen."

He went and washed the sleep from his eyes and tramped out to the lot to hitch up Bess.

Jubilee was a little surprised when he drove by for her; she wondered that he'd go that far off without having said anything about it. But he explained to her how the Lord had showed him when and where to enter His Kingdom. "Well, then, we're a-bound to go!" she agreed, and got ready quick as ever she could. She had belonged to the church since she was big enough to repeat a text, and he could tell she'd be glad when he had the thing settled in his mind.

The first hymn had been sung when they reached Grundy church, and the preacher was making his first long prayer. Rove pushed toward a bench of rough-sawed lumber at the very back—as well make the most of being a sinner while it lasted.

He took a good look at the way things appeared from here. Casting his eyes forward under their lashes during prayer, he could see how the hair curled against the women's necks or straggled in drake's tails if they were too old or too worked to care. Through a side window he had a view of Knob Mountain dark against the sunset sky—from up in front

in this church the mountain didn't show, nor did the graveyard, unless
a person looked back over his shoulder. Where Rove stood now he could
have read the letters on the gravestones had it been broad day, and he
liked the way some man's and woman's had leaned toward one another
in the spring-thawed earth.

He'd miss the things to be enjoyed from the back of a church, even
though he might keep his mind better on preaching. As the people sank
to the benches at close of the prayer he had a glimpse of Abner from
back and side—one sight that wouldn't be forced on him when he himself sat to the front.

Brother Pullen gave the pitch of another song with a tuning fork,
and Rove joined in the first verse of "There's a Great Day Coming"
while Jubilee found the place in a broken-back songbook. It was as good
as a fiddle tune. Some thought such songs were a little too much like
music for a church; folk had been known to say that a tuning fork was
a blasphemy. Brother Pullen had heard what they said and preached
once about it. He'd called on them to notice the Devil never made use
of one, neither for dances nor merry-go-arounds. Still, a good many on
Grundy Crick said the world would come to its end with such goings
on in God's temple. They went to the meetings to see it happen.

The Grundy preacher was beating with his hymnbook up and down
against his palm as the "Amen" corner dragged behind—". . . a *great
day coming by* and *by!"* When he had rallied them he kept moving his
hands in time to the song, but he closed his mouth and saved his own
breath.

That would have been reasonable if he'd been keeping it for the next
prayer, but he called on another to make the supplication. Rove was a
little disappointed in the man the Lord had picked to reach his soul.
He would have liked the preacher that brought him in to be more
zealous. Most would have sent up three or four long prayers themselves
and worked their voices to a right pitch for preaching. However, as
soon as the man was good into his sermon he recognized that saving
his words was this one's way of girding his loins for the Lord's work.
With his people grateful to rest their feet and catch breath after all the
prayers and singing, Brother Pullen was as fresh as a man that just had
his sleep out and washed his face in a cold running spring. Nor he
didn't spare them any. He told what a hard time people have until the
Lord wears them down to saintliness even if it takes their whole life;
he commenced to spend his strength as to bade them think of their
remissness. Rove settled back to listen, since plainly this was going to
be a preachment worth giving up to.

The light of the early spring day still lingered as Brother Pullen set
forth what a long and dusty road man travels here below, with rocks

reaching out to trip him around every turn and whenever he lifts up his eyes. "And yet if he don't lift up his eyes and tell where he's a-going, he's liable to take a wrong turn—and where will he be then? It ain't the grassy lane that's the right way, neither. If he wants to come out at the pearly gate, a man has to take the rockiest, stoniest path. The sun bears down on such a path with twice the heat it does on the one that is edged with roses and overshaded with ellum trees. That rocky way is twicet as steep, too, and the higher you go the hotter and dustier it gets!" Rove began to wish he hadn't heard what the Way was like before he set foot in it.

Brother Pullen wiped his face with his shirt sleeve and went to the water-bucket shelf and lifted out the dipper. He swallowed down two gourdfuls before he started in again: "Besides, that road steepens as you go upward! If it was that hard to begin with, there's many a person wouldn't start out!" Rove looked at Abner and saw how his lids hung heavy above his eyes, like he'd just come in from a long, hard walk. It made him too feel tired and sleepy.

The preacher related how the steep and rocky road leads to the finest meadow pastures and the rose-and-ellum one to the jumping-off place. Then, as soon as he'd finished with how fine it was at the end of that long, shoe-wearing climb, Preacher Pullen rolled back his cuffs, took another drink from the gourd dipper, and got down to business. He undertook to paint a picture of the fiery pit you never would have suspected lay at the end of that shaded lane, and he did it so well, before long Rove was sweating like he'd spent a day in the field.

He looked around, and there were other folk the same way. They couldn't get to the bucket of water like the preacher did when he was overcome by his own words and they felt hell-fire lick closer and hotter. Abner ran his finger around his neck and whipped off sweat like it had been a June day. The back of Cleet Melcher's shirt looked wringing wet and his tears were ready to overflow.

At the cry for mourners, people crowded one another in the aisle, while the preacher continued to call on anybody else that needed to be saved from that dreadful thirst to come down and seek after the water that quencheth it forever. Becky Hooper's eyes searched the congregation for one who might be ready to glean in the harvest, and Rove let his gaze slip away from hers as Brother Pullen commenced to pray. He would have given a whole lot for whatever dregs of brackish water might be left in that bucket on the corner shelf, but he still held back from the drink everlasting. The preacher's talk about hell-fire had become so familiar, with a winter long of meetings, as soon as he finished a cool breeze from the door had commenced to dry Rove's shirt. By the end of the prayer he'd lost all fear of a hereafter.

What hung in his mind and wouldn't let go was that picture of the rough and dusty road he'd have to walk right now if he joined the church, and it ten times as rugged as any he ever trod! The nearest he had been to a fiery pit was a burning brush pile after him and Pa had been grubbing forth sumac sprouts, but he knew as well as anybody what it was to broil on a steep road in the noontime sun. If the way to Heaven was like that, he'd chance it not to set foot on it for a while longer.

CARRY NATION'S EARLY LIFE IN MISSOURI

HERBERT ASBURY

Herbert Asbury was born in Farmington, Missouri. His father and grandfather were Methodist ministers, and he was a collateral descendant of Francis Asbury, first Methodist bishop ordained in America. Herbert was educated in Elmwood Seminary, Baptist College, and Carleton College, all in Farmington; but he reacted definitely against all this pious background. He learned vivid and effective writing on various newspapers, but chiefly on those of New York. His special field, it has been said, was the portrayal of "the shadier side of great American cities." His work in both biography and history was characterized, however, by scholarly investigation of his subjects.

Carry Amelia Moore was born in Kentucky in 1846, but she grew up in Missouri. Soon after the incidents related in the following narrative, she married David Nation (1877; divorced 1901), and she moved with him to Kansas in 1889. Kansas was then a prohibition state, and about 1900 Mrs. Nation began her spectacular career of wrecking places in that state and others where intoxicating liquors were sold. She usually used a hatchet for her purposes, and Carry Nation and her hatchet became a symbol of militant prohibitionism throughout the country.

The following passage in Asbury's biography tells of Carry's first marriage (at Holden, Missouri) and of its sequel; here we find much of the motivation for her later career.

In 1865, when Carry Nation was nineteen years old, Dr. Charles Gloyd, a young physician whose father was a Justice of the Peace at

Newport, Ohio, came to Belton, Missouri, with the intention of teaching until he could decide where to practise his profession. Through the influence of Carry Nation's father he obtained a country school near Belton, and boarded with her family. At first he was just another person for whom she had to cook and wash, but when she learned that he spoke several languages and possessed a very superior education, she began to stand in awe of him. The awe soon turned to reverence, and the reverence to adoration, but no words of love passed between them until one evening when he came upon her in a darkened hallway. He seized her hand and softly stroked it, and as she stood trembling in apprehension he spoke endearingly and kissed her upon the lips. Carry Nation was shocked and horrified. Never before had she been kissed or her hand been held, and now she had undergone both of these disturbing experiences within a few minutes. For a moment she was unable to speak, and then she snatched her hand from his grasp, covered her face with her palms, and cried out:

"I am ruined! I am ruined!"

But a repetition of the disaster convinced her that she was far from being ruined, and a wave of gratitude and love swept over her when Dr. Gloyd assured her that his intentions were honorable, and that he would at once ask for her hand in marriage. He did so next day, but Mrs. Moore was greatly displeased and violently objected, for she had planned to marry her daughter to a prosperous young farmer of the neighbourhood. Carry Nation was forbidden to sit alone in a room with Dr. Gloyd, to accompany him to social functions, or to converse with him unless in the presence of her father or mother. The lovers were thus driven to subterfuge; they met clandestinely and carried on their courtship by writing letters. On the table in his room Dr. Gloyd kept a volume of Shakespeare's poems and plays, and at breakfast several times a week he performed the difficult feat of bringing the poet's name into the matutinal conversation, whereupon Carry Nation knew that he had left a letter for her within its leaves. She obtained the sweet missive while sweeping his room and making his bed, and read it surreptitiously.

This continued for three months, when Dr. Gloyd went to Holden, in Johnson county, Missouri, where he established an office and sent for his father and mother. He continued to correspond with Carry Nation, and often visited her in Belton, but her parents were still bitterly opposed to his suit. They warned their daughter that her lover was addicted to the use of intoxicants, and freely predicted that he would die in the torments of delirium tremens. It is customary for Carry Nation's detractors to say that she drove Dr. Gloyd to drink, but it is untrue, although she was perfectly capable of doing so and, had he not already been a drinking man, would doubtless have accomplished much in that direction. The truth is that Dr. Gloyd learned to drink heavily during the Civil War, in which he served as a captain of the 118th Ohio Volunteers. Carry Nation refused to believe that he drank to excess, and, anyhow, she was confident that if he possessed any bad habits her great love would conquer them.

So, with the characteristic "hard-headedness" of which her parents had so often complained when she was a child, she had her own way, and on November 21, 1867, she and Dr. Gloyd were married in Belton. But her wedding morn gave promise of the sorrow and trouble that were to come. The weather was cold and dank, a disagreeable mist fell slowly from the skies, and there were no brightness or ray of sunshine on the day which Carry Nation had expected to be the happiest of her life. Moreover, when Dr. Gloyd appeared for the ceremony it was obvious that he had been drinking; his face was flushed and his gait unsteady, and he mumbled the words of the service with downcast head. With Carry Nation's sensitivity to divine impression, it is not to be wondered at that she felt a foreboding of evil and disaster. She went to Holden with her husband, but almost immediately she found that he had changed; he was morose and sullen, and not at all the lover she had expected. "He seemed to want to be away from me," she wrote. "He used to sit and read, when I was so hungry for his caresses and love. I have heard that this is the experience of so many other young married women. They are so disappointed that their husbands change so after marriage."

Matrimony failed to perform the miracle of curing Dr. Gloyd, for when he married Carry Nation he was a confirmed alcoholic, and smoked immoderate quantities of tobacco. He continued to smoke too much, and drank even more than before, and the spree which had begun on his wedding day was prolonged almost without interruption until his death. At the very time when his bride felt that he should be almost constantly in her arms, he was cold and distant, and had neither time nor inclination for her society. For a little while Carry Nation accepted his plea of illness, but she learned the truth on the fifth day of her married life, when Dr. Gloyd staggered into the house, threw himself on the bed and went to sleep. She leaned over him to smooth his rumpled hair and straighten the pillow beneath his throbbing head, and the reek of whisky struck her full in the face. She knew then what had transformed him from a gay sweetheart into an irritable, misanthropic husband, and it is doubtful if she ever afterward knew a completely happy moment. "I cried most of the time," she wrote. "My husband seemed to understand that I knew his condition, for twice, with tears in his eyes, he remarked, 'Oh, Pet, I would give my right arm to make you happy!' " But instead of making her happy he made her miserable, and touched off the spark that eventually started her on her career of smashing and destruction. He seldom came home until long after midnight, and sometimes not at all; and night after night Carry Nation never closed her eyes, but sat by the window straining to hear the sound of his footsteps upon the deserted pavement, while downstairs the sign in front of his office rattled and groaned mockingly in the wind. His medical practice dwindled to nothing, for when sick people called him he was away drinking, and there was no one in the house save a lonesome, weeping, distracted bride. And often there was not enough food.

Carry Nation's unhappiness was soon increased by pregnancy, and driven almost mad by the thought that she was to bear a drunkard's child, she became a familiar and pathetic figure as she scurried frantically through the streets of Holden searching for her husband. But she found him infrequently, for when he was drunk he fled into the Masonic Lodge, which no woman was permitted to enter. To the Masons, and even to the church folk, she was a nuisance, because she besought the former to rescue Dr. Gloyd from rapidly approaching ruin, and implored the latter to pray for him, and to direct the might of the Lord against the saloon-keepers who laughed at her pleas not to sell him more liquor. God Himself was apparently unmoved by her petitions, though she spent many weary hours on her knees. The Masons likewise were deaf to her entreaties. They continued to drink with her husband and protect him behind the doors of their lodge rooms, while the best the minister and members of his flock could offer were horrified exclamations such as "Oh! What a pity for a young man like Dr. Gloyd to throw himself away!" But this was scant comfort to a young woman frightened and bewildered by the pangs of pregnancy, whose mind, already confused by inherent defects, was in a constant ferment of worry over a drunken husband. Conscious that she could not avert the wreck of her home and the collapse of all her rosy dreams of connubial bliss, Carry Nation began to sit alone and brood—and out of her brooding and misery grew an implacable hatred of the saloon, fraternal orders and tobacco, which throughout her life remained the symbols of her unhappiness. "The world," she wrote, "was like a place of torture. I know now that the impulse was born in me then to combat to the death this inhumanity to man."

Reports of Carry Nation's miserable life and of Dr. Gloyd's excessive drinking reached Belton, and her father visited her during the summer following her marriage. He found her with insufficient food and clothing, and on the verge of a nervous breakdown through worry and constant weeping. He took her home with him, although she protested bitterly against the separation from her husband, for despite his weaknesses she still loved him dearly. Once in Belton her mother said that she could never again have anything to do with Dr. Gloyd, and Carry Nation was helpless, for the time was near for the birth of her child and she knew that if her mother cast her out her husband would not support her. She wrote to him almost daily, imploring him to reform and sign the pledge, and promising that if he would do so she would return to him as soon as their child had been born. Her letters were filled with frantic yearning for a home of her own, and a desperate fear that she would lose his love. Twice he visited her at Belton, but her mother received him as a stranger, and he was not permitted to talk to his wife alone. Mrs. Moore also refused to notify him when Carry Nation was confined, and he did not know that he was a father until his daughter was six weeks old, when Carry Nation and her half-brother drove to Holden to get her trunk and other belongings, for her parents had decreed that the separation must be final. He begged her to remain, declaring that if she did not he would be unable to control his appetite for liquor, and would be a dead man within six months. She wanted to stay, even though it was clear that he was drinking more than ever and that his protestations of reform were empty gestures, but she dared not disobey her mother. And so she returned to Belton. Some six months later she received a telegram that he was dead. His father had died a few weeks previously, and his mother, old and feeble, was left alone with scant means of livelihood.

Carry Nation collapsed from grief and despair when she heard of her husband's death.

POLITICS AND PRESS

THE PRESS AND POLITICS IN EARLY MISSOURI

Edwin C. McReynolds

Edwin C. McReynolds was born near Springfield, Missouri, in 1890. He attended high school at Pierce City and then took his A.B., M.A., and Ph.D. degrees at the University of Oklahoma, where he became a member of the History faculty 1943–1960. He is presently a member of the Cottey College faculty, Nevada, Missouri.

The passage that appears here is taken from Dr. McReynolds' Missouri: A History of the Cross-Roads State, *published in 1962.*

From the beginning of newspaper publication in Missouri, the press was a powerful factor in the intellectual and social life of the region. Newspapers also were important in the elections. The Irish-born printer Joseph Charless, who published the laws of Missouri Territory by a contract with Governor Meriwether Lewis, did not acquire suddenly the ability to create a sheet that was filled with dynamic news stories. The *Gazette* was short on current events and carried little advertising. During his best year of government contracts, Charless collected $1418.75. From readers of the *Gazette* he frequently accepted flour, pork, vegetables, and even old copper and brass in payment for subscriptions. Collection of money was difficult even from persons of prominence. Charless recalled that he once collected $47.00 of a $62.00 bill against John B. C. Lucas, and in 1816, Pierre Chouteau paid him $10.50 when the bill was actually $14.00.

Charless was opposed to Negro slavery and took a strong stand in the *Missouri Gazette* against the unmistakable current of public opinion favoring making Missouri a slave state. It was a losing fight; but the columns of the *Gazette* were always open to any person who wanted to express his views against slavery. It is interesting to note that Peter Blow, who became Charless' partner in the drug business, shared his unpopular opinion of slavery, and that Henry Taylor Blow, son of the druggist, president of the Iron Mountain Railroad, and head of an important lead and zinc business, joined Frank Blair in his attack upon slavery and became a leading partisan of Abraham Lincoln in St. Louis.

Most important of the contributions of Joseph Charless to the development of the American newspaper was his insistence upon freedom of the press. He was not the kind of person to submit tamely to any restriction upon his liberties.

One of the journalists who came to Missouri after the end of the Civil War and immediately became a force to be reckoned with in politics was William M. Grosvenor. His ancestors were Massachusetts immigrants one hundred years before the American Revolution. His father, Rev. Mason Grosvenor, was a graduate of Yale University and a professor of moral philosophy at Illinois College for many years. William spent the years 1851 to 1854 in Yale and at the age of twenty-four became editor of the New Haven *Palladium*. In 1861 he joined the Union Army and served as adjutant, captain, and finally colonel of the Louisiana Native Guards, Second Regiment, colored.

Back in New Haven, he became editor of the *Journal-Courier,* and in 1866 went to the St. Louis *Democrat*. For about seven of the nine years between 1866 and 1875, Grosvenor held the position of editor. He wielded strong influence in the repeal of Radical suffrage laws, the election of Carl Schurz to the United States Senate, and the election of Gratz Brown as governor. More than any other person, Grosvenor was responsible for exposing the tax frauds in connection with the St. Louis Whisky Ring. The prosecution of one hundred federal inspectors and distillers in 1875 and the many convictions that resulted from Grosvenor's investigations broke up the Whisky Ring.

In 1875 he became economic editor of the *New York Tribune* and continued in that position for twenty-five years, to the time of his death. His biographer describes him as a man of great physical strength, with "magnificent head and shoulders."

Perhaps enough has been told of Carl Schurz to indicate his connection with reform politics in Missouri. He was one of the great journalists who found it impossible to remain entirely aloof from party campaigns. His versatility in languages gave him a great advantage as a campaign speaker, and the fact that he was equally eloquent in German and English made him indispensable in gaining the support of new German citizens. He was also the author of a number of books, including a two-volume *Life of Henry Clay* and three volumes of *Reminiscences.*

Schurz was humorous, gay, good-natured, and hard to discourage. His charming manners and his complete lack of bitterness in political campaigns made many friends for him, even among persons who were unable to keep up with the rapidly shifting opinions reached by his independent mind. The versatility of the journalist-politician, who could do so many things well in the generally accepted group of related interests—public addresses, campaign organization, and administration—is shown by his reputation as an amateur pianist.

He was distinguished in almost everything that he attempted. As secretary of the interior, he introduced civil service examinations and merit promotions in his department well in advance of requirements of the law. He gained recognition for his enlightened treatment of the American Indians, who had been assigned to his department. He was interested in the protection of the public domain, and his administration of the department gave impulse to the movement for establishing national parks.

Emil Preetorius, editor of the *Westliche Post,* George Knapp, born in New York and transplanted to Missouri as a child in 1819, and Walter Barlow Stevens, editor of the *Globe-Democrat* for twenty years, were among the great journalists who worked in the state during the generation after the Civil War. Stevens was one of the most influential of the Washington correspondents after 1884, and in 1901 became secretary of the Louisiana Purchase Exposition Company.

Hungarian-born Joseph Pulitzer, the son of a prosperous merchant of Magyar-Jewish descent and an Austro-German mother—a beautiful and intelligent woman whose maiden name was Louise Berger—came to America in 1864, when he was seventeen years old, to fight in the Union Army. He had been rejected in England for military service in India and in France for service in the Foreign Legion because of defective eyesight. In New York harbor Pulitzer and his companion on the voyage entered without going through the regular routine for immigrants, by dropping into the water and swimming ashore.

Young Pulitzer succeeded in enlisting as a soldier for one year. Company "L" of the Lincoln Cavalry was recruited largely from boys of German descent, but in this unit he was not an immediate success. Perhaps because of his youth or his scrawny physique he became the object of many practical jokes in the company. On one occasion he struck a corporal who was involved in the hazing, and was saved from punishment by the action of Captain Ramsey, who enjoyed playing chess with him. The young Hungarian saw action at Antioch, Liberty Mills, Waynesboro, and Beaver Dam Flats.

By October, 1865, he had been mustered out of the army and was supporting himself by means of various jobs—mostly rough manual labor. He paid five dollars for passage on a steamer down the Mississippi River, to a job with "good pay." Forty miles below St. Louis, he and the other men, who had been deceived about obtaining employment, were put ashore. They walked back to St. Louis.

Joseph Pulitzer wrote the story of this adventure and succeeded in having it published in the *Westliche Post.* A farmer who gave the young man food and shelter for a night offered him whisky, chewing tobacco, and smoking tobacco, all of which he declined. Next morning as he departed, the farmer said: "Young feller, you seem to be right smart and able, for a furriner. But let me tell you, you'll never make a successful American until yer learn to drink, chew, and smoke."

In 1867, Pulitzer received a certificate of naturalization and became a notary public. Afterwards he was admitted to the bar, but did not practice law. At the Mercantile Library he met many prominent men, and he joined a chess club, of which Emil Preetorius and Carl Schurz were members. As a reporter on the staff of the *Westliche Post,* Pulitzer found himself. One of his associates was Henry M. Stanley. Schurz and Preetorius were joint editors, and Louis Willich was city editor. In this company of newspapermen, some of whom were potentially great, the young Hungarian was outstanding for his dynamic energy and his devotion to work.

In 1870 he ran for the state assembly as a Republican, in a district that had regularly returned Democratic members, and was elected. In the legislature as in his editorial writing, Pulitzer was independent and outspoken against corrupt politics. "The *Post* and *Dispatch* will serve no party," he declared, in his first issue of the merged newspapers, and he based his career upon that independent slogan. His service in the Missouri constitutional convention of 1875 gave to that body a strong impulse toward thoughtful liberalism.

By 1881, Pulitzer was the sole owner of the St. Louis *Post-Dispatch.* In the previous year he had supported Hancock as the Democratic candidate for President and worked diligently in the campaign. James A. Garfield was elected by a narrow popular margin—9,464 in a total of 8,898,968 votes —but by a substantial majority in the electoral college. The Democratic candidate carried all former slave states, and in Missouri his popular majority was over 55,000.

PULITZER AS A "SHOOTIST"

WALLACE GRUELLE

Wallace Gruelle was a young Missourian who served in 1870 as legislative reporter for the St. Louis Dispatch.

The three Gruelle dispatches here reproduced illustrate two matters: (1) the corruption and rough-and-tumble nature of politics in the Reconstruction Period following the Civil War, and (2) the fact that the mild-mannered, cultivated young Pulitzer could adapt himself to the conditions in which he found himself—that he was, then and always, the pragmatist in both politics and journalism.

*In 1869 Pulitzer, age 22, had been nominated by a Republican cau-
cus as the candidate of that party for a seat in the legislature at Jefferson City. The district was strongly Democratic, and the nomination was
regarded as a kind of joke on the young German immigrant who was
continually rushing about St. Louis streets in quest of news for the*
Westliche Post. *But Pulitzer surprised the prognosticators by getting
himself elected by a substantial majority.*

*The young newsman found the legislature swarming with lobbyists,
who controlled much of the law-making. Shocked by his discoveries of
graft and corruption in the activities of the County Court of St. Louis,
he not only exposed them in the* Westliche Post *(for which he continued
to write while at the capital) but also introduced a bill to discharge
the Court as an administrative body. Captain Edward Augustine, who
had received from the Court a contract to build a new Poor House that
seemed likely to cost a million dollars before it was completed, was on
hand to lobby against Pulitzer's bill. Pulitzer was then a slender, boyish
chap, Augustine a giant of a man. The first piece here presented tells
what happened the evening of January 27, 1870; the second is a reply
to the story about the encounter that appeared in the* Missouri Democrat
*and is entitled "A Card" in order to make it a personal statement; and
the third is a supplementary "color story." All are taken from the*
Dispatch *for January 27, 28, and 29, 1870.*

*Repercussions of the shooting were sensational. The House debated
a resolution to appoint a committee to investigate, but defeated it as a
matter unworthy of its attention. "If a member attended a wine party
and happened to kiss a pretty girl there, should the House investigate?"
one member asked. But Pulitzer was finally arraigned in court and
fined $100. With costs, the penalty ran to some $400, a large sum then
for the young man to pay. But sympathizers, including several prominent personages in his home city, made up the sum; in later years
Pulitzer paid back every dollar to these friends in need.*

*In fact, the incident made the young man something of a hero in
both Jefferson City and St. Louis. His bill passed the legislature, and
Augustine lost his contract. "It was the first hit I ever made," said
Pulitzer many years later.*

*More about Pulitzer's Missouri career will be found in the preceding
selection entitled "Press and Politics in Early Missouri." Later he went
on to greater fame as editor and publisher of the* New York World,
there to introduce a new era in the history of American journalism.

Jefferson City, Jan. 27, 1870—To-night, about half past 7 o'clock,
Mr. Pulitzer shot at and wounded Mr. Augustine in the office of the

Schmidt Hotel. It appears that Mr. Pulitzer—and, by the way, I am
on Pulitzer's side, not because he is a newspaper man, but he is a clever,
affable gentleman, whose portrait I intend to paint some day, and he
voted right on the Richland County bill—had sent an article to the
Westliche Post, at which Mr. Augustine took offense, and mildly told
Mr. Pulitzer that he was a liar. Mr. Pulitzer cautioned Mr. Augustine
against using such strong language. Mr. Pulitzer left the hotel and got
a pistol and returned and went for Mr. Augustine. Had not his pistol
been knocked down, Missouri would have been in mourning this day
for a slaughtered loyal son. As it was, only two shots were fired, one of
which took effect in Augustine's leg. Augustine struck Pulitzer on the
head with a Derringer, or some other kind of pistol, cutting his scalp
and ending the battle. Mr. Pulitzer was arrested and gave bond for his
appearance before the City Magistrate of Jefferson City.

A CARD

Editors of Dispatch:

In the Jefferson City correspondence of the *Democrat* this morning
Gerald is more severe than just on Mr. Pulitzer. I want it understood
in the beginning that I am not Mr. Pulitzer's special companion. I know
the correspondent of the *Democrat* to be a perfect gentleman. I don't
believe he would do any man a wrong intentionally; yet, misled doubtless by rumor, he has done Mr. Pulitzer injustice in making the following statement: "As he moved to the sidewalk he met two or three gentlemen of the press and said: 'If you wait a little while, you'll have an
item.'" The idea conveyed is that Mr. Pulitzer told the gentlemen of
the press, who happened to be T. D. Rapp and myself, before he left
the hotel or as he was leaving it, to "Wait awhile"; which is correct.

The whole thing is this: Understanding that a meeting of the St.
Louis delegation was to be held in the parlor of Schmidt's Hotel, Rapp
and I went down there. We found several German members and Mr.
Augustine talking over an article which had appeared in the *Westliche
Post* and of which Mr. Pulitzer was the author. He had ascribed Mr.
Augustine's visit to Jefferson City to improper motives and that gentle-
man was correspondingly indignant.

Mr. Pulitzer entered from the street door, went up to them and asked
what was the subject of discussion. Some one answered "you." Mr.
Augustine then spoke to him and told him that in writing what he did
about him to the *Westliche Post* he was a liar, or words to that effect.
Mr. Pulitzer told him to be more cautious in his language. Mr. Augustine, very excited, told him he was a "d——d liar." Mr. Pulitzer then

left the crowd and came over to where Waters, of Ray; Moon, of Livingston and T. D. Rapp and myself were standing. I said to him, "Pulitzer, why didn't you knock that man down when he called you a d———d liar? You must keep up the *esprit du corps,* man." Pulitzer replied: "Oh, it's all about the County Court." In a minute or two he left the house.

About five minutes afterwards I had a message to send off and asked Mr. Rapp if he felt like walking to the telegraph office with me. He said he had no objections. We started, and about twenty feet from the door we met Mr. Pulitzer returning to the hotel. It was then he told us to come back, that we would get a good item. Thinking he alluded to the meeting of the delegation, I told him we would be back in a few minutes. At High Street we separated, going down that street to the telegraph office. When about half way across the square I met three of the committee clerks of the House, all of them out of breath and running. One of them told me to go to Schmidt's Hotel and I would get an item. I told him I had just left Schmidt's. He said a shooting scrap had occurred. I turned back and found that Pulitzer had shot Augustine.

I am no upholder of assassination, but because a man unfortunately gets himself into a scrape, I do not see the necessity of hounding him down. Politically Mr. Pulitzer and I are enemies. Personally we are friends. I have stood by him and I will stand by him. I may not justify the step he took, but then I want justice done the man. His case may be bad enough in its best aspect, but I cannot see the necessity of making it worse than it really is.

> Respectfully,
>
> WALLACE GRUELLE.

Jefferson City, Jan. 28th, 1870—The exciting topic this morning is the shooting affair at Schmidt's Hotel. I think this is overdone. At least, Pulitzer is blamed more than he ought to be. As I told him last night, after he reached his room, I had a great notion to shoot him for aiming at Augustine's breast and hitting him only in the leg. Bad marksmanship is to be deprecated on all occasions, and when a member of the press— and a legislator, to boot—essays to burn gunpowder I want him to go the whole hog.

As I am the political guardian of Pulitzer, I have got him all right on important questions—his cue is to vote "no" whenever Mr. McGinnis, who sits directly in front of him, votes "aye." I will have to practice him at pistol shooting—have to make him understand that when he wants to shoot a gentleman he must take distance at such a pace that the party to be shot cannot knock the pistol down with his hand. Shooting is a

science and ought to be scientifically done. I am going to turn the alley-
way of Miss Lusk, just back of my room, into a shooting gallery and put
Pulitzer under a severe course of training for about two weeks, day and
night, and I will bet, at the end of that time, he can snuff a candle at
ten steps. If he can't, I now and here pledge you my word of honor
that I will shoot him myself.

                                                    WALLACE GRUELLE.

THE EDITOR'S REWARD

JOHN HENTON CARTER

*John Henton Carter was a St. Louis journalist, poet, and novelist. His
verse had something of the homespun quality that distinguished the
better-known Will Carleton. He sometimes used the pen name "Commodore Rollingpin."*

Commodore Rollingpin's Illustrated Humorous Almanac *was published annually for more than twenty years before it was made a monthly
in 1895. It did not last long as a monthly; after that it was a quarterly,
1897–1898, and ended with an annual number for 1899. For many
years annual editions, handsome with chromolithography, were devoted
to the St. Louis fall festival, the Pageant of the Veiled Prophet.*

The following verses are taken from Duck Creek Ballads. *The President referred to is, of course, Grover Cleveland, and the date 1893.*

A journalist from Duck Creek, of the ancient Bourbon school,
Whose chief ambition is to yearn for Democratic rule,
With beaming brow, and sprightly gait, stepped from an early train,
And hastening to the White House, proceeded to explain:

"My father was a Democrat, likewise my grandsire, too,
And all my readers know I print a paper that's true blue.
I hold man's highest aim should be to propagate the creed,
And sow and till with patient hand the Monticello seed.

"I helped to run you in, you know, just eight long years ago,
And toiled with others that you might succeed yourself, also.
And after having skipped a term, you're seated in the chair,
I think that I may safely say I helped to put you there.

"Your picture hangs upon my wall, with that of Mrs. C.
And baby Ruth, and every week, I freely puff all three.
I've named a boy, also two girls, in honor of the same,
And feel that I have started them upon the road to fame.

"But now my paper, like my wife, is needing a new dress,
Not that I think of them the more, nor of the children less.
So I've come on with signature, a little place to seek——"
And drawing forth his parchment, he wisely ceased to speak.

The Presidential eye was thrown upon the mighty list.
"You'll have to take your turn," he said, "in the official grist."
And then he tossed the document upon a pile near by,
So large it filled the Capitol, and rose into the sky.

They parted, and the editor sought the outgoing train,
And on his pass was landed safely at his home again,
Where he still does noble battle against his party's foes,
But his paper and his family are wearing their old clothes.

MR. BRYAN, THE COUNTRY EDITOR, AND THE TELEPHONE

HOWARD R. LONG

Howard R. Long is a native Missourian. After receiving his B.J. degree at the University of Missouri, he edited the Crane Chronicle *for several years. He then became general manager of the Missouri Press Association, serving at the same time as a professor of journalism at the University. He received his degree of Doctor of Philosophy in the Department of Rural Sociology, working under Professor C. E. Lively. For health reasons, he took up active, full-time farming for some years, but he was able to return to an academic career in the 1940's, bringing to his work at Southern Illinois University his unusual talents for organization and for individual teaching.*

Professor Long is a leading authority on the community newspaper in this country and in England. His quarterly called Grassroots Editor *publishes material in this field, and it is from that magazine that the following article is taken.*

Reprinted from the *Grassroots Editor.* By permission of the publisher.

Robert Walton was a leading Democrat in Howard County, Missouri, when that party was the only one with names on the ballot. He lived in Armstrong, and during most of his life he edited the *Herald,* a country weekly distinguished mainly for its political regularity. Bob's personal heroes, naturally enough, were the Democratic leaders of state and national stature.

A few years before his death, Mr. Walton stood with me at the counter of his newspaper office looking out upon the village street while he told me a story which I think should be recorded somewhere as a very minor, though an interesting, footnote of American history.

Back around the turn of the century Bob Walton, one summer morning, was looking out of that same window, toward the dingy little depot squatting by the Alton tracks, when a livery team trotted into view. In the buggy were a driver, and a stranger, whom the editor at first recognized only as no man who cast his vote in Howard County. Yet there was something familiar about the stocky figure, the massive head, and the wide mouth beneath the plain straw hat.

Recognition! Stopping only to seize pencil and pad, Bob hurried across to the stranger.

"Aren't you Mr. Bryan? And what are you doing at Armstrong with no arrangements in advance?"

"Why, yes, my name is Bryan, and I am here to catch the train for Chicago. Had a Chautauqua engagement in Fayette."

"But Mr. Bryan, why didn't you tell us you were coming? There are hundreds of people hereabouts who would give anything to shake your hand!"

"I am sorry, Mr. Walton, there just didn't seem to be time. I move around so much, I never know today where I will be day after tomorrow."

"Well, Mr. Bryan, now that you are here, won't you please make a speech? It would mean so much to us!"

Mr. Bryan looked up and down the street. He saw the proprietor of the general store leaning in the doorway, an old Negro dozing on the station platform, a lone horse at the hitchin' rack, and no other living things—not even a dog and his fleas.

The great man sighed.

"If we only had a crowd! If we only had a crowd!"

"I'll get you a crowd, Mr. Bryan! If you'll make the speech I'll get you a crowd. People will come from miles around to hear you talk!"

"No, I'm afraid not. In two hours my train is due. On a day like this all the farmers are in the field. There is no time to go out and bring them in."

"But, Mr. Bryan, if there were two hundred people, three hundred, maybe five hundred, would you make us a speech?"

"Of course, my good friend, of course! But forget about that and help me find some victuals."

"Mr. Bryan, I'll see that you get an early dinner and before you have finished your blackberry pie we'll have the street full of people, right here in Armstrong!"

"How can you do that? Burn down the town?"

"No, we'll telephone. Armstrong has a brand new system. All the farmers use telephones now. I'll have Central give the long ring on every party line. She'll tell the womenfolks to clang the dinner bells. When the men get to the house they'll hurry right on to town with whatever horseflesh they have in harness. You just wait!"

In seconds, it seemed, all of the villagers—men, women, and children—were clustered before the railroad station. But it was a puny crowd. A few minutes more and a horse, still wearing the harness for drawing a double shovel plow, galloped into town. Astride the animal was an elderly man, a veteran of the Confederacy. The child clinging to the old man's waistband, was, no doubt, a grandson thirsting for the true word of the Democratic faith. By this time dust was rising from the country roads. The farmers were on the march. They came riding in buggies, in surreys, in farm wagons. Later a few straggled in on foot. But they came, the women in sunbonnets and aprons, the men still wearing the grime of their work. Within the hour, such a crowd as the village of Armstrong had never seen was at hand and clamoring for "the speakin' " to begin.

Finally Bob Walton said, "Mr. Bryan, how is this for a crowd?"

"The best I've seen, Mr. Walton, since the campaign of ninety-six. Have the boys pull that hay rack right over here and I'm ready."

"You don't need an introduction, Mr. Bryan, but may I have the honor?"

"It would be my honor, Mr. Walton."

And that is how it came about that William Jennings Bryan made his great address at Armstrong, Missouri. In his excitement Bob Walton neglected to record the text. Thus the words are long forgotten. But it was the crowning speech of a great career, Mr. Bryan's greatest oration. The good people of Armstrong and vicinity were sure it was.

The Chicago train was late that day, but when the engineer whistled for the station, Mr. Bryan was still on his hay wagon. At least his shoes were there. Mr. Bryan himself was in the heights, explaining to the poor farmers of Howard County the glory of the common man.

LITTLE DIXIE

ALBERT EDMUND TROMBLY

A note on Professor Trombly will be found in connection with a group of his poems in our earlier section on "Other Cities and Towns in Missouri."

Following is the title poem in a book of Trombly's verse published as Volume XXVIII of the University of Missouri Studies.

It's the heart of Missouri, blooded of three,
Virginia, Kentucky, and Tennessee.
It's a tall spare man on a blue-grass hoss.
It's sugar-cured ham without raisin sauce.
It's coon dog, coon, persimmon tree.
It's son or brother named Robert E. Lee.
It's tiger stalking a jay-hawk bird.
It's the best hog-calling that ever you heard.
It's fiddler fiddlin' you out of your seat,
Fiddler fiddlin' you off your feet.
It's a bluebird singing in a hawthorn thicket.
It's vote to a man the Democratic ticket.
It's crisp brown cracklin's and hot corn pone.
It's catfish fried clean off the bone.
It's hominy grits and none of your scrapple.
It's mellow pawpaws and the Jonathan apple.
It's sorghum sweetenin' and belly-warming corn.
It's old Jeff Davis a-blowin' on his horn.
Unreconstructed it rares and bites
At touch of a rein that would curb its rights.
It's come in, stranger, draw up a chair;
There ain't no hurry and we'll all get there.

TRUMAN AND HISTORY

HARRY S. TRUMAN

A Missouri Reader would be incomplete without a selection from Harry Truman's Memoirs. Truman was born in Lamar, Missouri. Following his service as an artillery officer in the First World War, he studied law in Kansas City, where he became presiding judge of the Jackson County Court 1926–1934. He served Missouri in the United States Senate 1935–1945; he was inaugurated Vice-President in 1945, and succeeded a few months thereafter to the Presidency, following F. D. Roosevelt's death. He was returned to the White House after a brilliant campaign in 1948. After his retirement he came back to Independence, where the Truman Library was erected to house his own papers and works dealing with other Presidents and with the history of the country.

It seems fitting to present in this place a passage from Volume I of the Memoirs dealing with his childhood, and especially his early passion for the study of history—an interest that continued to be important in his life.

We had wonderful times in that neighborhood from 1896 to 1902. Our house soon became headquarters for all the boys and girls around. We had a large front yard, and our back yard was surrounded by a high board fence to keep the stock safely off the street. Usually there were goats, calves, two or three cows, my pony, and my father's horses to be taken care of. The cows had to be milked and the horses curried, watered, and fed every morning and evening. In the summertime the cows had to be taken to pasture a mile or so away after morning milking and returned the same evening. The goats and calves had to be taken to the big public spring at Blue Avenue and River, two blocks south of our house, for water.

There was a wonderful barn with stalls for horses and cows, a corncrib and hayloft in which all the kids met and cooked up plans for all sorts of adventures, such as trips to Idlewild, a sort of wilderness two blocks north, and pigtail baseball games which I umpired because I couldn't see well enough to bat.

It was a very happy time, not fully appreciated until a long time afterward. There was a woodpile on which my brother and I had to work after old Rube, a good old colored man with a limp, had sawed the cord wood into the proper length for the cooking stove. The wood had to be split and carried to the wood box in the kitchen for "Aunt" Caroline's use in making cookies, corn bread, and all sorts of good things to eat.

Like us, Jim Wright and the McCarrolls were interested in raising pigeons. We had fantails, pouters, and many kinds of common everyday pigeons. We carried on quite a trading business in pigeons, chickens, cats, and pups. My mother was very patient with us and our pals and always came to our defense when we went a little too far and the various fathers decided to take a hand.

We also had a garden, which had to be weeded in season and a yard to be mowed and raked too. Somehow we managed to get most of the chores done which had been laid out by my father and still have time to play and enjoy the company of our pals too.

After a while we began to grow up. The gang scattered here and there, and shortly the serious business of education, jobs, and girls began to take all our time.

Education progressed, and we learned geometry, music, rhetoric, logic, and a smattering of astronomy. History and biography were my favorites. The lives of great men and famous women intrigued me, and I read all I could find about them.

We had an excellent history teacher, Miss Maggie Phelps, and an English teacher, Miss Tillie Brown, who was a genius at making us appreciate good literature. She also made us want to read it.

Our science teacher was Professor W. L. C. Palmer, who became principal of the high school and afterward superintendent of all the schools. He married our mathematics and Latin teacher, Miss Adelia Hardin.

I do not remember a bad teacher in all my experience. They were all different, of course, but they were the salt of the earth. They gave us our high ideals, and they hardly ever received more than forty dollars a month for it.

My debt to history is one which cannot be calculated. I know of no other motivation which so accounts for my awakening interest as a young lad in the principles of leadership and government.

Whether that early interest stemmed partly from some hereditary trait in my natural make-up is something for the psychologists to decide. But I know that the one great external influence which, more than anything else, nourished and sustained that interest in government and public service was the endless reading of history which I began as a boy and which I have kept up ever since.

In school, history was taught by paragraphs. Each great event in history was written up in one paragraph. I made it my business to look up the background of these events and to find out who brought them about.

In the process I became very interested in the men who made world history. The lives of the great administrators of past ages intrigued me, and I soon learned that the really successful ones were few and far between. I wanted to know what caused the successes or the failures of all the famous leaders of history.

The only way to find the answers was to read. I pored over Plutarch's *Lives* time and time again and spent as much time reading Abbott's biographies of famous men. I read the standard histories of ancient Egypt, the Mesopotamian cultures, Greece and Rome, the exploits of Genghis Khan and the stories of oriental civilizations, the accounts of the development of every modern country, and particularly the history of America.

Reading history, to me, was far more than a romantic adventure. It was solid instruction and wise teaching which I somehow felt that I wanted and needed. Even as a youth I felt that I ought to know the facts about the system of government under which I was living, and how it came to be.

It seemed to me that if I could understand the true facts about the growth and development of the United States Government and could know the details of the lives of its presidents and political leaders I would be getting for myself a valuable part of the total education which I hoped to have someday. I know of no surer way to get a solid foundation in political science and public administration than to study the histories of past administrations of the world's most successful system of government.

While still a boy I could see that history had some extremely valuable lessons to teach. I learned from it that a leader is a man who has the ability to get other people to do what they don't want to do, and like it. It takes a leader to put economic, military, and government forces to work so they will operate. I learned that in those periods of history when there was no leadership, society usually groped through dark ages of one degree or another. I saw that it takes men to make history, or there would be no history. History does not make the man.

History showed me that Greece, which was not as big as the state of Missouri, left us ideas of government that are imperishable and fundamental to any society of people living together and governing themselves. It revealed to me that what came about in Philadelphia in 1776 really had its beginning in Hebrew times. In other words, I began to see that the history of the world has moved in cycles and that very often we find ourselves in the midst of political circumstances which appear to be new but which might have existed in almost identical form at various times during the past six thousand years.

Especially in reading the history of American Presidents did I become aware of the value of knowing what has gone before. I learned that the idea of universal military training, which was being hotly debated when I was in my teens, had first been recommended by President Washington in 1790. I learned of General McClellan, who traded his leadership for demagoguery and eventually defied his commander in chief, and was interested to learn how President Lincoln dealt with an insubordinate general.

These lessons were to stand me in good stead years later, when I was to be confronted with similar problems. There were countless other lessons which history taught that would prove valuable to me. There was the miserable performance of the Committee on the Conduct of the War in the 1860s, which did such a poor job for the federal government that Douglas Freeman, talking about his biography of Robert E. Lee, told me the committee was worth several divisions to the Confederacy. I was thoroughly familiar with the antics of that committee, and as chairman of the Senate special committee to investigate the defense effort in the 1940s, I avoided every pitfall into which my predecessors had fallen.

I learned of the unique problems of Andrew Johnson, whose destiny it was to be thrust suddenly into the presidency to fill the shoes of one of history's great leaders. When the same thing happened to me, I knew just how Johnson had coped with his problems, and I did not make the mistakes he made.

History taught me about the periodic waves of hysteria which started with the witch craze during colonial days, produced the abominable Alien and Sedition Acts of the 1790s, flourished again in the Know-Nothing movement, the anti-Masonic hysteria, anti-Catholicism, the Ku Klux Klan, the Red scare of 1919. When the cycle repeated itself during my administration in the form of anti-Communist hysteria and indiscriminate branding of innocent persons as subversives, I could deal with the situation calmly because I knew something about its background that students of history would know but perhaps not appreciate. When we are faced with a situation, we must know how to apply the lessons of history in a practical way.

I was beginning to realize—forty years before I had any thought of becoming President of the United States—that almost all current events in the affairs of governments and nations have their parallels and precedents in the past. It was obvious to me even then that a clear understanding of administrative problems presupposes a knowledge of similar ones as recorded in history and of their disposition. Long before I ever considered going into public life I had arrived at the conclusion that no decisions affecting the people should be made impulsively, but on the basis of historical background and careful consideration of the facts as they exist at the time.

History taught me that the leader of any country, in order to assume his responsibilities as a leader, must know the history of not only his own country but of all the other great countries, and that he must make the effort to apply this knowledge to the decisions that have to be made for the welfare of all the people.

HORSES, MULES, DOGS, AND 'COONS

THE HORSE IS KING

LEWIS ATHERTON

Lewis E. Atherton was born in Bosworth, Missouri, in 1905. He received his bachelor's, master's, and doctor's degrees from the University of Missouri, and became a member of that institution's History faculty in 1936.

Dr. Atherton has published widely in the fields of the economic and social history of the United States. The following paragraphs are taken from his book entitled Main Street on the Middle Border.

Village life moved at the pace of horse-drawn transportation. Tourist homes, tourist courts, garages, filling stations, and stores selling automobile accessories lay in the future. There were no concrete curbs, and parking meters were nonexistent; and small-town workmen would have been baffled at the idea of painting parking lines in streets consisting of dust or mud.

The presence of horses was evident everywhere. Droppings in the streets and town stables attracted swarms of flies, and narrow-rimmed wheels of wagons and buggies cut gaping ruts during rainy seasons. Hitching posts, connected with iron chains, surrounded the village square. Until business growth necessitated removal of hitching lots to the edge of business districts, farmers tied their teams around the courthouse square, let down check reins to ease the tired necks of their horses, and walked across the street to do their trading. Thirsty farm teams quickened their step when they approached town pumps and watering troughs, which also doubled as fire-fighting equipment.

Horses were sentient beings, capable of affection, and an unwritten code censured their abuse. In cold and rainy weather farmers paid the modest fee necessary to stable their teams in commercially operated feed barns and livery stables. The occasional drunk who forgot his team was roughly criticized by the village paper after some citizen had removed them late at night to a livery barn for food and shelter.

Even within the town itself business and social life depended on horse-drawn transportation. Most citizens had horse-and-carriage barns at the rear of their homes to shelter driving equipment. Commercial drays hauled freight to and from the depot, did heavy moving for local citizens, and made daily deliveries for stores unable to afford their own private wagons. Most stores, however, owned single-horse, spring wagons, with business advertisements painted on the sides, which made morning and afternoon deliveries to residential areas. Younger clerks enjoyed driving these conveyances at speeds beyond the limits of safety demanded by elderly residents of the town. Local hotel hacks, pulled sometimes by as many as four horses, rushed back and forth from depots at speeds supposed to impress travellers with their efficiency. By loading sample trunks of travelling salesmen smartly and with dispatch, sounding their horns sharply, and dashing off before a rival hack could clear the depot platform, drivers scored a point in favor of the establishment which they represented. Peddling carts, ice wagons, and sprinkler carts moved more sedately, much to the pleasure of children who begged fruit and small chunks of ice or played in the streams of water being sprayed on dusty streets.

Livery stables served those who could not afford to own rigs or who had temporary and unusual demands. Young people courted and eloped with livery stable teams, and circus agents drove them leisurely round the countryside to post bills. Drummers employed drivers and rigs to haul their sample trunks on two- and three-day side trips to hamlets lacking railroad connections. Picnics, celebrations and fairs in nearby towns, baseball trips, sleighing in winter, funerals—all these and more called for livery-stable teams.

A good bay trotter and a fine buggy appealed to the young man of the 1870's much as the convertible does to his great-grandson. At the peak of its development, a truly fine buggy was an expensive item. Polished and varnished ash shafts, rubber-tired wheels with shiny brass inner rims, brass lamps decorated with large glass rubies, and patent-leather dashboards pleased the eye. Even the harness had its charms—gleaming tan leather with brass fittings, rainbow-colored celluloid baubles, and ruby rosettes. The current generation will never know the thrill of spending $1.75 on a horse and buggy for an afternoon and evening of dating. The carriage with its fast team, yellow fly nets, linen lap robe, and beribboned whip lifted the spirit of the young blade as he drove up and down Main Street with one foot hanging over the body bed and a cigar at an angle in his mouth. Loafers shouted at him and received the expected quip in reply, commented on his extravagance, and wondered at his destination. A touch of the whip and he was on his way. With one horse pacing and the other trotting, he passed the fragrant slaughter-house at the edge of town and on to the meeting with his best girl.

Men loved a fast horse and a reputation for permitting no rival to pass. To curb this passion, town ordinances provided fines for careless and reckless driving. Gallatin's charter of 1857 specifically authorized punishment for "furious riding of any horse or animal" within the limits of this Missouri city. In spite of such laws, citizens still complained about fast driving. . . .

As a focal point in the age of horse-drawn transportation, the livery stable had a form, a personality, and an odor as distinctive as that of its twentieth-century successor, the garage and automobile showroom. Brick construction, feed chutes connected directly with the hayloft, and running water in stalls and washrooms marked the more pretentious establishments. Most, however, were large, boxlike structures of graying unpainted wood, with oversized doors to permit carriages to enter the central ramp. A few had signs in front, perhaps a horse's head with crossed whips carved in wood, but, as a rule, the only decorations were tin advertising strips of patent remedies for horseflesh nailed at random to exterior walls. All stables had the same mingled smell of horse urine and manure, harness oil, feed and cured hay.

A small office near the door contained a battered desk, a pot-bellied stove, a few chairs, a cot, and a lantern hanging on a wooden peg for the use of an attendant who was on duty twenty-four hours a day to wait on customers and to guard against the constant threat of fire. A slate on the wall near the office or just within listed the names of horses out on trips and rental charges. So far as possible, customers were held accountable for abusing horses by furious driving, for turning rubber-tired conveyances so short as to fray the rubber against the buggy bed, for failing to feed horses on long trips, and for other injurious acts. Some stables posted slogans to encourage better care of equipment:

> Whip Light,
> Drive Slow.
> Pay Cash
> Before You Go.

and all gave careful instructions to new patrons.

Well-equipped livery stables possessed a surprising variety of vehicles. Fancy buggies and curved sleighs were rented out for single dates; fringed surreys served for double-dating and more prosaic family trips. Carryalls, with seats along the sides and entrance steps in the rear, were used on special occasions—for Sunday School picnics, to carry visiting ball teams to hotel and the playing field, to take elderly ladies to the cemetery on Memorial Day, and in Autumn to taxi passengers to the fair grounds. Light spring wagons hauled drummers and their sample trunks on visits to country stores and hamlets. Of more somber mien were the hearses, with black enclosed sides and oval windows, fringe and plumes, and elaborate box lights. Hearses decorated in white were preferred for children's funerals. Perhaps one or more of the local doctors kept a team and glass-enclosed coupe at the livery stable. Hotel hacks, the town watering cart, and vegetable wagons added to the variety of conveyances parked along the walls.

Stalls were to the rear, from which horses were led up cleated ramps to the main floor for hitching. A second-floor loft over the stables facilitated the forking down of hay used for feed. Harness for each animal hung on wooden pegs at the front of his stall. Somewhere in the building was the washroom where buggies were washed and wheels were greased. Curry combs, hair clippers, sponges, axle grease, harness soap, and pitchforks were scattered through the building at points most convenient for their use. . . .

The livery barn was universally condemned by pious mothers who rated it only slightly above the town saloons. Its robust life shocked those refined people who spoke of bulls as "gentleman cows." Unlike twentieth-century automobile dealers, who move in country-club circles, livery stable owners generally ignored high society. Addicted to slouchy attire, sometimes noted for profanity, they were numbered among the few local men of property who avoided religious activities and booster movements. Since the usual explanations—stinginess, a choleric disposition, or free-thinking religious principles—did not apply in their case, they puzzled even their own contemporaries. For these mothers, however, it was enough that they were hard to understand and did not practice the finer points of accepted social conduct. The livery stable also served as a loafing place, especially for those most addicted to betting on horse races. Checkers and playing cards were often in evidence, and liquor was tolerated within limits. Most horrible of all, stallions were offered at service as long as public opinion would tolerate it, usually only until mothers of impressionable boys learned of the presence of "gentleman horses" within the city limits. . . .

Probably no other loafing place in town provided so fine a setting for tall stories, and there the town liars competed for supremacy. They told of working for the contractor who built Niagara Falls, of ice worms ruining a whole summer's supply of ice, and of the half-believable hoop snake. Stories of Civil War exploits appealed to an audience composed in large part of veterans, who could relish the ludicrous overtones [such as are found in this bit from *The Gilded Age*, by Mark Twain and Charles Dudley Warner]:

Still another told of coming on the battle field of Gettysburg on a gunboat in a driving snow storm. It was the morning of the third day of the battle. He had been drinking gun powder in his whiskey to make him brave, and he performed such feats of daring and valor that General Meade, with tears in his eyes, shook his hand and said, "Abel, I won't forget this."

Youngsters found additional attractions. Horseshoe nails could be bent into rings; old bottles and junk lying around the premises were collected and sold. And when the "Tom shows" *(Uncle Tom's Cabin)* came to town the trained dogs which would chill the local audience by baying on Eliza's trail generally were housed at one of the local livery stables.

Nineteenth-century midwestern civilization was obviously geared to the strength and limitations of horse-drawn transportation. The horse accounted for the carriage sheds and barns in residential sections, for livery and feed barns, for stockyards, harness shops, and blacksmith shops, for the many small carriage factories in country towns, for hitch racks, town pumps, and watering troughs. Cemeteries and schools were laid out with horse-drawn transportation in mind. The horse played a major part in determining trade areas, and his potentialities helped determine nineteenth-century recreational patterns.

KATE AND OTHER MULES

THAD SNOW

Thad Snow was born in Indiana, but in 1910 he bought a farm in Mississippi County, in southeastern Missouri, and lived there the remainder of his life. In his latter years he exercised his authentic literary talent in writing about his farming experiences for newspapers and magazines.

The mule had no better eulogist than Mr. Snow proves himself in Chapter XIV of his book From Missouri, *which we present through the kind permission of his daughter, Mrs. Robert G. DeLaney, who still lives on the farm near Charleston.*

I have written about hogs, sheep, cattle and my stock dogs. It is even more desirable to write about mules, because they are a vanishing race of noble animals and before long there will be no one left who knows much about them, or can give them the just praise they have earned.

I think the plowlands of the Eastern Seaboard States and even of Pennsylvania, Ohio and Indiana were cleared and plowed in the stumps mainly by oxen, because oxen move more slowly than horses and have more patience with all that happens while breaking in stump land. But mule power broke in the Delta. Oxen were too slow for pioneering in this century. In a way mules blend the virtues of oxen and horses. They are fast like horses but patient like oxen, which made them just right for the Delta.

Mules come in all sizes, shapes and colors. That is because their papas, who are vulgarly called jackasses, come in all sizes and shapes and colors; and their mamas who, of course, are brood mares, are likewise variable. You mix these two more or less alien bloods and you can have anything from a five-hundred-pound mountain pack mule, like I've seen here and there in foreign parts, up to sixteen-hundred-pound "wheel" mules like I used to see on dirt-moving jobs such as levee building. You can have them four feet high at the withers or six feet high, depending on their parentage and how the strange blood mixture turns out.

They say that a mule has no "pride of ancestry, and no hope of posterity." I don't know about the "hope" of posterity, but it is certainly true that they never have any. I've asked why mules do not reproduce and I've been told very wisely that it is because they are "hybrids." That explains nothing to me, because mules have everything it takes, so far as I can see, and seem to take a normal interest in such matters.

Most farmers of the Delta liked to work medium-sized mules that weighed from one thousand to twelve hundred pounds. While the Delta was in process of clearing and up until about 1930 the mule dealer was the biggest businessman in town. We raised no mules. They were all shipped in from the North. In the late winter and early spring thousands were shipped in to replenish the supply, and to increase the supply as more and more acres were cleared for the plow. Also hundreds were shipped out. The old worn-out ones went down farther south where cotton was a one-mule, one-Negro enterprise.

When the mules began to come in, everybody went around to the big sales barn to look them over; then for two or three months the mule barn was the center of business and social activity. Mules were practically all sold on credit—nothing down—and one year to pay. Almost anybody could buy a team on those terms. Such generous terms were all right for the dealer, because he sold them unbroken as three- or four-year-olds, and if the farmer took them out and broke them to work and kept them in good shape they would be worth $50 to $100 more as five-year-olds, in case the dealer took them back for non-payment. Theoretically, at least, a good managing farmer could have his work mules for nothing, because he could trade his five-year-olds back for four-year-olds each spring and draw boot every time, and finally whittle his note clear down in the course of years. I don't happen to remember anybody who managed quite that well.

Almost always work mules ran loose in the barn lot and were not tied up at all. They did not have stalls as horses commonly had in the

North. Usually hay was fed in racks in the sheds of the barn and the corn fed in troughs out in the lot, and most often the mule lot was a big one. There are several reasons for handling and feeding them that way. A mule likes to eat a bit of corn, and move over and eat a bit of hay, then go to the water trough and drink a little water. Perhaps he'll make the rounds a dozen times before he calls it a meal. He thinks this deliberation in his eating and drinking is good for his digestion, and I guess it is.

Then mules are particular about their toilets and sanitary arrangements. You bring in a mule from work and the minute you take off his bridle he flops down and rolls, and curries his hide. If the lot is good and dusty, so much the better. The dust absorbs sweat and he shakes it all out of his hair after each roll. He may want to roll a half dozen times during the noon hour. But he must roll on clean ground. He likes it dusty but it must be clean. So by common agreement mules always choose one corner of their lot for their "out back." They go there every time. This is an admirable thing to do but it is sometimes amusing to watch a mule solemnly leave his feed trough and go to the corner to attend to his business. This gives another mule the same idea, then he walks over, and so on and so on. The whole lot of twenty or thirty mules may go through the routine, one after the other. There is no crowding, no confusion, and no embarrassment.

I have indicated that cattle stealing was a great sport in Swampeast Missouri. But a greater sport was catching up mules in the morning. Usually I worked thirty mules from one lot. Fifteen boys and men would gather at the lot just before sunup. The mules were rested and the fun was on. The boys would go in with their bridles, and then action began. Around and around the lot they would go, carefully avoiding, however, the "out back" corner. The boys would yell out the names of their mules, and thrash their butts and sometimes their faces with the bridles, as they raced by. The yelling was the main thing and the mules seemed to like it. Finally one would be caught, then another and another, and pretty soon the rest would stop and take their bridles with decorum. Sometimes when the air was right and sound carried well we'd stop to listen. From miles around we could hear men yelling and thrashing at their mules just before sunrise. It was really the greatest sport of the Delta, and the only sport I know of that was played only at daybreak. Neither the mules nor the men went in for it much at catching-up time after the noon hour.

Relatively few people now living know much about mules. Only some oldsters like me have been so happily circumstanced as to have known hundreds of them personally and associated with them in intimate terms. Soon they will be almost mythical characters, known only by tradition and perhaps in poetry and song. Already there is a tradition forming, I believe, that mules were all pretty much alike, that their heels were eager and deadly, and that they were "as stubborn as a mule." I know I can't stop a tradition after it gets going, nor turn it one way or the other, and I would not generalize about mules any more than I would about people. But the thought occurs to me that as a class, or as a species—if mules can be called a species—they are managing their disappearance from off the face of this troubled earth in an exemplary fashion. They bray no hymns of hate, and do not destroy each other with bombs or even with heels. They just disappear with no fireworks, and with the least possible ostentation. On the other hand people prate peace and bray war, and make the greatest possible to-do about their own mutual destruction.

The tradition is that mules kick and that they are stubborn. With no general intent to buck the tradition but in justice to the hundreds of mules that I've worked with, I must say that no mule has ever kicked me except in a friendly, companionable way. Of course occasionally one has thrown a hind foot my way, but never to hurt me. I have actually, a few times, caught a mule's hind hoof in my hand and shaken it, like I would yours, because it was just the mule's way of saying "How do you do." . . . As for being stubborn, that depends on what you mean by that word. Most mules don't like to go where they ought not to go, and will argue the matter. Often it has turned out that I was wrong and the mule was right. Maybe it is not so much stubbornness as deliberation or even wisdom. Statesmen and particularly diplomats like to take what they call "calculated risks" of one sort and another. A risk is a risk to a mule.

Mules are not just mules. Each is an individual, and has character and personality of his own. Some are great-minded and some petty and small-minded, like people. Probably I have utterly forgotten ninety-nine out of a hundred people whom I've known. Not so with the mules I have known. Most of them I have forgotten, of course, but I believe I could recall a hundred mules to my mind, remember their names, and if I were an artist, paint their pictures not only to get their lines and colors, but to bring out their several and highly diverse personalities.

Kate was far and away the finest, smartest, handsomest, most scornful mule I ever owned. She was an aristocrat in the correct sense of the word. She was smarter than I was and had better breeding, and she knew it. If she finally gave me her respect, that was all. She gave her affection neither to me nor to any other mule, except only to her gentle work mate who was named Liz. She merely tolerated the rest of us. We were not in her class. Neither was Liz, but Kate loved her and never took advantage of her in any way. If, as sometimes happened, we hitched Kate with some other mule, she'd snap that mule back against the load on every hard pull, but with Liz she always kept her end of the double-tree a bare inch ahead.

She was a bright, almost cherry-red bay fifteen and three quarters hands high and weighed only about eleven hundred pounds. Her legs were trim and shapely. Her mother was obviously a thoroughbred, and her father certainly was not just another Spanish Jack. He was a Spanish Don or Grandee, for she had a slightly Roman nose, which is a pretty sure sign of noble blood in a mule, coming from the paternal side. Her eyes were wide spaced and extra full and a dark liquid brown. She stepped high and always with precision. Her ears were long and extra well pointed, and she kept them straight up and faced forward. I think she held her head higher than any mule I ever knew, but she could see a pebble in her path, just the same, because her eyes were so full and widely spaced. Always she gave one the impression that she saw and understood everything, and largely disapproved.

I bought Kate when she was a five-year-old, from a farmer who told me he thought he had the best mule he ever saw and the best worker, when he could catch her and get a bridle on her. He said that he had had her tied up for three months and that he had learned how to bridle her, but nobody else could. He said nobody could catch her in a lot, and he was tired of fooling with her. She had never been ridden.

I bought her on sight and said I'd take her with me if he'd lend me a bridle so I could ride her home, and lead my saddle mare. He was skeptical but said he would bridle her for me. I watched him do it, while he explained the principles involved. Kate would take the bit like any other mule, but she would not allow anybody to take hold of her ear and pull it into the headstall in the usual way; instead one must raise the wrist, gradually bending the big ear over little by little and pulling the headstall clear over it so it could flip upright on its own power. The second ear had to be handled with equal care but bent somewhat differently. This delicate technique is hard to explain but I learned it by watching once and doing it twice under direction. It is well that I learned it, because Kate lived twenty-six years, and to her dying day she could be bridled only by someone who knew how to give her ears the special consideration she thought was their due. A good many "warm blooded" mules are persnickety about their ears.

Kate didn't object much when I jumped on her and before we got home I could see that she liked it. We settled the matter of catching and bridling her out in the lot after about two hours of argument. That is, we settled it so far as we two were concerned. It was months before any one of my men could catch Kate or bridle her except when I was on hand to hold up my right hand and say "Kate."

Now some white-haired old mule driver like me might read this, and he would want to know how I could possibly have got a mule like Kate to stand in the lot for her bridle in two hours of argument. Well, I could do it because she was not only arrogant and scornful but highly intelligent. When I got home with her I unbridled her in the runway of the barn which was about twelve feet wide and fifty feet long. I left her there to get her bearings for thirty minutes. Then I entered with her bridle in my left hand and about twelve feet of half-inch rope in the other. I approached her, raised my right hand and said "Kate," as impressively as I could. As I came near she danced about, then whirled and flashed by me to the far end of the barn. I didn't say a word and didn't try to stop her. If I had she would have run right over me. Then next time I approached her I raised my hand and said "Kate" like before, but the second she started to dance I flipped her under the belly with the rope.

I'm afraid I must stop to explain (not to the old-timer) what can be done with a twelve-foot light strap or a half-inch rope. I've seen expert mule skinners not only flip off tufts of hair but split a mule's hide. It is an art. I was only moderately good at it. I suppose Kate danced, whirled and flashed by me fifty or possibly a hundred times. I approached her slowly every time and raised my hand. I didn't raise my voice when I said "Kate," but each time she started to dance I put a little more bite in the business end of the rope. I was trying to get over to her the idea that this was going to go on forever unless she stood stone still for the bridle.

Finally she did stand like a statue for me to bridle her. There was no halfway business about it. She showed not the slightest fear of me. She didn't surrender; she just quit because it was the only sensible thing to do. I rubbed her soft nose on my cheek, scratched her forehead and under her jaws and petted her all over. I took the bridle off and left her alone to think it over, and after a while I came back with the bridle and without the rope. She stood like a haughty angel; then I led her out in the lot and turned her loose.

What do you suppose she did? A mule man would know. She rolled, of course. She rolled on one side, then on the other, and got up and shook the dust out. She got up and down a dozen times till she was dry and shiny. The poor dear hadn't had a good roll for months, because she had had to be kept tied up all the time. For months I bridled her every time myself, and every time I approached her I held up my right hand and said "Kate." Then I risked letting Mose Feezor try it, while I stood by. Mose was my best hand so I had let him work her and Liz. Kate seemed to like Mose moderately well. One day Mose tried it on his own and got the job done.

Kate worked more days and hours than any other mule, because she could do every job better and was always ready. She was never sick, lame or tired. She was a fast, straight walker but would slow down when she plowed new ground. We used ten-inch Rose Clipper plows for breaking new ground, on which we welded erect eight-inch knife-edged cutters to slice through the roots. If a big root or decayed stump had any "give" to it Kate would set herself and tear through it, but if it felt solid she stopped instantly and backed up so the plow could be pulled out and thrown around.

In corn-planting time Kate got relief from heavy work, because she and Liz always planted, day after day. They made rows that were straight as a line. In stump land Kate laid off the rows with a single-stock bull tongue, and Liz came behind with a single drill. No matter how thick the stumps were Kate's rows always were forty inches wide, and stretched out clear across the field in a perfectly straight line. I have no idea how she did it. She'd go around a big stump and get back exactly in place, so all the driver had to do was to swing his single-stock around and get it back behind Kate. We could see that she kept one big eye cocked down at her last furrow to get the spacing exact, but we never saw her look ahead to check on the over-all straightness of her line; but there was never a bow or bend. No man that ever drove her claimed to know how she did it, and none ever claimed the credit for making straight rows.

We used Kate and Liz regularly in the logging. They could load any log in the woods without block and tackle. We had one enormous cypress log that was five and a half feet through at the butt. We laid off of it for a long time aiming to borrow block and tackle. But one morning Mose Feezor said he was tired of waiting, and was going to load that log. I went to the woods with him and found he had cut extra-long skids. Kate and Liz pulled the log up a few inches on the skids and let it back just to be sure the chains were placed right, then set themselves and took it clear up on the wagon. There is no describing how mules look and act on a pull of that sort. They do not stand up and just pull. They get down with their bellies close to the ground. We call it "scratching" because they move their feet rapidly and only an inch at a time. There is fast movement every instant, and it is thrilling to see.

We loaded many cars of alfalfa throughout the winter, and hauled in the mud with four-mule teams. Often the mud was axle deep and we could haul only thirty-two bales on a wagon. Sometimes I'd have a dozen boxcars set out on a siding. It was slow and mean work to bring the empty cars up to the loading place, and to move the loaded ones on up out of the way. We did this with heavy steel "pinch bars" that had sharp edges to go under the wheels and shaped so you could pry down on them and get enough power to move a car a little bit at a time. It was slow business.

One day one of the haulers said he had heard that a strong enough mule that knew how to get down and "scratch" and stay with it could be hitched alongside a car at the middle, then if the mule scratched long enough the car would start moving. He hadn't seen anything like that but had heard it, and it may have been just a tall tale. I didn't take much to the idea but the boys wanted to try it. They thought Kate could do it if it was possible at all. So we hitched her to a rod in the middle of a boxcar. Kate eyed that big boxcar, and said "What the hell!" as plain as could be. She leaned against her single-tree and nothing happened. She stopped and cast her big eyes up at the car and at us boys to see if we were really in earnest. She saw that we were. I said, "Kate," reassuringly, and Mose who held her line said in his squeaky voice, "Git down and scratch." Kate got down and scratched. She threw clouds of cinders in our faces and after a while that car moved. The rest was easy. Kate walked it a hundred yards to our loading place with the greatest of ease. It was hell to start but easy to pull.

After that we had no more use for "pinch bars." It was easy to see that Kate liked her new job. But one day she failed to move a car on the first try. I sent a boy up on the car to make sure he had loosened the brakes, and went all around the car to see that they were loose, and that there was no stone or cinders on the track. I asked the boy to be dead sure he had uncoupled the car from the one behind, and he threw the top lever clear over to show me. Then I asked Kate to try it again.

She scratched and scratched till I thought her great heart must burst. I have never seen anything like it. At last the car moved, then more movement, and Kate finally straightened up and walked on. We were all watching Kate, and none of us had noticed until she was well on her way that she had two cars, and not one. The second car had not come uncoupled. The pin still held by an inch, with the uncoupling lever thrown clear over. I doubt if any other mule ever performed such a labor.

Kate was admired and bragged about by every man who worked her or ever saw her work. It didn't turn her head. She mellowed a little, I think, as the years went by; but she remained aloof to the end. Her work was her interest in life, and she gave it all that she had.

Our great thinker, Thorstein Veblen, coined many words and phrases that are now embedded in our language; among them was the phrase "the instinct of workmanship" which he thought was one of mankind's praiseworthy attributes. Kate had it.

THE HOUN' DOG OUTLASTS THE MULE

HALLIE M. BARROW

Hallie M. Barrow was born at Fairfax, Missouri. She was educated in the St. Joseph schools and at Simmons College, Boston, Massachusetts. Since her marriage she has lived near Maysville.

Never was there a more thorough Missourian. A lover of the state's customs and people, she wrote a column about them for the St. Joseph News-Press *for some years; for almost a decade she broadcast a program on Missouri rural and folk topics by radio.*

The article here presented was published in the Kansas City Star, *March 12, 1960.*

Reading about the "Missouri Waltz" recently brought to mind the enthusiastic promotion given another competitor for the official state song. The unsuccessful number was pushed by the Missouri Fox Hunters associations and its title was, "Makes No Difference If He Is a Houn', They've Gotta Quit Kickin' My Dog Aroun'." [This had been the campaign song of Champ Clark when he was a candidate for the Democratic nomination for President in 1912. The song was a hit at the Baltimore convention, but it was not enough to win him the nomination over Woodrow Wilson.]

A veteran of the First World War remembers the tune as the regimental march of the Sixth Missouri Infantry, later consolidated with the old Third to make the 140th Infantry, 35th Division. Played with abandon on a bitter winter dawn in camp, it added materially to the rigors of combat training in Oklahoma.

The competition was strong, early in this century, between the mule and the foxhound as a symbol of Missouri. More fine mules were shipped from Missouri than any other state. More fine foxhounds were shipped from Missouri than any other state.

[*Editor's note:* The Forty Years Ago column on this page last Monday morning said that Thomas B. Hudspeth of Sibley had listed $4,567 profit from the sale of foxhounds in his income tax return.]

The foxhound men wanted the new national highway being laid across the state to be called "The Houn' Dog Trail," at least in Missouri. They lost when it was designated Highway No. 36. Then they wanted their "Houn' Dog" song to be made the state song. They lost to "The Missouri Waltz"—and no move has been made, to date, in behalf of the Elvis Presley classic, "Houn' Dog."

The Red Ranger, a fox hunter's journal, was published monthly at Rushville, Missouri, for over a quarter of a century. The mules had no magazine or official publication of their own, but articles about them had appeared in many magazines from the *Saturday Evening Post* on down. A book among the best sellers of its time was MacKinlay Kantor's *The Voice of Bugle Ann.* Bugle Ann was a Missouri Ozark hound.

Each of these Missouri products had a go in Hollywood. *The Voice of Bugle Ann* was made into a highly entertaining movie. Then the late Bob Burns came to the American Royal and from a show ring full of champion mules, he picked "Champ Clark" to be sent to Hollywood in a special stock truck, along with a mule understudy, to perform with Bob Burns in *I'm From Missouri.* It was just about a draw so far.

Then the First World War started and there was no question which was the most popular. The fox hunters meekly subsided, for every nation in the fray wanted Missouri army mules. The largest mule barns in the world were built at Lathrop, Missouri, right in the midst of a very hot foxhound section. From Lathrop, Missouri mules were shipped by the hundreds of thousands all over the world.

One of the catchy war songs of that era had a picture on its cover of a farm boy leaving for service. His parents were bidding him farewell at the gate and out in the barn lot the boy's mule was braying and kicking the daylights out of a rail fence. The title was "Good-by Ma, Good-by Pa, Good-by Maud With Your Old Hee-Haw." The American Royal became the largest and best mule show in the world. Excelsior Springs put on a "Mulesta," right after the Royal, three days of glorifying the Missouri mule. Mules were tops.

Then the pendulum swung to the other extreme.

The tractor pushed the mules off the farm. In the Army jeeps and helicopters ended many a GI's transportation problems and improved his language. Mule classes were discontinued at the American Royal. The sight of a mule was as rare as a horse and buggy. There was even some talk of putting a few mules in Swope Park so the next generation could at least say, "Once at the zoo we saw a mule."

But they'll see many a foxhound as they motor through the country.

Foxhounds hunt in packs and a farmer is about the only sportsman who can keep from three to 30 hounds at his home. Furthermore, the farmer need not buy a lot of special hunting clothes, boots, and equipment or go far away from his home and business for his fox hunt. Likely, his hounds can pick up a fresh scent right at the farmer's henhouse door.

All the preparation he has to make on any good trailing evening is to grab up an old hat and coat his wife has been threatening to burn, take his old steer horn off its peg on the porch, and blow a few mellow toots to call his hounds and to notify his neighbors and their hounds to meet him at the rendezvous, the old hay stack on the bluff over the creek. This is the farmers' country club.

They will spend the best part of the night in rare good fellowship, listening to the sweetest woodland music known, a pack in full cry. There is no head waiter or other service.

An old gallon bucket hangs from a tree fork. The first one to arrive starts a campfire, takes the bucket and fills it at a nearby spring. He adds coffee from a supply cached in a bee tree cavity, and the aroma of boiled coffee floats over the moonlit scene. It's just potluck after the coffee is made. If one of the farmers has butchered he may bring a sack of hamburgers, sausage cakes, or a few slices of sugar-cured ham to broil over the coals, and pull from his pockets some hunks of cold corn bread.

Young foxhounds have sweet soprano voices. Older hounds have deep, chesty altos, and for each turn and twist of the fox, the hounds have inflections, variations, and modulations. Each man knows his own hounds' voices, and from the musical message the hounds send to the hilltop, he can picture every move of the chase.

The foxhounds have never been asked to appear at the American Royal but they have "sponsored" a most unusual entertainment which resembles the old-fashioned chautauqua. The farmers owning foxhounds will nearly all belong to their county fox hunt associations, and once a year they meet and run their hounds in competition.

The Platte-Clay Fox Hunters Association has held its 50th meet at Dearborn, Missouri. This association owns eight acres of virgin timber. In a grassy valley the members have built an open air theater with covered stage and dressing rooms, a modern cook shack, a recreation hall, and an office. These annual hunts last three days. The farmers bring their families and camp out. There is just about everything in the line of camp equipment from the latest station wagon and trailer with every camping gadget known, on down to tents and just plain bedrolls.

With all the campers, it looks much like an old chautauqua ground. But the programs on the stage and in the big tent are not by paid professional talent, as with the chautauquas of the 1890's. The farm wives are members of extension clubs, and the farm children belong to 4-H clubs, F.F.A. and Audubon societies. They put on pageants, musical contests, style shows, judging demonstrations, plays, all kinds of sports, even to a rodeo and religious services. The men hunt for three days in peace. The farmers, their families, and their hounds have a wonderful time . . . and even the fox seems to enjoy the chase. No one carries a gun, as the object of the chase is not to kill the fox but to enjoy the sport and the music and behavior of the hounds.

Old fox hunters are not surprised their hounds have won the last round of the battle with the mules. As one of them summed it up:

"Our hounds sort of ran with their tails between their legs all during the war years, but a good hound never quits a trail."

THE HOUND-TUNER OF CALLAWAY

RAYMOND WEEKS

Raymond Weeks was Professor of Romance Languages at the University of Missouri 1895–1908, and later held a similar position for more than a decade at Columbia University. He was a poet and short-story writer. His stories deal mainly with Missouri people and customs. This story appeared in The Midland *for December, 1926.*

Before the War Between the States, the inhabitants of Missouri used to speak of Callaway County, and the unregenerate still do so. The minority, however, to which I am proud to belong, call the county the Kingdom of Callaway. Here is the origin of this name: Missouri seceded from the Union at the war. Later, the Yankees, by a succession of unscrupulous accidents such as always befall the ungodly, obtained possession of St. Louis and Jefferson City, called together an illegal legislature, and had it vote for the return of the State to the Union. Among the counties, Callaway alone possessed the courage which goes with virtue, refused to return to the Union and seceded from Missouri. Thus, you see, the Kingdom of Callaway came into existence.

To look at, the Kingdom of Callaway does not amount to much. It is composed of none too fertile hills, with laps of valleys in between. There are no mines, no factories, few industries and little agriculture, although mendacious travelers have averred the contrary. Boone, Audrain and the other fat, lazy counties lying at the feet of the Kingdom, speak of it with contempt. None the less, its people are the most heroic on the globe. Man does not live by bread alone.

About thirty years ago, it was my privilege to ride twice across the Kingdom of Callaway, and to talk with its inhabitants. They are few in number, and, like all noble souls, live much amongst the glories of the past. They are set in their ways, as befits a proud, unfortunate race, and they refuse to "smile as the wind sits." Their tongue is not voluble,

except when they speak of the degenerate populations which surround
the Kingdom. At such times, they draw from the hidden recesses of
the past a vocabulary which leaves nothing to the imagination, and hurl
fragments of this vocabulary upon the crapulous counties couchant at
their feet. In calmer moments, they will tell you that, if there is any
good blood in these counties, it strayed, or was stolen, from Callaway;
and heavens knows that, in the matter of good blood, Callaway leads
the world, so much so that every family in the Kingdom descends from
the ancient kings of Scotland, England, Ireland, Wales or France, and
some families descend from several of them at once. The traveler is
touched to see coagulated in a single realm the descendants of so many
noble lines.

Turning from history, and examining the inhabitants of the Kingdom
as they now are, we are struck by their many creditable superstitions.
But it would take too long even to begin to name them. Turning now
from their superstitions to something else, we are struck by the glorious
traditions of this people. They believe, for example, that their ancestors
discovered fire and music; that they were the first to shoe horses and
mules in the modern manner, by nailing the horse shoe to the hoof;
that they invented lightning, gunpowder and steam; and that Robert
Fulton was a native of Callaway—in fact, they named their capital Fulton in his honor.

As for music, we may readily accept the local tradition. The men,
women and children of the Kingdom of Callaway possess voices which
carry farther than any other voices in the world. While there are no
pianos or guitars or other degrading instruments, one notes the survival
of the ancient harp, of which the piano and guitar are degenerate descendants, and one finds quantities of dulcimoors and old fiddles and
twanging jewsharps and mournful hunting horns, such as exist nowhere
else. Besides—and this all travelers admit—the voices of the mules are
more musical here than elsewhere; and as for the hounds, well! until
you have heard the baying of a pack over the hills and little valleys of
Callaway of a moonlight night, you have heard nothing! There is none
of the hoarse, ridiculous, broken bellowing, none of the inconsequential,
stupid yelping, which you hear in less favored countries, but a veritable
harmony, so strange, so sweet, so primitive, that every fibre in you
quivers and shivers, and tears start to your eyes!

The improvement in the hounds of Callaway probably began about
a century ago, but it was destined to receive its great impetus from the
genius of one man, who previous to the War Between the States was
known as Uncle Josh. He was born about 1806. It is said that, as a
baby, he was given a hound as a pillow, and it is certain that he grew
up with dogs as his constant companions. Between him and them—to

the honor of both—existed perfect sympathy. A strange dog would run to him as a frightened child to its mama. He spoke their language. He understood their traditions, superstitions, prejudices, resentments, hatreds, longings, ambitions. Consider what it means to be a lost dog! How his body trembles! How his heart aches! How sore his paws are! How covered he is with mud and dust! What hunger! What loneliness! What homesickness! Imagine that you are that lost dog, then think of meeting a gentle, strong spirit, at whose word and touch your lostness, your ugliness, your despair drop from you in the twinkling of an eye. You are in the arms of a tender and sure friend, who is at the same time a magical physician. Such were the gifts of Uncle Josh.

He made a great discovery about 1848, the year near which his daughter and only child was born. Long before this, he had become locally famous as a trainer of hounds. A few distinguished men before him in the history of the world had, it is true, advanced the education of these noble animals, but he surpassed them. His love for dogs was greater; he wished them perfect. He had found that by his voice alone —he had a voice of wonderful carrying power—by a strange, crooning chant, he could get dogs to do almost anything. Recognizing soon the vastness of the field of dog study, he decided to limit his labors to hounds. After a while, he became so skillful that he could correct in the baying of an ordinary hound the "break" which is so distressing. And then—then he invented the tuning-fork! I do not mean that he was the first to invent this instrument, but that he reinvented it—invented it all over again, with the charm of a newly created marvel in a newly created country. And what a use he made of it! In Asia and Europe, the tuning-fork has never realized its possibilities. It was a disappointment from the start. It never became much more than a toy. In the Kingdom of Callaway, it became the national emblem.

Uncle Josh manufactured the forks with his own hands, and called them hound-forks. He graduated them, until he could express in notes of ravishment all the deep emotions of the canine heart. With a set of the hound-forks in his saddlebags, he was now seen journeying about Callaway, training hounds. Success and glory came, immense, dazzling, as you would have felt, if you could have heard one of his well-trained packs baying in the distance of a moonlight night, or if you could have seen him sitting on his horse under a tree, listening to the hounds, and from time to time singing in a low sweet voice his favorite hymn:

> On the other side of Jordan,
> In the sweet fields of Eden,
> Where the tree of life is blooming,
> There is rest for you.

His reputation spread, and he refused many offers to descend to the low counties and train hounds. The rich barbarians who lived in those counties were, and have remained, crazy about fox-hunting, without ever knowing the first elements of the art. One result of Uncle Josh's refusal to train outside the limits of Callaway was to make it the hound centre of the United States, and indeed of the world. Previously, the only exports of Callaway were limited quantities of mules, wild honey and whiskey. Now orders for hounds poured in more rapidly than they could be filled. The Callaway hound had become famous.

When the War Between the States broke out, Uncle Josh had already commenced what promised to be famous experiments with mule-forks. Except for the war, he would have made the universe his debtor by a new application of his great invention.

The beginning of the war found him a man of about fifty-five, with a long gray beard. He had recently become a widower. Despite his age, he shouldered his rifle and rode away to do his duty, leaving his daughter, aged thirteen, with his sister. When the rump legislature, got together by the Yankees, voted Missouri back into the Union, he made a brief apparition in his native county, and, to the plaudits of the entire population, including the dogs, led the Revolution which established the Kingdom of Callaway. He was chosen King against his will. He issued a royal edict that all dogs should be chained up for twenty-four hours (otherwise, they would have followed him), kissed his daughter and his sister good-bye, and hastened to rejoin his command in the Confederate Army. Much as he hated bloodshed, he fought like a demon, became a colonel, wept like an infant at the fall of the Confederacy, and at last returned home on foot, his uniform in rags and on his breast an immense beard which was no longer gray.

He met a more personal grief on his arrival in the Kingdom. He found the population in tears over the flight of his daughter, Peggy. (That, by the way, is a name which ought to be proscribed. Have you ever known a girl by that name with whom you did not fall in love? Society owes men something!) Peggy, then, had run away with a graceless fellow named Sam Black, who was not even born in Callaway! Girls are such fools! Sam had joined the Confederate army at the eleventh hour, just in time to get a uniform and a briar scratch, had fled to the confines of the Kingdom as to a neutral Power, had seen Peggy—and her beauty did the rest.

A word about Peggy.

You may have dreamed in favored moments of a beautiful woman, you may possibly have seen one, but never one her equal. Nor have you ever heard, in dreams or out of dreams, a voice like hers—a low, vibrant voice, with an unconscious, pellucid promise of ineffable things.

Her beauty was that of the dark-eyed, fair-skinned type which has wrought most of the havoc in history. Add to this that at seventeen her form had the soft rotundity of a woman's. Such was Peggy, as described to me by the inhabitants of the Kingdom.

You can imagine how the old man loved her, how shocked he was at her flight.

After a few days devoted to affairs of state, the King set out on a sublime quest—the search for Peggy. He took from a cache sufficient gold and silver to fill a money belt, had shod a young, powerful horse, named Robert in honor of General Lee, tossed into the saddlebags a change of linen and his best set of hound-forks, also his hunting horn, and rode softly away in the dead middle of a moonless night, accompanied by a hound escort of eight noble beasts.

The inhabitants knew of the King's departure. They chained up the dogs, in order that the Kingdom might not be depopulated. These intelligent animals too knew what was happening, and, whether chained in the open air or in cellars, kitchens, or barns, they heard Robert's step in the night and the soft-padded paws of the eight fortunate hounds, and threw themselves, howling and whining, as far as their fetters would allow. And so it went from hamlet to hamlet, from cabin to cabin—a progressive rattling of chains and howling of dogs, until long after the old man and his silent escort had left behind them in the darkness the Kingdom of Callaway.

The King unhesitatingly rode toward the west, for he knew that human thistle-down blows in that direction; he felt that Peggy and her abductor were somewhere between the Kingdom and the Kansas frontier. But what an immense territory to traverse!

Following the road when there was one, when not, riding through primeval forests and dense thickets, going around marshes, fording muddy streams, he made his way westward, simulating, especially at night, a fox hunt, for he felt sure that if Peggy could hear the baying of trained hounds from back home and the music made by her daddy, the hound-tuner, she would come to him. Many times the dwellers in an isolated log cabin heard in the darkness the baying of what seemed a pack of celestial hounds, the deep *toom! toom!* of a horn, and a strangely modulated humming: *ding, ding, ding; ting, ting, ting; ling, ling, ling.* Then, if they were near enough, they heard the voice, as if it were, of an old man calling: "Peggy! Peggy!"

In the daytime, he stopped to inquire at every house, tavern and village. The inhabitants looked with astonishment and sympathy at this old man in a torn Confederate uniform, with gray hair that reached his shoulders and a great white beard, with sad, sleepless eyes, and with an escort of mud-spattered hounds. At first, he always inquired if they had seen his daughter, a very pretty girl, who was eloping with a young man, but later, when he had lost nearly all of his hounds, he no longer spoke of her as *his* daughter, but as that of a sick friend. You see, one's social position could be told by the number of dogs which accompanied one. When he had only two or three hounds left, and when his uniform was only a flutter of rags, he became ashamed to say that he was the father of the beautiful girl he sought.

Throughout his search, the King never abandoned a hound to die in the woods. If the animal fell ill, or broke or injured a leg, he lifted him carefully to the saddle, and carried him until he could leave him in safety at a cabin. He usually camped part of the night in the forest, near a spring or brook. He kept his saddlebags stocked with ham, bacon and bread, which he shared generously with his escort. There was always grass for the horse. When he passed the night at a house, his money was refused, for such was the hospitality of the time.

It was about a month after he set out that he obtained his first news of the fugitives. They were, he learned, on foot, but occasionally got a "lift" from town to town or house to house. They had a long start of him, but he did not give way to discouragement. Sometimes a fortnight passed with no news, then a woman at a cabin would say:

"Wy! yase, they wuz hyah. They stopped the night with us."

"Did they say where they were going?"

"No, suh."

"Which way did they go from here?"

"Right on west, suh."

Finally, one Sunday morning, a man told him that he had seen them a week before, and that they had asked how far it was to Blufton. He rode straight to Blufton, seven miles distant, and entered the town, followed by two hounds, which to say the least, had lost their beauty. It was the hour for church, and the pitiful looking old man was seen by nearly all the inhabitants. At the main hotel they refused him admission, but he was received at a less reputable one when he planked down a gold piece. He took as good a room as the house possessed, paid two darkey boys for currying and rubbing down his horse, and tidied himself up a bit.

The next morning he walked about the little town, inquiring after the fugitive pair. Many remembered seeing them only a few days before, but no one knew where they had gone. Had they remained on the north bank of the Missouri, or had they crossed to the southern bank? Or had they perhaps taken a boat for what the King still called Westport Landing—a name which had been changed to Kansas City? No one could tell. He learned that a boat which had recently gone up the river would be due at Blufton on the return trip in three days. He devoted this interval to a search of the country around the little town. No news whatever of Peggy!

When the steamer tied up at the wharf on its return trip, he was the first to leap aboard. Yes, the captain remembered the beautiful girl and the young man. They had taken passage with him to Kansas City, where they had disembarked. A few days later, the old man, his precious Robert and his brace of remaining hounds disembarked in turn on the flat rock which formed the landing at Kansas City. The teeming, jostling levee received them with smiles of amusement, but the King merely swept with eagle eyes the faces before him, made brief inquiries at all the warehouses, stood a moment looking at the immense clay bluffs on whose top and beyond lay the young town, then rode resolutely up the steep, narrow street cut through the bluffs. He passed a day in visiting the stores, hotels and saloons on the Market Square, Grand Avenue and Main Street, and another day in the remainder of the town. No news! The fugitives must have found on the levee or at the Market Square a trader or farmer just starting for Westport or the interior.

It was now late August—three months since he had started on his quest. He was ill and felt very old, hardly able to sit a horse, but he set out resolutely to search the great, fertile region which extends from the river on the north to the prairies on the south, and from Independence on the east to the Kansas line on the west. He resolved to cover this territory systematically. Some days he could hardly drag, but he did his work well, though slowly. He inquired at every cabin, house, store or tavern, and of every person whom he met on those wild roads.

Day after day ended in discomfiture, and night after night without a discovery, yet he searched on in desperation, for he knew that he was at the jumping-off point: if the fugitives were not in the territory he was examining, it would mean that they had joined one of the caravans which started from Independence and Westport to cross the Great Desert. When he saw a caravan, he thought that Peggy was perhaps in one of the covered wagons. He questioned the drivers, and peered into as many wagons as possible. Some person was base enough to steal one of the old man's two remaining hounds. Undiscouraged, he continued his search with every ounce of failing strength.

The conclusion of the King's great search was related to me by Joe Holloway, a middle-aged black man, who had been a slave of Mr. James Holloway of Jackson County. As a boy, I never missed an opportunity to talk with him, as with all those who could tell of what we already called the old time. And few could entertain me so well as honest Joe, who knew something of the Indians and the French and the great caravans that used to start from Westport for the mountains beyond the Desert, and who knew all that was to be known of the early

families of our region. Then, too, it was a pleasure just to hear him
talk. His dialect walked upright, unaided and unashamed. To attempt
to represent his pronunciation by means of the alphabet is almost a
crime, for the result will be nearly as shocking as a transcription of your
dialect or mine would be. None the less, I am going to try, and if
there is one of you who possesses from childhood a knowledge of the
dear old dialect, and who has besides a profound, honest voice and a
great, generous heart, let him read aloud what Joe told me one day
when I found him seated by the Mormon Spring.

After a few moments' conversation about indifferent things, Joe
said to me:

"Did you heah the mockin' buhd singin' las' night in the moonlight?
Hit's mos' onusual, an' made me think of anothah night in Augus' a
long time ago—hit mus' o' ben twelve aw fohteen yeahz ago, jus' aftah
the close of the waw.

"Ole Massah James Holloway, who built the Holloway house in 1835,
'd been injoyin' poh health faw a numbah of yeahz, an' wuzn't able
to sleep much o' nights. He liked 'speschully to set out in the yahd of a
moonlit night in summah, an' he wuz a-settin' thah the night I'm speakin' of. Hit mus' o' ben wal pas' midnight, when he heahd the bayin' of
a houn' an' the *toom! toom!* of a hawn off yondah in his woods. He call
to Mistah Benjie, his son: 'Benjie come down heah quick an' go with
me!' but Mistah Benjie, he fas' 'sleep, so Massah Jim get up an' hurry
off alone, right up thet-a-way, beyont the family burin' groun' that you
know. He wuzn't afeahd o' nuthin', Mass' Jim, an' I've seen him do
wuss things than thet on the blackes' night the Lawd evah sent.

"Wal! he hurry, he hurry, tell he stop undah a young sycamoh to
wait faw the hunt to pass, an' befoh he could see hit comin' heahd a
hummin' an' a buzzin', the stranges' soun' thet mawtal evah heahd. Any
othah man 'cep' Massah Jim 'd a' tuhned an' run. An' then he seen come
into sight a big gray hoss an' on his back a man with a great white
beahd, an' he held in front o' him a bright metal fawk thet he struck
ev'ry time hit wuz goin' to stop hummin'. Mass' Jim step out into the
moonlight, an' the strangah rein in his hoss. They wuz two ole men
face to face.

" 'Good ev'nin',' says Mass' Jim.

" 'Good ev'nin',' says the strangah.

" 'Thet's a queah musical enstrument you have thah,' says Mass' Jim.
'What is it, if I may enquiah?'

" 'Hit's a houn'-fawk,' says the othah, an' he show two othas hangin'
frum the pommel o' the saddle by the side of the big hawn.

" 'I nevah seen such a enstrument,' says Mass' Jim. 'I reckon you
ain't frum these pahts?'

"A shadah seem to pass ovah the strangah's feachuhs befoh he
ansuhd:

" 'Nosuh, I'm from the Kingdom of Callaway. Back home they call
me Uncle Josh, the houn'-tunah.'

" 'You mus' have wondahful foxes in the Kingdom of Callaway, if
you've chased one clean heah,' says Mass' Jim.

" 'Yessuh,' says the ole man, 'I've followed one frum Callaway heah.'
He lean on the pommel o' his saddle an' seem a thousan' mile away in
his thoughts, an' on the othah side of his hoss, a little in front, set a
houn'-dog with his tongue out, an' the moonlight slipt down sof'ly an'
fell aroun' them. Mass' Jim didn't speak faw some time. He seen thet
the ole man woh a Confed'rit unifohm which wuz mos'ly rags. Mass'
Jim 'ad los' a boy, his oldes', in the Confed'racy. He pitied the ole man,
who seemed mighty weak, an' he step fohwahds an' laid his han' on his
ahm right kinely.

" 'Come an' be my gues' tonight,' he says. 'I live right ovah yondah.
I'll call a niggah woman an' one o' my men, an' we'll have some suppah,
an' I've got some mighty good tobaccy!'

" 'You'z very kine,' says the strangah, 'but I've wuhk to do.'

" 'I ain't got nothin' to do faw a month,' says Mass' Jim, 'I'll he'p
you! I know ev'rybody in this section an' ev'ry foot o' country.'

"Thet seem to decide the ole man, so they come ovah to the house,
an' Mass' Jim come to the quawtahs an' bahn, so'z to be shoh thet his
hoss wuz well kyahd faw, an' his dog nevah lef' him. By the time him an'
me an' Jiminy, what wuz the name o' the houn'-dog, come back to the
house, suppah wuz neahly ready. Aftah suppah, the ole man an' Mass'
Jim set out in front o' the house an' light thah pipes, an' me sets by 'em
on the groun' to listen to the convuhsation.

"The ole man tell how he envent the houn'-fawks an' make heaps o'
money trainin' houn's to bahk hahmoniously, like music, an' to be
gen'rally polite. Then come the waw, an' when hit wuz ovah, he
retuhned to the Kingdom of Callaway, an' if the daughtah of the King
hadn't jes' runned away with a young fellah named Sam White, as I
remembah. So to please the King, he staht out to fine huh. The King
think thet she won' be able to resis' retuhnin' if she heah the houn's an'
the houn'-fawks like huh'd always heahd them back home, an' if she
see Uncle Josh, thet she's knowd all huh life. So the King send Uncle
Josh away with eight aw ten houn's, the bes' in the Kingdom, an' with
plenty o' money, an' Uncle Josh take along his houn'-fawks an' his hawn,
what wuz also well known to the King's daughtah. Uncle Josh ride an'
ride an' seek an' seek. Hit mus' be a thousan' miles from heah to the
Kingdom of Callaway, an' he covahs all thet distance an' loses all his
houn's 'cep' Jiminy.

"Massah Jim wuzn't no fool. He didn't say much while the ole man wuz a-tellin' his story, but he jes' set a-lookin' at him. Aftahwahds he tole us all heah at home thet ez he listen to the ole man settin' thah in the moonlight, hit come ovah him suddently thet the ole man hissef wuz the King of Callaway, an' so he wuz!

"Frum that minit, Massah Jim wuz tuhmined to he'p fine the King's daughtah, no mattah how much trouble hit might give him. They set thah talkin' faw good two hours, an' then they went to bed, but I don' think Mass' Jim slep' much.

"Wal! they did'n' get up tell tohds ten o'clock the nex' mawnin'. The King of Callaway, faw him hit wuz, wan' to staht right off suhchin', but Massah Jim and his daughtah, Miss Naomy, wouldn' heah to hit, an' puhsuade him to wait tell aftah dinnah.

"At dinnah Mass' Jim say to him,

" 'I ain' nevah heahd sech houn' music as thet-thah Jiminy o' yourn kin make! Hit mus' come, I reckon, frum them wondahful houn'-fawks an' frum your genius in usin' them.'

"The ole man set thah smilin' an' seemin' to fawgit his troubles, so powahfully polite wuz he, 'speshully whah thah wuz ladies, an' Miss Naomy wuz settin' at his right han', so he says smilin':

" 'I reckon thet houn's is houn's.'

" 'Wal!' says Mass' Jim, 'we's got a pahsel o' wuthless houn's, an' we'll be mighty obliged, Naomy an' me, if you'll retuhn in a few days an' give 'em some trainin'.'

" 'I promise,' says the ole man. A cloud seem to pass ovah his face, then he went on: 'I jes' wan' to 'zamine the country frum Wes'poht to the Kanzus line. I knows thet the King's daughtah 'd nevah set foot on the soil of Kanzus, leas'wise I don' think so. If I don' fine huh, I shall espec' you to he'p me, like you said you would.'

" 'Shoh I will!' says Mass' Jim. 'We all will, an' we'll fine huh!'

"So the King rid away with Jiminy runnin' along by the hoss as proud as Lucifah. When they wuz gone, somethin' occuhd to me all of a suddent, an' I says to Mass' Jim:

" 'Mass' Jim, I jes' happem remembah thah's a strange young man an' a puhty gal ovah at the Johnsing place.'

"He tuhn to me right quick:

" 'Who tole you that?'

" 'Rachel'—thet's my wife—'she heahd hit frum Hildy. They been thah faw moh 'n a week, an' she tole jes' this mawnin'.'

"Miss Naomy look at huh paw, then she take huh hat an' go ovah to Missis Beccy Johnsing's—you know the house—an' inside of an houah she come back, walkin' fas', an' she say to huh paw an' huh brothah Benjie, says she: 'Hit's them!'"

" 'How 'd you know hit's the King's daughtah?' says Mass' Benjie, takin' the question right out o' his paw's mouth.

" 'I seen huh!' says she scawnfully. 'A bline man could see thet she's a princiss! Beccy intaduced me!'

"Then ev'rybody began askin' questions all to wunst!

" 'I'll tell you how she is,' says Miss Naomy. 'She's thet puhty thet hit 'd be a muhcy to the men to kill huh right now! You nevah seen anything blackah than huh hah, an' huh eyes is blackah still an' as sof' as black velvit! She don't look to be moh 'n a chile o' fifteen, but she has the fawm of a woman. An' huh voice, hit moh beautiful than she is! The moment you heah hit, you wan' to follah huh fawevah! I kin ondahstan' now thet Queens ain't like othah wimmin!'

" 'Did she seem happy?' ax Massah Jim.

" ' Yes an' no. I axt huh if they wuz a-goin' to remain with us, an' a cloud seem to pass ovah huh, an' she didn't ansuh faw awhile, then she said they's goin' to jine a caravan in a few days faw the Fah Wes' an' frum that minit she nevah smile again as long as I stay.'

" 'We musn' let huh iscape,' says Mass' Jim. 'Sen' Rachel ovah ev'ry day—twicet a day—to ax Miss Beccy what their plans is.'

"Wal! Rachel go ovah ev'ry day, an' Miss Beccy come down an' see we all the secont day—thah wuzn' no grandah lady in these pahts, an' a widah, the moh's the pity! An' when she heahd thet she had at huh house Princiss Peggy, daughtah of the King of Callaway, she become almos' as ixcited as us, an' she entahd into the plan to prevent the Princiss from iscapin'. Hit was arranged thet the fust night aftah the retuhn of the King we'd remine him of his promise to lead a hunt like he do in the Kingdom, to show us how it ought a be done. The moon 'd be jest about full then, we calclated, an' we'd sawt o' guide the hunt 'roun' tell hit 'd pass neah the Johnsing house, an' we felt shoh thet the Princiss 'd come to her paw if she heahd him suddent-like in the night an' realized thet he'd jouhnied all the way frum the Kingdom of Callaway jes' to fine huh.

"Miss Beccy an' the ladies of our fambly wuz so ixcited thet they walk up an' down the room, an' Miss Beccy say: 'Nevah in my life did I heah of anything so s'blime as what thet ole man's done! How I wisht I could see him!' An' Miss Naomy says: 'Don' call him an ole man, Beccy, call him the King!' An' Miss Beccy reply: 'He *is* a King!'

"But those plans wuz not relized. The day aftah the King set out to covah the country 'tween Wes'poht an' Kanzus hit commence to rain stiddy, what I call rainin', an' hit continue all night an' all the nex' day. Massah Jim, he thet res'less he set by the windah an' cuss somethin' awful, an' then he light his pipe an' walk about the house cussin' some moh, an' Miss Naomy sayin': 'Hesh, Paw!' Wal! the King had calclated to retuhn the ev'nin' o' the thuhd day, but he didn't.

" 'Long about two hours to sundown o' the thuhd day, hit become suddently hottah 'n blazes. Young like you is, you nevah seen nothin' like hit. Waves an' billahs o' heat roll ovah us frum the south, an' hit become so dahk thet we had to light candles an' lamps, an' Mass' Jim carrin' on wuss than evah an' cussin' ev'rything in the State of Missouri. An' then hit *did* rain! Bahrals an' hogsheads an' rivahs o' watah fell out o' the sky all to wunst, an' a night come down thet wuz a night! Hit wuz so black thet a preachah couldn't a seen a sinnah two foot frum him, iksep' faw the flashes o' lightnin' thet follahd each othah ev'ry three seconts, an' the thundah wuz like the jedgment day.

" 'Bout an hour aftah suppah, they wuz thet worrit an' nahvous thet they sen' me ovah to Miss Beccy's to enquiah if thah wuz any news. I tuk with me a stout hickry cane faw to he'p keep me frum fallin' an' push the branches out o' my face. Lawd! Hit wuz jes' like swimmin'! I thought moh 'n wunst I'd nevah get thah, but at las' I seen in a flash o' lightnin' the red brick house, an' I reach the shed behine the kitchen. I wait thah half an hour faw the watah to run off o' me, then I knock on the doh, an' Hildy call: 'Who's thah?' an' she wouldn't opem the doh till I name myse'f.

"Miss Beccy come in direc'ly she knowd I wuz thah, an' she shoh wuz pale! She hadn't no news, no moh 'n we all. She walk up an' down the big kitchen, an' wring huh han's. I ax whah the Princiss wuz, an' she say she wuz cryin' up stahs in the room what she an' the young fellah occupy. The room wuz in the back ell o' the house, an' opemd on the gal'ry.

"Wal! the stawm continue wuhs than evah, an' us three an' Bessie, the othah suhvant, wuz thah alone in the kitchen, 'spectin' the hull house to fall, when I thinks I heah the bayin' of a houn' an' I raise my han' an' say: 'Listen!' An' shoh anuff, in between them claps o' thundah we heahd the bayin' of a houn'!

"We throw opem the doh an' resh out undah the shed what wuz opem at both en's. The houn' wuz a-comin' up frum the low groun' tohds the branch, a little to the southwes' o' the house, right through them scattahd fruit-trees this side the awchuhd—you knows the spot. An' suddently we heahd the hummin' o' one o' them houn'-fawks—an' in a flash o' lightnin' we seen the King! He wuz ridin' with his head bent fohwahds, but we seen his great white beahd clingin' all ovah his breas' in the rain. Robaht—thet wuz the name of his handsome gray hoss, what wuz named aftah Gen'ral Lee—Robaht wuz a-breastin' the stawm somethin' beautiful, an' we seen his eyes like fiah. The King hadn't seen the house, 'cause the rain an' the branches wuz beatin' his face. An' all the time we heahd the bayin' o' Jiminy an' the unuhthly hummin' o' the houn'-fawk, an' wunst the ole man's voice callin': 'Peggy! Peggy!'

"Jes' as they come abres' o' the co'nah o' the house, we heahd a suddent movement up stahs an' bah feet runnin' along the gal'ry an' down the stahs, an' we heahd the voice o' the Princiss screamin': 'Daddy! Daddy!' We seen huh by the flashes run out into the stawm with huh black hah flyin', an' Robaht, when he heahd huh, stop proud-like with his neck ahched, an' the King raise his head an' see huh an' fall out o' the saddle like he shot, an' he fall right into huh ahms. We all resht out o' the shed. You nevah heahd a chile cry like the Princiss did, an' we wuz all weepin', 'cep' the King, who lay thah onconscious in huh ahms, an' the houn' dog Jiminy a-leapin' all ovah the Princiss an' a-kissin' huh. He knowd who they'd ben lookin' faw, an' so did Robaht!

"We all he'p to tote the King into the house, an' we lay him down on the floh o' the kitchen, with his head in the Princiss's lap, an' he give no sign o' life. An' the Princiss set thah on the floh weepin' an' beggin' him to speak to huh. Miss Beccy flew to the pantry, callin' awdahs to Bessie an' Hildy. Miss Beccy nevah had huh s'periah faw makin' toddy, an' in no time she wuz kneelin' down an' puttin' spoonfuls o' hot toddy in the King's mouth. At las' he opem his eyes, an' the fust thing he seen wuz the face o' his chile bendin' ovah him. He said a wuhd, an' the Princiss held him in huh buzzum like he wuz a baby, an' she kep' on kissin' him an' sobbin' ovah him, tell at las' we heahd the wuhds she wuz tryin' to say to him: 'Daddy! fawgive me! I ain' nevah goin' to leave you no moh!' He couldn't speak, but he put his ahms up 'roun' huh. Miss Beccy wuz still kneelin' on the floh, givin' him frum time to time a spoonful o' toddy. Huh puhty dress wuz wringin' wet, an' thah wuz watah all ovah the floh, but what did thet mattah? Aftah some minits, the King opem his eyes an' look a long time at his daughtah, an' then says: 'I don' know whah I is an' I don' kyah, so I have you.'

"Then Hildy an' Bessie, the othah suhvant, drug in an ahmchyah, an' we lif' the King tendahly an' place him in it, an' the Princiss cuddle up in his ahms, with huh puhty bah feet showin', an' they whispah to each othah.

"By this time, thah wuz coffy ready an' things to eat, but the King an' the Princiss wuz thet happy they couldn't eat nothin'. Jiminy, he jus' set thah by the ahm-chyah with shinin' eyes, the proudes' dog you evah seen! We try to get him to eat, but he wouldn't eat in company, so we invite him out into the shed, an' he shoh wuz hungry! One of the men 'd already put Robaht in the stable an' rub him down an' give him a big ration o' oats an' hay.

"The Princiss had done whispahd to the King whah he wuz an' how

Miss Beccy wuz one o' the grandes' ladies in the wuhld, an' he felt ashamed of all the trouble he'd caused an' of his rags. He whispahd some moh with his daughtah, an' then said to Miss Beccy, timidlike, not supposin' thet she knowed thet he wuz a King:

" 'Madam,' says he, 'I feel ashamed of all the trouble I have caused you. I can' thank you anuf! I shall nevah fawgit you as long as the good Lawd allows me to live. If you will pahdon me, I mus' be goin'. The stawm won' hahm me now.'

"Miss Beccy stan' thah an' laugh in the sweet way she had, an' say:

" 'Allow you and this deah chile to go out into the night an' stawm? We don' do things thet-a-way at this house. We've lots o' room! Remain with us as long as you kin. Your presence honahs this roof!'

" 'Hit's you who honahs us, Madam,' says the King. 'I would remain, only I promist Mistah Holloway to retuhn this evenin' if possible, an' heah hit is I don' know how many hours in the night, naw how many miles to the Holloway fahm.'

"Miss Beccy smile right sweet at thet an' say:

" 'Hit's less 'n a mile to the Holloway fahm. I'll tell you—let's all go ovah thah aftah while, if the stawm allows! They mus' be worrit to death, faw hit's nigh on two hours sence Joe lef' them. Joe,' says she tuhnin' to me, 'couldn' you ride the—' I reckon she wuz goin' to say 'the King's hoss,' but she check huhse'f—'couldn' you ride the beautiful gray hoss aw one of ourn, an' tell 'em the good news, an' we'll follah latah, if we kin, in the kerridge?'

"I go out an' saddle Robaht, an' I ride like wile. He wuz a powahful hoss, wuz Robaht, an' smahtah than a man. What joy when I got home an' resht in with the news! The ole house wuz a-buzzin' with noise in a minit—preparations in the kitchen, an' most o' the fambly runnin' up stahs to dress. In less 'n an hour, heah come the othahs in the kerridge, an' Bessie an' Hildy too, 'cause you couldn't o' kep' 'em away. Miss Becky had loaned the Princiss some shoes an' stockin's, 'cause she wouldn' go back to huh room. Thet young fellah what 'd been he'pin' to haul wood on the Johnsing place, she nevah seen him agin. He lef' the nex' day—j'ined a caravan faw the Fah Wes'.

"All the suhvants on this fahm wuz thah to he'p in the preparations faw dinnah, as wuz Bessie an' Hildy. You nevah seen a dinnah prepahd quickah an' bettah. Sech a dinnah! We'll nevah see hits like agin, faw them times is gawn. The dinnah wuz what you might call complete, frum fried chicken an' hot biscuit down the line to pickles an' jellies an' presuhvs an' cakes an' pies, an' o' cohs thah wuz hot coffy an' cream, an' Massah had got out two bottles o' the bes' wine evah drunk this side o' Saint Louis. An' then thah wuz the gues's, faw hit's the gues's thet sets off a feast!

"Wal! we kep' the King an' the Princiss with us faw nigh a fawt-night, an' hit wuz a time of onendin' festivities. We kep' opem house ev'ry day, an' Miss Beccy wuz heah mos' o' the time, bless huh! We wuz jes' one big fambly. The King an' Jiminy give a lesson ev'ry day to our houn's, an' all of us went along to see. These woods wuz alive with us happy folks. Wal! them houn's of ourn, they jes' wuship the King frum the fust! He train 'em with his voice, an' he train 'em with his eye, an' he train 'em with his houn'-fawks, an' Jiminy he'p him all the time.

"Sev'ral times a day, the King an' the Princiss come heah to the Mawmon pool, an' they walk along han' in han', jes' like lovahs. They use to set right heah whah we is this minit, me an' you, an' sometimes we heah them singin' togethah in a low voice

On the othah side o' Jawdan,
In the sweet fiel's of Eden,

an' the soun' wuz so sweet thet we had to cry.

"When hit wuz gettin' neahly time faw their depahchah, the King 'lowed he'd ride ovah to Wes'poht an' buy a hoss faw his daughtah, but bless you! We didn' do things thet-a-way! Massah Jim 'd done selected the bes' an' gentles' ridin' hoss in his paschas, an'd bought a fine side-saddle an' bridle. He present them all to the Princiss, who threw huh ahms 'roun' his neck an' kist him an' say she goin' to call him 'Uncle Jim,' an' she done so in speakin' an' writin', faw she writ often aftah she got back to the Kingdom of Callaway. Wal! the day come when they rid away side by side, huh an' the King, with Jiminy trottin' along by the hosses. We all try to smile, but we wuz weepin'. Right ovah yon-dah whah the drive tuhns into the Lockridge Road is the spot whah we seen them faw the las' time, tuhnin' an' wavin' to us, an' probably re-peatin' their invitation to come down to the Kingdom o' Callaway for the remaindah of our nachral lives."

EULOGY ON THE DOG

GEORGE G. VEST

George Graham Vest was born in Kentucky in 1830 and was graduated from Centre College in that state in 1848 and from Transylvania University's law school in 1853. Shortly thereafter he set out to seek his fortune in California, as did so many adventurous young men in those years; but his arm was broken in a stagecoach accident near Georgetown, Missouri, and while he was recuperating in that village he was asked to defend a Negro boy accused of murder. He won an acquittal in court, but the boy was later taken from the jail and lynched, and Vest was notified that he had better leave town. "That made me feel as though I wanted to stay," he remarked later, and accordingly he set up a law office in this small Pettis County village. Two years later, however, he moved to the larger town of Boonville, where he practiced law and politics. Early in the Civil War a group of militant Missourians elected him to the House of Representatives in the Confederate Congress, and later he was made a senator in that body to represent Kentucky. After the war, Vest took up the practice of law in Sedalia.

In 1869 Charles Burden, a farmer in Johnson County, accused his neighbor and brother-in-law, Leonidas Hornsby, of shooting and killing his favorite hound, Old Drum, on suspicion of sheep-killing, and asked fifty dollars damages. Three trials with decisions against the plaintiff preceded the final one at Warrensburg before the Court of Common Pleas on September 23, 1870. In this famous trial, the defendant was represented by T. T. Crittenden, later governor of Missouri, and Francis M. Cockrell, who served his state in the United States Senate for thirty years. The plaintiff's legal staff included Vest, his law partner, Col. John F. Philips, later federal judge for the Western District of Missouri, and Col. Wells Blodgett, a state senator and later general solicitor for the Wabash Railroad.

The climax of the trial was Vest's address to the jury, which has become a classic as "Eulogy on the Dog."

It has been said that this address drew tears from the eyes of members of the jury and others in the crowded courtroom, and that some jurymen wished to grant ten times the damages asked. But the plaintiff was happy with his fifty-dollar verdict. Then four days later the defendant filed for a new trial; this was refused, but an appeal was granted to the First District Court of Missouri, which required appellant to give $1,500 for appeal to the Supreme Court. Eventually the decision of the Court of Common Pleas was upheld, and the fine was paid September 18, 1872.

Professor Icie F. Johnson, of Central Missouri State College, has made a detailed examination of the various theories in regard to the first printing of the Vest "Eulogy" and has decided that the place and date are conjectural. It was doubtless written out from the memory of hearers some years after its delivery, and perhaps approved by Vest himself.

Vest moved to Kansas City in 1877 and two years later was elected to the United States Senate, in which he served for twenty-four years.

Senator Vest was somewhat below average height, but had broad shoul-
ders and a large head topped by a thatch of red hair. All his associates
agreed that he was "a born orator."

A fine statue of Old Drum was erected on the courthouse lawn in
Warrensburg in 1956, with a bronze plate presenting the "Eulogy."
The dedication was attended by four thousand people, and the main
address was made by John M. Dalton, later to be Missouri's governor.

Gentlemen of the Jury:—The best friend a man has in this
world may turn against him and become his enemy. His son or daughter
that he has reared with loving care may prove ungrateful. Those who
are nearest and dearest to us, those whom we trust with our happiness
and our good name, may become traitors to their faith. The money that
a man has he may lose. It flies away from him, perhaps when he needs it
most. A man's reputation may be sacrificed in a moment of ill-considered
action. The people who are prone to fall on their knees to do us honor
when success is with us may be the first to throw the stone of malice
when failure settles its cloud upon our heads. The one absolutely unselfish friend that man can have in this selfish world, the one that never
deserts him, the one that never proves ungrateful or treacherous, is his
dog.

Gentlemen of the jury, a man's dog stands by him in prosperity and
in poverty, in health and in sickness. He will sleep on the cold ground,
where the wintry winds blow and the snow drives fiercely, if only he
may be near his master's side. He will kiss the hand that has no food to
offer, he will lick the wounds and sores that come in encounter with the
roughness of the world. He guards the sleep of his pauper master as if
he were a prince. When all other friends desert he remains. When riches
take wings and reputation falls to pieces he is as constant in his love as
the sun in its journey through the heavens. If fortune drives the master
forth an outcast in the world, friendless and homeless, the faithful dog
asks no higher privilege than that of accompanying him to guard against
danger, to fight against his enemies, and when the last scene of all
comes, and death takes the master in its embrace and his body is laid
away in the cold ground, no matter if all other friends pursue their
way, there by his graveside will the noble dog be found, his head between his paws, his eyes sad but open in alert watchfulness, faithful and
true even to death.

DOGS, 'COONS, AND SNIPES

H. J. BLANTON

Notes about H. J. Blanton, long editor of the Monroe County Appeal, *will be found in this book in connection with other sketches of Missouri life at the close of the nineteenth century that are used in preceding sections. It is pleasant to end our anthology with two more nostalgic sketches (by no means without value as social history) from Blanton's* When I Was a Boy. *The first is from the Second Series of these collections, and the other from the First Series.*

WHEN DOGS WERE DOGS

When I was a boy dogs were dogs. This means that the dog was treated like a dog, instead of as a member of the family, as at present.

Practically every family had a lot of children. The children always wanted dogs, and this wish most always was gratified. But the dog's place was out of doors during the day time and under the house at night. Thus, in order to have fun with the dog during the day, the children, too, had to stay out of doors, which was helpful to their health.

No store carried canned dog food during that era. Commercial dog food had not been processed until comparatively recent years.

Nowhere was there a tax on dogs.

No store carried dog harness, dog blankets, dog collars or dog trappings of other sorts. There were no society dog shows, or dog events of other sorts.

All this does not mean that the dog played an insignificant part in the old-time scheme of things. Far from it.

Rabbit hunting, the favorite Saturday diversion for boys, required the co-operation of dogs. During that period the matter of converting forests into fields was reaching a climax in our locality. In every neighborhood there were large stretches of brush heaps that remained after the clearing. Most of the heaps were about four feet high and about 12 feet in diameter. They made wonderful fires when the time came to reduce them to ashes.

As a refuge for rabbits the brush pile had no equal. On arriving at the field a boy would mount the nearest brushpile, jump up and down, while shouting at the top of his voice. Usually, a frightened rabbit

Reprinted from *When I Was a Boy,* First and Second Series, by H. J. Blanton. By permission of Edgar P. Blanton.

would dash out into the open and head for another brushpile, with yelping dogs trying hard to overtake him. Sometimes the dogs would win. Other times the rabbit would outdistance them. Always, there would be hard running and much excitement among the boys. With slight intermissions for rest or lunch, this would continue all through the day. Usually, at least several rabbits would be carried home as trophies of the chase.

In the business section of our village, dogs furnished sport for early risers most every morning. Rats abounded in most of the basements and stores. Most every night, a lot of them would be caught alive in traps. All up and down the street, clerks would empty the traps outside, and there would be much cheering as waiting dogs closed in for the kill.

Dogs also were necessary for coon fights that were held in public halls from time to time. A live coon would be turned into the arena, where it would be attacked by the dog that had been selected for the first round of the battle. Cheering men and boys would stand three or four deep around the walls, some partisans of the dog, others cheering for the coon. The game little animal seldom gave ground, meeting every onrush of the dog with one of his own. If the dog got the worst of it, as he often did, and went yelping back to his master, there was much ridicule for both man and dog. This, in turn, led to fights among the men, and more fun for the spectators.

But the odds were too great for the coon. After two or three dogs had been taken on, he began to weaken, and eventually was killed in battle. It was terrible sport, doubly so because of the fact that the coon was not given a fighting chance for his life.

Dogs seldom had rabies in those days. If bitten by what was suspected to be a mad dog, the victim was kept filled with whiskey until a mad stone could be obtained. These articles were very scarce. Long journeys usually had to be made to where one could be found. This stone was a hard rocklike formation, which once in a long time was discovered in the stomach of a deer. Applied to the wound made by a dog or snake, it was credited with drawing into its porous surface such deadly poisons as it might contain. More people died from too much liquor in their stomachs than from too much poison in their veins.

Most every community has the tradition of a dog which made its way back to the old home after being transported to a new home a hundred or a thousand miles away. When the Blanton family moved from Howard County to Monroe in the early '70s, it brought Old Dick, the family dog, along. Two weeks later, Old Dick disappeared. Letters from the old neighborhood later brought news of his return. He evidently could not adjust himself to his new environment.

A much more remarkable case occurred when John T. Hook, America's foremost trainer of saddle horses, had his stables on the Paris fair grounds. He sold a fine horse to a customer in Montana, to whom he gave a dog the man had taken a fancy to. Horse and dog, with an attendant in charge, were shipped to Montana by train. The attendant returned by train the following week. Three months later, to Hook's great amazement, the dog, footsore and lean, but barking joyously, came back to the stables.

How animals, without chart or compass, make such trips has always been a mystery. It is doubly so when the dog was shut up in a boxcar on the outward trip and had no opportunity to get landmarks into his mind. The only word for it is "instinct," though nobody really knows what that is.

Unfortunately for the horse, a noble animal no longer needed on the farm, commercial dog food is now a staple article in drug and grocery stores. It is mostly made from horsemeat. Thus, millions of old Dobbins which otherwise would live lives of leisure in lush bluegrass pastures, go on foot into city abattoirs, and come out in cans. Buyers pay $1\frac{1}{2}$ cents a pound for the horse. As the dog food he is a source of great profit for a new industry.

In the pre-dog-food era, the dog was expected to get his living on scraps from the family table. It was an era in which everybody had meat three times a day and in which scraps were more plentiful. However, if the family dog failed to satisfy his appetite from the pan at his own back door he would get additional supplies from neighborhood dogs he was able to whip away from what they had been given.

The most despised individual in every community is the dog poisoner. Being a villain and sneak by nature, he spreads his bait by trickery and stealth while the family is away from home. Usually, the dog gives him a playful reception and licks the hand that is about to slay it. Then, having gained the dog's confidence, he plants his poisoned meat and sneaks home to gloat over what is about to happen. A life sentence in the penitentiary would be too good for criminals of this type.

COON AND SNIPE HUNTING

When I was a boy two activities in the deep woods were very popular with men and boys. One was coon hunting. The other was snipe hunting.

In those days there was little or no market for coon pelts, so instead of hunting those game animals for the money that could be earned, men and boys—and dogs—hunted them for the fun which followed when a connection could be formed between coon and dog. Moonlight nights always were selected for the hunt. Several axes and several dogs were taken along. Thus, when a coon could not be dislodged from a tree by nimble climbers, the tree was chopped down. Scores of the finest forest trees were destroyed in Monroe County most every season because coons had taken refuge in them as the hunters approached.

To fell one of those trees was no small task. In fact, two or three hours of hard chopping by expert axmen was required. As for the owners, nobody ever thought of asking their consent. No sooner would the tree crash to the ground than hunters and dogs closed in on the coon. The fight which followed more than compensated for all the labor and effort that had gone before. Eager dogs always found in the coon a worthy foe. Usually, he could hold his own with most any dog in the pack, provided the other dogs were held back in order to give him a sporting chance.

Nothing was quite so embarrassing to a hunter as to see his dog turn tail and go yelping away after the coon had gotten the best of him. By turning the dogs loose one at a time the contest could be prolonged until the game coon was worn out and killed.

Two or three times during the winter a coon fight would be staged in Margreiter's Hall in Paris, where the Odd Fellows Hall now is. An admission fee would be charged. My father always attended and would take all his boys. As sporting events these town coon fights provided more excitement than those out in the woods. This was because dog owners and spectators usually became involved before the evening was over.

Men and boys would be herded around the walls, leaving the center of the hall for coon and dog. Human fights would be provoked by efforts of an owner to assist his dog or to rescue it when the coon was getting the best of it.

Snipe hunting, I believe, has become a lost art. Nothing else provided quite so much mirth for the local community. Four things were required for a snipe hunt. First, a greenhorn from the city. Second, two candles. Third, a board on which to set them. Fourth, a bag for the snipe.

As a preliminary, however, it was necessary for local conspirators to talk snipe hunting in the presence of the city slicker. This fired him with zeal for the sport. Then, having worked him to a high pitch of anticipation, the conspirators would choose a very dark night for the hunt and invite him to go along.

In wagons the hunters would drive several miles into the country, then walk two or three miles through pastures and brush into the heart of distant deep woods. The board would be placed flat on the ground. A lighted candle would be set on each end of it. The greenhorn would crouch behind the board and hold the opened sack in position to catch the snipe when the others drove them in from the darkness. Then the town men, who usually were reinforced by a number of farm men and boys, would drift out into the night.

The city slicker thought they soon would return, driving large coveys of snipe into the candle-lighted sack he was holding. Instead, they made a bee line to their wagon and hurried back to town. The city man usually remained on the job until the candles burned out. Then, thinking his companions had become lost, he would shout himself hoarse in an effort to locate them. Finally, he would give up and start back to town on foot. Usually he would get lost and spend the balance of the night wandering around in circles. At daybreak he would totter up to some farm house, where he would be given a good breakfast and directions to his destination. Along about noon, worn out and bedraggled, he would get back to town, only to find all the citizenry waiting to greet him with ribald laughter.

It was further proof that there really was one greener thing than a country man in a big city, that being a city man out in the country. The victim usually joined the conspirators and helped at the job of interesting another city visitor in the thrilling sport of snipe hunting.